THE POETICAL HEROES

OF

SIR WALTER SCOTT.

Sir R. H. ANSTICE, K.C.B., M.A.

THE POETICAL HEROES

OF

SIR WALTER SCOTT.

BY

Sir ROBERT H. ANSTICE

KENNIKAT PRESS
Port Washington, N. Y./London

THE POETICAL HEROES OF
SIR WALTER SCOTT

First published in 1917
Reissued in 1970 by Kennikat Press
Library of Congress Catalog Card No: 70-113329
ISBN 0-8046-1007-X

Manufactured by Taylor Publishing Company   Dallas, Texas

I.—INTRODUCTION.

"O wake once more! how rude soe'er the hand
    That ventures o'er thy magic maze to stray;
O wake once more! though scarce my skill command
    Some feeble echoing of thine earlier lay;
Though harsh and faint, and soon to die away,
    'And all unworthy of thy nobler strain,
Yet if one heart throb higher at its sway,
    The wizard note has not been touched in vain.
Then silent be no more! Enchantress, wake again!" [1]

In the opening sentence of my former treatise on "The Heroes of the Iliad," I mentioned the intense, almost unsurpassed, attraction which, in my boyhood, I felt towards that glorious poem, adding, however, a possible exception, viz., the poems of Sir Walter Scott. To the latter, I think, I must give the palm (*i.e.*, as to the attraction the poems possessed for me); I could, and can still, repeat by heart pages of those lovely productions; no other poetry had such a charm for me as these. I certainly inherited this liking from my parents, who loved Scott's poems, and were never weary of repeating extracts from them. I think that the first poetry that I ever learnt by heart was the scene in the "Lay of the Last Minstrel" of the conflict between the young boy and the bloodhound. This poem indeed was, I think, the favourite one with my parents, but, much as I loved it, it was not the one (or, at any rate, is not at the present time) that possessed the greatest attraction for me. That poem is "The Lady of the Lake"; none, in my opinion, of Scott's poetical works can compare in beauty and charm with this lovely composition. The characters in it, also, are the most attractive of all; there is none that, so to speak, "jars" on one here, as does in the case of Marmion, for instance. I shall, however, go into this particularly later on, as I proceed to bring before my readers the

_____

(1) Opening verses of "The Lady of the Lake."

prominent characters in each poem. I therefore term my treatise "Scott's Poetical *Heroes*," though the treating of them involves a summary of the poem in which they respectively appear. I am not, however, attempting to deal with the whole of the poetical works of Sir Walter Scott—such a work would be endless; I only intend to bring before my readers the principal poems, those which constitute such a pleasing reminiscence of my boyhood; these I will attempt to portray in the following order, viz. :—

(1) "The Lay of the Last Minstrel."
(2) "The Bridal of Triermain."
(3) "Marmion."
(4) "The Lady of the Lake."
(5) "The Lord of the Isles."
(6) "The Vision of Don Roderick."
(7) "Rokeby."

Scott is not the favourite poet of the Scottish people, though, of course, appreciated by them; the writings of Burns appeal far more to their national character and feelings, but to English people the case is different. All, with very few exceptions, I am convinced, love the poems of Scott; and what constitutes the charm of his writings to us English is, I think, his marked impartiality, which is by no means a strong point with Scottish writers, even at the present day, when dealing with relations or comparisons between themselves and their southern brethren. Scott is a notable exception to this; dearly as he loves his own nation, Scotsman as he is to the very core, he has yet a corner in his heart for England; he evidently has a respect and affection for that nation; and he must win the heart of every English reader by the way in which he appeals to their good feeling and sense of right, after relating the defeat at Bannockburn in his poem "The Lord of the Isles," on which I will enter into detail hereafter in my comments upon that ballad. I may mention that this very impartiality was unfavourably commented upon by a Scottish reviewer at the time of the publishing of the aforesaid poem.

In the poems on which I am about to comment, though the Scottish element predominates, that of England is brought in considerably; in fact, the scene of the different poems is laid pretty equally in the two countries; those of "Rokeby" and the "Bridal of Triermain" are laid entirely in England, the one in Yorkshire, the other in the English Lake District; in the former, an Irish element is also introduced, the only instance of such in the poems that I can remember, with the exception of the "Dark Eth O'Connor" of Bannockburn. In "Marmion," the scene is laid partly in Northumberland, partly in the south-east of Scotland; in "The Lay of the Last Minstrel," in the Border country, on the Scottish side entirely; but, with regard to the characters, a strong English element is introduced. The events of "The Lord of the Isles" take place partly in the western isles of Scotland, latterly in the neighbourhood of Stirling. Lastly, as to my favourite poem, "The Lady of the Lake." The scene of that charming production is laid chiefly in the Central High-lands of Scotland, the lovely scenery of the Trossachs, the latter portion in the town of Stirling. No English character is introduced into this poem, with the exception of the soldier of the guard in Stirling Castle, John of Brent, an English refugee, one of those of whom the poet says—

> " And merry England's exiles came,
> To share, with ill-concealed disdain,
> Of Scotland's pay the scanty gain."

To these I have also added the "Vision of Don Roderick," a subject which stands alone. It is, in fact, simply a brief epitome of the history of Spain.

I will now, therefore, attempt to run through the events, characters, &c., of the poems which I have mentioned, in suc-cession, attempting, to the best of my ability, to delineate the chief features, &c., of the principal characters, trusting that my efforts may secure the appreciation of my readers in my thus attempting to summarise these lovely poems—

> " How rude soe'er the hand
> That ventures o'er their magic maze to stray." (2)

(2) Scott's " Lady of the Lake," introductory verses.

THE LAY OF THE LAST MINSTREL.

II.—THE LAY OF THE LAST MINSTREL.

> " Sweet Teviot ! on thy silver tide
>   The glaring bale-fires blaze no more ;
> No longer steel-clad warriors ride
>   Along thy wild and willowed shore ;
> Where'er thou wind'st by dale or hill,
> All, all is peaceful, all is still,
>   As if thy waves, since Time was born,
> Since first they rolled upon the Tweed,
> Had only heard the shepherd's reed,
>   Nor started at the bugle-horn." [3]

This poem was one of the first great efforts in this line by
Sir Walter Scott, "his first purely literary and original ex-
periment," as one of his biographers terms it. I can well believe
that it was his most favourite poetical work, for the scene is laid
in the Border country of Scotland, that lovely region of the
vales of Tweed, Teviot, Ettrick, and Yarrow, where he spent the
greater portion of his life, and which he dearly loved. The
inscription on his statue at Selkirk (placed by Scott in the mouth
of the aged "Last Minstrel") clearly shows this—

> " By Yarrow's stream still let me stray,
>   Though none should guide my feeble way ;
> Still feel the breeze down Ettrick break,
>   Although it chill my withered cheek."

The same biographer narrates a touching event at the close
of Sir Walter's life. He had gone abroad for his health, but
returned home stricken by a mortal illness. But the arrival at
his dearly beloved home (Abbotsford) seemed to awaken a spark
of life in the dying poet ; he rallied for a time, and his relatives
even entertained hope of his recovery. But it was but a dying
spark ; he sank again, lingered for a few weeks, and died on
September 21st, 1832.

(3) " Lay of the Last Minstrel," Canto IV., ver. 1.

The subject of the poem is chiefly an illustration of the manners and customs of the Borderers as they existed about the middle of the sixteenth century. Scott's hero of the poem, William of Deloraine, is an exact illustration of what they were : uneducated, rude, unscrupulous, with little or no sense of religion; [4] on the other hand, brave, daring, and possessed of generous feelings even towards their bitterest foes. [5] Scott well describes them in his poem of "Marmion"—

> "Not so the Borderer: bred to war,
> He knew the battle's din afar,
>   And joyed to hear it swell.
> His peaceful day was slothful ease;
> Nor harp, nor pipe, his ear could please,
>   Like the loud slogan yell.
> On active steed, with lance and blade,
> The light-armed pricker plied his trade—
>   Let nobles fight for fame;
> Let vassals follow where they lead,
> Burghers, to guard their townships, bleed,
>   But war's the Borderer's game.
> Their gain, their glory, their delight,
> To sleep the day, maraud the night,
>   O'er mountain, moss, and moor;
> Joyful to fight they took their way,
> Scarce caring who might win the day,
>   [If] Their booty was secure." [6]

These Borderers, both English and Scotch, appear to have acted entirely independently of the Governments of their respective countries; they raided and preyed on each other, notwithstanding that England and Scotland might have been at

(4) " Penance, father, will I none;
    Prayer know I hardly one;
    For mass or prayer can I rarely tarry,
    Save to patter an Ave Mary,
    When I ride on a Border foray:
    Other prayer can I none;
    So speed me my errand, and let me be gone."
                    " Lay of the Last Minstrel," Canto II., ver. 6.

(5) See Canto V., ver. 28, 29.

(6) " Marmion," Canto V., ver. 4.

peace at the time; in fact, this state of things existed some time after the Union of the Crowns.[7] Of course, during war, their services were engaged by their respective countries.

The state of the inhabitants in the vicinity of either side of the Border was, therefore, one of continual tension; a raid from either side might occur at any moment; their dwellings were never safe; and, in the poem, we find Watt Tinlinn, who lived on the Border stream, the Liddel, in reporting the advance of the English invading force, thus speaking—

> "They crossed the Liddel at curfew hour,
> And burned my little lonely tower;
> The fiend receive their souls therefor!
> It had not been burned this year and more." [8]

The Borderer appears to think that he had done very well in keeping his tower untouched for a whole year.

Strange to say that, notwithstanding this constant mutual robbing, burning, and plundering, the English and Scottish Borderers do not appear to have entertained any great animosity against each other. They appear to have looked upon this as the natural state of affairs; if a man were plundered on the one side of the Border, he had only to recoup himself from the other; and I have read (I forget where) of the case of a farmer on the Scottish side, who, having been robbed of a certain number of cattle by some English forayers, simply got a sufficient party together, crossed the Border, recouped himself from the nearest farm with the exact amount of which he had been robbed, and so returned home. One would think that, had all been actuated by this spirit, an accommodation would not have been difficult.

The feeling among them seems to have been more like that between hostile armies, where the soldiers on both sides entertain no personal feelings of hostility against each other. The friendly meeting of the English and Scottish Borderers in the fifth canto of the poem resembles greatly that of the British and French

(7) It must be remembered, however, that, with the exception of owing allegiance to the same sovereign, the governments of the two countries were entirely independent for more than a century after the Union of the Crowns.

(8) "Lay of the Last Minstrel," Canto IV., ver. 6.

soldiers at the battle of Talavera in 1809, when, during an interval in the battle, they met to quench their thirst at the stream, they maintained a perfectly friendly intercourse, even exchanging flasks.

Another peculiar feature of this poem is the introduction of witchcraft, or "gramarye," as it is termed, and which, with the exception of the "Bridal of Triermain," does not appear in the other poems. The Lady of Branksome herself deals deeply in the "black art"; [9] we have also the departed spirit of the wizard, Michael Scott, and Lord Cranstoun's goblin page, "of Gilpin Horner's brood."

Lovely as the poem is, it, together with that of "Marmion," has not escaped severe criticism. Lord Byron, in his "English Bards and Scotch Reviewers," lashes it with bitter sarcasm, in this fashion—

> "Thus Lays of Minstrels—may they be the last—
> On half-strung harps whine mournful to the blast,
> While mountain spirits prate to river sprites,
> That dames may listen to the sound at nights;
> And goblin brats, of Gilpin Horner's brood,
> Decoy young border nobles through the wood;
> And skip at every step, Lord knows how high,
> And frighten foolish babes, the Lord knows why;
> While high-born ladies in their magic cell,
> Forbidding knights to read, who cannot spell,
> Despatch a courier to a wizard's grave,
> And fight with honest men to shield a knave."

I will again touch upon this later. Lord Byron's greatest objection to Scott appears to be that the latter received money for the publishing of his poems, of which I myself cannot see the harm. He says, in the afore-mentioned production—

(9) The poet, however, describes the Lady as practising the superior, or "white" magic; *i.e.*, knowledge of controlling spirits, without entering into any compact with them.

> "I trust right well,
> She wrought not by forbidden spell;
> For mighty words and signs have power
> O'er sprites in planetary hour:
> Yet scarce I praise their venturous part,
> Who tamper with such dangerous art."
>
> "Lay of the Last Minstrel," Canto VI., ver. 5.

> "No! when the sons of song descend to trade,
> Their bays are sear, their former laurels fade.
> Let such forego the poet's sacred name,
> Who rack their brains for lucre, not for fame."

Did Lord Byron, then, never receive money for the publication of his own poems? I should be curious to know.

As is seen by the title, Scott places the poem in the mouth of an aged minstrel, supposed to be the last of his race, which had all died out. The old man is, as we should now say, "out of date"—

> "The last of all the Bards was he,
> Who sung of Border chivalry;
> For, well-a-day! their date was fled,
> His tuneful brethren all were dead;
> And he, neglected and oppressed,
> Wished to be with them, and at rest."

Not only so, but—

> "The bigots of the iron time
> Had called his harmless art a crime; "

referring, doubtless, to the Puritan rule in the time of Cromwell.

The old minstrel is described as seeking and obtaining hospitality at Newark Castle, on the Yarrow, then the residence of Anne, Duchess of Buccleuch and Monmouth, widow of the unfortunate Duke of Monmouth, who perished on the scaffold in the reign of James II. The period would, therefore, lie in the reign of William III., as the poet says—

> "A stranger filled the Stuart's throne; "

and the events related by the minstrel are supposed to take place about 150 years previously, viz., in the reign of Edward VI.[10] The minstrel, in return for the hospitality which he receives, offers to sing an old ballad relating to the family of the Duchess—

> "He could recall an ancient strain,
> He never thought to sing again."

(10) " Lay of the Last Minstrel," Canto IV., ver 24:
> " And this fair boy to London led,
> Shall good King Edward's page be bred."

His request is granted, and we now proceed to the events and characters recorded in the ballad.

The scene of the poem is laid at Branksome Tower, on the river Teviot, about three miles above Hawick: a note to the poem states that this residence had been the property of the Scotts of Buccleuch since the reign of James I. (of Scotland). The proprietress at the period of the poem is Dame Janet Beaton (or Bethune), widow of Sir Walter Scott of Branksome, who had been slain in Edinburgh by the rival clan of the Kerrs, with whom the Scotts were in deadly feud. The lady was descended from the Bethunes, a French family from Artois; [11] her father, says the poet, was learned in the "black art"—

> "He learned the art, that none may name,
>   In Padua, far beyond the sea.
> Men said he changed his mortal frame
>   By feat of magic mystery;
> For when, in studious mood, he paced
>   St. Andrew's cloistered hall,
> His form no darkening shadow traced
>   Upon the sunny wall!"

His daughter inherited his impious knowledge, and this gift of "gramarye" which she possesses forms a prominent feature in the ballad. She is described as a courageous, haughty, and vindictive woman; she sheds no tear over her murdered husband's bier; she broods deeply over vengeance—

> "Vengeance, deep brooding o'er the slain,
>   Had locked the source of softer woe;
> And burning pride, and high disdain,
>   Forbade the rising tear to flow;"

and it is not until her son, a little child—

> "Lisped from the nurse's knee—
> 'And, if I live to be a man,
> My father's death revenged shall be',"

that her tears at length find vent.

Such was the training of a child in those days; the Divine

(11) See notes *e* and *k* on the poem.

edict, "Vengeance is mine, I will repay," was little heeded in the sixteenth century.

The opening of the poem discovers the lady in her "secret bower," which none dare enter but herself; and, by the magical power with which she is gifted, she hears a "sullen, moaning" sound, which resolves itself into the voices of the spirits of the river and the mountain, which dialogue has not escaped the scathing pen of Lord Byron—

> "While mountain spirits prate to river sprites,
> That dames may listen to the sound at nights."

In my mind, however, the lines are very beautiful; we know the opening—

> RIVER SPIRIT—"Sleepest thou, brother?"
>
> MOUNTAIN SPIRIT—   "Brother, nay—
> On my hills the moonbeams play."

The dialogue is too lengthy to write down here,[12] I can only give the substance: they debate on the grief of Margaret of Branksome, daughter of the lady, who is pining for her lover, which lover is at feud with the clan of Buccleuch. She has therefore committed the offence, in those days unpardonable, of bestowing her affections on one who is at enmity with her family. The spirits confer together—"Is there any hope?" says one; "No," says the other, "not until ' pride be quelled, and love be free.' " These words are enough to rouse the anger of the lady, and she exclaims in her indomitable pride, thus defying them—

> "Your mountains shall bend,
> And your streams ascend,
> E'er Margaret be our foeman's bride!"

The above now requires explanation. These Border clans were often at desperate feud among each other, independently of the common enemy on the other side of the Border. In this case, as I have before mentioned, the Scotts of Buccleuch were at

---

(12) " Lay of the Last Minstrel," Canto I., ver. 15 to 18. The reader of this treatise should have a copy of the poem beside him.

deadly feud with the Kerrs of Cessford; how it arose, we are not told; a mere trifle, likely enough, roused it. The clans met at Halidon, near Melrose, and a desperate fight ensued, in which the Scotts seem to have had the worst of it. The hatred engendered by this defeat was no doubt increased by the murder of Sir Walter Scott, already noticed—

> "While Cessford owns the rule of Carr,
>   While Ettricke boasts the line of Scott,
>   The slaughtered chiefs, the mortal jar,
>   The havoc of the feudal war,
>   Shall never, never be forgot!"

In this battle, on the side of the Kerrs, fought Henry, Lord Cranstoun, of Crailing, in Teviotdale; he was therefore included by the Scotts in the feud. This nobleman falls deeply in love with Margaret of Branksome, the "Flower of Teviotside," and his love is returned, but these unfortunate lovers, suited for each other in every way, see no prospect of the fulfilment of their hopes on account of this wretched feud. Cranstoun would doubt-less have gladly come to an accommodation, but the pride and hatred of the Lady of Branksome are unconquerable; she would rather see her daughter dead than wedded to the foeman of her house.

She is rendered uneasy by the revelation of the spirits, in spite of her indomitable pride; and, firm in her purpose, deter-mines to seek further enlightenment. She proceeds to the Castle Hall, crowded with her retainers; and I take the opportunity of noting Scott's description of the garrison of a Border castle in those days. Branksome held, according to Scott, 29 knights, an equal number of squires, and again of yeomen—

> "Nine-and-twenty knights of fame
>   Hung their shields in Branksome Hall;
> Nine-and-twenty squires of name
>   Brought them their steeds from bower to stall;
>   Nine-and-twenty yoemen tall
>   Waited, duteous, on them all;
>   They were all knights of mettle true,
>   Kinsmen to the bold Buccleuch."

I cannot understand, however, why Scott makes the number

of each to be 29 instead of 30, for he states that 10 of each were always on duty, fully armed, with horses ready saddled, to mount at a moment's notice; this would divide the force into three reliefs, as customary at the present day. Perhaps Scott added a leader to each order; this, however, he does not mention. We see, then, these men constantly on the watch, not only against attack from the English Border, but also, doubtless, from the hostile clan.

The lady finds here her little son, the child whom we have lately seen vowing vengeance upon his father's murderers. "Young Hopeful" is bestriding the truncheon of a spear, riding round the hall in imitation of a Border forayer, and evidently looking forward to the time when he will be old enough to take his part in robbing, burning, and plundering, like the rest; his action is looked upon with high approval by the warriors present and by his mother herself. Such, as I before said, was the training of children at that period; but let us, in all fairness, remember the age in which these people lived, and not look upon their actions from a twentieth century point of view.

The lady now calls out one of her retainers, one William of Deloraine, who occupies a very prominent position in the poem. He is a perfect example of what the Border trooper was in those days, the attributes of whom I mentioned in a former page. The following lines describe the man exactly—

> " A stark moss-trooping Scot was he,
> As e'er couched border lance by knee:
> Through Solway sands, through Tarras moss,
> Blindfold, he knew the paths to cross;
> By wily turns, by desperate bounds,
> Had baffled Percy's best blood-hounds;
> In Eske, or Liddel, fords were none,
> But he would ride them, one by one;
> Alike to him was time, or tide,
> December's snow, or July's pride;
> Alike to him was tide, or time,
> Moonless midnight, or matin prime:
> Steady of heart, and stout of hand,
> As e'er drove prey from Cumberland;
> Five times outlawèd had he been,
> By England's king and Scotland's queen."

It will be noted, by the latter line, that these Borderers by no means confined their raids to the hostile country; Deloraine, as is seen, was outlawed by his own sovereign.

Lord Byron is very severe in his comments on the character of Deloraine. He describes him as "a happy compound of poacher, sheep stealer, and highwayman," forgetting, as is so often the case, the age in which the Borderer lived. Deloraine is, as I said, a thorough type of his class; he has his good qualities; he is thoroughly courageous and ready to face death, even if it be on the gallows. He is also not devoid of generous feelings, as we shall see later. It is very unfair to him, as I think, to compare him to Marmion, as Lord Byron does, saying that Marmion is exactly what Deloraine would have been had the latter been able to read and write. Now the two men are entirely different; Marmion is a man of high position, a baron of England, well educated; to such as he, the crime which he commits is utterly inexcusable.[13] Deloraine is merely a "stark moss-trooper," and acts according to his lights, and the manner in which he, together with many others, has been trained.

The lady has full confidence in the trustworthiness of Deloraine; she despatches him on a mission to Melrose, with these instructions—

> "In Melrose's holy pile
> Seek thou the monk of St. Mary's aisle.
> Greet the father well from me;
> Say that the fated hour is come,
> And to-night he shall watch with thee,
> To win the treasure of the tomb."

She warns him earnestly, at the same time, not to look into any book or scroll the monk might give him—

> "If thou readest, thou art lorn!
> Better hadst thou ne'er been born."

The Borderer assures her that he cannot read a line, "were't my neck verse at Hairibee"—*i.e.*, the last prayer on the gallows

(13) I shall go into this when I am dealing with the poem of "Marmion." I would also refer the reader to my comments on the similar difference between Oswald Wycliffe and Bertram Risingham in the poem of "Rokeby."

at Carlisle. Deloraine seems to look upon this end in much the same manner as does the highwayman, Dick Turpin, in W. H. Ainsworth's novel of "Rookwood"—

> "And what if at last, boys, he come to the crap,[14]
>   Even rack punch has some bitter in it;
> For the 'mare with three legs,' [15] boys, I care not a rap,
>   'Twill be over in less than a minute!"

Deloraine starts on his errand, and his ride is beautifully described in the poem; [16] he reaches Melrose in safety, and here the first canto ends.

Another personage (though not in the land of the living) is now brought before us, of whom we must say a few words before we proceed with our narrative.

This personage is no other than the famous wizard, Michael Scott. The original of the character was Sir Michael Scott of Balwearie, who lived in the thirteenth century, and was one of the ambassadors who, on the death of Alexander III. of Scotland, were sent to Norway to bring the heiress, the Maid of Norway, to Scotland, her inheritance.[17] Scott, however, by poetical licence I suppose, makes him live more than 200 years later than he actually did. He was the author of many scientific works, and, being thus in advance of his age, was looked upon, as a matter of course, as a wizard. We know the legend of himself and his familiar spirit, whom he had to keep in employment, lest the demon should destroy him, one of the tasks being the dividing of the Eildon Hill into the three peaks, which now stand out so picturesquely above the valley of the Tweed, near Melrose. The wizard got rid of the demon at last by setting him the endless task of making ropes of sand. He is supposed to have been buried in Melrose Abbey (his tomb is still pointed out), and his magical books with him: to obtain one of these from the tomb of the wizard was the weird mission of Deloraine.

I think no ruined abbey in the kingdom, with the exception,

---

(14) The gallows.

(15) The gallows.

(16) "Lay of the Last Minstrel," Canto I., ver. 25 to 31.

(17) See note *y*, "Lay of the Last Minstrel."

perhaps, of Fountains, can compare in beauty with that of Melrose. In contemplating the remains of these beautiful structures, I am always possessed with a feeling of indignation against those vandals who have wantonly reduced them to their present condition, for the ruins that remain show clear tokens of the glorious beauty of those edifices as they once were. In the case of Melrose, as Baddeley informs us, it was not only the fanatics of the time of John Knox who ruined the building, but the inhabitants of the town itself in a much later period, who "regarded it as a quarry, from which they could obtain stones ready cut for the erection of their houses." [18] It is carefully kept now, as are all other buildings of this nature, but too late to have prevented all this wanton mischief.

Scott's opening lines of the second canto, describing the appearance of the Abbey by moonlight, are very beautiful—

> "If thou wouldst view fair Melrose aright,
> Go visit it by the pale moonlight;
> For the gay beams of lightsome day
> Gild, but to flout, the ruins grey.
> When the broken arches are black in night,
> And each shafted oriel glimmers white;
> When the cold light's uncertain shower
> Streams on the ruined central tower;
> When buttress and buttress, alternately,
> Seem framed of ebon and ivory;
> When silver edges the imagery,
> And the scrolls that teach thee to live and die;
> When distant Tweed is heard to rave,
> And the owlet to hoot o'er the dead man's grave;
> Then go—but go alone the while—
> Then view St. David's [19] ruined pile;
> And, home returning, soothly swear,
> Was never scene so sad and fair!" [20]

(18) "Baddeley's Guide to Scotland" (Part III., Lowlands), p. 148.

(19) David I. of Scotland, founder of the Abbey.

(20) As a child, on first hearing this portion of the poem, I was told that Sir Walter Scott, being complimented by a friend on those beautiful lines, who observed that the poet must be thoroughly acquainted with the appearance of the Abbey by moonlight, from the frequent visits he must have paid to it under such conditions, replied that he had never seen the Abbey by moonlight in his life. I can hardly credit this; such lovely lines can only have been produced from the poet's own personal observation.

Deloraine is immediately admitted, as the Scotts of Buccleuch were great benefactors of the Abbey, and is ushered into the presence of the monk of St. Mary's aisle, an old man, of one hundred years of age. He delivers his message word for word as the Lady gave it him; the monk's horror is great; it is a superstitious age, and the prying into forbidden things, "what heaven and hell alike would hide," is considered a great sin, entailing punishment hereafter—

> "Wouldst thou thy every future year
> In ceaseless prayer and penance drie,
> Yet wait thy latter end with fear—
> Then, daring warrior, follow me."

The answer of Deloraine is characteristic, and recorded in a former note [21]—"Speed me my errand, and let me be gone," he says, and the monk proceeds to the chancel of the Abbey. The Abbey is now in its full glory, though the disastrous days are close upon it.

They enter through a small postern door (which yet exists) from the old Abbey garden; the chancel is beautifully lighted up by the moonlight, which shines through the stained glass of the oriel east window. The monk points out upon it the figure of St. Michael the Archangel, with the red cross in his hand, which cross, at a certain hour of the moon's passage, will cast its shadow upon the tomb of the wizard. They sit down, therefore, and commence their weird vigil, and the monk now mentions his intimacy with Michael Scott, and relates how the wizard, on his death-bed, repented of his former practices, and sent for the monk; to the latter he gives his last instructions, viz., to bury him in Melrose Abbey, his Book of Magic being buried with him, which Book is never to be removed unless required by the Lord of Branksome, of whose family the wizard evidently was; the Book to be returned when the need was past. He was to be buried under the shadow of the cross of St. Michael, his patron saint—

> "That his patron's Cross might over him wave,
> And scare the fiends from the Wizard's grave."

(21) See note 4.

The monk is relating his weird experience of the night in which he buried the wizard, when the bell tolls one, and superstitious terror strikes itself into the heart of Deloraine.

The shadow of the cross now points to the wizard's grave, which Deloraine proceeds to open. A light bursts forth from a lamp which is kept constantly burning in the tomb,[22] and the figure of Michael Scott is seen—

> "A palmer's amice wrapped him round,
> With a wrought Spanish baldric bound,
> Like a pilgrim from beyond the sea."

The Book is in his hand.

Not long is Deloraine permitted to gaze upon the body; the monk makes this appalling announcement—

> "Now speed thee what thou hast to do,
> Or, Warrior, we may dearly rue;
> For those, thou mayst not look upon,
> Are gathering fast round the yawning stone!"

Deloraine takes the Book in terror, and closes the tomb; darkness ensues, for the moon is now gone down. They grope their way back to the monk's cell, but not without some terrible indications of the presence of "those they may not look upon"—

> "'Tis said, as through the aisles they passed,
> They heard strange noises on the blast;
> And through the cloister-galleries small,
> Which at mid-height thread the chancel wall,
> Loud sobs, and laughter louder ran,
> And voices unlike the voice of man;
> As if the fiends kept holiday,
> Because these spells were brought to-day."

The monk dismisses the knight, and sends him on his way, with these words—

> "'Now hie thee hence,' the Father said,
> 'And when we are on death-bed laid,
> O may our dear Ladye, and sweet St. John,
> Forgive our souls for the deed we have done!'"

(22) How the lamp is kept burning in this position without opening the tomb to replenish it, Scott does not explain.

It is no wonder that, after the experiences of this terrible night, together with his own mental torment, that the old monk, aged a hundred.years, is found dead in his cell next morning.

Equally depressed is Deloraine, but he is of sterner stuff; he, however, speeds away from the vicinity of the Abbey as quickly as he can—

> "His joints, with nerves of iron twined,
> Shook, like the aspen leaves in wind."

He rejoices to see the daylight—

> "Full fain was he when the dawn of day
> Began to brighten Cheviot grey;
> He joyed to see the cheerful light,
> And he said Ave Mary, as well as he might."

The poet passes like a flash, and quite naturally, from the midnight gloom of the Abbey, the weird tomb, and "the voices unlike the voice of man," to bright sunlight, the singing of birds, and a lover's meeting. Henry, Lord Cranstoun, and Margaret of Branksome meet secretly in the woods of the Tower, the usual vows are exchanged, and the suitability of the lovers to each other, but for this unhappy feud, is again shown—

> "He was stately, and young, and tall;
> Dreaded in battle, and loved in hall:
> And she, when love, scarce told, scarce hid,
> Lent to her cheek a livelier red;
> When the half-sigh her swelling breast
> Against the silken riband pressed;
> When her blue eyes their secret told,
> Though shaded by her locks of gold—
> Where would you find the peerless fair,
> With Margaret of Branksome might compare!"

It will be noted that the aged harper, at this period of his recitation, deprecates the mention of "love"—

> "Its lightness would my age reprove;
> My hairs are grey, my limbs are old,
> My heart is dead, my veins are cold—
> I may not, must not, sing of love."

However, a cup of generous wine being presented to him by a wily page, which "swelled his old veins, and cheered his soul," he manifests a very different view of the "tender passion"—

> "Love rules the court, the camp, the grove,
> And men below, and saints above;
> For love is heaven, and heaven is love."

We turn from this exaggerated contemplation of the "tender passion" to a very different subject, and introduce an extraordinary creature, who takes a prominent part in the actions of the remainder of the poem. This is Lord Cranstoun's "Goblin Page," an ill-favoured, malicious dwarf, described as "scarce an earthly man." The introduction of this creature is, I think, a weak point in the poem, and somewhat merits the satire of Lord Byron—"goblin brats," as he says, "of Gilpin Horner's brood"—for the idea of this imp is taken from a certain Gilpin Horner, who appeared suddenly at a Border farm-house, stayed for a while, and then disappeared as suddenly. This dwarf appears to have suddenly sprung out upon Lord Cranstoun in a lonely glen, fastened himself upon him in spite of the Baron's endeavours to shake him off, and continued in his service since. Though "waspish, arch, and litherlie" (*i.e.*, lazy), he is faithful to his master, and on one occasion gives him timely warning when a party of the Scotts were assembling to take him prisoner. Whether goblin, imp, or elfin dwarf, "scarce an earthly man," this creature is connected in some manner with the wizard, Michael Scott, and is in some kind of subjection to him, from which bondage he has escaped for a time, hence his continual cry of "Lost! lost! lost!" Scott does not enlighten us upon this point, but we will deal with the matter further hereafter.

A distant sound is heard, and the lovers part hurriedly; Lord Cranstoun mounts his horse and rides off, soon, however, to enter into a very different meeting. He has not gone far when William of Deloraine appears, returning from his mission to Melrose. On the feudal enemies discovering each other, the inevitable conflict takes place. Not on equal terms, we should say, for Deloraine's steed, and he himself also, must have been greatly wearied by the midnight ride. However, he rides head-

long at his foe, "like a bull in a china shop," as we should say,
and deals the Baron a terrible blow on the helm, without,
however, unhorsing him. Cranstoun, on the other hand, severely
wounds the Borderer, the horse of the latter stumbles and falls,
and Deloraine lies insensible. Cranstoun upon this orders the
Dwarf to remain beside the wounded man, staunch the wound,
and convey him to Branksome—

> "His noble mind was inly moved
> For the kinsman of the maid he loved."

The Baron himself speeds away as fast as he can, for he is
in danger here—

> "Unless the swifter I speed away,
> Short shrift will be at my dying day."

The Goblin Page obeys his master, but with no good will,
for "small was his pleasure to do good." He discovers the Book
on the wounded man and manages to open it, but not for long,
for the outraged shade of the wizard appears on the scene—

> "He had not read another spell,
> When on his cheek a buffet fell,
> So fierce, it stretched him on the plain,
> Beside the wounded Deloraine.
> From the ground he rose dismayed,
> And shook his huge and matted head;
> One word he muttered, and no more—
> 'Man of age, thou smitest sore!'"

We wonder that the wizard did not take the opportunity of
snapping up his fugitive slave, as he did a few days later.

The Dwarf has, however, had time to read enough to give
him increased power in working mischief, which is his delight,
i.e., the power of changing the appearance of himself, and
others with him, in the eyes of other people. Thus, when he
conducts the wounded man to Branksome Hall, the warders
believe that there only passes "a wain of hay." He flings
Deloraine down before the door of the Lady's bower and takes
himself off. The Lady discovers Deloraine, tends him herself,

and declares that he shall be "whole man and sound within the course of a night and a day."

In the meantime, the Goblin Imp is working more mischief. He meets the young heir of Branksome, and decoys him into the wood, appearing to the latter as one of his comrades, while to the warders at the gate the two appear as "a terrier and lurcher passing out."

The Dwarf decoys the boy far into the wood, when, on passing a running brook, the spell is destroyed, and the Imp resumes his own shape; he scowls upon the child, and disappears in the forest.

And now ensues a scene in which, as I said in the introduction, is comprised the first poetry which, as I think, I ever learnt by heart : I can repeat the lines now. It is the encounter of the child with a bloodhound, which animals were, at this period, constantly used on the Border-side to hunt down fugitive raiders.

The child strays deeper into the wood, and has entirely lost his way, until—

> "He heard the mountains round
> Ring to the baying of a hound.
> And hark! and hark! the deep-mouthed bark
>   Comes nigher still and nigher;
> Bursts on the path a dark blood-hound,
> His tawny muzzle tracked the ground,
>   And his red eye shot fire.
> Soon as the 'wildered child saw he,
> He flew at him right furiouslie.
> I ween you would have seen with joy
> The bearing of the gallant boy,
> When, worthy of his noble sire,
> His wet cheek glowed 'twixt fear and ire;
> He faced the blood-hound manfully,
> And held his little bat on high;
> So fierce he struck, the dog, afraid,
> At cautious distance hoarsely bayed,
>   But still in act to spring."

The encounter is interrupted by an archer appearing on the scene, who, seeing the dog checked, at once infers that the quarry has come to bay. He draws his bow, without looking at

what he is aiming, when he is checked by his more observant
comrade, who calls out—

> "Shoot not, hoy!
> Ho! shoot not, Edward—'tis a boy!'"

The speaker advances, and in him we have, for the first time
in the poem, the example of an English Borderer, and the re-
presentation is by no means unfavourable.   He is described as—

> "An English yeoman good,
>   And born in Lancashire.
> Well could he hit a fallow deer
>   Five hundred feet him fro';
> With hand more true, and eye more clear,
>   No archer bended bow.
> His coal-black hair, shorn round and close,
>   Set off his sun-burned face;
> Old England's sign, St. George's cross,
>   His barret-cap did grace;
>
> .   .   .   .
>
> His buckler scarce in breadth a span,
>   No longer fence had he;
> He never counted him a man
>   Would strike below the knee."

He is a true descendant of Robin Hood, a true type of the
stalwart English yeoman whose prowess won so many victories for
England in the middle ages,[23] and a native of that county whose
gallant soldiers turned the day at Flodden.

The child, recognising the red cross—the badge of England,
the hereditary foe—struggles hard in the strong grasp of the
yeoman, who instantly discerns the high lineage of the boy, and
perceives that they have a "prize" now who will serve as a
suitable hostage in the ensuing controversy, of which we shall
hear.   The boy himself declares this, stating that he is "the
heir of the bold Buccleuch," and threatens the hated Southron
with death if he does not release him—

(23) "Not the Norman nobility, not the feudal retainers, won the battles of
Crécy and Poitiers, for they were fully matched in the ranks of France: but the
yeomen who drew the bow with strong and steady arms, accustomed to its use in
their native fields, and rendered fearless by personal competence and civil freedom."
("Hallam's Middle Ages," I., page 75).

> "If thou dost not let me go,
> Despite thy arrows and thy bow,
> I'll have thee hanged to feed the crow!"

The answer of the Englishman is amused and sarcastic—

> "Gramercy, for thy good will, fair boy!
> My mind was never set so high."

He admires the boy's spirit, and predicts that—

> "If thou are chief of such a clan,
> And art the son of such a man,
> And ever comest to thy command,
>   Our wardens had need to keep good order:
> My bow of yew to a hazel wand,
>   Thou'lt make them work upon the Border."

He takes the child away to convey him to Lord Dacre, one of the English wardens, who, as we shall shortly see, is now on the Border preparing for a hostile inroad into Scotland and an attack upon Branksome Tower. Scott does not enlighten us as to what brought these two Englishmen (no more are mentioned) thus into the heart of an enemy's country. They appear to have been only in pursuit of game, not on reconnoitring duty.

Meanwhile the Goblin Imp has taken the shape of the young heir at Branksome Tower, and, as might be expected, makes himself a general nuisance all round, until they all think that "the young Baron is possessed." The Lady is occupied, in the meanwhile, in tending the wounded Deloraine, so knows nothing about this, and the elvish Page takes very good care to keep out of her way.

It is now the evening of this eventful day, all appears peaceful and restful—

> "The air was mild, the wind was calm,
>   The stream was smooth, the dew was balm;
> E'en the rude watchman on the tower,
>   Enjoyed and blessed the lovely hour."

A single light, twinkling on a neighbouring hill, is sufficient to destroy this state of restful calm. All is now bustle and commotion, for the garrison know well what this light means; it is "the beacon blaze of war," indicating an impending attack from the English Border. They fly to arms, scouts are despatched immediately to reconnoitre the position of the enemy, and also to rouse the friendly clans. The word is, "Mount, mount, for Branksome, every man!" Their own beacon is lighted and taken up by the neighbouring hills, till the warning reaches the city of Edinburgh itself.

There is as yet doubt as to what the nature and strength of the invading force might be, and some think it is only an ordinary foray, but in the morning there is evidence of some important news, for one Watt Tinlinn, from the Liddel side (the Border river), is seen approaching. The nature of this hardy Borderer convinces the garrison that this can be no ordinary raid that had driven him from the little tower he occupied; the "gateward" says—

> "Right sharp has been the evening shower
> That drove him from his Liddel tower;"

and the same gateward adds his opinion, "I think 'twill prove a warden-raid," i.e., a raid conducted by the warden in person.

This conjecture is soon found to be true, for the stalwart Borderer arrives, with his "small and shaggy nag," bearing his wife and two children, the wife gaily decorated and bearing her husband's bow and arrows, he himself being armed with spear and axe, the usual Scottish weapons.

He reports an invasion of no less than 3,000 English troops, headed by both wardens, Lords Howard and Dacre; he repeats the words I have already quoted, showing that he thought he had done very well in keeping his tower unscathed by the enemy for a whole year.[24]

The numerous retainers of the clan now come pouring in to their chief's aid—

> "There was saddling and mounting in haste,
> There was pricking o'er moor and lee;
> He that was last at the trysting place,
> Was but lightly held of his gay ladye."

(24) See page 9.

The principal chiefs of those mentioned are Sir John Scott of Thirlstane, with his motto, "Ready, aye ready," and an aged knight, Sir Walter Scott of Harden; for all his age, he is a thorough old "moss-trooper," and leads the foray with the best of them. We shall hear of these two chiefs later.

The whole armed population of that portion of Scotland lying between Hawick on the east, the river Esk on the south-west, and extending to St. Mary's Loch on the north, appears to have obeyed the summons of the Lady of Branksome—

> "The Ladye marked the aids come in,
>   And high her heart of pride arose;
> She bade her youthful son attend,
> That he might know his father's friend,
> And learn to face his foes."

It may well be conceived that the wretched Imp, who had taken the form of the young heir of Buccleuch, had no desire to face the formidable Lady, with her powerful learning—

> "He counterfeited childish fear,
>   And shrieked, and shed full many a tear."

The Lady, astounded and wrathful at hearing this, orders Watt Tinlinn to remove the degenerate child to Rangleburn, "e'er the clan his weakness view." Tinlinn has no easy task; his horse, conscious of the uncanny burden he carries, becomes terribly restive, and—

> "It cost Watt Tinlinn mickle toil
> To drive him but a Scottish mile."

At length, however, they cross a running brook, the Imp resumes his own shape and flies, with his usual cry of "Lost! lost! lost!" not unscathed, however, for Tinlinn sends an arrow after him and wounds him in the shoulder.

Tinlinn has barely time to reach Branksome on his return when indications of the approaching enemy are heard. Scott has already described in beautiful lines the gathering of the clan of Scott to the aid of its chief; in equally beautiful lines does he now describe the advance of the English force. The "light forayers" come first, then follow the "Kendal archers all in green," and Lord Dacre's billmen supporting the archers, all, as in the present day, marching to the sound of music, the minstrels playing "Noble Lord Dacre, he dwells on the Border." Some German mercenaries follow, armed, as seems to have been peculiar at that time, with guns instead of bows and arrows; and lastly, the "men-at-arms," or cavalry, which bring up the rear under Lord William Howard, termed by the Scots "Belted Will," from the broad and studded belt which he wore—

> "So rode they forth in fair array,
> Till full their lengthened lines display;
> Then called a halt, and made a stand,
> And cried, 'St. George for merry England!'" [25]

Two fresh persons are now introduced into the scene, the English wardens, Lords Dacre and Howard, and their characters are very different. Lord Dacre is hot-tempered, fiery, and incautious in action; more of a soldier than a general, somewhat like old Marshal Blucher; he is, moreover, impatient of counsel, and somewhat vindictive also. Lord Howard is a more pleasing character. In action he is equally brave,[26] but more cautious, and in policy more calculating than his hot-tempered colleague. He also appears to be a perfect gentleman in the best sense of the word, courteous and generous. Scott presents a high portrait of him—

> "Accepted Howard, than whom knight
> Was never dubbed, more bold in fight,
> Nor, when from war and armour free,
> More famed for stately courtesy."

This is a striking instance of the poet's impartiality, to which I have before drawn notice.

The opposing forces are now fronting each other—one from the plain, the other from the castle—when the seneschal of the castle rides forth, with willow wand in hand, the sign of truce. The English lords meet him; he asks the reason of their invasion during a period of Border truce, in haughty terms, and with

---

(25) "Lay of the Last Minstrel," Canto IV., ver. 16 to 19.

(26) "Who, in field, or foray slack,
 Saw the 'blanche lion' e'er fall back?"

threat of retaliation. This rouses the anger of Lord Dacre, but Howard, with cooler head, replies to the seneschal, and desires to communicate with the Lady in person. She appears, therefore, on the walls, and the English herald declares to her the cause of grievance. He produces the young heir of Buccleuch, now a prisoner in the hands of the English.

The grievance is that William of Deloraine had, during this period of Border truce, plundered the lands of one Richard Musgrave, in Cumberland, and slain the brother of that chief. They demand, therefore, that Deloraine should suffer "march-treason pain," and make the extravagant demand that 200 English soldiers be admitted into the castle of Branksome; if this is denied, they will at once storm and take it, removing the boy to London as a prisoner. I should conjecture that this demand came from Lord Dacre, against the opinion of his more moderate brother warden.

As might be expected, the Lady distinctly, haughtily refuses this arrogant demand, stating, however, that William of Deloraine would either purge himself by oath of the charge, or, in alternative, would be prepared to meet Musgrave in single combat—

> "Through me, no friend shall meet his doom;
> Here, while I live, no foe finds room.
> Then, if thy Lords their purpose urge,
> Take our defiance loud and high;
> Our slogan is their lyke-wake dirge,
> Our moat the grave where they shall lie."

These defiant words clinch matters, both sides prepare for battle, and in another moment the conflict would have been in full play, when suddenly a horseman gallops up to the English lords. This man is an exile from England, and he brings dire news to his countrymen; no less than 10,000 Scots are advancing to the relief of the castle, under command of the Earls of Douglas, Home, and other notable Scottish warriors—

> "An exile from Northumberland,
> In Liddesdale I've wandered long;
> But still my heart was with merry England,
> And cannot brook my country's wrong;

> And hard I've spurred all night, to show
> The mustering of the coming foe."

Lord Dacre, with his usual hot-headedness, takes no heed of this news, and orders an immediate assault—

> "Level each harquebuss on row;
> Draw, merry archers, draw the bow;
> Up, bill-men, to the walls, and cry,
> Dacre for England, win or die!'"

But here, however, his cooler colleague, Lord Howard, firmly interposes. This rash advance into the midst of an enemy's country, without any reconnoitring, except to their immediate front, has probably been undertaken by the hot Lord Dacre against the advice of his brother warden, but here the latter speaks out strongly. An attack at this moment would be sheer madness; they will shortly be outnumbered by about three to one, besides the garrison of Branksome; an immediate retreat would have been the only course to take, only, fortunately, there is a better way to get out of the difficulty. "Accept the Lady's offer," says Lord Howard, "and let the matter be decided by single combat"—

> "Let Musgrave meet fierce Deloraine
> In single fight; and if he gain,
> He gains for us; but if he's crossed,
> 'Tis but a single warrior lost:
> The rest, retreating as they came,
> Avoid defeat, and death, and shame."

Even Lord Dacre cannot help admitting the wisdom of this counsel, but he yields with a very bad grace. Very probably there have been strained relations before between these two lords, being men of such different temperaments; this affair widens the breach, and destroys any semblance of friendship—

> "But ne'er again the Border-side
> Did these two lords in friendship ride;
> And this slight discontent, men say,
> Cost blood upon another day."

The English herald again proceeds to the walls, and tenders acceptance of the Lady's offer, viz., single combat between

Musgrave and Deloraine; should the former be victorious, the young heir of Branksome should remain in English hands as a hostage for his clan, if the latter, the boy should be restored to his mother. In either case, the English force should be permitted to retire to the Border unmolested.

The acceptance of the terms is received with satisfaction by the garrison; this is a private feud, and all, doubtless, to do them justice, are glad to avoid unnecessary bloodshed. The Lady is the sole exception; by her hidden art, she knows of the approaching reinforcements, but does not venture to disclose her knowledge, though one would have thought that her retainers were perfectly aware of its source, and would not, indeed, have objected to it when it brought them such advantage. We have already seen that no one ever dared to cross the threshold of the Lady's bower except herself.

The terms of conflict are made without any difficulty; the combat is to take place early next day, and, strangely enough, on foot, with axe and knife—not on horseback. The "tournament" was doubtless dying out, but we have seen an instance of the latter kind of conflict in the case of Cranstoun and Deloraine.

Hardly had the terms of the truce been settled, when the Scottish reinforcements appear—

> "Thick clouds of dust afar appeared,
> And trampling steeds were faintly heard;
> Bright spears, above the columns dun,
> Glanced momentary to the sun;
> And feudal banners fair displayed
> The bands that moved to Branksome's aid." (27)

Announcement of the truce is made to the leaders of the reinforcing troops, and the hospitality of Branksome Tower is tendered to them; it is also offered to the English lords, and their reception of the invitation is characteristic of each— Howard accepts cordially, Dacre, chagrined at being thwarted in his wishes, prefers to rest in his tent.

(27) I think Scott excels particularly in his poetry which describes the advance or gathering of armies.

A scene is now introduced, very remarkable, very pleasing, and very characteristic of the "old Border day." While the leaders of each party are being entertained in the castle, the men, both English and Scotch, nationally bitterly hostile to each other at this period, meet individually in a perfectly friendly fashion—

> "They met, and sate them mingled down,
> Without a threat, without a frown,
>   As brothers meet in foreign land:
> The hands, the spear that lately grasped,
> Still in the mailèd gauntlet clasped,
>   Were interchanged in greeting dear;
> Visors were raised, and faces shown,
> And many a friend, to friend made known,
>   Partook of social cheer."

But, had any "sign of war been seen," this peaceful intercourse would in a moment have been changed to dire conflict—

> "Those bands, so fair together ranged,
> Those hands, so frankly interchanged,
>   Had dyed with gore the green:
> The merry shout by Teviot-side
> Had sunk in war-cries wild and wide,
>   And in the groan of death;
> And whingers, now in friendship bare,
> The social meal to part and share,
>   Had found a bloody sheath."

Such were the characteristics of this extraordinary period; in this instance, however, peace prevails, and—

> "In peaceful merriment, sunk down
> The sun's declining ray."

A little episode occurs that night which we must touch upon before proceeding to the scene of the combat; this is another meeting of Margaret of Branksome with her lover, Lord Cranstoun. The latter is introduced into the castle by the magic spell of his Goblin Page, who makes him appear as a "knight from Hermitage." The lovers meet, and are happy for the time being, but Lord Cranstoun had come into the castle for another purpose besides that of meeting his lady-love, one very important, and which we shall presently discover.

All arrangements have been made for the combat on the following morning, but here a difficulty occurs. In spite of the Lady's skill, Deloraine has not yet recovered from his wound,[28] and a dispute now ensues between the two principal chiefs, Thirlestane and Harden (before mentioned), as to which should act as substitute in the conflict. The dispute is getting very warm, and is causing the Lady a great deal of anxiety, when, fortunately, it is settled by the appearance (apparently) of Deloraine himself, fully armed and ready for battle. The Lady believes that her skill has been successful after all, and is satisfied.

The usual ceremonies are now gone through, the proclamation of each combatant is duly made, and the two warriors join in the deadly conflict—

> "And in mid list, with shield poised high,
> And measured step and wary eye,
> The combatants did close."

The warriors are evidently both in the prime of health and vigour, and the combat is long and desperate; at length the Scottish champion deals a fatal blow, and Musgrave falls dying to the ground—

> "He strives to rise—Brave Musgrave, no;
> Thence never shalt thou rise again!"

The end is not long in coming—

> "The death pang's o'er—
> Richard of Musgrave breathes no more."

All are now pressing round the victor, who still stands gazing on his dead foe, and seems not to hear their congratulations, when, on a sudden, a terrifying interruption occurs; a "half-naked, ghastly man" appears on the scene, running up in haste—

> "He crossed the barriers at a bound,
> And wild and haggard looked around,
> As dizzy, and in pain;
> And all, upon the armèd ground,
> Knew William of Deloraine!"

(28) See page 24.

Amid the general amazement, the marshals of the lists rush to the victor—

> "'And who art thou,' they cried,
> 'Who hast this battle fought and won ? '
> His plumèd helm was soon undone—
> 'Cranstoun of Teviot-side !
> For this fair prize I've fought and won'—
> And to the Ladye led her son."

The Lady fervently embraces her rescued boy, but cannot bring herself as yet to address his deliverer. Cranstoun has done her a great service, but the feeling of the feud still clings to her, and reconciliation is a bitter pill to swallow. However, she must feel that, had Cranstoun not appeared, the issue of the fight might well have been otherwise; Deloraine, even if he had been able to take part in the conflict, has only just recovered from his wound; Thirlestane and Harden, the latter especially, are aged,[29] and would hardly have been a match for Musgrave, in the prime of his vigour. Had it not been for Cranstoun, then, her son would probably have been lost to her for ever. This her friends, the Earls of Angus (Douglas) and Home, put before her;[30] and Howard, generous enemy as he is, adds his entreaties to theirs; the whole clan also are in favour of a foregoment of the feud. She therefore at length yields, but evidently reluctantly; however, when she does yield, she does so thoroughly—

> "She looked to river, looked to hill,
>   Thought on the Spirit's prophecy,[31]
> Then broke her silence stern and still—
>   'Not you, but Fate, has vanquished me;
> Their influence kindly stars may shower
> On Teviot's tide and Branksome's tower,
>   For pride is quelled and love is free.'—
> She took fair Margaret by the hand,
> Who, breathless, trembling, scarce might stand;
>   That hand to Cranstoun's lord gave she—

(29) Thirlestane joined James V. in his ill-fated invasion of England in 1542; the events of the poem probably take place some nine or ten years later.

(30) The Earls of Angus and Home were probably the wardens of the Scottish Border. On an incursion like this, headed by the English wardens, they would at once gather to oppose it, and we note that Lords Home and Dacre (a warden of each side) are appointed marshals of the lists for the single combat.

(31) See page 13.

> ' As I am true to thee and thine,
> Do thou be true to me and mine !
>   This clasp of love our bond shall be;
> For this is your betrothing day,
> And all these noble lords shall stay,
>   To grace it with their company.' "

All, therefore, is ended satisfactorily, and before we close the scene of the combat we have a pleasing episode to contemplate before the body of Musgrave is borne away by his comrades. William of Deloraine appears here in his best attributes. Rough "moss-trooper" as he is, given, as all his class, to robbing, burning, and plundering, he has his "better side," to which I have before alluded; and here we have it, in the poet's own words—

> " He was void of rancorous hate,
>   Though rude, and scant of courtesy ;
> In raids he spilt but seldom blood,
> Unless when men-at-arms withstood,
> Or, as was meet, for deadly feud."

He is not much pleased at having his place in the combat taken by Lord Cranstoun, "this new ally," but he sees what advantage had been gained by his (Cranstoun's) interposition, and, therefore, "greets him right heartily." And now, as he looks down on the body of his old enemy, Richard Musgrave, his mixture of hatred for old wrongs and respect for a gallant foe are wonderfully mingled; these are some of the most favourite lines to me, and, I think, may well be repeated at length—

> " Now, Richard Musgrave, liest thou here !
>   I ween, my deadly enemy ;
> For if I slew thy brother dear,
>   Thou slewst a sister's son to me ;
> And when I lay in dungeon dark,
>   Of Naworth Castle, long months three,
> Till ransomed for a thousand mark,
>   Dark Musgrave, it was long of thee.
> And, Musgrave, could our fight be tried,
>   And thou wert now alive, as I,
> No mortal man should us divide,
>   Till one, or both of us, did die.

Yet rest thee God! for well I know
I ne'er shall find a nobler foe.
In all the northern counties here,
Whose word is snaffle, spur, and spear,
Thou wert the best to follow gear.
'Twas pleasure, as we looked behind,
To see how thou the chase couldst wind,
Cheer the dark blood-hound on his way,
And with the bugle rouse the fray!
I'd give the lands of Deloraine,
Dark Musgrave were alive again."

So we take leave of this prominent character in this poem of Sir Walter Scott's; this thorough type of the marauding Borderer of the period, of his faults, of his good qualities; and I think that, with this latter delineation of his character as thus written, we may take William of Deloraine to be, with all his faults, something above that in which he is depicted by Lord Byron—"a happy compound of poacher, sheep-stealer, and highwayman." It must be remembered, also, that it is not fair to look upon Deloraine and his like through "twentieth century spectacles."

I think myself that Scott might well have ended his poem here, for the events have practically come to an end, and ended satisfactorily. The conflict has been settled honourably to both parties; the Scottish champion has won his cause, and restored the heir of Buccleuch to his mother, who has at last sanctioned the betrothal of her daughter to her lover, Lord Cranstoun, who is the deliverer of her son. The English have secured their safe retreat into their own country, with the loss of but one man, and Deloraine, in this last scene, has displayed his best qualities. There is, however, the wretched Goblin Page (the blot on the poem, as I think) to be disposed of, and Scott disposes of him in the last canto, in a most unexpected and startling manner.

The sixth canto of the poem is taken up by the betrothal feast,(32) which takes place after the spousal rites, which, according to the custom of the period, have to be celebrated before the actual marriage takes place. I may take the opportunity of saying that the poet states that the marriage of

(32) See page 36.

"Teviot's Flower and Cranstoun's heir" actually does take place shortly afterwards, and we may presume that the happy pair "lived happily ever afterwards." I mention this now, and here drop the matter, following the example of the poet, who merges the events in the weird scene which closes the poem.

The betrothal feast, then, is at its height; the wine flows, the minstrels play, and all is mirth and gaiety.

The wretched Goblin Page, who has found his way back to the castle with his master, Lord Cranstoun, now, when the wine flows freely and "the blood runs hot and high," strives to do all the mischief he can, of which he never loses an opportunity. In the hall, he succeeds in rousing a quarrel between Conrad of Wolfenstein, leader of Lord Dacre's mercenaries, and a certain Hunthill, styled "Dickon Draw-the-sword," a characteristic Border nickname. The dispute arises from the loss of some horses by Conrad, which the Dwarf suggests were stolen by Hunthill; the controversy ends with Conrad's striking Hunthill with his gauntlet. The principal chiefs succeed in appeasing the quarrel for the time being, but Conrad is found slain a fortnight later, and it is significantly suggested that, from that time, "Dickon wore a Cologne blade."

The Dwarf, having now succeeded in his treachery satisfactorily to himself, sneaks off to the buttery, where the retainers are feasting. Watt Tinlinn, whom we have met before, is conspicuous here, and is pledging another Borderer, who boasts of another characteristic nickname, "Arthur Fire-the-braes." The Dwarf owes Tinlinn a bitter grudge for the wound the latter has given him,[33] and at once turns his baleful attention upon him. The Imp taunts him, steals his food and liquor, and finally stabs him in the knee with a bodkin. There is a terrible outcry then—

> "The startled yeoman swore and spurned,
> And board and flagons overturned;
> Riot and clamour wild began;
> Back to the hall the Urchin ran;
> Took in a darkling nook his post,
> And grinned and muttered, 'Lost! lost! lost!'"

It is his last prank.

(33) See page 28.

The minstrels are now called, as was the custom in those days, and their songs occupy some pages of the poem. It would take up too much space to enter into the details, but two of them may well be recommended to readers—the first is a tragical ballad relating to the love of an English lady for a Scottish knight, commencing—

> "It was an English ladye bright,
>   (The sun shines fair on Carlisle wall,)
> And she would marry a Scottish knight,
>   For Love will still be lord of all; "

and ending tragically—

> "Now all ye lovers, that faithful prove,
>   (The sun shines fair on Carlisle wall,)
> Pray for their souls, who died for love,
>   For Love shall still be lord of all!"

The second is an equally tragical ballad, relating the death of the Lady Rosabelle, the heiress of the St. Clairs of Roslin, by drowning in the Firth of Forth. The burial place of the St. Clairs is the lovely chapel of Roslin, the "gem" of the south of Scotland. The poem ends thus—

> "There are twenty of Roslin's barons bold
>   Lie buried within that proud chapelle;
> Each one the holy vault doth hold—
>   But the sea holds lovely Rosabelle!

> "And each St. Clair was buried there,
>   With candle, with book, and with knell;
> But the sea-caves rung, and the wild winds sung,
>   The dirge of lovely Rosabelle."

It is during the singing of this last ballad that a mysterious darkness overshadows the hall, which the guests hardly notice until the close of the song—

> "It was not eddying mist or fog,
> Drained by the sun from fen or bog;
>   Of no eclipse had sages told;
> And yet, as it came on apace,
> Each one could scarce his neighbour's face,
>   Could scarce his own stretched hand behold."

Horror seizes upon all, while the Goblin Page is heard to mutter "Found! found! found!" At that moment comes a bright, vivid flash of lightning, which strikes full on the spot where the Dwarf is crouching; it is followed by a most terrible peal of thunder, and—

"When ended was the dreadful roar,
The elvish Dwarf was seen no more!"

The guests, as may be imagined, are in the utmost terror; some have heard a voice, some have seen a hand, some an arm, and some a portion of a garment. But none in all that assembly are so terrified as is William of Deloraine; this sturdy Borderer, who would have faced a whole troop of hostile forayers without a shadow of fear, is now in a state of abject terror; he has seen more than any, and he shudderingly declares that he has seen—

"A shape with amice wrapped around,
With a wrought Spanish baldric bound,
  Like a pilgrim from beyond the sea;
And knew—but how, it mattered not—
It was the wizard, Michael Scott."

Such is the end of this wretched Goblin Page, and, as I have already stated, Scott does not enlighten us as to the relation between this creature and the departed wizard. However, on the motion of the Earl of Angus, it is agreed that a pilgrimage should be made to Melrose Abbey to offer up prayers for the soul of Michael Scott. The last lines of the poem give the description of the pilgrimage, and conclude with Scott's translation of the grand hymn, "Dies Iræ"—

"O! on that day, that wrathful day,
When man to judgment wakes from clay,
Be THOU the trembling sinner's stay,
Though heaven and earth shall pass away!"

A few words in conclusion. I have already drawn attention to the severity with which Lord Byron criticises the poem, which is evidently in Scott's mind when he says—

> "And little reck I of the censure sharp
> May idly cavil at an idle lay." [34]

Indeed, the portion of the poem relating to the Goblin Page, his pranks, and his connection with the wizard, Michael Scott, is, as I consider, grotesque, and is the weak point of the work, which here lays itself open to the scathing sarcasm of the rival poet. But I am of opinion that Lord Byron does not do justice to the poem as a whole. What can equal the beauty of the lines describing the Abbey of Melrose by moonlight ? The gathering of the clans, also, to the aid of their chief, the advance of the English force, the approach of the Scottish reinforcements, the single combat, the lament of Deloraine over Musgrave, are all beautifully told; and more than all do I think the opening lines of many of the cantos worthy of the highest praise; for example, the lines with which the fourth canto opens, and with which I have headed this portion of my treatise—

> "Sweet Teviot! on thy silver tide,
> The glaring bale-fires blaze no more; "

And last, and most beautiful of all, are those glorious lines in which the poet expresses his love for his native country, and more especially for that part of it in which he lives, [35] and with which lines in detail I may well conclude my treatise—

> "Breathes there the man, with soul so dead,
> Who never to himself hath said,
> This is my own, my native land !
> Whose heart hath ne'er within him burned,
> As home his footsteps he hath turned,
> From wandering on a foreign strand !
> If such there breathe, go mark him well ;
> For him no minstrel raptures swell ;
> High though his titles, proud his name,
> Boundless his wealth, as wish can claim ;
> Despite those titles, power, and pelf,
> The wretch, concentred all in self,
> Living, shall forfeit fair renown,
> And, doubly dying, shall go down
> To the vile dust, from whence he sprung,
> Unwept, unhonoured, and unsung.

(34) " Lady of the Lake," concluding stanzas.

(35) See page 7.

"O Caledonia! stern and wild,
Meet nurse for a poetic child!
Land of brown heath and shaggy wood,
Land of the mountain and the flood,
Land of my sires! what mortal hand
Can e'er untie the filial band
That knits me to thy rugged strand!
Still, as I view each well-known scene,
Think what is now, and what hath been,
Seems as, to me, of all bereft,
Sole friends thy woods and streams were left;
And thus I love them better still,
Even in extremity of ill.
By Yarrow's stream still let me stray,
Though none should guide my feeble way;
Still feel the breeze down Ettricke break,
Although it chill my withered cheek;
Still lay my head by Teviot stone,
Though there, forgotten and alone,
The Bard may draw his parting groan."

THE BRIDAL OF TRIERMAIN.

III.—THE BRIDAL OF TRIERMAIN.

> " Know, too, that when a pilgrim strays,
>   In morning mist or evening maze,
>   Along the mountain lone,
>   That fairy fortress often mocks
>   His gaze upon the castled rocks
>   Of the Valley of St. John;
>   But never man since brave De Vaux
>   The charmèd portal won:
>   'Tis now a vain illusive show,
>   That melts whene'er the sunbeams glow,
>   Or the fresh breeze hath blown." [1]

In this charming little poem we are transported into new ground,
viz., to that most lovely corner of England, the English Lake
District, where the mountain scenery equals in beauty that of
the Highlands of Scotland or of North Wales, though confined
to a much smaller area, which latter feature, however, has many
advantages. "To the pedestrian who prefers beauty to excitement," says Baddeley, who knew every inch of the district, "the
small scale of the English Lake scenery is an invaluable boon.
It gives him that infinite variety which is, as it were, the 'salt'
of his exertions. In a six days' tour he can wander from lake to
lake, and from valley to valley, and see so many utterly different
views that he may think he has exhausted the district. The
leisurely tourist, however, may roam for six weeks, or even
months, and still find fresh scenes of beauty to delight his eyes." [2]
The district is, indeed, the Paradise of the pedestrian; he can
wander at will without fear of being obstructed, as would often
be the case in the Highlands of Scotland, when the tourist en-
croaches on some grouse moor or deer forest.

The main action of the poem takes place in the Valley of
St. John, that lovely vale which lies between the village of

(1) "Bridal of Triermain," Conclusion, ver. 1.

(2) "Baddeley's English Lake District," Introduction, p. xiii.

Threlkeld, at the foot of Saddleback, and the northern end of Thirlmere Lake : a stream, termed St. John's beck, issues from the lake, flows through the above-named valley, and joins the river Greta at Threlkeld. The valley is bounded on the east by the ridge of Helvellyn, termed here the Helvellyn Dods ; and from the slope of this ridge, near the Thirlmere end of the valley, stands out a curious rocky mound, termed the "Castle Rock," from its fancied resemblance to a ruined castle. It is with this rock that we have to deal in the poem ; with its resemblance to a castle I shall have more to say hereafter, from my own personal experience. At present, I will go through the events of the poem, the idea of which is, of course, derived from the fairy tale of the "Sleeping Beauty."

The hero of the poem is a certain Roland, Baron de Vaux, of Triermain, which, as the note mentioned below says, is a· fief of the Barony of Gilsland, in Cumberland. The family of De Vaux was an ancient one, and readers of the Waverley Novels will remember that a scion of that family appears in "The Talisman," as an officer of Richard Cœur de Lion. The branch of the family on which the fief of Triermain was bestowed held it for several centuries, and the eldest sons were successively during this period named Roland,[3] so that the hero of this poem is no special historical character.

This Baron is a warden of the Border-side, and evidently a man of great prowess, for, at the opening of the third canto of the poem, we find that his absence on the "venturous quest," of which we shall hear in due course, gives great encouragement to the raiders from the Scottish side of the Border. He is repre-sented to us, first, as resting after one of these frequent Border forays—

> "He had been pricking against the Scot,
> The foray was long and the skirmish hot;
> His dinted helm and his buckler's plight
> Bore token of a stubborn fight."

This warlike Baron is at present unmarried, and appears likely to remain so, for he requires such a catalogue of good qualifications in his future bride as would very rarely be found

(3) See note c, "Bridal of Triermain," Canto I.

in one and the same person. We give them in detail, for they are beautifully rendered in the opening lines of the poem—

> "Where is the maiden of mortal strain,
> That may match with the Baron of Triermain ?
> She must be lovely and constant and kind,
> Holy and pure and humble of mind,
> Blithe of cheer and gentle of mood,
> Courteous and generous and noble of blood—
> Lovely as the sun's first ray,
> When it breaks the clouds of an April day;
> Constant and true as the widowed dove,
> Kind as a minstrel that sings of love;
> Pure as the fountain in rocky cave,
> Where never sunbeam kissed the wave;
> Humble as maiden that loves in vain,
> Holy as hermit's vesper strain;
> Gentle as breeze that but whispers and dies,
> Yet blithe as the light leaves that dance in its sighs;
> Courteous as monarch the morn he is crowned,
> Generous as spring dews that bless the glad ground;
> Noble her blood as the currents that met
> In the veins of the noblest Plantagenet—
> Such must her form be, her mood and her strain,
> That shall match with Sir Roland of Triermain."

We shall see, however, that Sir Roland, in spite of all his extravagant requirements, is at once attracted and hopelessly captivated by the first lovely face he sees; and that the lady of his choice certainly does not possess the whole of the attributes above depicted.

We left the Baron resting after his Scottish foray; at dawn of day, however, he wakes in a state of great excitement, and inquires hastily of his retainers in this fashion—

> "Hearken, my merry-men ! What time or where
> Did she pass, that maid with her heavenly brow,
> With her look so sweet and her eyes so fair,
> And her graceful step and her angel air,
> And the eagle plume on her dark-brown hair,
> That passed from my bower e'en now ? "

Both the minstrels and men-at-arms assure him that they have neither heard nor seen anything. The Baron, therefore, summons his page, Henry, whose life he had saved at the sack of the castle of Hermitage, in Liddesdale, during one of his forays into Scotland. The boy is, therefore, devoted to him; and he dispatches him at once to Lyulph's tower, on the bank of Ulleswater Lake. The poet makes this tower, at this period, tenanted by a learned sage of that name; from him the Baron hopes to obtain information regarding the lovely vision which he has seen.[4] The page pursues his way; he passes "red Penrith's Table Round," and "Mayburgh's mound and stones of power," and follows the course of the river Eamont to Ulleswater; thence, following the bank of the lake, he encounters the "hoary sage." He quickly delivers the message of his master, and the sage, after due reflection, gives his reply, and relates a narrative into which we will now enter.

Lyulph at once replies as to the individuality of the lady seen in the vision—

> "That maid is born of middle earth,
>   And may of man be won,
> Though there have glided since her birth
>   Five hundred years and one."

Before we enter upon Lyulph's tale, I would point out the fact that this 500 years seems to me a very narrow margin. The period of the poem appears to be about the same as that of "The Lay of the Last Minstrel," viz., about the middle of the sixteenth century; therefore, 500 years would only bring us back to the period of the Norman Conquest. The hero of the ensuing tale is King Arthur, and, if this monarch ever existed, it must have been during the Roman occupation of Britain, and somewhat early in that period, viz., while the ancient British kings still waged war against the Roman and Anglo-Saxon invaders. Scott, in the poem, mentions both of these nations as being successfully encountered by King Arthur—

> "Twelve bloody fields, with glory fought,
>   The Saxons to subjection brought;

(4) Baddeley states that the name of the tower was derived from Ulf, or L'Ulf, a former Baron of Greystoke, who also gave his name to the lake. Scott, indeed, terms Ulleswater, Ulfo's Lake.

> Rython, the mighty giant, slain
> By his good brand, relieved Bretagne;
> The Pictish Gillamore in fight,
> And Roman Lucius, owned his might."

Therefore, I should say that twelve hundred years would not be too many to record.

The opening of the tale shows to us King Arthur taking a solitary journey, in the character of knight-errant, as is so often represented regarding him and his Knights of the Round Table. He is riding down the valley of Threlkeld, skirting the base of the mountain, Saddleback. This mountain is here incorrectly termed by the poet "Glaramara," the real poetical name being "Blencathara." Glaramara is one of the Borrowdale mountains.[5] A beautiful description is given of the mountain—

> "Rock upon rocks incumbent hung,
> And torrents, down the gullies flung,
> Joined the rude river that brawled on,
> Recoiling now from crag or stone,
> Now diving deep from human ken,
> And raving down its darksome glen."

The king pursues his way past Threlkeld, when there suddenly opens upon him—

> "The narrow valley of Saint John,
> Down sloping to the western sky,
> Where lingering sunbeams love to lie."

(5) This is not the only case in which Scott makes these curious mistakes; in one of his lesser poems, "Helvellyn," he describes the view from the summit of that mountain—

> "On the right, Striding-edge round the Red-tarn was bending,
> And Catchedicam its left verge was defending."

So far correct; but he states that—

> "One huge nameless rock in the front was ascending."

I can personally affirm that there is no "huge rock" whatever in the gap between Striding-edge and Catchedicam (pronounced Catchcam). The ground here is entirely unobstructed.

Also, in describing the Chase in "The Lady of the Lake," Scott mentions the "mountain high, the lone lake's western boundary," stating that the "huge rampart barred the way." Now, the pass of the Trossachs lies perfectly open, and unobstructed at the western end of Loch Achray.

The Castle Rock lies fully open to the king's view, and here he sees, not a pile of rocks, but an actual castle—

> "With airy turrets crowned,
> Buttress, and rampire's circling bound,
> And mighty keep and tower."

Surprised to see a castle in the midst of such a wild district, Arthur rides forward to reconnoitre, deeming the mysterious edifice to be the habitation of—

> "Wizard stern, or goblin grim,
> Or pagan of gigantic limb,
> The tyrant of the wold."

The place is wrapped in grim silence; no sound is heard—

> "Save that awakening from her dream,
> The owlet now began to scream,
> In concert with the rushing stream,
> That washed the battled mound."

This silence sinks upon the king's spirits, and he hesitates before he winds his horn. At length he does so, and the castle gates are flung open. He is received by very different inmates to what he expected—

> "A band of damsels fair!
> Onward they came, like summer wave
> That dances to the shore;
> A hundred voices welcome gave,
> And welcome o'er and o'er!"

These syrens speedily divest the monarch of his armour, and escort him to the hall, where he is confronted with the lady of the castle. This lady, Guendolen, is but half human; her father is a "genie of the earth," bitterly hostile to mankind, and he has trained his daughter to draw Christian knights from their duty and "sink them in sinful sloth and shame." She practises these shameful arts for a long time, when she is all in a moment subdued at the presence of Arthur, with whom at the first glance she falls desperately in love—

> " While up the hall she slowly passed,
> Her dark eye on the king she cast,
>   That flashed expression strong;
> The longer dwelt that lingering look,
> Her cheek the livelier colour took,
> And scarce the shame-faced king could brook
>   The gaze that lasted long.
> A sage, who had that look espied,
> Where kindling passion strove with pride,
>   Had whispered, ' Prince, beware !
> From the chafed tiger rend the prey,
> Rush on the lion when at bay,
> Bar the fell dragon's blighted way,
>   But shun that lovely snare !' ''

Into this dangerous snare the king falls for a while—"mirth into folly glides, and folly into sin"—he neglects his public duties, forgets his wife (who, however, was no better than himself in that respect), and continues for months in the arms of his paramour—

> " Thus, week by week, and day by day,
> His life inglorious glides away,
> But she, that soothes his dream, with fear
> Beholds his hour of wakening near."

This hour is bound to come, and the lady is not slow to perceive the symptoms of its approach. She strives to stave it off with the usual feminine devices, but in vain. Arthur at length speaks hesitatingly of his kingly duties, which must call him from her side; she does not attempt to dissuade him, for she feels it would be useless, but she gives him a reproachful look, which indicates that she is convinced that he intends to desert her and (that inevitable result of their intercourse) the child that is to be born by her. Arthur hastens to re-assure her, and makes this extraordinary compact with her—

> " Eager he spoke—' No, lady, no !
> Deem not of British Arthur so,
> Nor think he can deserter prove
> To the dear pledge of mutual love !
> I swear by sceptre and by sword,
> As belted knight, and Britain's lord,
> That, if a boy shall claim my care,
> That boy is born a kingdom's heir;

> But, if a maiden Fate allows,
> To choose that maid a fitting spouse,
> A summer-day in lists shall strive
> My knights—the bravest knights alive—
> And he, the best and bravest tried,
> Shall Arthur's daughter claim for bride.'"

At dawn the next day Arthur appears, now clad in his long-discarded armour, setting out on his return to his kingly duties. But he does not get clear of the castle precincts without another encounter with Guendolen. She encounters him—

> "Attired like huntress of the wood:
> Sandalled her feet, her ankles bare,
> And eagle-plumage decked her hair."

Her love has now evidently turned to hate, and she seeks to destroy him. She offers him a cup of fiery liquor, the draught, as she calls it, "which Genii love!" The monarch accepts the cup, and is about to drink, when, fortunately for him, a drop escapes, and falls on his charger's neck; the horse is madly terrified—

> "Screaming with agony and fright,
> He bolted twenty feet upright."

The spilt liquor burns all the herbage wherever its drops alight. Guendolen has failed in her purpose against the king's life; she has as yet taken no notice of the oath which he had sworn; but, having failed now, she stores it up for future ill, as we shall presently see.

The maddened horse carries his rider up the vale at frantic speed, and stops, through sheer exhaustion, at the top. Arthur now gazes back upon the Castle Rock, but no castle was to be seen—

> "Nor tower nor donjon could he spy,
> Darkening against the morning sky;
> But, on the spot where once they frowned,
> The lonely streamlet brawled around
> A tufted knoll, where dimly shone
> Fragments of rock and rifted stone."

The king returns to Carlisle, and forgets these former incidents in the discharge of his kingly duties—

"And cares, that cumber royal sway,
Wore memory of the past away."

We now enter upon another phase of the narrative.

We pass over a period of fifteen or sixteen years, during which King Arthur has gained renown for himself in all parts. The Saxon, the Roman, the Pict have succumbed to his power—

"And wide was through the world renowned
The glories of his Table Round."

To him appeal all those who have suffered wrong from "tyrant proud, or faitour strong," and such appeal is never made in vain.

For the purpose of hearing such appeals, Arthur holds a solemn court at Whitsuntide, or Pentecost. This appears to be the great yearly festival at this period, for we read before that the king starts on his knight-errant trip "when Pentecost was o'er," evidently, as we should now say, taking a holiday after the great function was concluded.

The meeting we are now entering upon seems to have been very important, for every knight under Arthur's rule is, unless abroad, ordered to be present; and at this meeting the usual tournaments or jousts, with other games and pastimes, take place, with, of course, the usual attendance of minstrels. The poet mentions as being present the names of many well-known knights in the history of King Arthur's Round Table.

While the jousts, games, and merriment are at their full height, an incident takes place which startles the king—

"A Maiden on a palfrey white,
Heading a band of damsels bright,
Paced through the circle, to alight
And kneel before the king.

.   .   .   .

Her dress like huntress of the wold,
Her bow and baldric trapped with gold,
Her sandalled feet, her ankles bare,
And the eagle-plume that decked her hair."

It will be remembered that this was the exact dress worn by Guendolen in her last meeting with the king; and this, combined, doubtless, with the likeness in features, inclines Arthur for a moment to believe that he again beholds his former love. But a moment's glance discovers the mistake, and establishes the individuality of the maiden—

> "But 'twas a face more frank and wild,
> Betwixt the woman and the child,
> Where less of magic beauty smiled
>   Than of the race of men;
> And in the forehead's haughty grace,
> The lines of Britain's royal race,
>   Pendragon's you might ken."

She is Gyneth, daughter of Arthur and Guendolen, and she prefers her petition, which is no less than the fulfilment of the king's oath to her mother on his last night at the Castle of St. John.[6] The hand of the now deceased Guendolen is in this; if she cannot injure the king himself, she will do so through his followers.

The king receives his daughter with affection, and swears to fulfil his vow, which he proceeds to do on the moment—

> "Up! up! each knight of gallant crest!
>   Take buckler, spear, and brand!
> He that to-day shall bear him best,
>   Shall win my Gyneth's hand.
> And Arthur's daughter, when a bride,
>   Shall bring a noble dower;
> Both fair Strath-Clyde and Reged wide,
>   And Carlisle town and tower."

A scene of great excitement ensues—

> "The helmets glance, and gleams the lance,
>   And the steel-weaved hauberks ring."

The loveliness of the maiden has the same effect on the Knights of the Round Table as it has on the hero of the poem centuries later; all other considerations are thrown aside for the purpose of winning her—

(6) See page 51.

> "Nor love's fond troth, nor wedlock's oath,
>   One gallant could withhold,
> For priests will allow of a broken vow,
>   For penance or for gold."

The whole of the knights throng into the lists, eager to win the coveted prize, with the exception of three, in whose case other attractions exceed those of the stranger maiden; two of these, however, are no better than the rest, for they "love their neighbours' wives"; the third, however (and we turn to him with relief), "loves his own." This latter knight, Sir Caradoc, appears, indeed, to have incurred the ridicule of this profligate court for his purity—

> "What time, of all King Arthur's crew,
>   (Thereof came jeer and laugh,)
> He, as the mate of lady true,
>   Alone the cup could quaff."

He was the only
> "One of that fair court
> Was true to wedlock's shrine."

He is the one bright spot in this dark cloud of profligacy and infidelity.

On seeing his knights assembling for battle, Arthur's apprehensions are aroused; these are all doughty warriors, and will not part without desperate conflict and bloodshed; he therefore admonishes his daughter, while putting the warder of battle into her hand, as "the queen and umpire of the martial scene"; he earnestly urges her, if the strife becomes warm and threatens bloodshed, to throw the warder down, stop the fight, and place the matter of choosing a suitable husband for her in the king's own hands—

> "But, Gyneth, when the strife grows warm,
> And threatens death or deadly harm,
> Thy sire entreats, thy king commands,
> Thou drop the warder from thy hands.
> Trust thou thy father with thy fate,
> Doubt not he choose thee fitting mate;
> Nor be it said, through Gyneth's pride
> A rose of Arthur's chaplet died."

Gyneth, however, schooled by her mother, makes a haughty reply, and refuses to submit to this restriction—

> "But think not she will e'er be bride
> Save to the bravest, proved and tried;
> Pendragon's daughter will not fear
> For clashing sword or splintered spear,
> Nor shrink, though blood should flow."

The king yields reluctantly; he will not violate his oath; but he recognises at last Guendolen's hand in this—

> "Too late I mark, thy mother's art
> Hath taught thee this relentless part.
> I blame her not, for she had wrong;
> But not to these my faults belong.
> Use, then, the warder as thou wilt;
> But trust me, that, if life be spilt,
> In Arthur's love, in Arthur's grace,
> Gyneth shall lose a daughter's place."

The fight commences, and lasts long, for, as I have said, the combatants are doughty warriors, well skilled in battle, and while their armour holds true, the combat is bloodless, and—

> "It seemed their feathered crests alone
> Should this encounter rue."

But this cannot last; the combat becomes more serious, and blood begins to flow; soon knights begin to fall, and no less than twenty warriors lie "gasping on the ground." Arthur is in despair; Gyneth even is overcome with terror and remorse—

> "But still she deemed her mother's shade
> Hung o'er the tumult, and forbade
> The sign that had the slaughter stayed,
> And chid the rising tear."

So, unhappily for herself, she continues on in her ruthless course.

Many warriors of renown have fallen, but now the climax arrives—a kinsman of the wizard Merlin is slain—

> "Vanoc by mighty Morolt pressed,
> Even to the confines of the list,
> Young Vanoc of the beardless face,
> (Fame spoke the youth of Merlin's race,)
> O'erpowered at Gyneth's footstool bled,
> His heart's blood dyed her sandals red."

The end is now come; the wizard Merlin suddenly arises from the earth in the midst of the lists, and stays the combat. He sternly pronounces doom on the "fair cause of mischief"—

> "Long shall close in stony sleep
> Eyes for ruth that would not weep,
> Iron lethargy shall seal
> Heart that pity scorned to feel.
>
> .   .   .   .   .   .
>
> Thou shalt bear thy penance lone,
> In the Valley of Saint John,
> And this weird shall overtake thee—
> Sleep, until a knight shall wake thee,
> For feats of arms as far renowned
> As warrior of the Table Round."

The doom instantly takes effect; Gyneth, in spite of her efforts, falls to sleep before them all, and this is beautifully rendered by the poet—

> "Slow the dark-fringed eyelids fall,
> Curtaining each azure ball,
> Slowly as on summer eves
> Violets fold their dusky leaves.
> The weighty baton of command
> Now bears down her sinking hand,
> On her shoulder droops her head;
> Net of pearl and golden thread,
> Bursting, gave her locks to flow
> O'er her arm and breast of snow."

Her loveliness arouses relenting in the breast of her angry father, and renewed incitement to combat to the warriors, but this lasts not long; Gyneth vanishes into "necromantic night." She is borne to the mystic castle in the Vale of St. John, to "dree her weird" till the time appointed.

Lyulph concludes his tale by relating the dangers and difficulties that would beset any one attempting to release the Sleeping Beauty. First, to the ordinary eye of mortal no castle is to be seen in the valley—

> "Not at every time or tide,
> Not by every eye descried.
> Fast and vigil must be borne,
> Many a night in watching worn,
> Ere an eye of mortal powers
> Can discern those magic towers."

Of the numbers who came to the rescue of the maiden, in the time immediately succeeding this incident, many withdrew in despair; no castle is to be seen. A few persevered, and this was the result—

> "Of the persevering few,
> Some from hopeless task withdrew,
> When they read the dismal threat
> Graved upon the gloomy gate.
> Few have braved the yawning door,
> And those few returned no more.
> In the lapse of time forgot,
> Well-nigh lost is Gyneth's lot;
> Sound her sleep as in the tomb,
> Till wakened by the trump of doom."

We now enter upon the third and final phase of the poem, the events of which occupy the whole of the third canto; and we turn with relief from the profligate court of King Arthur to the gallant hero of the tale. Sir Roland de Vaux is, as I think, a character to be greatly admired. He is courageous, faithful, firm, and steadfast; when he has entered upon an undertaking, he never swerves from his purpose until the object is fulfilled; he pursues his way steadfastly to the end; no perils daunt, no hardships dishearten, no temptations beguile him away; he will die sooner than fail. This we shall see constantly as we accompany him on his venturous quest.

He is evidently a man of upright character, and we have seen that he requires an infinity of virtues in the lady he may choose for his bride; no ordinary woman will satisfy him. But here human nature is too strong for him; the appearance of Gyneth in his dream at once disperses all his former requirements; this syren exercises the same influence over him as she did over King Arthur's knights, and he determines to win her or die—

> "For, by the blessèd rood I swear,
> If that fair form breathe vital air,
> No other maiden by my side
> Shall ever rest De Vaux's bride!"

No sooner has he heard Lyulph's tale than he determines to attempt the release of the imprisoned maiden; and, characteristically, he vows to succeed or perish in the attempt—

> "When first I took this venturous quest,
> I swore upon the rood,
> Neither to stop, nor turn, nor rest,
> For evil or for good."

How nobly he fulfils this resolve we shall now see. Regardless of all other considerations, not heeding that his absence lays the Border open to the attacks of Scottish raiders, with but one fixed purpose in his mind, he proceeds to the Valley of St. John; and his long, lonely watch here constitutes the first stage of his trials. He had been warned by Lyulph, as we have seen, that he must not expect to see the castle at once; [7] long, weary watching must be endured before that wondrous appearance may be discerned by him. He turns his eyes to the Castle Rocks at once, and keeps a constant watch upon them, but for a long while without result. It is not to be wondered at that he often fancied that the rocks were changing into the form of a castle, but ever is he deceived—

> "Ever he watched, and oft he deemed,
> While on the mound the moonlight streamed,
>   It altered to his eyes;
> Fain would he hope the rocks 'gan change
> To buttressed walls their shapeless range,
> Fain think, by transmutation strange,
>   He saw grey turrets rise.

(7) See page 58.

> But scarce his heart with hope throbbed high,
> Before the wild illusions fly,
>   Which fancy had conceived,
> Abetted by an anxious eye
>   That longed to be deceived."

He examines the rocks closely, and even climbs to the summit of the mound, but with no result; he discovers nothing—

> "Save that the crags, so rudely piled,
> At distance seen, resemblance wild
>   To a rough fortress bore."

This wearying stage of the quest has disheartened many former adventurers, but not so our hero. He continues firm in his purpose, and at length his perseverance is rewarded.

He has been on his weary watch for about a month, and the moon is now on the wane. It is a wild, stormy night, and De Vaux has taken shelter in the little cave in which he passes the night. He has fallen into broken slumber, when a sound is heard which thoroughly awakens him; it is nothing less than the tolling of a bell; the sound is repeated twelve times, and awakens echoes in the surrounding mountains. A "thought of fear" comes into our hero's mind, and no wonder; such a sound in this lonely place, far from human habitation, might well inspire terror into the bravest; but this thought quickly passes, his enterprise rushes on his mind—

> "But lively was the mingled thrill
> That chased the momentary chill,
>   For Love's keen wish was there,
> And eager Hope, and Valour high,
> And the proud glow of Chivalry,
>   That burned to do and dare."

In the black darkness of the night, however, De Vaux can do nothing, when, suddenly, a weird light appears upon the scene; a great meteor arises, and for a short space illumines the valley. It shines full upon the mound of rocks, and there, at length, appears the marvellous sight which our adventurer had so long desired—

"What sees he by that meteor's lour ?—
A bannered Castle, Keep, and Tower,
　Return the lurid gleam ;
With battled walls and buttress fast,
And barbican, and ballium vast,
And airy flanking towers, which cast
　Their shadows on the stream."

De Vaux rushes out from his cave, and makes his way towards
the mound at his utmost speed, but it is loo late : the mystic light
fades and dies away, and black darkness again settles down upon
the valley. The knight winds his horn, and receives, indeed, a
reply, but a second summons remains unanswered; he searches
vainly for the mound throughout the night, and when morning
dawns there is no semblance of a castle, but only the usual pile of
rocks.

Roland has failed for a time, but his failure does not dishearten him. He has indeed gained one thing. His long, weary
watch may well have inclined him to doubt whether Lyulph's tale
may not merely have been a tradition, handed down from age to
age; but, if so, this revelation reassures him; the castle is there,
without a doubt, and he is determined not to stir from his post
until he reaches it.

Another long, weary month of watching without result drags
by; and then, at length, a second opportunity occurs.

The moon is again on the wane, the period at which, as it
seems, the appearance usually takes place. Just at the break of
day, a mist arises, and enshrouds the pile of rocks. A breeze,
however, springs up and shakes this veil of mist, without entirely
dispersing it, and through the rifts thus made the form of the
castle is dimly seen. Roland loses not a moment; he rushes
towards the mound, but it would appear as if he were to be
baffled again, for, before he can gain it, "the rocks their shapeless
form regain." An unearthly laugh ensues from the mountain
spirits, rejoicing at the warrior's failure. This does not in the
least terrify him; it only rouses his anger, and makes him more
determined than ever. He makes an angry reply, and hurls his
axe at the rocks; a fragment is detached, and falls thundering
down into the stream below; its fall lays bare a rude, rocky kind

of staircase, which Roland hastens to climb, and arrives upon a platform, where at length his long, patient perseverance is rewarded.

Full in view before him stands the much-sought-for castle, not in mist or meteor light, but in the full light of day—

> "No misty phantom of the air,
> No meteor-blazoned show was there;
> In morning splendour, full and fair,
> The massive fortress shone."

The knight, so far, has gained the object of his quest; he has obtained the reward of his patience; but now, at this stage, his courage has to be tested. Lyulph had spoken of—

> "The dismal threat
> Graved upon the gloomy gate."

This inscription now appears before him. It applauds his patience, but adds this sinister warning—

> "View it o'er, and pace it round,
> Rampart, turret, battled mound;
> Dare no more! to cross the gate
> Were to tamper with thy fate;
> Strength and fortitude were vain;
> View it o'er—and turn again."

This warning deters not our brave warrior in the least; he pushes the gate open, and enters a vaulted passage, but no sooner is he within when—

> "An unseen arm, with force amain,
> The ponderous gate flung close again,
> And rusted bolt and bar
> Spontaneous took their place once more,
> While the deep arch with sullen roar
> Returned their surly jar."

Even this appalling incident does not terrify our bold hero; it only arouses in him a certain grim humour—

> "Now closed is the gin, and the prey within,
> By the Rood of Lanercost!
> But he that would win the war-wolf's skin,
> May rue him of his boast."

He proceeds on his way, and enters the outer court of the castle, and here another obstacle confronts him. Between him and the main building lies a broad, deep moat, with no means of crossing except by swimming. De Vaux is in full armour; he cannot swim in it; he must either remain where he is, or proceed on his way unarmed. He hesitates not a moment; he flings away his armour (retaining, however, his good sword), and swims the moat.

And now comes the last and most terrible trial of his courage; he is without armour, and imprisoned within the walls of the castle. On emerging from the moat, he enters a large hall, decorated with portraits of ancient heroes and their deeds, which for a while invite his attention and delay his progress, but not for long. He proceeds to a door at the farther end of the hall, in which there is a "wicket-window grate," through which the knight peers before adventuring further.

He beholds a sight sufficient to appal the bravest warrior. He sees four savage African maidens, armed and accoutred, and each leading a Lybian "tiger" [8] by a leash of gossamer. As he opens the wicket, signs of hostility at once appear in these terrible inmates—

> "Each grisly beast 'gan upward draw,
> Rolled his grim eye, and spread his claw,
> Scented the air, and licked his jaw."

A weird song from the savage guardians of these beasts, denoting their dire hostility to mankind, by no means tends to allay the terror of the beholder—

> "Rash Adventurer, bear thee back!
> Dread the spell of Dahomay!
> Fear the race of Zaharak,
> Daughters of the burning day!
>
> .   .   .   .   .   .
>
> Ours the scorpion, ours the snake,
> Ours the hydra of the fen,
> Ours the tiger of the brake,
> All that plague the sons of men.

(8) Scott, doubtless, writes for effect: he must have known, as we do, that there are no tigers in Africa; nor do I think the term "tiger" is ever applied to the African leopard as it is to the jaguar of South America.

> Ours the tempest's midnight wrack,
> Pestilence that wastes by day—
> Dread the race of Zaharak!
> Fear the spell of Dahomay!''

And now how does our bold hero receive this terrifying warning, and the equally appalling spectacle of these savage beasts thirsting for his blood? In a manner characteristic of himself, he deems that his latter end is now approaching; he must either face these dire foes and their equally savage guardians, or die a lingering death of starvation. He, without hesitation, chooses the honourable course, reminding himself of the oath he swore on first setting out on this venture [9]—

> " My forward path too well I ween
> Lies yonder fearful ranks between;
> For man unarmed, 'tis bootless hope
> With tigers and with fiends to cope—
> Yet, if I turn, what waits me there
> Save famine dire and fell despair ?—
> Other conclusion let me try,
> Since, choose howe'er I list, I die.
> Forward, lies faith and knightly fame;
> Behind, are perjury and shame.''

With this gallant resolve, he draws his sword, seizes a banner from the wall for further protection, and boldly enters the hall.

Two tigers are at once let loose upon him from both sides; he baffles one by flinging the banner over it, and pierces the other through with his sword. Here his danger ceases; the Amazons restrain the remaining beasts, and our hero passes safely through a door at the other end of the gallery. No pursuit is attempted; and here the maidens encourage him on his further journey, as we shall again more than once find to be the case, when the ordeal is safely passed. Their song now expresses their rejoicing at being freed from their long, weary watch by Roland's bravery and encouragement to him to proceed—

> " Warrior! thou, whose dauntless heart
> Gives us from our ward to part,
> Be as strong in future trial,
> Where resistance is denial.''

[9] See page 59.

The song dies away, and the knight pursues his way. The courage of our hero has now been thoroughly proved, and there is no further trial for him in this respect; it has now to be seen whether he is equally proof against temptation, *i.e.*, "where resistance is denial." All further obstructions to him are (with one exception) of this nature. He arrives at a "lofty dome," which—

> "Flashed with such a brilliant flame,
> As if the wealth of all the world
> Were there in rich confusion hurled."

Gold, silver, jewels, lie piled about in heaps, under the guardianship of four maidens, the "daughters of a distant land" (evidently South America), who proffer all this wealth to our hero, on bended knee, thus describing it—

> "See the treasures Merlin piled,
> Portion meet for Arthur's child."

The first offers—

> "Clots of virgin gold!
> Severed from the sparry mould;"

the second, "pearls that long have slept"; the third—

> "Rubies blazing bright,
> Here the emerald's fairy green,
> And the topaz glows between;
> Here their varied hues unite,
> In the changeful chrysolite;"

the fourth, diamonds—

> "While their glories I expand,
> Shade thine eyebrows with thy hand.
> Mid-day sun and diamond's blaze
> Blind the rash beholder's gaze."

The offer of this wealth has no more effect on the purpose of our hero than has the peril lately passed; he waves it aside, and passes on, declaring—

> "De Vaux of wealth saw never need,
> Save to purvey him arms and steed,
> And all the ore he deigned to hoard
> Inlays his helm, and hilts his sword,"

and thus he leaves them.

The next temptation is that which, centuries before, had overcome King Arthur, and made him neglect his kingly duties for many months, viz., that of sinful pleasure; but we shall find that the Knight of Triermain is made of sterner stuff in this respect than was the king.

De Vaux arrives at a lovely courtyard, with a fountain in the centre, and "a fair arcade" on either hand, garnished with "alleys and bowers, for sun or shade"; but, significant fact as to where his duty lies, he sees, full in front of him, a door, which—

> "Low-browed and dark, seemed as it led
> To the lone dwelling of the dead,
> Whose memory was no more."

The knight stops for a moment to slake his thirst at the fountain, and, while thus engaged, he is aware of the presence of several maidens, evidently from the East, as—

> "Their hue was of the golden glow
> That suns of Candahar bestow."

These syrens immediately begin to exercise their wiles upon the knight, tempting him to rest on his way till the following day—

> "Stay, O stay!—in yonder bowers
> We will braid thy locks with flowers,
> Spread the feast and fill the wine,
> Charm thine ear with sounds divine,
> Weave our dances till delight
> Yield to langour, day to night.
> Then shall she you most approve,
> Sing the lays that best you love,
> Soft thy mossy couch shall spread,
> Watch thy pillow, prop thy head,
> Till the weary night be o'er—
> Gentle Warrior, wouldst thou more!—
> Wouldst thou more, fair Warrior?—she
> Is slave to Love and slave to thee."

Our hero is equally proof against this temptation, as he was against that of riches, but he is without austerity in his nature—

> "As round the band of syrens trip,
> He kissed one damsel's laughing lip,
> And pressed another's proffered hand,
> Spoke to them all in accents bland,
> But broke their magic circle through:
> 'Kind Maids,' said he, 'adieu, adieu!
> My fate, my fortune, forward lies.'"

He breaks from them, and vanishes beneath the dark archway before mentioned; and here, as on a former occasion, he receives encouragement to pursue his way, now that the temptation has been withstood. He hears the voices of the maidens singing after him—

> "Fair Flower of Courtesy, depart!
> Go, where the feelings of the heart
> With the warm pulse in concord move;
> Go, where virtue sanctions love!"

The next ordeal which awaits our hero tries him more than any. This darksome door admits him to a series of ruined, dangerous vaults, in the "wildered maze" of which he wanders for a time. There is no light, except that of mine-fires—

> "Whose fearful light the dangers showed
> That dogged him on the dreadful road.
> Deep pits, and lakes of waters dun,
> They showed, but showed not how to shun.
> These scenes of desolate despair,
> These smothering clouds of poisoned air,
> How gladly had De Vaux exchanged,
> Though 'twere to face yon tigers ranged!"

and the following is a proof that this dire experience tried the warrior more than anything he had yet undergone—

> "Nay, soothful bards have said,
> So perilous his state seems now,
> He wished him under arbour bough,
> With Asia's willing maid."

But at length his hardships come to an end; he hears a trumpet call, and a voice chanting a lay which seems to call him to future glory—

"Son of Honour, theme of story,
Think on the reward before ye!
Danger, darkness, toil despise;
'Tis Ambition bids thee rise.

. . . . . .

Lag not now, though rough the way,
Fortune's mood brooks no delay;
Grasp the boon that's spread before ye,
Monarch's power, and Conqueror's glory!"

This indicates another temptation, that of sovereign power,
and it proves to be the last. Following the sound, the knight
gains a staircase, which leads him again to upper air and a lofty
hall, in which stand four maidens, evidently of Europe. Three
of these bear the emblems of sovereignty—crown, sceptre, and
globe; the fourth, a native of "Merry England," stands apart,
leaning on a harp; she bears nothing of the above-mentioned
symbols of royalty, but, in her hand, a simple laurel wreath.

Our hero is now subjected to his last temptation. The three
foremost maidens kneel down to him as to a monarch, and proffer
the symbols of royalty and sovereignty—

"O'er many a region wide and fair,
Destined, they said, for Arthur's heir."

Will he yield to this temptation? It sounds plausible; his
quest is evidently nearly over, and would it not be right to secure
a wide domain for his intended bride, the daughter of King
Arthur? But no; if these thoughts ever crossed his mind, they
are speedily dispelled; he remembers his oath—

"Neither to stop, nor turn, nor rest,
For evil or for good."

This apparent good, plausible as it seems, stands in the way
of his course, and must be rejected. He refuses these brilliant
offers with his usual firmness—

"'Rather,' he said, 'De Vaux would ride
A Warden of the Border-side,
In plate and mail, than, robed in pride,
A monarch's empire own;

> Rather, far rather would he be
> A free-born Knight of England free,
> Than sit on Despot's throne.'"

He passes on, therefore, unscathed, and as he goes the fourth maiden lays her hand upon her harp and breaks forth into a stirring, triumphant song, which shows the warrior that his trials are now ended, and that he is about to attain the goal of his wishes—

> "Quake to your foundations deep,
> Stately Towers, and bannered Keep,
> Bid your vaulted echoes moan,
> As the dreaded step they own.
>
> "Fiends! that wait on Merlin's spell,
> Hear that foot-fall! mark it well!
> Spread your dusky wings abroad,
> Boune ye for your homeward road!
>
> "It is His, the first who e'er
> Dared the dismal Hall of Fear;
> His, who hath the snares defied,
> Spread by Pleasure, Wealth, and Pride.
>
> "Quake to your foundations deep,
> Bastion huge, and Turret steep!
> Tremble Keep! and totter Tower!
> This is Gyneth's waking hour."

The end has come. De Vaux enters a bower, "where milder light through crimson curtains fell," and here he finds the object of his quest—

> "Deep slumbering in the fatal chair,
> He saw King Arthur's child!"

He sees her exactly as she has been described in Lyulph's tale—the warder still in her hand, Vanoc's blood on the hem of her dress, and her hair falling over her shoulders—and here for the first time does doubt and a kind of fear come over him—

> "Trembling in his fitful joy,
> Doubtful how he shall destroy
> Long-enduring spell;

> Doubtful too, when slowly rise
> Dark-fringed lids of Gyneth's eyes,
> What those eyes shall tell.
> 'St. George! St. Mary! can it be,
> That they will kindly look on me!'"

At length, he kneels and takes her hand in his, but, as he does so, a loud thunderclap is heard, which wakes the maiden, the castle walls burst asunder and melt away—

> "But beneath their mystic rocks,
> In the arms of bold De Vaux,
>   Safe the Princess lay!
> Safe and free from magic power,
> Blushing like the rose's flower
>   Opening to the day;
> And round the Champion's brows was bound
> The crown that Druidess had wound,
>   Of the green laurel bay."

This was all our hero had gained—the Princess and the wreath of victory, but this was all that he would desire, for, as the poet says—

> "Where should warrior seek the meed,
> Due to high worth for daring deed,
>   Except for Love and Fame!"

The poet ends here abruptly; we know nothing of the intercourse between De Vaux and the rescued Princess, we only know that—

> "Our lovers, briefly be it said,
> Wedded as lovers wont to wed,
>   When tale or play is o'er;
> Lived long and blessed, loved fond and true,
> And saw a numerous race renew
>   The honours that they bore."

This is satisfactory, for, as I before said, the lady by no means approaches the high ideal required by the Baron of Triermain in his future bride; indeed, her character in Lyulph's tale is by no means a pleasing one, but we may hope that her punishment, her "sleep of many a hundred year, with gentle dreams beguiled," may have improved and softened her disposition.

On the other hand, the character of the hero of the poem, Sir Roland de Vaux of Triermain, is a very attractive one. He is, I think, the ideal of what a brave, nay, a Christian knight should be. He is possessed of great courage, steadfastness, and firmness against temptation; he never swerves an inch from the path which he has taken; these qualities carry him safely through all the dangers, difficulties, and temptations to which he is exposed; he obtains the reward of his toil, and the laurel wreath of victory in consequence.

Before I conclude my treatise, I would say a few words regarding the Castle Rock and its resemblance to an actual castle, which forms the great feature of the poem. The Rock itself, as I said before, is a round "tump" of a hill standing out from the main Helvellyn range, covered partly with turf, through which the bare rock appears in parts.

In my mind, in looking at it from the Thirlmere end of the vale, there is no appearance of a ruined castle at all, and, but for the poem, the idea of such would never occur to the beholder. From the Threlkeld end, there, in general, may be a slight resemblance, but not much; there are no jagged rocks which may suggest resemblance to ruins; it is merely, as I said, a rounded rock. I have, however, within the last two years, undergone an experience which surprised me. I was travelling in the train, and had just passed Threlkeld station, when the setting sun shone full upon the Rock, the front of which, thus lit up, had exactly the appearance of a ruined castle. The mound is here only seen for a moment from the train. This is not to be confounded with another appearance of the castle to me, some years before, which I will relate hereafter. It may, however, have been somewhat different in appearance in Scott's time. In fact, it must have been so, according to the following extract which I quote from the notes to the poem :—[10]

"We now gained a view of the Vale of St. John, a very narrow dell, hemmed in by mountains, through which a small brook makes many meanderings, washing little enclosures of grass ground, which stretch up the rising of the hills. In the widest part of the dale, you are struck with the appearance of an ancient, ruined castle, which seems to stand on

(10) The extract is taken from " Hutchinson's Excursion to the Lakes."

the summit of a little mount, the mountains around forming an amphi-theatre. This massive bulwark shows a front of various towers, and makes an awful, rude, and Gothic appearance, with its lofty turrets and ragged battlements; we traced the galleries, the bending arches, the buttresses. The greatest antiquity stands characterised in its archi-tecture; the inhabitants near it assert it is an antediluvian structure.

"The traveller's curiosity is roused, and he prepares to make a nearer approach, when that curiosity is put upon the rack by his being assured that, if he advances, certain genii who govern the place, by virture of their supernatural arts and necromancy, will strip it of all its beauties, and, by enchantment, transform the magic walls. The vale seems adapted for the habitation of such beings; its gloomy recesses and re-tirements look like the haunts of evil spirits. There was no delusion in the report; we were soon convinced of its truth; for this piece of antiquity, so venerable and noble in its aspect, as we drew near, changed its figure, and proved no other than a shaken, massive pile of rocks, which stand in the midst of this little vale, disunited from the adjoining mountains, and have so much the real form and resemblance of a castle that they bear the name of the Castle Rocks of St. John."

This is a very remarkable statement, and does not, as I have said, carry out the actual appearance of the rounded "tump" of rock, known as the Castle Rock. I will, however, relate another experience of my own, which, as I think, solves the question and shows the actual origin of the poem.

Some years ago, I was staying at Keswick, and had rambled one afternoon up to the slope of Skiddaw. On returning by the ridge which connects the above mountain with the wooded hill of Lattrig (termed Skiddaw's cub), I stopped for a moment by a memorial stone to two shepherds (father and son, if I recollect rightly), having on it a very appropriate epitaph—

> "Great Shepherd of the chosen flock,
> These men have left our hill,
> Their feet are on the Living Rock,
> O guard and keep them still."

It was about sunset, and a lovely evening. I had paused about this place, and turned my eyes towards the Valley of St. John (about three miles distant), with the setting sun behind me. Over there, in the spot where the Castle Rock should be, I saw the exact appearance of a castle, just as it is described in the poem—a gateway, with two flanking towers, and a keep behind.[11] I kept my eyes on this appearance, which seemed to shimmer in the sunlight, until the light of the setting sun faded away. This appearance, as I think, must have formed the original idea of the poem; Scott must have seen it from this point, as I did, and have visited the Rock afterwards. Hence he would have taken his idea of the Castle Rock from this appearance, and not from any fancied resemblance to a castle in the rock.

It will be noted that from this point the Rock had an appearance of a castle in entire preservation; from Threlkeld, it appears as a ruined one. In both cases, the appearance was caused by the setting sun shining full upon the Rock.

This, then, is therefore the probable solution; this is what the poet is thinking of when he concludes his work with these lines—

> " Know too, that when a pilgrim strays,
> In morning mist or evening maze,
>   Along the mountain lone,
> That fairy fortress often mocks
> His gaze upon the castled rocks
>   Of the Valley of Saint John;
> But never man since brave De Vaux
>   The charmèd portal won.
> 'Tis now a vain illusive show,
> That melts whene'er the sunbeams glow,
>   Or the fresh breeze hath blown."

(11) " Embattled high and proudly towered,
  Shaded by ponderous flankers, lowered
  The portal's gloomy way."
                    Canto III., ver. 15.

MARMION.

IV.—MARMION.

" A royal messenger he came,
Though most unworthy of the name,
A letter forged ! St. Jude to speed !
Did ever knight so foul a deed !
At first in heart it liked me ill,
When the king praised his clerkly skill.

. . . .

' 'Tis pity of him too,' he cried,
' Bold can he speak, and fairly ride ;
I warrant him a warrior tried.' "

SUCH is the comment passed upon the character of the hero of the above poem by the old Scottish Baron, Archibald Douglas, Earl of Angus, termed "Bell-the-Cat"; a man none too scrupulous in his deeds, provided they assume the nature of open warfare ; but averse to a mean, treacherous act, such as forgery—a crime, however, by no means uncommon in the sixteenth century, at the commencement of which the events of the poem take place.[1]

It is a fair, unbiassed estimate of the character of the man who is the principal personage of the poem on which I am about to attempt to comment : that of, on the one part, a mean, treacherous scoundrel, on the other, of a gallant, fearless warrior, foremost in the fight, and ready to die for his country's cause. Such characters are, indeed, by no means uncommon in history, and I venture to refer my readers to a former treatise, in which I commented upon the character of Ahab, King of Israel. The latter and our present subject, Marmion, are by no means dissimilar in their characters, as we shall see as our narrative of the poem proceeds.

As in the "Lay of the Last Minstrel," so in the case of "Marmion," we have the scathing criticism of Lord Byron, who says, "Marmion, the hero of the later romance, is exactly what

---

[1] " Marmion," Canto VI., note *m.*

William of Deloraine would have been, had he (Deloraine) been able to read and write." This, as I think I said in my former treatise, is hardly fair on Deloraine: the two characters are entirely different; the one is simply the type of a Border moss-trooper, acting according to his own lights, and possessing certain redeeming qualities; the other is an educated man, in high position, one who ought to have been far above the despicable act which we shall shortly relate. Lord Byron practically repeats the comment of the Earl of Angus on Marmion, when he says—

> "Next view in state, high prancing on his roan,
> The golden-crested, haughty Marmion.
> Now forging scrolls, now foremost in the fight,
> Not quite a felon, yet not half a knight;
> The gibbet or the field prepared to grace,
> A mighty mixture of the great and base."

The events of the poem, as I have said, take place at the commencement of the sixteenth century, and conclude with a beautiful description of the Battle of Flodden, in A.D. 1513. In fact, Scott himself terms the poem "A Tale of Flodden Field," and heads it with an extract from Leyden—

> "Alas! that Scottish maid should sing
> The combat where her lover fell!
> That Scottish bard should wake the string,
> The triumph of our foes to tell!"

Lord Marmion, the hero of the poem, is described as—

> "Lord of Fontenaye,
> Of Lutterward, and Scrivelbaye,
> Of Tamworth tower and town."

He is, himself, a fictitious character, and the family to which he is supposed to belong (who had formerly possessed the above-named estates) had been extinct for many centuries previous to the period of the opening of the poem.[2] In this instance, therefore, the poet was in no danger of offending any existing members of the family by portraying one of their ancestors as an unscrupulous scoundrel.

(2) "Marmion," Canto I., note z.

It will be well, I think, before entering into the narrative of the poem, to describe the events connected with the crime committed by Marmion, which, although mentioned constantly in the course of the poem, really occurred before it opens. They are related, first, by Constance de Beverley, the nun whom Marmion had seduced and persuaded to leave her convent, in her own words—

> "I listened to a traitor's tale,
> I left the convent and the veil,
> For three long years I bowed my pride,
> A horse-boy in his train to ride";

secondly, by the Abbess of St. Hilda to Ralph de Wilton, the victim of Marmion's crime; and, lastly, De Wilton himself relates his own adventures to his lady-love.

The tale runs as follows: Marmion, wearying of his abducted nun, falls in love with another lady (or, rather, with her lands and heritage), the Lady Clara de Clare, of the house of the powerful Earl of Gloucester. This lady is, however, beloved by, and returns the love of, the youthful Sir Ralph de Wilton before mentioned. Marmion is, however, the more powerful suitor, and high in favour with the king, Henry VIII., who supports him in his suit; and, utterly unscrupulous as he is, he attempts to ruin his rival by declaring him a traitor, in that he (De Wilton) had been in league with a certain Martin Swart, who had been associated with, and fought on the side of, Lambert Simnel, the pretender to the crown in the reign of Henry VII.; and, to prove his assertion, Marmion challenges De Wilton to single combat— "the ordeal of battle." The latter owns that he had known Swart, but denies that any treasonable correspondence had passed between them, "merely a scroll of courteous compliment." De Wilton dispatches his squire to his residence to bring this scroll; when produced, however, the packet is found to contain several treasonable letters. These letters had been, at Marmion's instigation, forged by the wretched girl whom he had abducted from the convent; she meets De Wilton's squire, drugs him with wine, and, while he is in that state, substitutes the forged letters for the genuine scroll. She does this, evidently, in the hope of regaining Marmion's favour, and also, doubtless, with the intention of holding him in her power, "as privy to his honour's stain." The squire confesses this, when too late; no one believes his statement except the Lady Clare.

The only hope, therefore, for De Wilton now is to accept Marmion's challenge, and seek to prove his innocence by ordeal of battle; and here, alas! he fails. He is confronted by a formidable antagonist; Marmion is a trained veteran; he has fought at Bosworth Field, and evidently on the side of the Earl of Richmond (afterwards Henry VII.), which would account for his being so high in favour with Henry VIII. This battle (Bosworth) took place in 1485; therefore, if we assume that Marmion "fleshed his maiden sword" there, he would, at the period now in question (1513), be probably fully fifty years of age. De Wilton, on the other hand, is evidently a youth, without the military training of his antagonist. Under these circumstances, the result is as might be expected, and it is an example to show how weak and void of proof were the boasted ordeals of those times.

> "Their oaths are said,
>   Their prayers are prayed,
>   Their lances in the rest are laid,
> They meet in mortal shock;
> And hark! the throng, with thundering cry,
> Shout, 'Marmion, Marmion, to the sky!
>   De Wilton to the block!'"

She (the Abbess) afterwards says of De Wilton—

> "To clear his fame in vain he strove,
> For wondrous are His ways above!
> Perchance some form was unobserved,
> Perchance in prayer or faith he swerved;
> Else how could guiltless champion quail,
> Or how the blessèd ordeal fail?"

The above lines are taken from the narrative of the Abbess of Whitby to De Wilton himself, who was in the disguise of a palmer; we shall touch on this interview later (Canto V., verse 21).

De Wilton lies senseless in the lists; he has failed in the ordeal, and his life is forfeit; but he is probably believed to be dead, and, therefore, an old retainer of his is permitted to remove his body; he recovers, and we shall hear of him again in the course of the narrative.

The Lady Clare, in despair at the thought of having to wed Marmion, whom she abhors, consigns herself to the care of the Abbess of St. Hilda, at Whitby, with the intention of taking the vows and becoming a nun. She is not, however, out of danger; Marmion is powerful, high in the favour of the king, who gives him his full support—

> "'Ho! shifts she thus?' King Henry cried,
> 'Sir Marmion, she shall be thy bride,
> If she were sworn a nun.'" (3)

However, the lady remains at the convent for the present, for, as war with Scotland was impending, the king dispatches Marmion on an embassy to the Court of Edinburgh.

In the meantime, the unhappy Constance finds her crime useless: far from regaining Marmion's favour, she finds him more infatuated than ever with the charms of Lady Clare; her threats, her entreaties are vain; she only irritates him with her reproaches; and, mad with jealousy and rage, she, by connivance with a recreant monk, endeavours to poison her rival: the attempt fails, but how, the poem does not state. Marmion, however, by some means (probably through the wretched monk above mentioned) learns of this attempt, and, enraged at this, and also wearied with her reproaches, treacherously betrays her to the monks of Holy Island, who seize the maiden during Marmion's march towards Scotland. To do Marmion justice, however, he did not contemplate the terrible fate that awaited her—the fearful punishment of those days inflicted on a perjured nun. He adjured the monks to do her no harm, and merely keep her in confinement, that thus he would be rid of her. But, in his inmost heart, he must have known what her fate would be, for we shall see, in the course of the poem, how his conscience smites him—

> "When Constance, late betrayed and scorned,
> All lovely on his soul returned."

(3) Scott rather anticipates the action of Henry VIII. in this matter; the king, at this period of his reign, was a strong supporter of the Church, so much so as to receive from the Pope the title of "Defender of the Faith": such a threat would not be characteristic of him at this time, not till a much later period.

The second canto of the poem relates her terrible fate, and I think it best to enter upon this now, instead of taking it in the general course of the poem, as it concludes the course of events which take place before the action of the narrative commences.

A "chapter of St. Benedict" is to be held at St. Cuthbert's Abbey, Holy Island, situated off the coast of Northumberland, consisting of the Abbot, the Prioress of Tynemouth, and the Abbess of St. Hilda's Abbey, Whitby—

> "For inquisition stern and strict,
> On two apostates from the faith,
> And, if need be, to doom to death."

These culprits are the unhappy Constance and the wretched monk above mentioned.

The poet describes the voyage of the Abbess of Whitby from her abbey to the Holy Isle; she is attended by five nuns and the heroine of the poem, the Lady Clare, now a novice of the abbey, whither she had fled to escape from the persecution of Marmion. The voyage along the coast of Northumberland is beautifully described—

> "And now the vessel skirts the strand
> Of mountainous Northumberland;
> Towns, towers, and halls successive rise,
> And catch the nuns' delighted eyes.
> Monk-Wearmouth soon behind them lay,
> And Tynemouth's priory and bay;
> They marked, amid her trees, the hall
> Of lofty Seaton-Delaval;
> They saw the Blythe and Wansbeck floods
> Rush to the sea through sounding woods;
> They passed the tower of Widderington,
> Mother of many a valiant son;
> At Coquet-isle their beads they tell
> To the good Saint who owned the cell;
> Then did the Alne attention claim,
> And Warkworth, proud of Percy's name;
> And next, they crossed themselves to hear
> The whitening breakers sound so near,
> Where, boiling through the rocks, they roar
> On Dunstanborough's caverned shore;
> Thy tower, proud Bamborough, marked they here,
> King Ida's castle, huge and square,

> From its tall rock look grimly down,
> And on the swelling ocean frown;
> Then from the coast they bore away,
> And reached the Holy Island's bay."

Holy Island, or Lindisfarne, stands about 1½ miles from the mainland, separated entirely at high water, but accessible when the tide is out—

> "For with the flow and ebb, its style
> Varies from .continent to isle."

On this occasion, it is high water when the Abbess and her nuns reach the island.

Passing by the reception of the guests, and the intercourse of the nuns of the two abbeys, each group vying with the other in relating the merits and exploits of their respective patron saints, we enter upon a dismal scene. We are conducted to a gloomy subterranean vault, hewn out of the rock on which the abbey is built—

> "It was more dark and lone, that vault,
> Than the worst dungeon cell;
>
> .   .   .   .
>
> This den, which, chilling every sense
> Of feeling, hearing, sight,
> Was called the Vault of Penitence,
> Excluding air and light,
> Was, by the prelate Sexhelm, made
> A place of burial, for such dead
> As, having died in mortal sin,
> Might not be laid the church within.
> 'Twas now a place of punishment;
> Whence if so loud a shriek were sent
> As reached the upper air,
> The hearers blessed themselves, and said
> The spirits of the sinful dead
> Bemoaned their torments there."

Few, with the exception of the Abbot himself, knew the way to this grim dungeon, for—

> "Victim and executioner
> Were blind-fold when transported there."

In this awful place, therefore, lighted only by a single cresset lamp, the three judges before mentioned are assembled to try the two wretched prisoners, whom I also mentioned before, viz., Constance de Beverley and the recreant monk; and the dread preparations for the awful punishment for relapsed monks and nuns, viz., that of burying alive, a penalty evidently derived from the laws of ancient Rome against relapsed vestal virgins, are vividly presented before us. We behold two dark niches in the wall, each furnished with a slender meal, to keep the wretched inmates alive for a short period; each guarded by two grim monks, as executioners—

> "Men who were with mankind foes,
> And with despite and envy fired,
> Into the cloister had retired,
> Or who, in desperate hope of grace,
> Strove, by deep penance, to efface
> Of some foul crime the stain."

Round these grim ministers of ecclesiastical justice lie the implements of their office—

> "Hewn stones and cement were displayed,
> And building tools in order laid."

The aspect of the three judges, and of the wretched culprits, is well described. The president, the blind old Abbot, designated "The Saint of Lindisfarne," sees nothing before him but what he deems his stern duty—

> "Nor ruth, nor mercy's trace is shown,
> Whose look·is hard and stern."

The Prioress of Tynemouth is also hard and stern, but the Abbess of St. Hilda is of a more tender disposition; this terrible work is not to her liking: she covers her face—

> "To hide her bosom's swell,
> And tear-drops that for pity fell."

The demeanour of the two prisoners also is very different: Constance, clad in the dress of a page, in the livery of Lord Marmion, faces her doom bravely; while the wretched monk cowers on the floor of the cell, moaning and howling for mercy, she "waits her doom without a tear."

There is little form of trial; the culprits are identified, and it would be useless to attempt to deny their crime. The old Abbot is about to pronounce sentence when Constance essays to speak, and he pauses to permit her to do so.

She owns her offence, and relates the story which I have already told regarding Marmion's crime and De Wilton's disgrace; and she declares that, should the last hope of her being restored to Marmion's favour have been destroyed, she would have betrayed him without the least hesitation—

> "Had fortune my last hope betrayed,
> This packet, to the king conveyed,
> Had given him to the headsman's stroke,
> Although my heart that instant broke."

She speaks with contempt of her dastard companion, and concludes bravely—

> "Now, men of death, work forth your will,
> For I can suffer and be still;
> And come he slow, or come he fast,
> It is but Death who comes at last."

She does not conclude, however, without launching a fiery bolt at her executioners, with a prophecy, which came only too true, of the impending attack of Henry VIII. on the monasteries—

> "Yet dread me, from my living tomb,
> Ye vassal slaves of bloody Rome!
> If Marmion's late remorse should wake,
> Full soon such vengeance would he take,
> That you shall wish the fiery Dane
> Had rather been your guest again.(4)

(4) Constance does not misjudge Marmion: mark his dying words—

> "I would the Fiend, to whom belongs
> The vengeance due to all her wrongs,
> Would spare me but a day!
> For wasting fire, and dying groan,
> And priests slain on the altar-stone,
> Might bribe him for delay."

Canto VI., ver. 31.

Behind, a darker hour ascends!
The altar quakes, the crosier bends,
The ire of a despotic king
Rides forth upon destruction's wing;
Then shall these vaults, so strong and deep,
Burst open to the sea-wind's sweep;
Some traveller then shall find my bones,
Whitening amid disjointed stones,
And, ignorant of priests' cruelty,
Marvel such reliques here should be." (5)

This terrible denunciation, together with her wild appearance, appals the judges for a while and strikes them dumb, for—

" Her figure seemed to rise more high,
Her voice, despair's wild energy
Had given a tone of prophecy."

But soon the Abbot recovers himself, and gives out the usual sentence of dismissal to the living tomb, "Vade in Pace!" (Go in Peace!)—

" Sister, let thy sorrows cease,
Sinful brother, part in peace!"

A veil is now drawn over the dread scene which follows: the judges retire, glad indeed to return to the upper air, but not before they have proof of the horrible work which is going on— "the shriekings of despair, and many a stifled groan." These are doubtless from the craven monk, for we may be certain that Constance meets her doom in silence. Stern, bigoted as they are (at least, two of them), they are yet human, and the terrible scene which they have passed through has a strong effect upon them—

" Even in the vesper's heavenly tone,
They seemed to hear a dying groan,
And bade the passing knell to toll
For welfare of a parting soul."

So closes the second canto, and here, I may say, also ends the preliminary portion of the poem, for, though the scene which I have described is included in the poem itself, it is but the climax

(5) A note in the second canto of the poem states that a female skeleton was found in the ruins of the Abbey of Coldingham; it was believed to be that of an immured nun.

of the events which take place before the actual narrative commences. This latter follows the steps of Lord Marmion on his embassy to the Scottish Court; his crossing the Border, his journey to Edinburgh, his sojourn at King James's Court; thence, on his return journey, his stay at Tantallon Castle, and his recrossing of the Border, only to meet his death on Flodden Field. To this narrative, therefore, I now proceed.

The first canto opens at the Border Castle of Norham, situated on the south, or English, side of the Tweed, about six miles above the town of Berwick-upon-Tweed. It is but a ruin now, but was then, "in the old Border day," a fortress of great importance, one of those stationed on the English Border to guard against the inroads of the ever-turbulent Scottish raiders. The governor of the castle is "Sir Hugh the Heron bold," who is described as "Baron of Twisell and of Ford, and Captain of the Hold." Why the poet terms him "Sir Hugh" we know not, for the note to the poem states that the original of this chieftain is Sir William Heron of Ford,[6] whose wife, Lady Heron, is now, according to the poem, at the Court of King James IV., and a favourite of that monarch, having been sent there as a hostage for her husband, who had slain a Scottish chieftain. We are not informed of the particulars of this arrangement, which certainly appears strange, especially at the period of which we are writing, when a man's life was held of little account. This, however, appears to be a fictitious statement, for another note to the poem states [7] that James did not make the acquaintance of this lady until he had entered England on his way to Flodden, and that his infatuation for her charms caused the fatal delay which brought on that defeat. We shall hear and see more of this Lady Heron as we proceed with the narrative of the poem.

The warder on the castle rampart hears a trampling of horse, and descries a troop approaching—a "plump of spears," as the poet describes it; a horseman issues from it, and gallops on to the castle gate to announce its approach. He blows his horn, and, like that of the Moor Calaynos,[8] "the note he blew, right

(6) Note *b*, ver. 13, Canto I.

(7) Note *x*, ver. 10, Canto V.

(8) See "Lockhart's Spanish Ballads."

well they knew": a guest of high importance is at hand, an
emissary of the king. The warder at once warns the governor,
who immediately gives orders for the guest's reception—

> "Now, broach ye a pipe of Malvoisie,
>   Bring pasties of the doe,
> And quickly make the entrance free,
> And bid my heralds ready be,
> And every minstrel sound his glee,
>   And all our trumpets blow;
> And, from the platform, spare ye not
> To fire a noble salvo-shot:
> Lord MARMION waits below."

The cannon thunders forth, the trumpets blow, the castle
gates are flung open, the guards salute, and we are now confronted with the hero (and villain) of the poem.

Lord Marmion, whatever his private character may have
been, is evidently a doughty warrior; he is no longer young; he
has been proved in many a fight, and as

> "The scar on his brown cheek revealed
>   A token true of Bosworth field,"

his age would, as I pointed out before, now certainly be not
less than fifty. His appearance is striking, and characteristic of
the trained warrior—

> "His eyebrow dark, and eye of fire,
>   Showed spirit proud, and prompt to ire;
> Yet lines of thought upon his cheek
> Did deep design and counsel speak.
>   His forehead, by his casque worn bare,
>   His thick moustache, and curly hair,
>   Coal-black, and grizzled here and there,
>   But more through toil than age;
>   His square-turned joints, and strength of limb,
>   Showed him no carpet knight so trim,
>   But, in close fight, a champion grim,
>   In camps, a leader sage."

Pity indeed that so noble an aspect concealed a heart
capable of the most unscrupulous villainy!

The following of this doughty warrior is worthy of himself—two squires (whom we shall frequently meet in the course of the narrative), four men-at-arms, armed with "halberd, bill, and battle-axe," and twenty yeomen archers, of whom—

> "Each one a six-foot bow could bend,
> And far a cloth-yard shaft could send;
> Each held a boar-spear stout and strong,
> And at their belts their quivers rung."

Above all waves Marmion's banner, with his crest—

> "A falcon hovered on her nest,
> With wings outspread, and forward breast."

Such is the chief, and such his following, who, as I said earlier, are now on their way on an embassy from the English monarch, Henry VIII., to the Scottish sovereign, James IV., to demand the reason of the force which the latter was now assembling in the south of Scotland.

A noble reception awaits the chieftain and his troop at Norham Castle; the garrison turns out "with musket, pike, and morion"; the welcome shot is fired, the minstrels play, and, as Marmion scatters the usual largesse around, they strike up a welcome—

> "Welcome to Norham, Marmion!
> Stout heart and open hand!
> Well dost thou brook thy gallant roan,
> Thou flower of English land!"

Marmion dismounts, and enters the castle hall, where the heralds announce him, and in such words that cannot be pleasing to him, for, as we shall see later, he is not absolutely devoid of conscience. They descant upon his late victory over De Wilton, they applaud his prowess to the skies, and conclude thus—

> "Place, nobles, for the Falcon-Knight!
> Room, room, ye gentles gay,
> For him who conquered in the right,
> Marmion of Fontenaye!"

He must have felt that there would have been a very different reception for him had they but known the truth.

He is now received by Sir Hugh Heron and conducted to the banquet, and here again he is unpleasantly reminded of his former misdeeds. Sir Hugh asks him the awkward question—

> "Where hast thou left that Page of thine,
> That used to serve thy cup of wine,
> Whose beauty was so rare ? "

His following description of this page evidently shows that Sir Hugh suspected the true sex of the supposed boy, and this allusion to the unhappy Constance naturally arouses Marmion's anger; he suppresses it, however, saying that he left the boy sick at Lindisfarne, and then retorts by asking Heron why his lady was not present at the board. Sir Hugh replies carelessly, as if he were utterly indifferent to the fact that Lady Heron was leading a very doubtful life at King James's Court—

> "Better loves my lady bright
> To sit in liberty and light,
>   In fair Queen Margaret's bower.(9)
> We hold our greyhound in our hand,
>   Our falcon on our glove;
> But where shall we find leash or band
> For dame that loves to rove ? "

Lord Marmion, as we have seen, is on his way to Edinburgh, on an embassy to the Court of Scotland, for the purpose above mentioned, for James IV. is now assembling an army for the invasion of England, choosing the opportunity, as was often the case, when the English king was at war with France, as was the case now. The pretext of James for war was, according to the poem, a very flimsy one—a mere Border foray, with which Henry had probably nothing to do; for, as I mentioned in my treatise on the "Lay of the Last Minstrel," Border warfare was carried on independently of the nature of affairs, whether of peace or war, between the two countries. Such constant warfare on the Border could, however, always furnish a pretext for a quarrel, such as under—

---

(9) This is Margaret Tudor, sister of Henry VIII. and wife of James IV., from whom the Stuart kings derived their title to the crown of England.

> " ' Our Borders sacked by many a raid,
> Our peaceful liege-men robbed,' he said;
> ' On day of truce our Warden slain,
> Stout Barton killed, his vassals ta'en—
> Unworthy were we here to reign,
> Should these for vengeance cry in vain;
> Our full defiance, hate, and scorn,
> Our herald has to Henry borne.' " (10)

But, in fact, James was but carrying out the constant policy of his predecessors—

> " For once the eagle England being in prey,
> To her unguarded nest the weasel Scot
> Comes' sneaking, and so sucks her princely eggs;
> Playing the mouse, in absence of the cat,
> To taint and havoc more than she can eat." (11)

Such a policy, however, had, before this, proved very disastrous to Scotland. England had more than once proved herself quite capable of coping with France and Scotland combined, and James might have remembered the invasion of England in 1346 by David Bruce, which ended in the defeat and capture of that monarch at Neville's Cross; also the several severe defeats of the Scottish allies, in their assistance of France against Henry V. and his successor.(12) National animosity, however, prevails against principles of cautious policy, and the unfortunate monarch, contrary to the counsel of his best advisers, proceeds upon his unhappy enterprise, which ends in a worse defeat than that of Neville's Cross, and his own death.

Henry VIII. was, doubtless, unwilling to enter into a war with Scotland while embroiled with France; he, therefore, sends Marmion, who, as we have seen, was his favourite, on an embassy to the Court of Scotland on the errand above mentioned, and also, doubtless, to make a last attempt to patch up a peace, if possible.

(10) King James's own words to Marmion, ver. 13, Canto V.

(11) See Shakespeare's " Henry V."

(12) They suffered severely at Crevant, Verneuil, and Rouvrai (1422 to 1429), where their allies, the French, evidently allowed them to bear the brunt of the battle; they gained, however, one advantage at Beaugé, where they surprised and defeated a party of English under the Duke of Clarence, brother of Henry V., which prince was here slain.

Marmion, therefore, on hearing that Lady Heron is at the Court of King James, at once offers to bear any message to her which her lord might wish to send; at the same time asking for the services of a guide to direct him in his march through Scotland. Heron at once offers him the services of his rough Borderers, who have many a time "harried" that part of Scotland, but Marmion explains that he is on a peaceful errand, and that, therefore, a different kind of guide would be more acceptable—

> "A herald were my fitting guide;
> Or friar, sworn in peace to bide;
> Or pardoner, or travelling priest,
> Or strolling pilgrim, at the least."

Heron thereupon mentions a certain Friar John of Tillmouth, who knew—

> "Each castle, town, and tower,
> In which the wine and ale is good,
> 'Twixt Newcastle and Holy-Rood."

This worthy, however, appears to have got into trouble in Scotland, being found in company with another man's wife; as Heron termed it, "teaching Dame Alison her creed." He barely escapes from the enraged husband, who threatens his life if he ever catches him on the Scottish side of the Border. This worthy friar, therefore, is naturally reluctant to be employed on this enterprise.

A youth named Selby, nephew to Sir Hugh, now suggests a solution of the difficulty. There is, he says, a "holy palmer" just arrived, who has journeyed to a number of places known in sacred history, also to many shrines at home, and—

> "Knows the passes of the North,
> And seeks far shrines beyond the Forth."

He is of an extremely ascetic character, a very different personage from Friar John—

> "Little he eats, and long will wake,
> And drinks but of the stream or lake.
> This were a guide o'er moor and dale;
> But, when our John hath quaffed his ale,

> As little as the wind that blows,
> And warms itself against his nose,
> Kens he, or cares, which way he goes."

Marmion at once accepts the services of the Palmer, who is summoned to the hall; and here we are confronted with the second most important personage of the narrative.

Ralph de Wilton, after his defeat by Marmion and consequent disgrace, had been rescued and tended by a faithful old retainer through his subsequent illness; he alone, of all, remains faithful to his former master—

> "Menials, and friends, and kinsmen fled
> From the degraded traitor's bed—
> He only held my burning head,
> And tended me for many a day,
> While wounds and fever held their sway."

On recovery, De Wilton assumes a pilgrim's dress, and, accompanied by this faithful old servant, journeys in many lands; at last the old man dies, and with his last breath entreats of his master a boon—

> "If e'er my deadliest enemy
> Beneath my brand should conquered lie,
> Even then my mercy should awake,
> And spare his life for Austin's sake."

How De Wilton fulfils this wish, and how that act of mercy benefits him, we shall shortly see. In the meantime, in the course of his travels, he arrives at Norham Castle in his palmer's dress, and is here confronted with that "deadliest enemy" above mentioned.

He enters the hall; his hardships have entirely changed his appearance, and his gaunt, haggard features afford to Marmion no suspicion of his identity—

> "Poor wretch! the mother that him bare,
> If she had been in presence there,
> In his wan face, and sun-burned hair,
> She had not known her child."

The supposed Palmer accept the office of guide, and Marmion departs on the following morning, dismissed with the same honours which greeted him on his arrival, and he enters Scotland under the guidance, which he little guesses, of his most deadly enemy.

The first day's march takes the party over the Lammermuir Hills to the village of Gifford, about four miles from the town of Haddington, a march of about 25 miles. This village, in which, in the poem, so many matters of interest occur, or are narrated, is, strangely enough, scarcely mentioned in the guide book,[13] which merely states that here is situated Yester Castle, the seat of the Marquis of Tweeddale. Of the weird hall in that castle, of the wizard Lord Gifford, of the ancient Roman camp where the mysterious conflict takes place, of all of which we shall hear anon, the book mentions nothing; in fact, the present mansion appears to be entirely modern. The camp, indeed, would appear to be entirely mythical, for there is not a note, even in the poem itself, affording any explanation. The party reaches this hamlet towards evening—

> "Before them, at the close of day,
> Old Gifford's towers and hamlet lay."

They are not admitted to the castle, the lord being absent, and his lady, left in charge, being unwilling to admit an unknown party. They, therefore, take up their quarters at the village inn, in which, however, there seems to be everything tending to the comfort and accommodation of even so large a party—

> "The village inn seemed large though rude,
> Its cheerful fire and hearty food
> Might well relieve his train."

They are soon settled comfortably to their meal in the spacious kitchen; mirth and jollity soon go their round; and here we are brought face to face with some of the good traits in the character of Marmion, over which, however, the shadow of his crime persistently lowers—

> "Theirs was the glee of martial breast
> And laughter theirs at little jest;
> And oft Lord Marmion deigned to aid,
> And mingle in the mirth they made:

(13) "Baddeley's Guide to the Lowlands of Scotland."

> For though, with men of high degree,
> The proudest of the proud was he,
> Yet, trained in camps, he knew the art
> To win the soldier's hardy heart.
> They love a captain to obey,
> Boisterous as March, yet fresh as May;
> With open hand, and brow as free,
> Lover of wine and minstrelsy;
> Ever the first to scale a tower,
> As venturous in a lady's bower;
> Such buxom chief shall lead his host
> From India's fires to Zembla's frost."

But, amidst all this mirth, the mind of Marmion little coincides with his outward pleasantry; the dark gaze of his enemy, the supposed Palmer, is sternly fixed upon him the whole time, and this strongly affects Marmion, who in vain attempts to frown the look down. De Wilton himself afterwards describes the incident—

> " And ne'er the time shall I forget,
> When, in a Scottish hostel set,
>   Dark looks we did exchange:
> What were his thoughts I cannot tell,
> But in my bosom mustered Hell
>   Its plans of dark revenge."

Not only does the gaze of the supposed Palmer have such strong effect on the mind of Marmion, but it also affects the spirits of the men, damping their previous mirth. One of them at length whispers to his comrade—

> " Saint Mary! saw'st thou e'er such sight?
> How pale his cheek, his eye how bright,
> Whene'er the fire-brand's fickle light
>   Glances beneath his cowl!
> Full on our Lord he sets his eye;
> For his best palfrey, would not I
>   Endure that sullen scowl."

Marmion at length, unable to endure that direful look, and also to cheer the drooping spirits of the men, calls upon one of his squires, Fitz-Eustace, to regale them with a lay. The answer of the squire awakens the conscience of the Baron, by lamenting the absence of the page, "Constant," by which name and in which disguise the unhappy Constance had accompanied the train—

> "No nightingale her love-lorn tune
> More sweetly warbles to the moon."

Fitz-Eustace then sings the favourite song of the supposed page, some of the words of which pierce Marmion's conscience to its very depths—

> "Where shall the traitor rest,
>   He, the deceiver,
> Who could win maiden's breast,
>   Ruin, and leave her?
> In the lost battle,
>   Borne down by the flying,
> Where mingles war's rattle
>   With groans of the dying,
>   There shall he be lying."

I have already mentioned the motives that actuated Marmion in his desertion of this unhappy maid and allowing the priests to capture her, giving them strict charge, however, to do her no harm, but merely to keep her in confinement. We have seen how the charge was kept; little did the priests care for the injunctions of Marmion; and indeed, in all probability, they would not, for their own sakes, have dared to remit the enjoined punishment.

It is no wonder that Marmion, conscience stricken, broods over his disgraceful act, for Constance was, and still is, his first love, his courtship of the Lady Clare being more for that lady's lands than for her person. The song so affects his imagination that he says to Fitz-Eustace—

> "Is it not strange, that, as ye sung,
> Seemed in mine ear a death-peal rung,
> Such as in nunneries they toll
> For some departing sister's soul?
>   Say, what may this portend?"

The Palmer answers (the first time he had opened his lips that day), "The death of a dear friend." The convent bell was indeed, at that very hour, tolling the knell of the unhappy Constance in far-off Lindisfarne; and the Palmer's words must have driven into the heart of Marmion the certainty of her death, although he strives to hide it from himself—

> "Gave I not charge
> She should be safe, though not at large ?
> They durst not, for their island, shred
> One golden ringlet from her head."

Well does the poet describe the gloomy, conscience-stricken state of Marmion—

> "His thoughts I scan not; but I ween,
> That, could their import have been seen,
> The meanest groom in all the hall,
> That e'er tied courser to a stall,
> Would scarce have wished to be their prey,
> For Lutterward and Fontenaye."

The Baron's gloomy brooding is interrupted by the host, who, incited by the words of the Palmer, which intimate that the latter is possessed of the power of divination, relates a legend of the neighbourhood—

> "Yet might a knight his fortune hear,
> If, knight-like, he despises fear,
> Not far from hence;—if fathers old
> Aright our hamlet legend told."

Before entering into the narrative of this legend, I must remind the reader of what I before stated, viz., that, strangely enough, nothing relating to it is mentioned in the guide book to Scotland, by Baddeley, who so seldom omits any subject of interest; the village itself of Gifford is but casually mentioned, together with the neighbouring Yester House; the "Goblin Hall" in that castle and the haunted camp in the neighbourhood are not mentioned at all; we must therefore conjecture that the legend, and all the facts connected with it, come entirely from Sir Walter Scott's imagination, together with his mythical hero Marmion.

The tale runs thus: Alexander III. of Scotland, shortly before his famous victory at Largs over the Northmen (A.D. 1263), while mustering his army to repel their invasion, arrives at Yester Castle to consult the then Lord Gifford, who is reported

to have been a wizard; the latter, emerging from the "Goblin
Hall" in the castle, in his wizard's dress, meets the king and
tells him that he (Lord Gifford) himself can give him no information as to "his kingdom's future weal and woe," but that if he
(the king) has sufficient courage to endure the ordeal, he may
compel the demon who holds the secret to divulge it—

> "But thou—who little know'st thy might,
> As born upon that blessèd night,(14)
> When yawning graves, and dying groan,
> Proclaimed hell's empire overthrown,—
> With untaught valour shalt compel
> Response denied to magic spell."

The monarch eagerly expresses his willingness to enter upon
the trial, and the wizard directs him to proceed to a neighbouring
ruined camp, enter by the south entrance, and wind his horn,
when the demon shall appear in the likeness of the king's worst
enemy, mounted and armed for the fight—

> "Couch then thy lance, and spur thy steed—
> Upon him! and St. George to speed!
> If he go down, thou soon shalt know
> Whate'er these airy sprites can show—
> If thy heart fail thee in the strife,
> I am no warrant for thy life."

The king, therefore, at midnight, proceeds to this haunted
camp, in which is space for conflict—

> "The breadth across, a bowshot clear,
> Gives ample space for full career."

He winds his horn, and forthwith appears a mounted figure in
armour, in the shape of Edward I. of England, then, according
to the poem, on crusade in Palestine,(15) and who afterwards,
although no foe to Alexander himself, became so, in after years,

(14) Good Friday. The note to the poem, note *h*, states that those born on
that day, or on Christmas Day, were supposed to have the power of "seeing
spirits, and even of commanding them."

(15) Sir Walter does not adhere strictly to history. Edward, as Prince of
Wales, would, at this period (A.D. 1263), be engaged in the Barons' War: his visit
to Palestine did not take place till after the close of that war (A.D. 1265).

to the latter monarch's nation. The combatants meet; Alexander fells his adversary to the ground, but does not himself escape unscathed; he receives a slight wound in the face. The king leaps from his horse, and, with sword in hand, compels the demon to reveal the future; he learns, therefore, of the impending glorious victory of Largs. The narrator concludes by stating that every year, on the anniversary of this fight, the king's wound bursts forth anew, Lord Gifford gibingly saying—

> "Bold as ye were, my liege, ye pay
> The penance of your start."

The host, in conclusion, declares that this adventure is still open to anyone courageous enough to undertake it, and that the "elfin warrior" is still to be met with at the haunted camp.

In Marmion's present gloomy, morbid mood, this narrative makes a great impression on his mind, and so disturbs him that he cannot rest, as he himself admits, when afterwards relating the circumstance—

> "'In vain,' said he, 'to rest I spread
> My burning limbs, and couched my head,
> Fantastic thoughts returned;
> And, by their wild dominion led,
> My heart within me burned.'"

His squire, Fitz-Eustace, resting in a stable loft, is suddenly aroused in the middle of the night by his master, standing fully armed beside his bed. Marmion orders him at once to saddle his (Marmion's) steed, as he intends to seek the elfin camp and ascertain if there be any truth in the legend. He enjoins strict silence upon the squire, for—

> "I would not, that the prating knaves
> Had cause for saying, o'er their ale,
> That I could credit such a tale."

With these words, Marmion mounts his steed and departs on his weird quest.

What now occurs is related by Marmion himself and by De Wilton, the actors in the scene, in different parts of the poem, but I prefer to relate at once what actually occurred.

De Wilton, in his palmer's disguise, had watched his enemy, and seen him ride forth fully armed; at once guessing his purpose, he seizes on the horse of the other squire, Blount, and the armour of others of the men, and also rides out to the haunted camp, arriving there about the same time as his enemy. On reaching the spot, Marmion, at the southern entrance, winds his horn; an answering blast is heard, and a mounted champion appears in the lists. The combatants meet; Marmion, as we know, is the more formidable warrior of the two, but he is not now himself; he is overcome by superstition, and also, perhaps, by a guilty conscience; as he himself says afterwards, on receiving his death wound at Flodden, "a sinful heart makes feeble hand." He also owns his superstitious terror, when relating the event afterwards—

> "I care not though the truth I show—
> I trembled with affright;
> And as I placed in rest my spear,
> My hand so shook for very fear,
> I scarce could couch it right."

The result is as might be expected under the circumstances; at the first shock, Marmion is unhorsed, and rolls on the plain. Looking up, he gazes on the face of his foe, and recognizes the features of his mortal enemy, De Wilton—

> "I knew the stern vindictive look,
> And held my breath for awe.
> I saw the face of one who, fled
> To foreign climes, has long been dead—
> I well believe the last;
> For ne'er, from visor raised, did stare
> A human warrior, with a glare
> So grimly and so ghast."

Marmion, therefore, believes that he sees a spectre, as the legend tells; he sees the supposed spectre wave its blade over him three times, and then disappear, as he thought, in answer to his own prayer—

> "But when to good Saint George I prayed,
> (The first time e'er I asked his aid,)
> He plunged it in the sheath;
> And, on his courser mounting light,
> He seemed to vanish from my sight."

Never had Marmion been so near to death; he was saved, not by the intervention of St. George but by the last dying wish of Austin, the old, faithful servant of De Wilton, of which we have treated before; [16] at the very instant of the latter's raising his sword to slay his enemy, he is reminded of the boon asked of him—

> "For the death-stroke my brand I drew,
> (O then my helmèd head he knew,
>   The Palmer's cowl was gone,)
> Then had three inches of my blade
> The heavy debt of vengeance paid—
> My hand the thought of Austin stayed,
>   I left him there alone."

De Wilton receives his reward for this act of mercy, as we shall see hereafter.

Marmion, as we have seen, has been overcome by superstition, and believes that he has been vanquished by a being of another world; we can, therefore, well understand his anger when, later, he discovers the truth—

> "'Ah! dastard fool, to reason lost!'
> He muttered: ' 'Twas not fay nor ghost
> I met upon the moonlight wold,
> But living man of earthly mould.—
>   O dotage blind and gross!
> Had I but fought as wont, one thrust
> Had laid De Wilton in the dust,
>   My path no more to cross.'"

Fitz-Eustace waits up, in great anxiety, for his master; the latter at length returns, showing unmistakable signs of his recent conflict and fall; he says not a word to his squire, however, but, throwing the reins of his horse to him, retires in silence.

There is great commotion in the morning, when not only do the retainers find the horse of Marmion in almost a dying state in his stall, but also that the horse of the squire, Blount, has been ridden in the night, and is in a terrible condition. An altercation ensues between Blount (the "sworn horse courser," as his master terms him, a much rougher character than Fitz-Eustace) and the

(16) See page 93.

host; heated on the part of the former, humorous on that of the latter. Lord Marmion, however, makes light of it all, which must have seemed strange to his followers; and it is also strange that the condition of Blount's horse does not impart to him (Marmion) a suspicion of the truth. He, however, takes no heed, and orders his troop to mount and continue their journey.

The train proceeds "through Humbie's and through Salton wood," but they have not proceeded far when they are met by another party, sent to meet them by King James; their leader is an historical character, "Sir David Lindsay of the Mount, Lord Lion King-at-Arms" (or Lion Herald). As to the latter distinction, Sir Walter Scott owns that he anticipates it by sixteen years; [17] it seems to have been a very great one, for the poet says—

> "Down from his horse did Marmion spring,
> Soon as he saw the Lion-King;
> For well the stately Baron knew,
> To him such courtesy was due,
>   Whom royal James himself had crowned,
>   And on his temples placed the round
>   Of Scotland's ancient diadem;
>   And wet his brow with hallowed wine,
>   And on his finger given to shine
>   The emblematic gem."

A fine description is given of the personal appearance and attendant following of this statesman and poet; he and Marmion meet with due courtesy.

The message of the Lion Herald is in effect that King James, although he has forbidden any English, under the present strained circumstances, to enter his Court, yet, out of courtesy to Marmion, he will make an exception in the latter's favour; the envoy, therefore, is enjoined to conduct the Baron to a fitting residence until he (the king) is ready to receive him.

Sir David conducts Marmion to Crichton Castle, which is situated on the banks of the Tyne, between 16 and 17 miles from Edinburgh, and considerably out of the Baron's direct route to

(17) This is not the only case of anticipation of honours in the poem: there is that of Bishop Gawaine Douglas, son of "Bell-the-Cat," on which I will touch later.

that city. This castle, like so many others, is now a ruin, and also, unlike others, not well known, for, as Baddeley tells us, it is strictly closed, and trespassers on the premises are threatened with prosecution. It seems, however, to have been different in Scott's time; the poet seems to know the castle well. He says—

> "Crichtoun! though now thy miry court
> But pens the lazy steer and sheep,
> Thy turrets rude, and tottered Keep,
> Have been the minstrel's loved resort.
> Oft have I traced within thy fort,
> Of mouldering shields the mystic sense,
> Scutcheons of honour, or pretence,
> Quartered in old armorial sort,
> Remains of rude magnificence."

This castle, at the time of which we write, is the property of Earl Adam Hepburn of Bothwell, grandfather of that Bothwell of ill-fame who is too well known in the history of Mary, Queen of Scots. This nobleman is now absent with his retainers with the king's army at Edinburgh; he is doomed shortly afterwards to perish on Flodden Field.

Marmion, in his absence, is received by the lady of the castle, and entertained with due courtesy; he remains here for two days, and, while here, he learns from Sir David Lindsay an extraordinary event, which we will now relate.

It was the custom of King James, in the month of June every year, to take up his residence in the palace of Linlithgow, to undergo penance on the anniversary of the death of his father, James III., the young prince having been persuaded to join the rebellion against the latter monarch, and been present at the battle of Sauchieburn, where he (James III.) was slain.[18] The young king, struck with remorse, enjoins upon himself severe penances, one being that of constantly wearing an iron belt, and also the annual penance at Linlithgow, where—

> " For now the year brought round again
> The day the luckless king was slain—
> In Katherine's aisle the monarch knelt,
> With sackcloth shirt, and iron belt,
> And eyes with sorrow streaming."

(18) Or, rather, that he was assassinated shortly after the battle.

With regard to this, Sir David remarks—

> "But June is to our Sovereign dear
> The heaviest month of all the year:
> Too well his cause of grief you know,—
> June saw his father's overthrow.
>
> .   .   .   .   .   .
>
> In offices as strict as Lent,
> King James's June is ever spent."

In the June, therefore, immediately preceding the date of the opening of the poem (August, 1513), King James is undergoing his usual penance in the church at Linlithgow, when an apparition manifests itself to him—

> "Stepped from the crowd a ghostly wight,
> In azure gown, with cincture white;
> His forehead bald, his head was bare,
> Down hung at length his yellow hair.
>
> .   .   .   .   .   .
>
> Seemed to me ne'er did limner paint
> So just an image of the Saint,
> Who propped the Virgin in her faint,—
> The loved Apostle John."

The apparition approaches the king, and addresses him in a hollow voice—

> "My mother sent me from afar,
> Sir King, to warn thee not to war,—
>   Woe waits on thine array;
> If war thou wilt, of woman fair,
> Her witching wiles and wanton snare,
> James Stuart, doubly warned, beware:
>   God keep thee as He may!"

Having said these words, the apparition vanishes—

> "Like sunbeam on the billow cast,
>   That glances but, and dies."

In spite of this warning, however, James is determined to proceed in the war.

In answer to this narrative, Marmion relates to Sir David

his own weird experience at Gifford, into the details of which
we have already entered.

By this time, instructions have arrived from the king to
conduct Marmion to his presence; on the following morning,
therefore, the two trains proceed on their way towards Edinburgh.

> "Early they took Dun-Edin's road,
> And I could trace each step they trode;
> Hill, brook, nor dell, nor rock, nor stone
> Lies on the path to me unknown."

Their route lies past the Braid Hills, to the south of the city,
and eventually they reach the summit of Blackford Hill, from
which a lovely view is obtained of the city of Edinburgh from
the south; this view obtained now by Marmion is quoted by
Baedeker, and this seems to be the only interest attaching to
either this or the Braid Hills, which do not seem to be visited
much by the ordinary tourist; in fact, in "Baddeley," the
supreme guide book, neither are mentioned at all. Blackford
Hill is now a public park, crowned by the National Observatory;
the Braid Hills are covered with the inevitable golf course.[19]
Scott, however, evidently loved Blackford Hill, for he says—

> "Blackford! on whose uncultured breast,
>   Among the broom, and thorn, and whin,
> A truant boy, I sought the nest,
> Or listed, as I lay at rest.
>   While rose, on breezes thin,
> The murmur of the city crowd,
> And, from his steeple jangling loud,
> Saint Giles's mingling din."

From this eminence a marvellous scene bursts upon Marmion.
On the "Borough Moor," lying between the city and the Braid
Hills (about two miles across), lay encamped the whole Scottish
army, destined for the invasion of England—

> "Thousands on thousands there were seen,
> That chequered all the heath between
>   The streamlet and the town;
> In crossing ranks extending far,
> Forming a camp irregular;

> .   .   .   .

> In these extended lines there lay
> A martial kingdom's vast array."

Scott well describes this martial array—the trampling of the horses, the clank of armour, &c.—also quaintly describing the rude artillery of the period—

> "And dire artillery's clumsy car,
> By sluggish oxen tugged to war";

a mighty contrast to our present Royal Horse and Field Artillery. He notes also the various banners streaming in the air, over which proudly floats the Royal Banner of Scotland, where "the ruddy Lion ramped in gold."

Marmion cannot restrain his admiration at the sight of this gallant host, although it is that of an enemy, and declares to Sir David Lindsay that he (Marmion) does not wonder that, with such a force, the Scottish king is determined to risk the chance of war, and that, were that host his, he would have no hesitation in leading them into battle—

> "Not power infernal, nor divine,
> Should once to peace my soul incline,
> Till I had dimmed their armour's shine
> In glorious battle fray!"

The "Lion King" is of a more peaceful disposition, and states his opinion that it were better that kings should appreciate the blessings of peace, and abstain from war, if possible.

Not only does the Scottish host excite the admiration of Marmion, but also the appearance of the city of Edinburgh itself, as it must that of everyone viewing that lovely city for the first time. It is, without doubt, the most picturesque city in the kingdom. The long, sloping ridge, ascending from Holyrood Palace through the quaint "Old Town," is crowned at length by the famous Castle, after which the ridge ends and descends abruptly from the very Castle walls; this sight attracts the eye of the observer, and can never, if he has any sense of natural beauty, be forgotten; nor, turning to more modern sights, can anything equal the lovely frontage of Princes Street, with the gardens in front. But my poor words are wholly inadequate to describe the beauties of this lovely city; I turn, therefore, to Sir Walter Scott, who thoroughly appreciated them, as he always did anything beautiful in aspect, whether it was of nature or art—

> "Such dusky grandeur clothed the height,
> Where the huge castle holds its state,
> And all the steep slope down,
> Whose ridgy back heaves to the sky,
> Piled deep and massy, close and high,
> Mine own romantic town !
> But northward far, with purer blaze,
> On Ochil mountains fell the rays,
> And as each heathy top they kissed,
> It gleamed a purple amethyst.
> Yonder the shores of Fife you saw;
> Here Preston-Bay and Berwick-Law;
> And, broad between them rolled,
> The gallant Firth the eye might note,
> Whose islands on its bosom float,
> Like emeralds chased in gold." [20]

So impressed is Marmion's squire, Fitz-Eustace, with the view, that he cries out enthusiastically—

> "Where's the coward that would not dare
> To fight for such a land ! "

The train cannot, however, linger here; they proceed on their way to the barriers of the camp. Sir David, on the way, while expressing admiration for the gallant host, cannot repress his misgivings of coming disaster. They were too truly to be fulfilled, for, like the Latins at Lake Regillus—

> "Foredoomed to dogs and vultures,
> That gallant army came."

The train, in due course, are admitted, on the Lion Herald's authority, and pass through the midst of the Scottish army. It is a fine array, and again excites the admiration of Marmion on a nearer view; but it is a most heterogeneous force, and this, doubtless, was one of the causes of the subsequent disaster.

---

[20] The poet, however, does not mention the nearer beauties of Arthur's Seat and Salisbury Crags.

Scott gives a most interesting description of the various races of men who composed the army—the "men-at-arms," or heavy cavalry, fully clad in plate and mail, mounted on powerful steeds, and armed with spear and battle-axe; the light cavalry, consisting of young knights and squires; the burghers, or burgesses, from the cities, on foot, armed, but with no badge of distinction as the knights, bearing pikes, two-handed swords, maces, and bucklers; the yeomanry, or peasantry, from the country, armed, some with spears, some with halberds, axes, cross-bows, or knives, and some even with a fire-arm, called a hagbut, which does not yet appear to have superseded the bow and arrow.

And now we come to two very important bodies of men fighting here under the same banner, but in difference of character and habits as far apart as the poles—these represent the Lowlanders and Highlanders of Scotland, who, as I hope to show when I take up my treatise on "The Lady of the Lake," were almost as hostile to each other as both were to the southern foe.

First, the Borderers. I have descanted fully upon them in my treatise on "The Lay of the Last Minstrel," so will not dwell long upon them, except to point out one of their striking characteristics. They cast covetous eyes on the rich arms, apparel, &c., of Marmion and his train, and long for an opportunity to attack and spoil them; and not only them (the enemy), but, indiscriminately, their own countryman, the Lion King—

> "Hist, Ringan! seest thou there!
> Canst guess which road they'll homeward ride?
> O! could we but, on Border-side,
> By Eusedale glen, or Liddel's tide,
>   Beset a prize so fair!
> That fangless Lion, too, their guide,
> Might chance to lose his glittering hide."

All is fish, as may be seen, that comes to their net.

Next, the Highlanders, an entirely different race of men, in manner and costume—

> "Just then the chiefs their tribes arrayed,
> And wild and garish semblance made,
> The chequered trews, and belted plaid,
> And varying notes the war-pipes brayed,
>   To every varying clan."

As with the Borderers, in "The Lay of the Last Minstrel," so, in "The Lady of the Lake," shall we come into contact with the Highlanders, who are there represented as entirely hostile to the Lowlanders or Saxons; it therefore appears strange that King James should have a contingent of these in his army. Their arms are broadsword, dagger, targe, and bows and arrows, but, with regard to the latter, the poet says—

> "But, O!
> Short was the shaft, and weak the bow,
> To that which England bore."

Lastly, the Islemen (also Celts), attached to these, armed with the "ancient Danish battle-axe."

If this force excites the admiration of Marmion, no less does the appearance of his own men attract attention from the Scottish warriors—

> "Fast ran the Scottish warriors there,
> Upon the Southern band to stare;
> And envy with their wonder rose,
> To see such well-appointed foes;
> Such length of shafts, such mighty bows,
> So huge, that many simply thought,
> But for a vaunt such weapons wrought;
> And little deemed their force to feel,
> Through links of mail, and plates of steel,
> When, rattling upon Flodden vale,
> The cloth-yard arrows flew like hail."

The bow, indeed, was the great weapon of England in the Middle Ages; to this was principally due her great victories in France and Scotland. A Scottish proverb states that an English archer carried in his belt 24 Scottish lives, meaning the number of arrows he bore: this acknowledgment of superiority is a decided proof of the formidable power of the weapon, for Scottish people, even now, are not given to acknowledge superiority in anything that is English.

Sir Archibald Alison, in the first chapter of his "History of Europe," very ably explains the reason of the efficiency of this particular weapon in England, viz., that this country possessed a class not known in Scotland or France—a yeoman or middle class, created by the Norman Conquest from the vanquished Saxons. Efforts were often made to introduce the use of the bow into Scotland, but they all failed, on account of the want of this particular class of men.[21] Robin Hood and his "merry men" represent this class in England; they were the progenitors of the victors of Crécy and Neville's Cross against France and Scotland; the familiarity with this formidable weapon enabled England to hold her own against the two above-named countries combined. Even at the period of the poem, the bow appears to be a superior weapon to the firearm.

Marmion, with his train, passes through the camp and enters the city of Edinburgh, which teems with martial preparations; Sir David provides fit accommodation for the English visitors till evening, when the king has announced that he will receive the English baron; and here we enter into a new phase of the poem, the reception of Marmion at the Scottish Court.

We are now introduced to Holyrood Palace in its palmy days, when the Scottish king held his Court there, in all its grandeur and brilliancy. Another century saw the end of these days; after the Union of the English and Scottish Crowns, the glories of Holyrood paled before those of the Court of St. James's. At the time of the Union, unthinking Scotsmen exulted under the idea that this Union conferred pre-eminence on Scotland over her ancient enemy, but the more intellectual men knew better; they said that, after all these centuries of strife, England had at last beaten them. Henry VII. of England, a far-seeing monarch, also saw the matter in this light: when doubts were expressed to him of the result of the possible future union, viz., that by it England would become subordinate to Scotland, he replied that there need be no fear, the lesser country must, of necessity, follow the greater.[22] And so it was; the first thing that James VI. did, on receiving the news of his accession to the throne of England, was to abandon his native country in all haste and proceed to London, to enter

(21) " Alison's History of Europe," Vol. I., page 75.

(22) These words were, doubtless, spoken at the time of the marriage of James IV. of Scotland with Margaret, daughter of Henry VII.; from that marriage, of course, the claim of the Stuart kings to the throne of England was derived.

upon his acquired inheritance. From that day the Scottish kings kept their Court at Whitehall or St. James's Palace; their visits to Holyrood were few and far between. Indeed, they alienated their subjects in Scotland as much as they did those in England; and a Scottish force was afterwards to be seen fighting on the side of the English Parliament in the great Civil War.[23] After the execution of Charles I., they did indeed give some help to his successor, but there was little loyalty, and it ended in disaster; only a small portion of them (chiefly Highlanders) were on the side of James II. when he was dethroned, and it was only this portion, with but few exceptions, who supported the two Stuart Pretenders in the eighteenth century.[24] It may indeed be said of Holyrood Palace, the famous ancient Court of Scotland's Kings— "Ichabod! thy glory has departed!"

Little did any thought of this disturb the gay revellers in the palace, now in the height of its glory. King James is giving a princely entertainment to the chiefs of his army, who have received orders to set out with their forces for England on the morrow. James IV. loved these entertainments, and this, the poet says, was his greatest, and, alas! his last—

> "Old Holy-Rood rung merrily,
> That night, with wassel, mirth, and glee:
>
> .   .   .   .   .   .
>
> The dazzling lamps, from gallery gay,
> Cast on the court a dancing ray;
> Here to the harp did minstrels sing;
> There ladies touched a softer string;
> With long-eared cap, and motley vest,
> The licensed fool retailed his jest;
> His magic tricks the juggler plied;
> At dice and draughts the gallants vied;
>   While some, in close recess apart,
>   Courted the ladies of their heart,
>   Nor courted them in vain;

(23) Indeed, the primary cause of the Civil War arose from the war of Charles I. with his Scottish subjects, when he was compelled to summon the English Parliament to obtain supplies.

(24) It was, of course, the religion of the later Stuart princes which debarred their claim to the sovereignty of both England and Scotland; but for this, their descendant might now be reigning in Great Britain.

> For often, in the parting hour,
> Victorious love asserts his power
> O'er coldness and disdain;
> And flinty is her heart, can view
> To battle march a lover true,—
> Can hear, perchance, his last adieu,
> Nor own her share of pain."

Many last adieux were, doubtless, spoken on that night; our thoughts turn to a similar scene in later ages, the Duchess of Richmond's ball before the battle of Waterloo.

We are now introduced to the brilliant, chivalrous, but unfortunate monarch, of whom we have often made mention, but have not yet met, who advances through the throng of courtiers to receive Marmion. He is gorgeously dressed, and the poet says that—

> "Marmion deemed he ne'er had seen
> A prince of such a noble mien."

It was indeed so, if his appearance were really as the poet describes it—

> "The Monarch's form was middle size;
> For feat of strength, or exercise,
>   Shaped in proportion fair;
> And hazel was his eagle eye,
> And auburn of the darkest dye,
>   His short curled beard and hair;
> Light was his footstep in the dance,
>   And firm his stirrup in the lists;
> And, oh! he had that merry glance,
>   That seldom lady's heart resists.
> Lightly from fair to fair he flew,
> And loved to plead, lament, and sue;—
> Suit lightly won, and short-lived pain!
> For monarchs seldom sigh in vain."

This latter phase of his character (similar to that of his descendant, Charles II.), indeed, proves to be his ruin; for, as I stated before, his delay at Ford Castle (at the outset of the ensuing campaign), dallying with Lady Heron, gave the Earl of Surrey time to collect a force slightly superior in numbers to that of the Scottish invader. The morality of his Court, indeed (again like that of Charles II.), appears to have been of a very low order.

The character of James appears to consist of a singular mixture of good and bad qualities; he has more of the chivalry of a knight-errant and courage of a soldier than the abilities of a general; he is "a wise legislator, energetic administrator, no unskilful diplomatist, a patron of learning, the Church, and the poor." On the other hand, he is "inconstant, extravagant, obstinate, and superstitious"; his obstinacy, like his gallantry, leads to his ruin, for he enters into this fatal campaign against the counsel of his ablest advisers. With all this, he is popular, and has more influence with his barons than the kings of his family usually had.[25]

The fate of James is more deplored by the Scottish people that that of any of the other sovereigns of that name;[26] but surely it is the most honourable, for he dies bravely in fair fight against the national enemy, while, of the others, the first of the name was assassinated, the second was killed by the accidental bursting of a cannon, the third, again, was assassinated after a battle against his own subjects, while the fifth died of a broken heart after a defeat more disgraceful than that of Flodden. The sixth (James I. of England) was the only one who experienced good fortune throughout; but he had none of the qualities which have, in spite of their glaring faults, spread a certain fascination, a certain charm, over the other Stuart kings. No one of them was ever a success as a ruler, yet no sovereigns have ever, in their misfortunes, had such devoted followers.

Lady Heron is here mentioned as being present with the king, if not as his mistress, at least on very familiar terms with him; but this, as I have more than once mentioned, is not in accordance with historical fact: James did not make the acquaintance of this lady until he had entered England. This amorous monarch is also on familiar terms with the Queen of France; and it is partly due to the influence of the latter that

(25) See "Dictionary of National Biography: James IV."

(26) That beautiful poem by Aytoun, "Edinburgh after Flodden," may possibly have some influence here.

he is entering on this unfortunate war with England; therefore, the influence of both these women is exercised in the cause, each of her own country,[27] to the king's ruin—

> "And thus, for France's Queen, he dressed
> His manly limbs in mailèd vest;
> And thus admitted English fair
> His inmost counsels still to share;
> And thus, for both, he madly planned
> The ruin of himself and land!"

He neglects his own queen, who, as the poet says, was in beauty and character far above them all. In this, again, he is a forecast of Charles II.

At the time of the arrival of Marmion, Lady Heron is playing upon the harp and singing the well-known ballad of "Young Lochinvar," which brings in the famous Netherby Hall, from which the young gallant abducts his lady-love from the bridal feast, where she is to wed "a laggard in love, and a dastard in war." [28] The king is in close attendance upon her—

> "And pressing closer, and more near,
> He whispered praises in her ear."

A glance of recognition passes between the lady and Marmion, which by no means pleases the king; and this contributes a harsh tone to his answer on reading the letter brought by Marmion; he expresses his determination on war with England,[29] and concludes thus—

> "Our full defiance, hate, and scorn,
> Our herald has to Henry borne."

A Scottish baron is standing near, a well-known character in the history of Scotland, Archibald Douglas, Earl of Angus, termed "Bell-the-Cat," whose opinion of Marmion I have quoted

(27) It will be remembered that England was at this time at war with France; it was therefore important to the latter country to obtain the assistance of Scotland.

(28) This story is repeated in the "Minstrelsy of the Scottish Border," in a poem named "Katherine Janfarie"; here, however, Lord Lochinvar is the intending bridegroom, and another gallant steals the bride away.

(29) See his words on page 91.

at the commencement of this treatise. His was a dreaded name
when he was in his prime, but he is now advanced in years, and
his best days are past. He was one of the foremost in attempting
to dissuade James from entering upon the war with England,
and this greatly angered the impetuous monarch, who told the
aged earl that, "if he were afraid, he might go home." [30] The
king now consigns Marmion to the hospitality of Douglas, at his
castle of Tantallon, until the return of his (the king's) herald
from England. James here repeats his former insult, describing
Douglas as—

> "A chief unlike his sires of old.
> He wears their motto on his blade,
> Their blazon o'er his towers displayed;
> Yet loves his sovereign to oppose,
> More than to face his country's foes."

This unworthy insult moves the aged baron to tears; this
at once disarms the anger of the king, who thereupon apologises,
and testifies to the great worth of Douglas, and Marmion takes
advantage of this change in the mood of James to attempt
to induce him to turn his thoughts to peace. This intervention,
however, only irritates the monarch, who repeats his intention
of marching on the morrow. He turns again to his revelry, and
leads Lady Heron forth to the dance.

We now turn to another matter. It will be remembered
that one of the judges of the unhappy Constance was the Abbess
of Whitby, who had attended at Holy Island for that purpose,
attended by a party of nuns, with whom was Lady Clare, who,
as before stated, had placed herself under the protection of the
Abbess to escape the persecution of Marmion; her intention was
to take the veil, and she was now a novice. [31] On their way
back, the ship in which they sailed was captured by a Scottish
privateer and conveyed to Edinburgh. James was too chivalrous
to detain these women in captivity, and he now takes advantage
of the return of Marmion and his train to England to place the

---

(30) According to historical fact, this incident took place shortly before Flodden;
on receiving this insult Douglas returned home, leaving, however, his two sons with
the king.

(31) See page 81.

party under his escort, little knowing that he had placed them in the hands of the man they hated and dreaded most of all men : the Abbess fears the vengeance of Marmion should he have learned the fate of Constance; while Clare finds herself placed in the power of the man who had, as she thought, slain her lover, and whom, of all others, she would gladly have avoided. It seems to her to be the dark night of despair, but the dawn is at hand.

We now return to De Wilton, of whom we have lost sight for a while; he had wished to leave the train of Marmion when they met with Sir David Lindsay, but the latter would permit no one to leave the band, and this proved fortunate for De Wilton, as we shall see.

In accordance with the above-mentioned arrangement, quarters had, by order of the king, been assigned to the Abbess and her nuns, adjoining those of Marmion. Seeing a pilgrim, a holy man, among the Baron's train, the Abbess enters into communication with him, saying she had a secret to reveal to him. She meets De Wilton, therefore (in his palmer's disguise), on a balcony overlooking the city : it is now night—

> "A solemn scene the Abbess chose;
> A solemn hour, her secret to disclose."

She relates to the supposed Palmer the tale I have already gone through,[32] regarding the treachery of Marmion towards De Wilton, and the latter's failure in the ordeal of combat. She says that she holds a packet of papers in her hands, the contents of which will completely clear De Wilton's honour. She does not confess how she has received these papers, but they must evidently have been handed over to her by the unhappy Constance in the latter's last moments.[33] The Abbess places the packet in the hands of the Palmer, urging him to give it to Wolsey, to place it before King Henry. We may imagine the feelings of De Wilton at this announcement; he cannot hide his emotion, and the Abbess is anxiously inquiring what affects him so strongly

(32) See page 79.

(33) See page 85. Constance had the packet in her hands at the time of her condemnation.

when an incident takes place which turns their thoughts in another direction.

On the top of the Cross of Edinburgh (now destroyed) appears a strange vision [34]—

> "Darkly did it seem as there
> Heralds and pursuivants prepare,
> With trumpet sound, and blazon fair,
> A summons to proclaim."

The terrible summons is in these words—

> "Prince, prelate, potentate, and peer,
> Whose names I now shall call,
> Scottish, or foreigner, give ear!
> Subjects of him who sent me here,
> At this tribunal to appear,
> I summon one and all:
> I cite you by each deadly sin,
> That e'er hath soiled your hearts within;
> I cite you by each brutal lust,
> That e'er defiled your earthly dust,—
> By wrath, by pride, by fear,
> By each o'er-mastering passion's tone,
> By the dark grave, and dying groan!
> When forty days are past and gone
> I cite you at your Monarch's throne
> To answer and appear."

The names of all those who are to fall on the fatal field of Flodden are now thundered forth, the first being that of the unfortunate King James, who, as we have seen, has disregarded a warning from Heaven, and on whom, therefore, the doom is now to fall.[35] The names of all his fated nobles follow, afterwards, that of Lord Marmion, then, lastly, is called out, "De Wilton, erst of Aberley"; but, on this latter summons, a voice answers in defiance—

(34) This incident is declared to be true; and, as the note to the poem says, is mentioned by all Scottish historians; even the fact of a man defying the ghostly edict is mentioned.

(35) See page 104. This appearance (*i.e.*, the one at Linlithgow) is described as "one of the best attested apparitions in history."

> "Thy fatal summons I deny,
> And thine infernal lord defy,
> Appealing me to Him on High,
> Who burst the sinner's yoke."

On this, the vision disappears; the Abbess falls prone in terror, and, when her nuns come to her aid, the Palmer is gone.

On the morrow, the Scottish army leaves Edinburgh for the English Border; the train of Marmion proceeds to Tantallon Castle, under charge of the Earl of Angus; while the Abbess, with her nuns and the Lady Clare, follow about half an hour's march in rear, under charge of Fitz-Eustace.

To do him justice, Marmion does not attempt to force his presence upon Clare, nor does he appear to have thought of using any violence, but rather to wait until the influence of her relatives and of King Henry may induce her to turn a favourable ear to his suit. He really covets Clare's lands more than her person; his true love is still with the unhappy Constance. His conscience also smites him for the crime he has committed—

> "Conquest, by that meanness won,
> He almost loathed to think upon,
> Led him, at times, to hate the cause,
> Which made him burst through honour's laws."

He is not without conscience, as we have already noted, and the above lines may lead us to believe that the crime of authorising the forgery, and his abduction and desertion of the unhappy Constance, were the only serious crimes in his adventurous career. He is unscrupulous, however, and is determined to retain Lady Clare in his possession, for the present, at least.

De Wilton, on the other hand, is full of exultation; having read the contents of the packet, which entirely exonerate him, a load is lifted from his mind, and his flow of spirits makes him forget his assumed character of a palmer—

> "But in that Palmer's altered mien
> A wondrous change might now be seen;
>   Freely he spoke of war,
> Of marvels wrought by single hand,
> When lifted for a native land;
> And still looked high, as if he planned
>   Some desperate deed afar.

His courser would he feed and stroke,
And, tucking up his sable frocke,
Would first his mettle bold provoke,
    Then soothe or quell his pride.
Old Hubert said, that never one
He saw, except Lord Marmion,
    A steed so fairly ride."

The party, in due course, arrives at North Berwick, and here that portion under Fitz-Eustace halts at a convent of Cistercian nuns, situated a little distance from the town. Here the squire has orders to leave the Abbess and her nuns until Lord Angus can obtain a ship to convey them back to Whitby. This arrangement, as may be supposed, is a great relief to the Abbess, as it delivers her and her nuns from the dreaded Marmion, but her relief is changed to horror when she finds that the Lady Clare is not to remain with her, but proceed on with the train of Marmion. Fitz-Eustace explains that—

" Lord Marmion hath a letter broad,
    Which to the Scottish Earl he showed,
    Commanding that, beneath his care,
    Without delay, you shall repair
    To your good kinsman, Lord Fitz-Clare."

At this announcement, Clare turns as pale as death, and the Abbess "loudly exclaims." Fitz-Eustace proceeds to re-assure them—

            "The lovely Clare
    Will be in Lady Angus' care,
        In Scotland while we stay;
    And, when we move, an easy ride
    Will bring us to the English side,
    Female attendance to provide
        Befitting Gloster's heir;
    Nor thinks, nor dreams, my noble lord,
    By slightest look, or act, or word,
        To harass Lady Clare.
    Her faithful guardian he will be,
    Nor sue for slightest courtesy
        That e'en to stranger falls,
    Till he shall place her, safe and free,
        Within her kinsman's halls."

Clare feels that she can trust Fitz-Eustace; and, to do Marmion justice, he fully acts up to the promise of his squire.

The Lady Abbess, however, lets loose the vials of her wrath upon Marmion, and calls upon the Prioress of the convent to curse him with "candle, bell, and book," but this the latter prudently declines to do. The Abbess, nevertheless, still inveighs furiously against Marmion with a flow of words which seem never to be coming to an end, when Blount, Fitz-Eustace's brother squire, rudely interposes—

> "Fitz-Eustace, we must march our band;
> St. Anton' fire thee! wilt thou stand
> All day, with bonnet in thy hand,
>   To hear the Ladye preach?
> By this good light! if thus we stay,
> Lord Marmion, for our fond delay,
>   Will sharper sermon teach."

Clare, therefore, submits to force, but declares that, sooner than wed Marmion, she will take her own life—

> "Yet one asylum is my own,
>   Against the dreaded hour;
> A low, a silent, and a lone,
>   Where kings have little power."

A touching farewell now takes place between Clare and the Abbess and nuns, and she departs under charge of the squires. In due course, they reach Tantallon Castle, situated on the coast, about two miles east of North Berwick—a most striking ruin in the present day. Scott well describes it—

> "Broad, massive, high, and stretching far,
> And held impregnable in war.
> On a projecting rock they rose,
> And round three sides the ocean flows;
> The fourth did battled walls enclose,
>   And double mound and fosse."

Here Marmion remains for a while, but he soon wearies of the inaction. Rumours reach him of the war in Northumberland, into the events of which we will enter hereafter. At length he hears that the two opposing forces are in close proximity to each other, and that there is every prospect of a battle taking place. Upon this, he determines to depart for the scene of action on the following day, not only because he chafes at his in-activity and longs for action, but that he has observed a change in the manner of the Earl of Angus towards him—coldness and lack of courtesy. The earl, doubtless, is not best pleased at having to harbour Marmion and his English troop in his castle; in this he only obeys the wishes of his king—

> " My manors, halls, and bowers shall still
> Be open to my sovereign's will,
> To each one whom he lists, howe'er
> Unmeet to be the owner's peer,
> My castles are my king's alone,
> From turret to foundation-stone."

But there is now another reason which increases Douglas's hostility to Marmion, and into this we will now enter.

The Lady Clare, in the meantime, remains in the care of Lady Angus; Marmion never intrudes his presence upon her, which, as I have said before, speaks well for him. She loves to wander alone upon the battlements, from which, as I myself know, a lovely view is obtained of the surrounding country. She has laid aside her convent dress at the wish of Douglas—

> " It were unseemly sight, he said,
> A novice out of convent's shade."

She is, therefore, again richly dressed " in all her loveliness." Her thoughts are sad ones, as may be imagined; hers seems to be a hopeless situation; but she is full of fortitude, and is determined never to yield to Marmion's will. She regrets her past quiet, convent life—

> " How different now ! condemned to bide
> My doom from this dark tyrant's pride;
> But Marmion has to learn, e'er long,
> That constant mind, and hate of wrong,
> Descended to a feeble girl,
> From Red De Clare, stout Gloster's Earl;
> Of such a stem, a sapling weak
> He ne'er shall bend, although he break."

It is on the evening of the day before the intended departure of Marmion that Clare is taking her usual lonely walk on the battlements, when she is astonished at seeing pieces of armour lying about, and, before she has time to recover from her surprise, she sees, to her astonishment and joy, her lover, De Wilton, standing before her, the one whom she had long deemed dead. We can well imagine the joy of the meeting, but can only imagine it; even the poet himself does not attempt to describe it—

> "Expect not, noble dames and lords,
> That I can tell such scene in words:
> What skilful limner e'er would choose
> To paint the rainbow's varying hues,
> Unless to mortal it were given
> To dip his brush in dyes of heaven ?"

De Wilton quickly relates his tale to his love, with which we are already acquainted; he tells her of his promise to his old servant, to spare his deadliest foe when that foe was at his mercy; how this had taken place, when he encountered Marmion in the field at Gifford, and that his mercy on that occasion served him in good stead, for, had he not spared his foe, he would never have met the Abbess of Whitby and received from her the packet which restored his good name. He concludes with saying that he has reported the whole matter to Douglas, who has believed his story, and intends to dub him knight anew that night. The earl has furnished him with armour, over which he is keeping watch, according to custom, before receiving knighthood; then, in the morning, once more a "belted knight," he will depart to join the English army.

The ceremony is performed in the chapel of Tantallon that night; Gawaine Douglas, Bishop of Dunkeld, son of the old earl, presides at the altar.[36] Wilton kneels, and Clare binds on his spurs and sword. Douglas dubs him knight—

> "Saint Michael and Saint Andrew aid,
>   I dub thee knight.
> Arise, Sir Ralph, De Wilton's heir !
> For king, for church, for lady fair,
>   See that thou fight."

(36) The note to the poem states that Gawaine was not a bishop at this period.

As De Wilton rises, a few kind words from the young bishop completely overcome him, and he sobs out—

> "Where'er I meet a Douglas, trust
> That Douglas is my brother."

The old earl, however, will not accept this; De Wilton must not forget his own nation, and that it is at war with that to which the Douglas family belongs—

> "I have two sons in yonder field;
> And, if thou meet'st them under shield,
> Upon them bravely—do thy worst;
> And foul fall him that blenches first!"

These two sons, alas! fell on that fatal field; the old earl survived them but a year.

Marmion arrays his troop in the morning to proceed to the English camp; he has not yet discovered the absence of the supposed Palmer. Douglas announces the safe departure of De Wilton to Clare, in a whisper, as he assists her to her horse—

> "Let the hawk stoop, his prey is flown."

Marmion, in the act of departing, bids adieu to Lord Angus, proferring his hand, but this the old earl haughtily refuses—

> "The hand of Douglas is his own;
> And never shall in friendly grasp
> The hand of such as Marmion clasp."

Marmion is at present not aware that the earl is acquainted with his guilty secret; but even if he had been, whatever his character might have been, his courage is indisputable; and, heedless of the dangerous position in which he now stands (for his train had left the castle), he breaks forth furiously and defies Douglas to his face—

> "And—'This to me!' he said,—
> 'An 'twere not for thy hoary beard,
> Such hand as Marmion's had not spared
> To cleave the Douglas head!"

> And, first, I tell thee, haughty Peer,
> He, who does England's message here,
> Although the meanest in her state,
> May well, proud Angus, be thy mate:
> And, Douglas, more, I tell thee here,
>   Even in thy pitch of pride,
> Here in thy Hold, thy vassals near,
> (Nay, never look upon your lord,
> And lay your hands upon your sword,)
>   I tell thee, thou'rt defied!
> And if thou saidst, I am not peer
> To any lord in Scotland here,
> Lowland or Highland, far or near,
>   Lord Angus, thou hast lied!'"

These are bold words indeed, especially in the perilous position in which Marmion now stands, and, as might be expected, they rouse the earl to a pitch of ungovernable fury—

> "And darest thou then
> To beard the lion in his den,
>   The Douglas in his hall?
> And hopest thou hence unscathed to go?—
> No, by Saint Bride of Bothwell, no!—
> Up drawbridge, grooms—what, Warder, ho!
>   Let the portcullis fall!"

It is a terribly dangerous predicament in which Marmion now stands, and he only saves himself from it by the mettle of his steed, his own dauntless courage, and incomparable horsemanship—

> "Lord Marmion turned,—well was his need,
> And dashed the rowels in his steed,
> Like arrow through the archway sprung,
> The ponderous gate behind him rung:
> To pass there was such scanty room,
> The bars, descending, razed his plume.
> The steed along the drawbridge flies,
> Just as it trembled on the rise;
> Not lighter does the swallow skim
> Along the smooth lake's level brim."

Lord Marmion reaches his band in safety, and shouts back defiance; Douglas threatens pursuit at first, but soon recovers himself. He then gives that wonderful epitome of Marmion's character with which I have headed this treatise.[37] Disgusted as he is with Marmion's foul deed, he yet gives the latter credit for his boldness and courage—

> " ' 'Tis pity of him too,' he cried,
>   ' Bold can he speak, and fairly [38] ride;
>   I warrant him a warrior tried.' "

In parting with this old warrior, I cannot omit his extraordinary statement that neither he nor his sons (except the bishop) could "pen a line." Indeed, he thinks the capability of writing to be a bad thing, for, in commenting on Marmion, he says—

> " At first in heart it liked me ill,
>   When the King praised his clerkly skill." [39]

It seems to me extraordinary that, in the sixteenth century, a nobleman in the position of the Earl of Angus could be thus illiterate.

Marmion now misses the Palmer, and makes inquiries; from his squires he hears the astounding news that they had seen the Palmer, at break of day, clad in armour, mount on the earl's favourite steed and ride away, Lord Angus himself wishing him God-speed, and that he (the Palmer)—

> " Much resembled that same knight
>   Subdued by you in Cotswold fight."

The whole truth now bursts upon Marmion, and he breaks forth into the passionate exclamation set forth on a former page.[40] He understands now the coldness of Douglas towards him, and he is not without uneasiness as to the consequences to

(37) See page 77.

(38) " Fairly," in the language of the period, means " excellently "; it is used in that sense in a previous incident in the poem. See Canto V., ver. xxvii., last line, *re* De Wilton's riding.

(39) Douglas does not seem to have known that the forgery was not committed by Marmion himself, but by Constance, at his (Marmion's) instigation. See page 79,

(40) See page 101.

himself; but this does not trouble him much, for he is unaware of the possession by De Wilton of the incriminating packet, which, as Constance said, might bring him (Marmion) to the block. He concludes—

> "A Palmer too!—no wonder why
> I felt rebuked beneath his eye:
> I might have known there was but one,
> Whose look could quell Lord Marmion."

A long ride lies before Marmion and his train, but at last they reach the convent of Lennel, situated on the Tweed, near Coldstream, and in the vicinity of Flodden Field.[41] Here they stay the night, which is to be Marmion's last night on earth. We now approach the final, culminating stage of the poem, which relates of the famous battle of Flodden; but before entering into the details as described in the poem, I must briefly touch upon a few historical facts connected with the campaign.

The scene of the battle of Flodden lies from five to six miles south of Coldstream, in the county of Northumberland. Flodden Ridge was the first position of the Scottish army on the eve of the battle, but, when the English commenced their flank movement the following morning (to be described hereafter), they (the Scots) shifted their ground in accordance, so as to approach the enemy more nearly; and when the English movement was completed, the Scottish army was posted on Branston Hill, which, therefore, should have given the name to the battle, rather than the neighbouring hill of Flodden, which was farther distant from the actual battlefield. The battle of Waterloo is a similar instance to this: the village of Waterloo is four miles distant from the actual scene of conflict.

On the 22nd August, 1513, James IV. crossed the English Border with the immense force we have already witnessed, varying by different accounts from 80,000 to 100,000 men. The campaign, which was to close so disastrously, seemed to open brightly, and with every prospect of success; there was no force

---

(41) The distance from Tantallon to Coldstream, as the crow flies, is about 35 miles; and, considering the state of the roads in those days, it must have been a very tiring day; neither men nor horses, one would think, would be in fit condition for battle the following day; no wonder they were worsted.

in Northumberland adequate to oppose the invading army, and had James acted with vigour and promptitude, he might have overrun the north of England, and the campaign have ended far differently from what it did. He commenced well; he had taken Wark and Norham Castles by August 28th, and afterwards he captured three armed fortresses, one being that of Ford, in the neighbourhood of the future battlefield. But here his fatal weakness, on which we have already commented, ruined him. He meets here Lady Heron, the lady of the castle, and, under the influence of her charms, he "wiled the precious hours away," and doubtless the lady acted purposely, with intent to delay him. While he was thus dallying, the greater portion of his immense host, weary of the inactivity, fell, as usual, to plundering, and deserted with their booty back to Scotland; hence his force dwindled away to about 30,000 men, or even less.

On the other hand, the English commander, though taken by surprise at first, acted with vigour and promptitude. The command in the north of England had been given to Henry Howard, Earl of Surrey, who was not only a daring warrior but a sagacious general; he was advanced in years, being now at the age of 70. He had before this been in charge of the Border, and had met James in an invasion of the north of England in 1497, when the latter retired. While James was thus dallying away the precious time at Ford, Surrey was rapidly collecting his forces together, and by September 8th had reached Wooler, about six miles from Ford and from Flodden Hill, where the Scottish army was now posted. This at length roused James, who at last joined his force and prepared for battle. He had now but 30,000 men, as I before said, while Surrey's force amounted to about 32,000.[42] Surrey's energy in thus raising a force superior to that of his enemy stands out in strong contrast to the dilatoriness of the unfortunate king.

On the memorable morning of the 9th of September, 1513, Surrey's headquarters were at Barmoor Wood, south-east of

(42) Accounts differ greatly as to numbers: some make the Scottish force still considerably superior to the English; R. White, in his "Battle of Flodden Field" (my principal text-book), reduces the numbers on each side by about 10,000 men, as we shall see shortly. However, I think we may take it for granted that the English force exceeded that of the Scots by 1,000 to 2,000 men.

Flodden Hill, and from this post he made an unexpected, at the same time important, strategical movement. The Scots were, as aforesaid, posted on Flodden Hill, an impregnable position, from which they had evidently no intention of moving; Surrey therefore determined to draw them out from thence, and force them to give battle. With this object, he suddenly moved his army to the north-west, then, wheeling round to the east, he crossed the river Till, by Twizel Bridge, near that river's junction with the Tweed, with his vanguard and artillery, while his rearguard crossed by a ford about a mile higher up the river. He brought his whole army across, without molestation from the enemy, and this movement placed his force between the Scottish army and the Border, thus cutting off their communication with their native country. This movement, he rightly calculated, must force James either to fight or to starve.

As this is the first action of the battle described in the poem, we will leave its details to the narrative, to which we now return.

On that eventful morning, Marmion, accompanied by his squires, ascends the tower of the convent, from whence he has a full view of the Scottish army stationed on the hill aforesaid, and soon he observes strong commotion in their ranks—

> "Their front now deepening, now extending,
> Their flank inclining, wheeling, bending,
> Now drawing back, and now descending,
> The skilful Marmion well could know,
> They watched the motions of some foe,
> Who traversed on the plain below."

This unsteadiness very clearly shows the vacillation of James; he is utterly undecided what to do. On the other hand, however, this constant movement may mean the changing of the position of the Scots from Flodden to Branxton Hill, as before noticed.

The quick eye of Fitz-Eustace detects the approach of the English host before Marmion perceives it; he exclaims exultantly—

> "Hark! hark! my lord, an English drum!
> And see ascending squadrons come
> Between Tweed's river and the hill,

Foot, horse, and cannon:—hap what hap,
My basnet to a 'prentice cap,
  Lord Surrey's o'er the Till!
Yet more! yet more!—how fair arrayed
They file from out the hawthorn shade,
  And sweep so gallant by!
With all their banners bravely spread,
  And all their armour flashing high,
Saint George might waken from the dead,
  To see fair England's standards fly."

Sir Walter Scott beautifully describes the flank march of
the English; their march through the defile, their crossing of
the bridge, and their issue into the plain above—

"High sight it is, and haughty, while
  They dive into the deep defile;
  Beneath the caverned cliff they fall,
  Beneath the castle's airy wall.
By rock, by oak, by hawthorn-tree,
Troop after troop are disappearing;
Troop after troop their banners rearing,
  Upon the eastern bank you see.
Still pouring down the rocky glen,
  Where flows the sullen Till,
And rising from the dim-wood glen,
Standards on standards, men on men,
  In slow succession still,
And sweeping o'er the Gothic arch,
And pressing on, in ceaseless march,
  To gain the opposing hill."

In equally beautiful lines does the poet blame the neglect of
James to attack the English while performing this hazardous
movement. The "vain knight-errant's brand" aptly describes
the character of the king in his military capacity—

"And why stands Scotland idly now,
  Dark Flodden! on thy airy brow,
Since England gains the pass the while,
And struggles through the deep defile?
What checks the fiery soul of James?
Why sits that champion of the dames
  Inactive on his steed,
And sees, between him and his land,
Between him and Tweed's southern strand,
  His host Lord Surrey lead?

> What 'vails the vain knight-errant's brand ?—
> O, Douglas, for thy leading wand!
>   Fierce Randolph, for thy speed!
> O for one hour of Wallace wight,
> Or well-skilled Bruce, to rule the fight,
> And cry—' Saint Andrew and our right! '
> Another sight had seen that morn,
> From Fate's dark book a leaf been torn,
> And Flodden had been Bannock-bourne ! "

Scott forgets, however, that Surrey took only half his host through this defile, the remainder passed over a ford a little higher up the river; this, therefore, considerably lessens the hazard of the movement. The writer of the note to the poem at this point, in mentioning the two crossings, says, however, "As the passage, both over the bridge and through the ford, was difficult and slow, it seems possible that the English might have been attacked to great advantage while struggling with these natural obstacles." The same writer also comments on the neglect of James to attack—"I know not if we are to impute James's forbearance to want of military skill, or to the romantic declaration which Pitscottie puts in his mouth, 'that he was determined to have his enemies before him on a plain field,' and therefore would suffer no interruption to be given, even by artillery, to their crossing the river." [43] If this latter statement be true, the king deserves unqualified censure; this decision cost him the ruin of his army and the loss of his own life. What would have been thought of Wellington if he had permitted the French to outflank him at Salamanca? Romance is out of place on the battlefield. But I am of opinion that the risk of Surrey was not so great as Scott implies, for Twizel Bridge is five

---

(43) With regard to the latter suggestion as to the action of James, the author of the "Battle-fields of Scotland" makes the following statement:—" Surrey, knowing the chivalrous character of the Scottish king, sent him a challenge, taunting him with a breach of honour in attacking a kingdom with whom he had sworn perpetual peace, and defying him to try on the following Friday the ' righteousness of the matter' between them." James, irresponsible as a "mediaeval knight-errant," accepts this challenge, and permits the English to pass the Till unmolested, in spite of the urgent entreaties of his generals to at least open fire upon them with artillery. The same author adds, " Chivalry, foolishness, if you will, played a much larger rôle in those events than the prosaic historian appreciates. James was a ' Don Quixoté '." He also terms James " a knight-errant, a dreamer," hence the declaration mentioned above.

miles distant from Branxton Hill (and on this the Scots were moving from Flodden Hill, the latter position being farther off still), and the ford is described as being "sufficiently shallow for the main body to pass over." [44] In fact, the probability is that the Scots did not reach their new position on Branxton Hill in time to prevent Surrey's movement. However this may be, Surrey has completed his flank movement successfully, and his force is now drawn up in order of battle—

> "The precious hour has passed in vain,
> And England's host has gained the plain;
> Wheeling their march, and circling still,
> Around the base of Flodden-hill." [45]

Marmion at once grasps the importance of this movement of the English; he feels certain that King James is now bound to fight, and that the battle may take place at any moment. He must therefore join Lord Surrey at once, and he determines to take the Lady Clare with him, to be left in rear of his lines during the battle, in spite of the remonstrance of the Abbot, who offers to take charge of her at the monastery, which would certainly have been the proper arrangement. Marmion refuses, muttering—

> "The pheasant in the falcon's claw,
> He scarce will yield, to please a daw;
> Lord Angus may the Abbot awe,
> So Clare shall bide with me."

The train therefore starts, crosses a ford on the Leat, and arrives in rear of the English army; here Marmion halts by a stone cross, and directs Blount and Fitz-Eustace to remain there, with ten of his band, to guard the Lady Clare; directing Fitz-Eustace, if the day goes against England, to convey the lady to Berwick. He addresses Clare courteously, but with a slightly veiled threat—

> "Here shalt thou tarry, lovely Clare:
> O! think of Marmion in thy prayer!
> Thou wilt not?—well—no less my care
> Shall, watchful, for thy weal prepare.

.   .   .   .

(44) "Battle of Flodden Field," by R. White.

(45) Branxton Hill.

But, if we conquer, cruel maid!
My spoils shall at your feet be laid,
    When here we meet again."

The two squires, with their men, are, naturally, greatly discontented at being left in this charge, and thus excluded from the fight, but Marmion heeds not, and, with the remainder of his train, makes his way to Lord Surrey. He is received cordially, and directed to the right of the English line, where his own retainers are stationed. His arrival there is received with the greatest enthusiasm—

"Where such a shout there rose
Of ' Marmion! Marmion!' that the cry,
Up Flodden mountain shrilling high,
    Startled the Scottish foes."

The opposing forces were now drawn up as follows, each in three bodies : the Scottish right wing, consisting of Highlanders from the West and Isles of Scotland, under the Earls of Lennox and Argyle, brave, but undisciplined, as we shall see. These were opposed by men from Cheshire and Lancashire, under Sir Edward Stanley. The Scottish centre was under the king himself, with many of his principal nobles and gentry, many of whom "fought as common soldiers." [46] The English centre was under Surrey himself; they consisted principally of men from Northumberland and Cumberland. In fact, all the northern counties of England furnished troops, and there were some contingents from the south. The Scottish left wing, with which, in the poem, we have principally to deal, consisted of Highlanders from Aberdeenshire, under the Earl of Huntly, and southern Borderers, under the Earl of Home. Opposed to these were troops under Sir Brian Tunstall, Lord Edmund Howard (son of the Earl of Surrey), and, according to the poem, Marmion. Lord Thomas Howard, Admiral of England, lay between this force and that of Surrey, opposed on the Scottish side by the Lords Montrose and Crawford. A reserve, under Lord Dacre, was posted in rear of the English army, a corresponding reserve being in rear of that of the Scots.[47] According to the authority I last quoted (from which

(46) " Battle of Flodden Field," by R. White.

(47) We hear nothing more of this Scottish reserve.

I draw many facts connected with the battle), the English force consisted of about 24,000 men, that of the Scots being doubtful, but probably about 2,000 less.

The moment in which Marmion joints the English right wing is that in which King James has at last determined to attack. The conflict had already commenced with artillery fire on both sides; Scott says—

> "Not in the close, successive rattle,
> That breathes the voice of modern battle,
> But slow and far between."

This does not, however, appear to have actually been the case; the artillery fire seems to have been very hot; that on the Scottish side was ill directed, and, the guns being posted far above the English position, the balls generally went too high; and probably the guns of that period could not be depressed sufficiently. On the other hand, the English fire was well directed and played havoc amongst the Scottish gunners, who were at length driven from their guns, their Master of Ordnance being slain. Irritated by this galling fire, James determined to end this state of things, and he therefore prepared to attack. On leaving Flodden Hill, his former camping ground, he had set fire to the refuse, &c., of his camp (not the tents, probably, as the poem says), and the smoke from this, driven across by the wind, obscured his movements, under cover of which he advanced against the enemy in full charge—

> "Volumed and vast, and rolling far,
> The cloud enveloped Scotland's war,
> As down the hill they broke;
> Nor martial shout, nor minstrel tone,
> Announced their march; their tread alone,
> At times one warning trumpet blown,
> At times a stifled hum,
> Told England, from his mountain-throne
> King James did rushing come.—
> Scarce could they hear, or see their foes,
> Until at weapon-point they close.—
> They close, in clouds of smoke and dust,
> With sword-sway, and with lance's thrust;
> And such a yell was there,
> Of sudden and portentous birth,
> As if men fought upon the earth,
> And fiends in upper air."

We are at present concerned only with the battle on the English right, with which Marmion is stationed; victory here inclines to the Scots. Tunstall is slain, and his force driven off; a desperate resistance is made by Lord Edmund Howard, who is unhorsed three times, and narrowly escapes being slain, but this force is also repulsed. According to the poem, the victorious Scottish wing, instead of turning to assist their own centre, disperses in pursuit and takes to plundering; they are, therefore, no further use in the battle. The real fact was far worse than this, as we shall see hereafter, when we come to the later phases of the battle—

> "But Fortune, on the right,
> With fickle smile, cheered Scotland's fight.
> Then fell that spotless banner white,
>   The Howard's lion fell;
> Yet still Lord Marmion's falcon flew
> With wavering flight, while fiercer grew
>   Around the battle-yell.
> The Border slogan rent the sky:
> A Home! A Gordon! was the cry;
>   Loud were the clanging blows;
> Advanced—forced back—now low, now high,
>   The pennon sunk and rose;
> As bends the bark's mast in the gale,
> When rent are rigging, shrouds, and sail,
>   It wavered 'mid the foes."

Blount can bear this no longer; he dashes off with the rest of the band to the rescue; they recover the pennon for a moment, but what can eleven men do? It falls again.

Fitz-Eustace is left alone with the Lady Clare, when, suddenly, the steed of Lord Marmion dashes by, riderless, with loose rein, and saddle covered with blood. On this, Fitz-Eustace gallops off also, and the lady is left alone in a terrible plight; she calls out the name of her lover despairingly, "Is Wilton there?" Again, more than once, she calls, but none hear or heed.

At this moment the two squires return, bearing their lord, desperately wounded. The plight of Marmion is terrible; they lay him down, unlace his armour, and remove his helmet, when a terrible spear wound is discovered, together with an equally fearful cut upon the head; he is evidently mortally wounded.

The air revives him for a moment; he cries out despairingly, but quickly recovers himself, as he thinks of his country's danger. He despatches the squires, one to Lord Surrey with report of the disaster, the other to Lord Dacre, commanding the English reserve [48]—

> "Yet my last thought is England's:—fly,
>   To Dacre bear my signet ring;
>   Tell him his squadrons up to bring.—
> Fitz-Eustace, to Lord Surrey hie:
>   Tunstall lies dead upon the field;
>   His life-blood stains the spotless shield:
>   Edmund is down;—my life is reft;—
>   The Admiral alone is left.
>   Let Stanley charge with spur of fire,
>   With Chester charge, and Lancashire,
>   Full upon Scotland's central host,
>   Or victory and England's lost."

The squires gallop off, and the dying man is left alone. He lies in silence for a while, then a "low moan" escapes him—

> "Is there none,
>   Of all my halls have nursed,
> Page, squire, or groom, one cup to bring
> Of blessèd water from the spring,
>   To slake my dying thirst!"

And now occurs a touching incident. Clare has suffered terrible wrong at the hands of the man who now lies helpless before her; he is the one whom she fears and hates more than any one on earth; but at that pitiful cry the best part of her woman's nature asserts itself—

> "Forgot were hatred, wrongs, and fears,
>   The plaintive voice alone she hears,
>   Sees but the dying man."

Here it is that those immortal words of Scott occur, words so true to life, the truth of which there is hardly a man has not experienced some time in his life—

(48) It is rather a mistake, however, on Scott's part, thus making Marmion issue orders as if he were commander-in-chief. He could not possibly know what had taken place on the English left: Stanley might also have been defeated, as far as he knew.

"O, woman! in our hours of ease,
Uncertain, coy, and hard to please,
And variable as the shade
By the light, quivering aspen made;
When pain and anguish wring the brow,
A ministering angel thou!"

The maiden takes the Baron's helmet and runs to the neighbouring stream, but finds it running full with blood. Of a sudden, however, she espies a "little fountain cell"—

"Where water, clear as diamond-spark,
In a stone basin fell.
Above, some half-worn letters say,
'Drink, weary pilgrim, drink and pray
For the kind soul of Sybil Gray,
Who built this cross and well.'"

She fills the helmet and returns to the dying man, and sees, with relief, a monk in attendance on him. A painful scene now ensues during the last moments of this bold, bad man. He inquires for Constance, stating that he will atone for the wrong he has done her. Clare has to confess that Constance is dead— "She—died at Holy Isle." Marmion knows well what this means; he remembers the Palmer's words at the inn at Gifford; [49] he springs to his feet, forgetting his wound, and breaks forth into these passionate words—

"'Then it was truth!'—he said—'I knew
That the dark presage must be true.—
I would the Fiend, to whom belongs
The vengeance due to all her wrongs,
Would spare me but a day!
For wasting fire, and dying groan,
And priests slain on the altar-stone,
Might bribe him for delay.'"

Terrible words from the mouth of a dying man! It will be noted that, to the last, his crime against Constance, his first and only love, alone seems to haunt him; his crime against De Wilton seems to be forgotten. After this terrible outburst, he

(49) See page 96.

sinks fainting to the ground; the favourite song of Constance, which, as will be remembered, Fitz-Eustace sang at the inn at Gifford,[50] now rings in his ears, and drowns the prayers and pleadings of the monk; the latter is in despair—

> "Avoid thee, Fiend !—with cruel hand
> Shake not the dying sinner's sand !—
> O look, my son, upon yon sign
> Of the Redeemer's grace divine;
> O think on faith and bliss !—
> By many a death-bed I have been,
> And many a sinner's parting seen,
> But never aught like this."

At this moment, however, an incident occurs which brings the dying man back for a moment to life again—an English war-cry is heard, which shows that the battle is now turning in favour of England. It is the moment when Sir Edward Stanley, having defeated the Scottish right wing, turns and falls upon their centre; of this we shall hear later—

> "The war, that for a space did fail,
> Now trebly thundering swelled the gale,
> And—Stanley ! was the cry:—
> A light on Marmion's visage broke,
> And fired his glazing eye:
> With dying hand, above his head,
> He shook the fragment of his blade,
> And shouted ' Victory !—
> Charge, Chester, charge ! On, Stanley, on !'
> Were the last words of Marmion."

His last moment is therefore relieved by the knowledge of his country's victory, and thus his spirit passes away. Though the terrible burst of vengeance in his last moments appals us, it is pleasing to see that he shows consciousness of, and some signs of repentance for, his crimes, with also some desire to make amends; with this comment, therefore, we say "Good-night to Marmion."

The monk places Clare on her horse, and conducts her from the battle-field to the chapel of Tillmouth on Tweed, where, the

(50) See page 96.

following morning, she has the good fortune to meet her kinsman, Lord Fitz-Clare.

We will now return to the details of the battle. Though the left wing of the Scots was, as we have seen, victorious, matters were turning out very differently in other parts of the field. We have seen that King James, instead of remaining in his former strong position, had broken from it, and made a furious attack on the enemy. The Scottish centre, under the king himself, attacks that of the English, under Surrey; there is a desperate fight for a while, an equally desperate conflict taking place at the same time between Lord Admiral Howard (to the right of Lord Surrey) and the Earls of Montrose and Crawford; neither side for a time gains the advantage, and the issue appears doubtful,[51] when the event is decided by the result of affairs on the English left.

We have seen that the Scottish right wing was composed of Highlanders from the West and Islands of Scotland, under command of the Earls of Lennox and Argyll; brave, headstrong, but undisciplined men; formidable in attack, but liable to panic—

> " There the western mountaineer
> Rushed with bare bosom on the spear,
> And flung the feeble targe aside,
> And with both hands the broadsword plied."

These were opposed by the pick of the English force, the men of Cheshire and Lancashire, under Sir Edward Stanley, men, as one narrator says, "well adapted for war, and exceedingly dexterous in the use of the bill and long bow." These send a shower of arrows upon the wild Highlanders, who, irritated by this galling fire, at length burst their ranks, rush madly down upon their foes, and encounter them in the manner depicted by the verses above. They are met, however, by the steady, disciplined billmen of Cheshire and Lancashire, against whom their wild rage expends itself in vain. The result is as might be expected : the steady resistance daunts the wild, enthusiastic Highlanders; panic succeeds to rage, and they break and fly;

(51) This is probably the time when, in the poem—
" The war for a space did fail."

they disperse, and are of no further use in the battle. Stanley, upon this, advances, and, on passing the Scottish line, wheels his force to the right, and falls upon the right flank of their centre, now, as we know, engaged in a desperate encounter with Surrey. About the same time, Lord Admiral Howard is successful in driving away Montrose and Crawford's force; he, then, also turns and attacks the left flank of the Scottish centre, which is now assailed in front and on both flanks.

And now, how about the victorious Scottish left wing ?—

> "Where's now their victor vanward wing,
> Where Huntley, and where Home ?"

According to the poem, they, on driving off the English right wing, had dispersed and taken to plunder, and were, therefore, of no more use to their countrymen than were the western Highlanders, but matters were worse than this. Some of the men, doubtless, dispersed and plundered, but Huntly and Home remained with the bulk of their force on the side of the hill without attempting to move. They were now confronted by the English reserve, under Lord Dacre, who had moved up into the place formerly occupied by the defeated English right wing, but no action appears to have taken place.[52] Huntly, indeed, suggested to Home that they should go to the assistance of the now pressed Scottish centre, but the latter would not move. Lord Home, in fact, is alleged to have said that he had done enough : he had fulfilled his duty in defeating the force opposed to him ; let the other portions of the army do the same. This is hardly credible, but I presume that the authority is good.[53] Huntly indeed made an attempt to relieve the centre, but he considered it hopeless, being probably outnumbered ; he therefore withdrew his forces. Home now did the same, without striking a blow ; the two earls withdrew their forces across the Border, with a large body of their troops entirely unscathed. No wonder that they

(52) According to one account, however, Huntly and Home succeeded in rallying a portion of their dispersed force ; and were returning to the battle-field, when they were met by Dacre and the English reserve, who attacked, defeated, and dispersed them.

(53) "Battle of Flodden Field," by R. White.

were looked upon afterwards in Scotland as traitors to their country. An English historian, Hollingshead, states that, had they attacked the English centre, they would probably have changed the fortune of the day.[54] There must have been something very wrong here, to prompt these noblemen thus to desert their king and their countrymen.[55]

Lord Dacre, on seeing the retreat of this force, at once advanced his reserve, and, executing a similar movement to those of Stanley and the Lord Admiral, wheeled it round and flung it upon the rear of the Scottish centre, which unfortunate body was now enclosed on all sides by the enemy. A desperate conflict ensues; the Scots resist bravely, but it is hopeless; Scott gives a grand description—

> "The English shafts in volleys hailed,
>   In headlong charge their horse assailed:
>   Front, flank, and rear, the squadrons sweep,
>   To break the Scottish circle deep,
>   That fought around their king.
>   But yet, though thick the shafts as snow,
>   Though charging knights like whirlwinds go,
>   Though bill-men ply the ghastly blow,
>   Unbroken was the ring;
>   The stubborn spearmen still made good
>   Their dark, impenetrable wood,
>   Each stepping where his comrade stood,
>   The instant that he fell.
>   No thought was there of dastard flight,
>   Linked in the serried phalanx tight,
>   Groom fought like noble, squire like knight,
>   As fearlessly and well;
>   Till utter darkness closed her wing
>   O'er their thin host, and wounded king."

On darkness falling, Surrey withdrew his forces; on the morrow, the Scottish host had dispersed and crossed the Border

---

(54) The historian, however, forgets Lord Dacre's force, which had not yet been engaged; these would probably have been quite sufficient to keep the Scottish left wing engaged.

(55) The name of the Earl of Huntly, however, appears in the list of the slain; he therefore personally probably joined the King in the centre, and fell beside him. The case appears to be the same with the Earls of Lennox, Argyle, Montrose, and Crawford, all of whom held commands. The rear of the Scottish centre was open until attacked by Dacre.

into Scotland as best they might; the battle was lost. By one account, the Scottish loss is stated to be from 8,000 to 10,000 men; that of the English, from 6,000 to 7,000. Anyhow, Surrey had suffered severely, and made no attempt at pursuit; indeed, he had no intention of invading Scotland; by King Henry's wish, he was only pursuing a defensive course; Henry had no desire to quarrel with Scotland.

The battle of Flodden is looked upon as the most disastrous event in the annals of Scottish history; not that there was any disgrace, with the exception of the case of Huntly and Home; otherwise, all fought bravely and did their duty. It was the loss of the king and of so great a number of the nobility which stamped the disaster so deeply upon the soul of the nation; the loss seems to be almost unparalleled in history—thirteen earls, one archbishop, two bishops, two abbots, and the Dean of Glasgow, fifteen lords and chiefs of clans, five peers' eldest sons, the French ambassador, &c. Only five Englishmen of rank fell, one being Sir Brian Tunstall.[56] "Red Flodden's dismal tale" is indeed the Jena of Scotland—

> "Tradition, legend, tune, and song,
>   Shall many an age that wail prolong:
>   Still from the sire the son shall hear
>   Of the stern strife, and carnage drear,
>   Of Flodden's fatal field,
>   Where shivered was fair Scotland's spear,
>   And broken was her shield!"

There is a mystery attaching to the death of King James, but it is almost universally accepted, and I think that there can be no doubt but that he died on the field during the terrible struggle at the end of the day. There seems to have been some doubt as to the identity of the body, as the spoilers were all about, who "stripped and gashed the slain." This probably gave Sir Walter Scott the idea of the extraordinary story regarding the body of Marmion, into which I shall shortly enter. But, however that may be, I think there is no doubt that the king died on the battle-field, the victim of his own rashness and obstinacy. The poet adopts this view—

(56) "Battle-fields of Scotland," by T. C. F. Brotchie.

" View not that corpse mistrustfully,
　Defaced and mangled though it be;
　Nor to yon Border castle high
　Look northward with upbraiding eye;
　　Nor cherish hope in vain,
　That, journeying far on foreign strand,
　The Royal Pilgrim to his land
　　May yet return again.
　He saw the wreck his rashness wrought;
　Reckless of life, he desperate fought,
　　And fell on Flodden plain;
　And well in death his trusty brand,
　Firm clenched within his manly hand,
　　Beseemed the monarch slain."

Returning finally to our tale, we must say a word regarding
our two lovers, De Wilton and Clare. Scott gives an exaggerated
account of Wilton's gallantry in the field, with evident consciousness that it is overrated; for instance—

" That, when brave Surrey's steed was slain,
　'Twas Wilton mounted him again."

Also, in the original manuscript of the poem, this line is
written—

" 'Twas said that he struck down the king";

but this line Scott afterwards altered, as evidently going rather
too far in the adulation of his hero.

However, Wilton doubtless bears himself well in the fight,
glad indeed at being again a "belted knight," with every prospect
of restoration to his former state, the stain against his honour
being completely wiped away. That this is the case is evident.
He doubtless presents the packet to Wolsey, according to the
advice of the Abbess, and is cleared in the eyes of the king. He
marries the Lady Clare, the ceremony being performed by
Cardinal Wolsey, in the presence of King Henry and Queen
Catherine, whose presence evidently shows that they desire to
show their confidence in De Wilton's innocence and their desire
to atone to him for the injustice done to him before. The
marriage of our lovers appears to be a perfect case of "living
happily ever afterwards," for—

> "Afterwards, for many a day,
> That it was held enough to say,
> In blessing to a wedded pair,
> 'Love they like Wilton and like Clare!'"

I now conclude with the extraordinary story which the poet relates with regard to the body of Marmion. It is stated that Fitz-Eustace conveyed a body, supposed to be that of Lord Marmion, to "moated Lichfield's lofty pile." It is buried with all due honours, and a monument raised to the memory of the noble Baron. But this body is not that of Marmion; it is that of a Scottish peasant who had followed his lord to Flodden; being mortally wounded, he drags himself to Sybil's cross, and there dies by the side of the body of Marmion—

> "The spoilers stripped and gashed the slain,
> And thus their corpses were mista'en;
> And thus, in the proud Baron's tomb,
> The lowly woodsman took the room."

The body of Marmion is buried by Sybil's cross and well, the spot where he died—

> "Less easy task it were, to show
> Lord Marmion's nameless grave, and low."

We now take leave of this extraordinary character, described by Lord Byron as—

> "Now forging scrolls, now foremost in the fight,
> Not quite a felon, yet not half a knight;
> The gibbet and the field prepared to grace,
> A mighty mixture of the great and base."

This very aptly describes Marmion's character as depicted by Sir Walter Scott—a treacherous villain on the one hand, a gallant warrior on the other. As I before mentioned, I think his character very greatly resembles that of King Ahab, on which I commented in a former treatise. Regarding the "gibbet or the field," it was well for Marmion that he fell on the field of battle, otherwise it was very probable that his head would have fallen on the scaffold when that incriminating packet had been produced by De Wilton; or, at least, he would have been disgraced for life. He is not devoid of conscience, as we have more than once seen; he wished that his crime could have been undone,[57] and in his last moments he wishes to atone for the wrong done to Constance. His courage also is indisputable; he, like Ahab, appears at his best on the field of battle, and his heart is thoroughly with his native country. Taking all these qualities into consideration, I think we may aptly conclude with the words of the poet—

> " When thou shalt find this little hill,
> With thy heart commune, and be still.
> If ever, in temptation strong,
> Thou left'st the right path for the wrong;
> If every devious step, thus trode,
> Still led thee farther from the road;
> Dread thou to speak presumptuous doom
> On noble Marmion's lowly tomb;
> But say, ' He died a gallant knight,
> With sword in hand, for England's right.' "

(57) See page 118.

THE LADY OF THE LAKE.

V.—THE LADY OF THE LAKE.

> " Where dwell we now ! See, rudely swell
> Crag over crag, and fell o'er fell.
> Ask we this savage hill we tread,
> For fattened steer or household bread;
> Ask we for flocks these shingles dry,
> And well the mountain might reply,—
> ' To you, as to your sires of yore,
> Belong the target and claymore !
> I give you shelter in my breast,
> Your own good blades must win the rest.'—
> Pent in this fortress of the North,
> Think'st thou we will not sally forth,
> To spoil the spoiler as we may,
> And from the robber rend the prey ?
> Ay, by my soul !—While on yon plain
> The Saxon rears one shock of grain;
> While, of ten thousand herds, there strays
> But one along yon river's maze,—
> The Gael, of plain and river heir,
> Shall, with strong hand, redeem his share.
> Where live the mountain chiefs who hold
> That plundering Lowland field and fold
> Is aught but retribution true ?
> Seek other cause 'gainst Roderick Dhu.''

THESE words represent the feeling of the Highland clans towards
the Lowlanders for centuries; the ancient hostility between the
Gael and the Saxon, the Celt and the Teuton; they show exactly
the feeling which actuated the Highland chiefs in their raids
into the Lowland country. The Saxons had rent their country
from them; and from that country, therefore, they considered
it their right to recoup themselves with that spoil, with those
necessaries, which they could not obtain in their own barren
mountains—

> " Spoil the spoiler as we may,
> And from the robber rend the prey.''

Such was their ruling principle, and we find that this state of things existed up to the middle of the eighteenth century.[1] The feeling of hostility, therefore, was as strong between the Highlanders and the Lowlanders as that of the latter towards the English; and the Scottish Lowlanders were, therefore, placed in a very awkward position, between the "auld enemy" in the south and the Highland foe in the north.[2] Hitherto our dealings have been with the English and Scottish Borderers, but now we turn to the Highlanders: no English appear in the poem with which we are now dealing, with the exception of a solitary individual, and, in place of the scenery of the Scottish Border, we are transported to the lovely scenery of the Central Highlands of Scotland, in Perthshire.

I have already said, in the preliminary words of my treatise, that, among all the poems of Scott, "The Lady of the Lake" is, and always has been, my favourite; it has a charm for me which the other poems do not possess, fond as I am of them. The lovely scenery in which the events of the poem take place is hardly equalled in all the beautiful districts of Scotland, extensive as they are. Few places, in my opinion, equal in beauty the drive through the charming wooded glen of the Trossachs, opening out at last, by the little inlet in the midst of the wood, to the glorious reach of Loch Katrine, with the imposing prospect of Ben Venue on the left, while, on the right, the crag of Ben A'an, "through middle air, heaves high his summit bare."

The characters, also, in the poem are, I think, more attractive than those in the former poems into which I have entered. There is no "elfin page," which character mars the otherwise lovely poem of "The Lay of the Last Minstrel"; there is no Marmion, with crime overshadowing his bravery and other good qualities. The "best side" of all the characters of the poem is prominently put forth—that of King James V. specially attracts; Roderick Dhu, the Highland chieftain, with his chivalrous faith,

(1) See Scott's novel "Waverley," where the herds of the Baron of Bradwardine are raided by Highland plunderers on account of his refusing to pay blackmail to their chieftain.

(2) The services of the Highlanders were sometimes, however, obtained against the common enemy, as I have already shown in my relation of the battle of Flodden.

is a superior character to that of Marmion or of William of
Deloraine; the gallant Lord Douglas, Malcolm Græme (lover
of Ellen, Douglas' daughter), the old minstrel, Allan-bane, all
attract us pleasantly; and last, but not least, there is the charming personality of the "Lady of the Lake" herself, Ellen Douglas.
I shall carefully portray all these characters in detail presently,
and we are glad to see that this lovely poem has escaped the
scathing pen of Lord Byron.[3]

The principal character in the poem is King James V. of
Scotland; and the portrait drawn of him is a very favourable
one, better, perhaps, than that monarch actually deserves; the
last lines of the poem depict him as a monarch should be. He
certainly had many good qualities, but he had failings also, the
most prominent of the latter being intense vindictiveness, which,
however natural the feeling might have been under the circumstances, was carried too far. He was an infant when he
succeeded to the throne; this entailed a long minority, always
so disastrous to a country. He was under the care—under the
rule, indeed—of successive Regents: first, of the Duke of
Albany, then of the Lord Douglas, Earl of Angus, who had
married the Queen Mother. The rule of this nobleman seems to
have been, as far as the young prince was concerned, a regular
tyranny, the latter being little more than a prisoner in the
hands of his step-father. This state of things was naturally most
galling to the high-spirited young king, who, in his seventeenth
year, managed to escape from this thraldom. Matters now
changed. James, having a large number of nobles at his back,
turned his wrath upon Angus and all the Douglas family; they
were banished from the kingdom, and their estates forfeited, the
king declaring that they should never enter Scotland again,
which, indeed, they never did during his lifetime. This feeling
of revenge the king kept up to the end of his life, and he carried
his vindictiveness so far as to lead him to a most cruel act.
Lady Glamis, sister of the Earl of Angus, was indicted for a
supposed plot against the king, of which she was probably, and,

---

(3) "English Bards and Scotch Reviewers" was, no doubt, published before
"The Lady of the Lake" appeared; otherwise Lord Byron, doubtless, would have
found some holes to pick in it.

indeed, as her judges believed, innocent; but, in spite of the entreaties of many of the nobles to spare her, James would not relent: she was burned alive on the Castle Hill of Edinburgh. This is, indeed, a dark stain on the king's character; but we are dealing not with historical facts, but with Sir Walter Scott's poem, and in this, as I said, the character of James is depicted most favourably; he is throughout brave, generous, and chivalrous.

The Lord Douglas of the poem is a fictitious character, as is also his daughter Ellen, the heroine; he is shown as taking refuge from the king's anger in an island on Loch Katrine, under the protection of a marauding Highland chieftain, Roderick Dhu (the black). Douglas is described as the "uncle of the banished earl," and therefore it is evident that Scott derives his personality from Sir Archibald Douglas of Kilspindie, who was High Treasurer during the rule of his nephew, the Earl of Angus. This noble was a favourite of King James, who gave him the name of "Grey Steel." This, however, did not exclude him from the penalties laid on his family; he was banished from Scotland with the rest. It is related that, doubtless relying on the old friendship, he returned to Scotland, sought James out, and prayed for forgiveness, but all in vain. The king took no notice of his entreaties, and at length banished him to France, treating him indeed in a very different manner from that with which James is described to have dealt with the Douglas of the poem—

> "Calmly we heard and judged his cause,
> Our council aided and our laws.
>
> .   .   .   .
>
> And Bothwell's Lord henceforth we own
> The friend and bulwark of our Throne."

Thirdly, we have the Highland chieftain, Roderick Dhu, a very prominent character in the poem—

> "The Saxon's scourge, Clan-Alpine's pride,
> The terror of Loch-Lomond's side."

This formidable chieftain is the head of the Clan of Alpine; he possesses all the faults and good qualities of his race. He is an unscrupulous marauder—he raids, burns, plunders, and slaughters; and this, as has been seen in the lines with which I have headed this treatise, he considers he has a right to do; he and his clansmen glory in their merciless deeds, which form part of the subject of their triumphal slogan—

> "Proudly our pibroch has thrilled in Glen Fruin,
>   And Banochar's groans to our slogan replied:
> Glen Luss and Ross-dhu, they are smoking in ruin,
>   And the best of Loch-Lomond lie dead on her side.
>   Widow and Saxon maid
>   Long shall lament our raid,
>   Think of Clan-Alpine with fear and with woe;
>   Lennox and Leven-glen
>   Shake when they hear agen,
>   ' Roderigh Vich Alpine dhu,[4] ho! ieroe!' "

With all his faults, however, the chief has his good qualities; there is a certain amount of chivalry in his character, he is strictly faithful to his word, and his courage is, of course, indisputable—

> "Yet with thy foe, must die, or live,
>   The praise that Faith and Valour give."

His character cannot be better depicted than in the words of Ellen Douglas, the heroine of the poem, whom the chief loves; which love she cannot return, although she feels friendship for him and gratitude for the shelter which he has afforded to her father; at the same time, she has a horror of his crimes. She says—

> "I grant him brave,
> But wild as Bracklinn's thundering wave;
> And generous—save vindictive mood,
> Or jealous transport chafe his blood:
> I grant him true to friendly band,
> As his claymore is to his hand:
> But O! that very blade of steel
> More mercy for a foe would feel:
> I grant him liberal, to fling
> Among his clan the wealth they bring,
> When back by lake and glen they wind,
> And in the Lowland leave behind,

(4) Black Roderick, son of Alpine.

> Where once some pleasant hamlet stood,
> A mass of ashes slaked with blood.
>
> .   .   .   .   .
>
> No! wildly while his virtues gleam,
> They make his passions darker seem,
> And flash along his spirit high,
> Like lightning o'er the midnight sky."

His fiery, vindictive temper had brought him into trouble before this; he appears to have been admitted into the Court at Holyrood, where, having an altercation with a certain knight, he stabbed the latter to death, for which act he was outlawed. Such is his condition at the opening of the poem.

He has now given shelter to the outlawed Douglas and his daughter, on account, doubtless, of their being in the same predicament as himself; but also because he is related to the Douglas family, Douglas having married the sister of the Lady Margaret, mother of the chieftain.

The Lady Ellen herself, young Malcolm Græme, her lover, and the old minstrel, Allan-bane, are very pleasing characters in the poem; to the narrative of which we now proceed.

The subject of the poem consists principally of one of the escapades of King James V., to which, it is said, this monarch was greatly addicted; and the one with which we have to deal nearly cost him his life. At the outset, however, the king is led into this adventure by accident: he is hunting, has outstripped his followers, and lost his way; he encounters, and is hospitably entertained by, the "Lady of the Lake," and, as might be expected, he loses his heart to her and is determined to seek her out again, greatly to his own peril; into the details of which adventure we are now about to proceed.

The opening scene is laid in the forest of Glen Artney, on the shores of Loch Earn, which lovely lake presents so charming an aspect, from end to end, from the railway between Oban and Callander, as the train winds down and emerges from Glen Ogle. It lies stretched like a map at our feet, while above it towers the lofty mountain, Ben Voirlich.

In this forest of Glen Artney, then, a noble stag has harboured for the night; he is aroused at early morn by the well-known sounds of the chase—

> " The deep-mouthed bloodhound's heavy bay
> Resounded up the rocky way,
> And faint, from farther distance borne,
> Was heard the clanging hoof and horn."

The rousing of the deer, his alertness, his attitude, and his bold burst of flight are beautifully described by the poet in these immortal lines which compose the first nine stanzas of the first canto.[5] He dashes away, and directs his course towards Uam-Var, a mountain in the neighbourhood of Callander. The pursuers follow hard on his track, but they have a formidable task before them. The quarry is evidently no ordinary one; the stag is in possession of full health and vigour; he leads them a terrible chase, and, by the time they have reached the neighbourhood of Uam-Var, more than half the hounds have fallen out, and a great number of the riders.

The stag is now pausing for a moment, contemplating his further course; he—

> " Pondered refuge from his toil,
> By far Loch Ard or Aberfoyle."

He chooses eventually the route which leads him to the glen of the Trossachs—

> " But nearer was the copse-wood grey,
> That waved and wept on Loch-Achray,
> And mingled with the pine-trees blue
> On the bold cliffs of Ben-venue."

With "fresh vigour," then, he again dashes off, leaves his pursuers behind, and gives them another desperate chase; he swims the river Teith more than once—

> " Twice, that day, from shore to shore,
> The gallant stag swam stoutly o'er."

The chase now pursues the well-known coach route from Callander to the Trossachs—along the shore of Loch Vennachar, across the opposing hill, past the Brig of Turk village (the "Duncraggan's huts" of the poem), down to the Brig of Turk

(5) I could, and still can, repeat the whole of the lines of " The Chase " by heart.

itself (the bridge which crosses the stream coming down from Glen Finlas), thence by the margin of the little Loch Achray—

> "Thus up the margin of the lake,
> Between the precipice and brake,"

until, at the farther end of the loch, the wooded gorge of the Trossachs opens out before them.

Along this route the stag leads his pursuers, who, one by one, give up as their horses fail to carry them further; and, by the time the Brig of Turk is reached, there are left but two hounds and one solitary horseman, the latter being the principal personage of the poem—

> "The headmost horseman rode alone."

This horseman, however, has by no means given up hope; he has not yet perceived the failing power of his steed, and his two hounds are—

> "Of black Saint Hubert's breed,
> Unmatched for courage, breath, and speed."

The stag, also, is evidently failing, and the hunter now—

> "Marked that mountain high,
> The lone lake's western boundary,
> And deemed the stag must turn to bay,
> Where that rude rampart barred the way." (6)

The hunter draws his knife and dashes on, fully expecting that the victory is now his; but there is life in the quarry yet, the vigour of the stag is evidently greater than that of either horse or hounds; he turns aside, and dashes into the glen of the Trossachs with a speed which entirely outstrips that of the hounds, then, disappearing from sight, he baffles them. At the same time, the gallant steed, his powers being utterly exhausted, suddenly collapses and falls to the ground. The rider, without thought of anything but the chase, tries to rouse him with spur and rein, but it is useless—

---

(6) I may mention here that this "huge rampart" does not exist: it is evidently introduced for poetical effect; the gorge of the Trossachs opens out unimpeded at the end of Loch Achray. A similar error occurs in Scott's little poem of "Helvellyn": there is no "huge nameless rock" in front of the Red Tarn.

> " For the good steed, his labours o'er,
> Stretched his stiff limbs, to rise no more."

The sorrow of his master then breaks forth in those immortal lines, which close this, the opening episode of the poem—

> " I little thought, when first thy rein
> I slacked upon the banks of Seine,
> That Highland eagle e'er should feed
> On thy fleet limbs, my matchless steed !
> Woe worth the chase, woe worth the day,
> That cost thy life, my gallant grey ! "

Our hero then proceeds to "wind his horn," which soon recalls his two hounds, wearied with their fruitless chase; he continues, however, to sound, on the chance of recovering some comrade who had fallen out in the race; this, however, proving of no effect, he proceeds on his way, but, strangely enough, he goes forward instead of retracing his steps, by which latter course he might have fallen in with some of his followers.

His course leads him through the lovely glen of the Trossachs, so well known to the modern tourist; the poet beautifully describes the nature of the glen, the mingled rocks, foliage, &c.—

> " Nor were these earth-born castles bare,
> Nor lacked they many a banner fair;
> For, from their shivered brows displayed,
> Far o'er the unfathomable glade,
> All twinkling with the dew-drop sheen,
> The brier-rose fell in streamers green,
> And creeping shrubs of thousand dyes
> Waved in the west-wind's summer sighs."

The adventurer threads his way through this tangled mass of rocks and trees—much thicker, doubtless, in those days than in the present time—until he reaches that now well-known lovely little inlet of water which inserts itself into the midst of the wood, the south-eastern end of Loch Katrine, where now the steamer starts on its trip along the lake. This place, at the period of the poem, is entirely closed in by rocks on all sides, and the hunter, having no boat, has no alternative but to scale the rocks, from the summit of which he may hope to see what lies in front of him. This he proceeds to do, by aid of the roots of the trees projecting from the rocks, and at length he reaches a point where, all of a sudden, the beautiful prospect of Loch Katrine bursts upon him—

> " And thus an airy point he won,
>   Where, gleaming with the setting sun,
>   One burnished sheet of living gold,
>   Loch-Katrine lay beneath him rolled ;
>   In all her length far winding lay,
>   With promontory, creek, and bay,
>   And islands that, empurpled bright,
>   Floated amid the livelier light ;
>   And mountains, that like giants stand,
>   To sentinel enchanted land."

Loch Katrine,[7] about $9\frac{1}{2}$ miles long, shows a great diversity of scenery. The most beautiful portion is doubtless at its south-eastern end, where it is merged in the wooded and mountainous scenery of the Trossachs glen. After emerging from this glen, and passing "Ellen's Isle " (the scene of the poem, to which we shall shortly come), the prospect becomes more tame, and is somewhat marred by the insertion of the Glasgow waterworks. Still, we have a grand prospect of mountain scenery in the distance ; Ben Lomond peers over a nearer ridge to the west-ward, while further away in front appear the mountains over-hanging Loch Lomond. The upper end of the lake, little known to tourists, emerges from the wild valley of Glen Gyle.

All this lovely scene bursts upon our hero for the first time, the long stretch of the lake appearing between those two mountains which stand forth as sentinels above the Trossachs glen—

> " High on the south, huge Ben-venue
>   Down to the lake in masses threw
>   Crags, knolls, and mounds, confusedly hurled,
>   The fragments of an earlier world ;
>   A 'wildering forest feathered o'er
>   His ruined sides and summit hoar,
>   While on the north, through middle air,
>   Ben-an heaved high his forehead bare."[8]

(7) Loch Catteran, or the Lake of the Robbers.

(8) From the summit of Ben A'n I have obtained a grand view of the Trossachs glen.

Our adventurer contemplates the lovely scene for some time, considering what a delightful spot it would be were it inhabited, but, as it is, he feels that he must probably make his couch for the night on the bare ground, with the chance also of falling in with some Highland robbers. From this predicament, however, he is unexpectedly relieved.

As a last chance, he again winds his horn, when, to his surprise, from beneath a neighbouring oak, where it has as yet lain concealed, a skiff shoots forth, propelled by a maiden; and here, for the first time, we are confronted with the heroine of the poem, Ellen Douglas, the "Lady of the Lake."

She stops her boat to listen for further sound, and the poet takes the opportunity of describing her charms in his own beautiful words—

> "And ne'er did Grecian chisel trace
> A Nymph, a Naiad, or a Grace,
> Of finer form, or lovelier face."

Her dress is that of the daughter of a Highland chieftain; this the poet describes, and thence touches upon her disposition—

> "And seldom o'er a breast so fair,
> Mantled a plaid with modest care,
> And never brooch the folds combined
> Above a heart more good and kind.
> Her kindness and her worth to spy,
> You need but gaze on Ellen's eye;
> Not Katrine, in her mirror blue,
> Gives back the shaggy banks more true,
> That every free-born glance confessed
> The guileless movements of her breast."

She now calls out, "Father!"—there is no answer; then, "Malcolm, was thine the blast?" On this, the hunter, emerging from the wood, says, "A stranger, I." The maiden, alarmed at first, thrusts her boat back from the shore, but is soon reassured by his appearance—

> "Not his the form, nor his the eye,
> That youthful maidens wont to fly."

And here the poet enters into a description of his hero, James V. of Scotland—

> "On his bold visage, middle age
> Had slightly pressed its signet sage,
> Yet had not quenched the open truth
> And fiery vehemence of youth;
> Forward and frolic glee was there,
> The will to do, the soul to dare,
> The sparkling glance, soon blown to fire,
> Of hasty love, or headlong ire.
>
> .   .   .   .   .   .
>
> His stately mien as well implied
> A high-born heart, a martial pride."

Also, when he explains his presence there, it is pointed out
that—

> "His ready speech flowed fair and free,
> In phrase of gentlest courtesy;
> Yet seemed that tone, and gesture bland,
> Less used to sue than to command."

The maiden at once proffers the stranger hospitality, and, to
his surprise, intimates that his visit was expected, for it was
foretold by her old minstrel, Allan-bane (whose acquaintance we
shall shortly make), who appears to have possessed what we
would now term "second sight."

She receives him into her boat, which, propelled by his
powerful arm, soon reaches that little island which, situated just
outside the Trossachs glen, is now known by the name of "Ellen's
Isle."

This small island is entirely covered with wood, and appears
to have been so at the period represented by the poem—

> "'Twas all so close with copse-wood bound,
> Nor track nor pathway might declare
> That human foot frequented there."

The maiden, however, soon discovers to the stranger a secret
path, winding through the wood, and at length opening into a
clearing, where a large building is seen, made of rude materials,
such as would now be termed a "log house." This house is no
less than the headquarters of the formidable Highland chieftain,
Roderick Dhu, who is absent on one of his forays at this time.
The house is tenanted by the Lady Margaret, mother of the

chieftain, and by the exiled Lord Douglas, his daughter, Ellen, and the old minstrel, Allan-bane. Douglas, as well as the chief, is absent at this period.

At the porch the maiden turns and archly addresses her guest—

> "On Heaven and on thy lady call,
> And enter the enchanted hall!"

He replies, in like humour—

> "My hope, my heaven, my trust must be,
> My gentle guide, in following thee."

On entering the hall, however, he is startled by the clang of "angry steel," but he soon finds that it is caused by the fall of an immense sword blade, which, with its scabbard, had been hanging against the wall, on the horns of a stag, which wall is covered with arms, hunting weapons, and trophies of the chase.

He raises the weapon, poises it, and, with his mind full of the exiled Lord Douglas, says—

> "'I never knew but one,' he said,
> 'Whose stalwart arm might brook to wield
> A blade like this in battle-field.'"

Ellen, in answer, mentions the vast strength of the owner, without, of course, divulging his name.

The stranger is now received hospitably by the mistress of the mansion, no questions being asked of him until he had refreshed himself, such being the laws of ancient hospitality—

> "Such then the reverence to a guest,
> That fellest foe might join the feast,
> And from his deadliest foeman's door
> Unquestioned turn, the banquet o'er."

At length he gives his name and rank; he calls himself "The Knight of Snowdoun, James Fitz-James," by which name we shall for the present know him. He speaks the truth partly, but disguising the true facts. The king later, as we shall see, explains to Ellen his partially true statement—

> " 'Tis under name which veils my power,
> Nor falsely veils—for Stirling's tower
> Of yore the name of Snowdoun claims,
> And Normans call me James Fitz-James."

Fitz-James, on his part, endeavours to find out the name and quality of his hostesses, but they parry all his endeavours. They soon retire, leaving him to his rest, Ellen concluding, in accompaniment to the harp, with singing that lovely lay commencing—

> "Soldier, rest! thy warfare o'er,
> Sleep the sleep that knows not breaking!"

She concludes with leading—

> "The lay,
> To grace the stranger of the day,"

in the following well-chosen words—

> "Huntsman, rest! thy chase is done,
>   While our slumbrous spells assail ye,
> Dream not with the rising sun
>   Bugles here shall sound reveillé.
> Sleep! the deer is in his den;
>   Sleep! thy hounds are by thee lying;
> Sleep! nor dream in yonder glen,
>   How thy gallant steed lay dying.
> Huntsman, rest! thy chase is done,
> Think not of the rising sun,
> For at dawning to assail ye,
> Here no bugles sound reveillé." (9)

The guest lies down to rest, but his sleep is not at first untroubled. The fall of the sword has disturbed him; and his thoughts constantly revert to the exiled Lord Douglas, mingled with the feelings he has already begun to entertain towards Ellen, in whom he fancies he sees a resemblance to Douglas. At length he wakes, and again fixes his eyes upon the sword. He rises, and walks outside to calm himself, thus soliloquising—

---

(9) "The Lady of the Lake" excels in the number of these beautiful minor poems enclosed, as it were, in the main one. It is a peculiar beauty which distinguishes this poem from others by Sir Walter Scott.

> " Why is it at each turn I trace
> Some memory of that exiled race ?
> Can I not mountain maiden spy,
> But she must bear the Douglas eye ?
> Can I not view a Highland brand,
> But it must match the Douglas hand ?
> Can I not frame a fevered dream,
> But still the Douglas is the theme ? "

He becomes calmer, however, and adopts the best course that he could take—

> " His midnight orison he told,
> A prayer with every bead of gold,
> Consigned to Heaven his cares and woes,
> And sunk in undisturbed repose ;
> Until the heath-cock shrilly crew,
> And morning dawned on Ben-venue."

He departs in the morning, sped on his way by the song of the old minstrel, Allan-bane—

> " Then, stranger, go ! good speed the while,
> Nor think again of the lonely isle."

But besides, should he ever return, he is assured of a welcome—

> " Or if on life's uncertain main,
> Mishap shall mar thy sail ;
> If faithful, wise, and brave in vain,
> Woe, want, and exile thou sustain,
> Beneath the fickle gale ;
> Waste not a sigh on fortune changed,
> On thankless courts, or friends estranged,
> But come where kindred worth shall smile,
> To greet thee in the lonely isle."

He is landed on the farther shore, and, accompanied by a guide, proceeds on his way, but not without a long and lingering look behind upon Ellen, as she sits by the side of the old minstrel. Here we take leave of Fitz-James for the present ; but he has not forgotten the "lonely isle" nor its occupant, and he is shortly destined to return again, at his great risk, and with a narrow escape of his life.

We now enter upon another episode of the poem, which is divided into six cantos; each canto generally represents a whole day. In the present case, however, I have brought the first episode of the narrative into the second canto, concluding with the departure of the stranger guest. In this canto we are introduced to the three other important characters of the poem—the banished Lord Douglas, Ellen's father, young Malcolm Græme, her lover, and the formidable Highland chieftain, Roderick Dhu.

Before these personages appear on the scene, however, there is an interval, which is occupied by a conversation between Ellen Douglas and her faithful attendant, the minstrel, old Allan-bane.

Ellen is ashamed to find that the departing stranger has lately occupied her thoughts to the exclusion of her lover, young Malcolm Græme; she therefore desires the minstrel to strike his harp to the "glory of the Græme." The old man attempts to do so, but is unable, on account of an overpowering depression of spirits. He is possessed, as we have seen, of the "second sight," and has also a strong belief in omens. The arrival of the stranger has doubtless brought on this feeling, for the falling of the sword, untouched, from its scabbard [10] foretold to him the coming of a secret foe. This, indeed, was true at the time being, though the clouds hereafter were happily cleared away.

Another foreboding, however, would doubtless be that of the approaching disaster to the clan under whose protection the exiles were, and the fear that this disaster would involve the family of Douglas in its fall.

Ellen cheers him, and their discourse then turns to their protector, Roderick Dhu, who was also madly in love with the maiden, so that, as she herself says—

> "And then for suitors proud and high,
> To bend before my conquering eye,
> Thou, flattering bard! thyself wilt say
> That grim Sir Roderick owns its sway.
> The Saxon scourge, Clan-Alpine's pride,
> The terror of Loch-Lomond's side,
> Would at my suit, thou know'st, delay
> A Lennox foray—for a day."

(10) See page 159.

She speaks in jest, but the old minstrel at once says that this is no theme for jesting; she is dealing with a very formidable character, whose love is to be feared as much as his hate, as he says—

> " But though to Roderick thou'rt so dear,
> That thou mightst guide with silken thread,
> Slave of thy will, this chieftain dread;
> Yet, O loved maid, thy mirth refrain!
> Thy hand is on a lion's mane."

She at once replies that, deep as is her gratitude to Roderick for his protection to her and her father, she cannot give him her love; that is another's—

> " Allan! Sir Roderick should command
> My blood, my life,—but not my hand ";

rather—

> " An outcast pilgrim will she rove,
> Than wed the man she cannot love."

She thus expresses her estimate of the chieftain's character, which I have already given on a former page; [11] not only does she not love him, but she fears him, not without reason, for, as the old minstrel points out, Roderick has already suspected Ellen's love for Malcolm Græme, and discord may break out at any moment.

Their conversation is interrupted by distant sounds, which gradually swell in strength on nearer approach, and soon indicate the arrival of the formidable Highland chieftain and his followers. They come in four barges, from the direction of Glen Gyle, and as they approach their "pibroch" [12] sounds louder and louder—

> " Ever, as on they bore, more loud
> And louder rung the pibroch proud.
> At first the sounds, by distance tame,
> Mellowed along the waters came,
> And, lingering long by cape and bay,
> Wailed every harsher note away;

(11) See page 151.

(12) Pipe music.

> Then, bursting bolder on the ear,
> The clan's shrill Gathering they could hear;
> Those thrilling sounds, that call the might
> Of old Clan-Alpine to the fight."

As the boats approach the island, the pipes cease; they are succeeded by the voices of the men, who chant forth the praises of their chief and of the emblem of the clan, the pine tree—

> "Ours is no sapling, chance-sown by the fountain,
>   Blooming at Beltane, in winter to fade;
> When the whirlwind has stripped every leaf on the mountain,
>   The more shall Clan-Alpine exult in her shade.
>   Moored in the rifted rock,
>   Proof to the tempest's shock,
>   Firmer he roots him the ruder it blow;
>   Menteith and Breadalbane, then,
>   Echo his praise agen,
>   'Roderigh Vich Alpine dhu, ho! ieroe!'"

Next comes the boasting of their late victories; nothing else, alas! but murder and rapine. I have given the words of this verse on a former page.[13]

Lastly, mingled with the praise of the chief, is the hope of the latter's union in marriage with the "rosebud that graces yon island"—

> "Row, vassals, row, for the pride of the Highlands!
>   Stretch to your oars, for the ever-green pine!
> O! that the rosebud that graces yon islands
>   Were wreathed in a garland around him to twine!
>   O that some seedling gem
>   Worthy such noble stem,
>   Honoured and blessed in their shadow might grow!
>   Loud should Clan-Alpine then
>   Ring from her deepmost glen,
>   'Roderigh Vich Alpine dhu, ho! ieroe!'"

A great reception is, of course, awaiting them at the island from the Lady Margaret (the chief's mother) and her female attendants; she summons Ellen, who is reluctantly obeying, when she (Ellen) is relieved from her embarrassment by a bugle

(13) See page 151.

call from the shore on the Trossachs side, which she knows to be
that of her father. At once springing aside, she summons to
her Allan-bane, the old minstrel—

> "'List, Allan-bane! From mainland cast,
> I hear my father's signal-blast.
> Be ours,' she cried, 'the skiff to guide,
> And waft him from the mountain-side.'"

Therefore, when Roderick lands and looks around for the form he
values more than all the welcoming crowd, he seeks in vain.
She has gone—

> "The islet far behind her lay,
> And she had landed in the bay."

Two other characters now appear upon the scene—the
banished Lord Douglas and Ellen's lover, Malcolm Græme.
Douglas had been on the chase, and, wandering up Glen Finlas,
had been in some danger—

> "For, all around,
> Hunters and horsemen scoured the ground."

These were, probably, some remnant of the late hunt,
searching for their lost monarch; there is, I think, no reason to
suppose that these had any inkling that the banished lord was
in the neighbourhood. There was, however, danger that they
might recognise him; and from this predicament he is delivered
by young Malcolm Græme, whom he encounters in the glen.
Græme is a ward of the king, and thoroughly loyal to his
sovereign, but, influenced, perhaps, by pity for the exile, and,
doubtless, still more so by his love for the latter's daughter, he
guides Douglas through the wood, not without some risk of
capture, and at length conducts him safely to the strand near
the island.

This favoured lover of the heroine only appears twice in the
poem, viz., on the present occasion, and, for a moment, at the
end; the poet, however, endows him with a superabundance of
good qualities: graceful in appearance, skilful in the chase, swift
of foot, of strong endurance, pleasing in character, and of such
courage and skill in arms that it was a popular saying that, were

he grown to manhood, he would be likely to vie in prowess with the formidable Highland chieftain, Roderick Dhu himself. No person, however, can be perfect; and, in conjunction with all these fine qualities, we see, as might indeed be expected, an element of conceit.

The party wend their way back to the island, where Roderick Dhu had already landed. Douglas, with a kind word to old Allan-bane, meets the chieftain, who, as may be expected, is not best pleased at the sight of Malcolm Græme, with whom, as is hinted,[14] unpleasantness has before arisen, on account, doubtless, of their mutual love to Ellen, and also, very probably, jealousy on the part of the chief, caused by the popular rumour mentioned above regarding the prowess of the youth. What the actual circumstance of this friction was is not, I think, distinctly stated. Roderick, however, in the meantime receives Græme courteously, the latter being his guest.

The first part of the day passes peacefully, when a message is brought to Roderick which disturbs that restless chieftain; in the evening, he discloses the purport to the assembled party. The news has reached him that the king is about to invade the Highlands. There is, indeed, no real warrant for this rumour, the fact being that the monarch, who is about to hold sports at Stirling, has despatched a force, under the Earls of Moray and Mar, to Doune, to guard against any possible attack from the Highland clans while the public attention is directed to the sports. This action, therefore, is entirely defensive, which is indeed confirmed by the king himself in the future interview with the chief, which we shall relate hereafter. The fact, however, that King James had lately shown himself very active in quelling the disorders of the Border robbers is quite enough to make Roderick believe that he (the king) was meditating similar action against the equally troublesome Highlanders—

> "This tyrant of the Scottish throne,
> So faithless, and so ruthless known,
> Now hither comes; his end the same,
> The same pretext of sylvan game."

(14) In the ensuing quarrel, Roderick says—

> "Back, minion! hold'st thou thus at naught
> The lesson I so lately taught?"

Roderick also declares that Douglas was recognised while in Glen Finlas; this, then, was probably another reason for this threatened invasion. On this, Douglas, believing his own capture to be the principal cause of the intended attack, declares his intention of withdrawing, with his daughter, from the island and seeking another place of refuge, so that he may draw away the threatened storm from Roderick and his clan.

The chief eagerly protests against this step, and now makes offer openly for the hand of Ellen, assuming that, by thus entering into alliance with Douglas, many allies would be gained, either for offensive or defensive warfare, as above expressed—

> "To Douglas, leagued with Roderick Dhu,
> Will friends and allies flock enow;
> Like cause of doubt, distrust, and grief,
> Will bind to us each western chief.
> When loud the pipes my bridal tell,
> The Links of Forth shall hear the knell,
> The guards shall start in Stirling's porch;
> And when I light the nuptial torch,
> ᷄housand villages in flames
> Shall scare the slumbers of King James!"

He moderates his tone, however, on seeing the fear and disapproval of Ellen, and the warning signs of his mother—

> "Nay, Ellen, blench not thus away,
> And, mother, cease these signs, I pray;
> I meant not all my heat might say.—
> Small need of inroad, or of fight,
> When the sage Douglas may unite
> Each mountain clan in friendly band,
> To guard the passes of their land,
> Till the foiled King, from pathless glen,
> Shall bootless turn him home agen."

At this direct offer of marriage and consequent alliance with the fiery chieftain, Ellen feels, as described by the poet, like one who, in a dream, desires to fling himself over a precipice—

> "Did he not desperate impulse feel,
> Headlong to plunge himself below,
> And meet the worst his fears foreshow?"

She, as we know, regards this marriage with the greatest
dread and aversion, but how is she to act ? What will the consequence be to her father if she refuses ? The alliance with this
Highland chieftain may be of the greatest advantage to Douglas ;
in case of success, favourable terms may be made with the king,
and the exile be restored to his estates and the royal favour. She
is half inclined to sacrifice herself, and Græme, seeing this, is
about to speak—which act would doubtless have precipitated the
impending quarrel—when the situation is saved by the interposition of Douglas himself. He is not the man to attempt to
control his daughter's wish in such a case, and, in spite of his
wrongs, he yet loves his king, and will not bear arms against
him. He speaks out in a manner worthy of himself, refusing the
proferred union and alliance—

> " ' Roderick, enough ! enough ! ' he cried,
> ' My daughter cannot be thy bride ;
> Not that the blush to wooer dear,
> Nor paleness that of maiden fear.
> It may not be—forgive her, chief,
> Nor hazard aught for our relief.
> Against his sovereign, Douglas ne'er
> Will level a rebellious spear.
> 'Twas I that taught his youthful hand
> To rein a stèed and wield a brand.
> I see him yet, the princèly boy !
> Not Ellen more my pride and joy ;
> I love him still, despite my wrongs,
> By hasty wrath, and slanderous tongues.
> O seek the grace you well may find,
> Without a cause to mine combined.' "

Whatever may have been the faults of Roderick Dhu, he
certainly possesses one redeeming quality : his love for Ellen is
deep, pure, and sincere. He is cut to the heart by this refusal of
his love, but he behaves like a man under the blow. He does
not break into an outburst of rage, as might have been expected
from one of his fiery temperament, but he wrings the hand of
Douglas in silence, and tears of despair actually burst forth
from this rugged warrior. Ellen also is pained by this strong
expression of feeling, for she has, as we know, feelings of regard

and gratitude towards the chief, and, not bearing to see his grief, she rises to leave the room.

Græme hastens to assist her, and on sight of his hated rival thus, as it were, usurping his place, the wrath of Roderick, hitherto restrained, bursts forth. He flings himself on Græme, lays hand on him, and drags him away; on which Græme, equally enraged, turns upon the chief, and the two grapple furiously together; but Douglas at once flings himself between them and drags them apart—

> "Madmen, forbear your frantic jar!
> What! is the Douglas fallen so far,
> His daughter's hand is deemed the spoil
> Of such dishonourable broil!"

The combatants part, but with hands on their swords, and still inclined for fight. Roderick, however, remembers that Græme is his guest, and sheaths his sword. His words, nevertheless, show that jealousy, as well as rivalry, animates him towards one who, as rumour asserted, might rival himself in prowess on attaining to manhood—

> "Rest safe till morning; pity 'twere
> Such cheek should feel the midnight air!"

He dares Græme to reveal all he knows of the position of Clan Alpine to the king, offering to him safe conduct at the same time. This Græme haughtily refuses, declaring that the chieftain's hold was safe, for—

> "The spot, an angel deigned to grace,
> Is blessed, though robbers haunt the place."

He takes an affectionate farewell of Douglas and Ellen, and, accompanied by old Allan-bane, proceeds to the shore, and, scorning even the aid of a boat, flings himself into the lake and swims to the mainland.

In this quarrel, I must confess, my sympathies are generally with Roderick; he behaves well under his terrible disappointment, while Græme, on the other hand, makes no allowance for the feelings of the chief, but shows the bitterest hostility to him, whose hospitality he had enjoyed during the day : he describes him as a "pride-swollen robber," refuses his courtesy and safe conduct, which were perfectly to be relied on, as we shall see later, and, in his pride and conceit, refuses even the aid of a boat—

> "Tell Roderick Dhu, I owed him nought,
> Not the poor service of a boat,
> To waft me to yon mountain-side."

In fairness to Græme, however, we must confess that Roderick was the aggressor; but, granting that, I do not think that Græme comes well out of this; he might have shown more respect to a man older than himself and also his host. However, we shall see no more of this youth till shortly before the conclusion of the poem.

Douglas, in accordance with his expressed intention no longer to endanger Roderick by his presence on the isle, withdraws, with his daughter, on the following morning to Coirnan-Uriskin, or the Goblin Cave, in a wild dell on the slope of Ben Venue; while the chief, still impressed with the idea (believing also, doubtless, that Græme intended to betray him) that invasion by the troops at Doune was imminent, and also to stifle his scathed feelings in the excitment of warfare—

> "To drown his love in war's wild roar,
> Nor think of Ellen Douglas more,"

proceeds to assemble his clan by sending round the "Fiery Cross," to the account of which event we will now proceed.

The third canto of the poem contains the description of the assembling of the clan by means of the method just mentioned, the "Fiery Cross" being two pieces of wood shaped together into that form, the ends having been set on fire and then extinguished in the blood of a slain goat. This is passed on by envoys, who relieve each other at certain places, forwarding this signal of assembly, each envoy being bound to carry the cross on, no matter what occupation, however important, he may be engaged in; this will be seen in the narrative hereafter. Thus, in a very short space of time, the cross would have traversed the whole clan, who would speedily assemble at the appointed meeting place. Each envoy merely showed the cross and named the place of assembly, and any clansman who failed to attend the summons (as the note to the poem says) "suffered the extremities of fire and sword, which were emblematically denounced to the disobedient by the bloody and burnt marks upon this warlike signal." The description of the rites, and the transmission of the Fiery Cross, are fully detailed in the canto into which we are now about to enter. This custom appears to have lasted up to the very end of the existence of the clans as fighting bodies, which took place after the campaign of 1745-46. As the poet says—

> " Yet live there still who can remember well,
>   How, when a mountain chief his bugle blew,
> Both field and forest, dingle, cliff, and dell,
>   And solitary heath, the signal knew;
> And fast the faithful clan around him drew,
>   What time the warning note was keenly wound,
> What time aloft their kindred banner flew,
>   While clamorous war-pipes yelled the gathering sound,
> And while the Fiery Cross glanced, like a meteor, round."

Roderick Dhu, as we have seen, is now determined to assemble his clan to resist the invasion, which he supposes to be about to take place, from the troops under the Earls of Moray and Mar, now mustered at Doune, to protect the royal sports at Stirling. His own wild thoughts, maddened by his rejection by Ellen, incline him to believe this muster of the royal troops as hostile to himself, and he rushes blindly into this war, hereafter to prove fatal to himself.

We see him, therefore, at early dawn on the morning succeeding the events just related, impatiently pacing the strand of the island, with his hand upon his sword, hardly able to restrain himself during the performance of the rite, which had to take place before the signal of assembly could be despatched—

> " The shrinking band stood oft aghast
> At the impatient glance he cast;—
> Such glance the mountain eagle threw,
> As from the cliffs of Ben-venue
> She spread her dark sails on the wind,
> And high in middle heaven reclined,
> With her broad shadow on the lake,
> Silenced the warblers of the brake."

Scott beautifully contrasts the wild, gloomy mood of the chief with the peace of the breaking dawn—

> "Mildly and soft, the western breeze
> Just kissed the lake, just stirred the trees;
> And the pleased lake, like maiden coy,
> Trembled, but dimpled not for joy."

In great contrast to this scene of peace is the dire ritual which now takes place, and which is performed by one well suited to the task, a wild, half-mad anchorite, named Brian the Hermit—

> "His grizzled beard and matted hair
> Obscured a visage of despair;
> His naked arms and legs, seamed o'er,
> The scars of frantic penance bore."

The birth of this mysterious being, who, although in priestly orders, is more Druid than Christian, is doubtful, his father being unknown; and the circumstances, in that superstitious age, point to the belief that that father is not an earthly being. His mother, it appears, "watched a midnight fold," on ground on which, in days gone by, a battle had been fought, of which the ghastly relics—rusty weapons, bones, &c.—lay around—

> "All night, in this sad glen, the maid
> Sate shrouded in her mantle's shade:
> She said, no shepherd sought her side,
> No hunter's hand her snood untied,
> Yet ne'er again to braid her hair
> The virgin snood did Alice wear;
> Gone was her maiden glee and sport,
> Her maiden girdle all to short,
> Nor sought she, from that fatal night,
> Or holy church or blessèd rite,
> But locked her secret in her breast,
> And died in travail, unconfessed."

It is no wonder that, under these circumstances, Brian became what he was. Estranged from his fellow-men, who taunted him with the mystery of his birth, he withdrew from them to the solitude of the mountains, and, in this gloomy, morbid life, began to fancy himself to be actually what was generally believed, the child of a supernatural being—

> "And sought, in mist and meteor fire,
> To meet and know his Phantom Sire!"

This, doubtless, affected his brain, and he began to see visions, some sanguinary, some caused by mirage—

> "Thus the lone Seer, from mankind hurled,
> Shaped forth a disembodied world."

He had, indeed, been admitted to the cloister for a while, and during that period obtained the order of priesthood; but, as I have said, his instincts were more those of a Druid than of a Christian priest; the restraint of the monastery became unendurable, and he broke loose and again hid himself in the mountains. He still retained, however, one link with the human kind, that with the Clan Alpine, to which his mother belonged; the welfare of the clan still moved his heart, and having seen, as he thought, signs of ill-omen towards it, he comes forth to warn his chief and to take part in the rite which follows.

This consists of the slaughter of a goat and the formation, as I have already described, of a cross of wood, which cross this grisly priest holds aloft, uttering a dire anathema on any clansman who, on beholding it, shall fail to obey the summons. The clansmen present echo it, with the cry, "Woe to the traitor, woe!" and—

> "Ben-an's grey scalp the accents knew,
> The joyous wolf from covert drew,
> The exulting eagle screamed afar,—
> They knew the voice of Alpine's war."

The priest then proceeds with the grim ritual; he sets fire to the ends of the cross, and proceeds with further anathema, which is now principally addressed to the women present—

> "While maids and matrons on his name
> Shall call down wretchedness and shame,
> And infamy and woe."

The women echo the curse as eagerly as did the men before—

> "Then rose the cry of females, shrill
> As goss-hawk's whistle on the hill,
> Denouncing misery and ill,
> Mingled with childhood's babbling trill,
> Of curses stammered slow."

Brian now concludes the rite by dipping the burning ends of the cross in the blood of the slaughtered goat, thus quenching the flames, pronouncing over it a more terrible anathema than before on the clansman failing to obey the signal—

> "When flits this Cross from man to man,
> Vich-Alpine's summons to his clan,
> Burst be the ear that fails to heed!
> Palsied the foot that shuns to speed!
> May ravens tear the careless eyes;
> Wolves make the coward heart their prize!
> As sinks that blood-stream in the earth,
> So may his heart's-blood drench his hearth!
> As dies in hissing gore the spark,
> Quench thou his light, Destruction dark!
> And be the grace to him denied,
> Bought by this sign to all beside!"

The rite is now concluded, and Roderick, who has with difficulty restrained his impatience during its performance, seizes the cross and hands it to his henchman, Malise, with these brief words—

> "The muster place be Lanrick mead—
> Instant the time—speed, Malise, speed!"

As we have just entered into a description of the rite which preceded the transmission of the Fiery Cross, so now we deal with its circulation through the clan, and the marvellous effect which its appearance excites among the clansmen. No matter on what occupation a clansman may be engaged, of whatever importance, whether of sorrow or of joy, he must leave it and repair without delay to the general muster place at the call of his chief.

To certain families of the clan the task evidently belongs of transmitting the Fiery Cross on from one station to another. The first on the route by which the emblem of war is now sent is the chief of Duncraggan, whose residence lies on the hill between the lochs of Achray and Vennachar. This is at no great distance from Loch Katrine, and the dispatch of Malise would seem to be but a preliminary course, to deliver the cross into the above-named chieftain's hands. The real mission of the henchman is, as we shall see, to reconnoitre the position of the enemy and also to discern the feeling of the neighbouring clans. However, Malise proceeds to rouse all those clansmen living around Loch Achray, and that most effectually—

> "Fast as the fatal symbol flies,
> In arms the huts and hamlets rise;
> From winding glen, from upland brown,
> They poured each hardy tenant down.
> Nor slacked the messenger his pace;
> He showed the sign, he named the place;
> And, pressing forward like the wind,
> Left clamour and surprise behind.
> The fisherman forsook the strand,
> The swarthy smith took dirk and brand,
> With changèd cheer, the mower blythe
> Left in the half-cut swathe his scythe;
> The herds without a keeper strayed,
> The plough was in mid-furrow stayed,
> The falconer tossed his hawk away,
> The hunter left the stag at bay;
> Prompt at the signal of alarms,
> Each son of Alpine rushed to arms;
> So swept the tumult and affray
> Along the margin of Achray."

Leaving the shore of the lake and this tumult behind him, Malise passes the Brig of Turk, and, ascending the hill beyond, comes upon the little hamlet, now termed the Brig of Turk village, which even at the present time presents the appearance described in the poem—

> "Duncraggan's huts appear at last,
> And peep, like moss-grown rocks, half seen,
> Half hidden in the copse so green."

Here, however, alas! the envoy comes upon a sad scene; he enters a house of woe. Duncan, chief of Duncraggan, who should have "sped the message on," is smitten down by death; whether by casualty or by disease is not shown; probably the former, as his death seems not to have been known to Roderick.[15] However that may be—

(15) It should be remembered, however, that the chief had only just returned from a distant foray.

> "A gallant hunter's sport is o'er,
> A valiant warrior fights no more."

The sorrowing family are gathered round the bier; above the funeral wail arises the mournful dirge of the coronach—

> "He is gone on the mountain,
> He is lost to the forest,
> Like a summer-dried fountain,
> When our need was the sorest.
> The font, re-appearing,
> From the rain-drops shall borrow,
> But to us comes no cheering,
> For Duncan no morrow!
>
> .　　.　　.　　.　　.　　.　　.
>
> Fleet foot on the correi,
> Sage counsel in cumber,
> Red hand in the foray,
> How sound is thy slumber!
> Like the dew on the mountain,
> Like the foam on the river,
> Like the bubble on the fountain,
> Thou art gone, and for ever!"

Entirely heedless of the mournful scene, the envoy rushes in and delivers his message—

> "The muster place is Lanrick mead;
> Speed forth the signal! clansmen, speed!"

The call is responded to without hesitation by Angus, son and heir of the deceased; in spite of his grief, he must forward the message; the duty to his chief comes first; and this he accepts as a matter of course. He rushes away with the cross, after a brief parting with his mother, who, indeed, does not attempt to detain him. She accepts the position as does her son, and, stern as she is in character, overcomes her sorrow for a time and calls her retainers to arms, like a true Highland clanswoman—

> "And short and flitting energy
> Glanced from the mourner's sunken eye,
> As if the sounds to warrior dear
> Might rouse her Duncan from his bier:
> But faded soon that borrowed force;
> Grief claimed its right, and tears their course."

We shall meet her again before the close of the poem.
The Fiery Cross now speeds on eastwards—

> "Ben-ledi saw the Cross of Fire,
> It glanced like lightning up Strath-Ire."

At length the envoy leaves the valley of the Teith, and proceeds
up the lovely Pass of Leny to the southern end of Loch Lubnaig,
opposite to the little mound crowned by the Chapel of St. Bride,
of which now only a few almost undistinguishable fragments
remain. Here Angus will find his successor, but he has first to
pass the Leny, then in full flood. He plunges in, undergoing a
terrible passage, encumbered as he is with the Fiery Cross, but
he stumbles through at length, and ascends to the chapel.

Here he enters upon a very different scene from that which
he had just left; there sorrow, here joy. The man whose duty
it is to carry the cross on, Norman, heir of Armandave, has just
been married to "Tombea's Mary," a young and lovely maiden.
The bridal procession is just issuing from the chapel; everything
betokens joy and gladness; when—

> "Who meets them at the churchyard gate ?
> The messenger of fear and fate ! "

Without heeding the joyous scene any more than Malise had
that of woe, Angus holds forth the cross to the bridegroom, with
the same ominous words—

> "The muster place is Lanrick mead !
> Speed forth the signal ! Norman, speed ! "

This is a more terrible ordeal than the former; the summons
to war might come as a relief to Angus, as it may cause him to
forget his sorrow for a while; but with Norman ! Just wedded,
he is torn from the embrace of his young and lovely bride at the
very moment of winning her—

> "And must the day, so blithe that rose,
> And promised rapture in the close,
> Before its setting hour, divide
> The bridegroom from the plighted bride ?

> O fatal doom !—it must ! it must !
> Clan-Alpine's cause, her Chieftain's trust,
> Her summons dread, brooks no delay;
> Stretch to the race—Away ! away !''

The pain, the wrench, must have been great, but he hesitates no more than did Angus. One glance at his bride, then, without venturing another, he seizes the cross and speeds forward on his appointed way, being consoled by the thought that he is doing his duty to his chief and to his clan—

> "Zeal for the clan and Chieftain burning,
> And hope, from well-fought field returning,
> With war's red honours on his crest,
> To clasp his Mary to his breast.''

Norman, however, does not forget the fact that he may never return, as indicated in the lovely little ode to his bride, which he now sings—

> "A time will come with feeling fraught !
> For, if I fall in battle fought,
> Thy hapless lover's dying thought
>   Shall be a thought on thee, Mary.
> And if returned from conquered foes,
> How blithely will the evening close,
> How sweet the linnet sing repose
>   To my young bride and me, Mary !''

He appears again in the poem, but it is not mentioned whether or not he returns in safety to his "bonnie bride."

In the meantime he speeds on with his symbol of war through the Braes of Balquidder—

> "The signal roused to martial coil
> The sullen margin of Loch Voil,
> Waked still Loch Doine, and to the source
> Alarmed, Balvaig, thy swampy course;
> Thence southward turned its rapid road
> Adown Strath-Gartney's valley broad,
> Till rose in arms each man might claim
> A portion in Clan-Alpine's name.''

Every valley sends forth its little band of men; from all

parts they assemble and converge towards the rendezvous, where,
by the evening, the whole clan is assembled; what their full
number was is not said, but we know that they were "by
hundreds prompt for blows and blood." A formidable force—

> "Each trained to arms since life began,
> Owning no tie but to his clan,
> No oath, but by his chieftain's hand,
> No law, but Roderick Dhu's command."

We now return to the above-named chieftain, and, at the
close of the third canto of the poem, we are pleased to see a
glimpse of the brighter side of his character, as he nears the
close of his stormy career. His love for Ellen Douglas is, as I
have before said, "deep, pure, and sincere." He has rushed
into this mad warfare to drown the thoughts of his love, but
Ellen is ever in his mind and he is constantly anxious for her
safety.

It will be remembered that Douglas, believing that this
impending warfare between Clan Alpine and the royal troops
is altogether on account of the chief's extending to him his
protection, has determined to withdraw with his daughter to
another place of refuge, and has, in accordance with this resolve,
moved to the Goblin Cave, in the pass of Bealach-nam Bo ("the
pass of cattle"), on the slope of Ben Venue. It seems to have
been as secure a spot as could be chosen, as it is guarded by the
strongest of all guards, Superstition—

> "Grey Superstition's whisper dread
> Debarred the spot to vulgar tread;
> For there, she said, did fays resort,
> And satyrs hold their sylvan court,
> By moonlight tread their mystic maze,
> And blast the rash beholder's gaze."

Roderick's mind is, as we have seen, full of Ellen; he
has already sent scouts towards the south (beyond the above-
mentioned pass) to assure himself that there was no danger of
an attack from that direction; and now he cannot refrain
from, if not seeing her, at least approaching her once more.
He is passing from the island with a few retainers to join the

main clan at the appointed gathering place, but, sending his men on, he turns off, with but a single page, towards the present refuge of Douglas—

> "Eve finds the Chief, like restless ghost,
> Still hovering near his treasure lost;
> For though his haughty heart deny
> A parting meeting to his eye,
> Still fondly strains his anxious ear
> The accents of her voice to hear."

As he loiters here, he suddenly hears the sound of the harp of Allan-bane, accompanied by the voice he knows so well: Ellen is singing a hymn to the Virgin Mary. Beautiful as are all the short poems of Scott—enclosed, as it were, in the main poem—in these, and especially in the poem we are dealing with, he, as I think, excels.[16] The hymn alludes to the present condition of Ellen and her father—

> "Ave Maria! Maiden mild!
> Listen to a maiden's prayer;
> .   .   .   .   .   .
> Maiden! hear a maiden's prayer;
> Mother! hear a suppliant child."

These lines, with a little different wording, run through the whole hymn. The position of Ellen and her father also permeates the lines—

> "The flinty couch we now must share
> Shall seem with down of eider piled,
> If thy protection hover there.
> The murky cavern's heavy air
> Shall breathe of balm if thou hast smiled.
> Then, Maiden! hear a maiden's prayer;
> Mother, list a suppliant child!"

The chief remains listening until the notes cease, then,

---

(16) In this third canto of the poem there are three of these little attached pieces, different entirely in character, but equally, in their own way, beautiful, viz. :—(1) The dirge or coronach of Duncan, chief of Duncraggan; (2) the ode of Norman of Armandave to his bride; and (3) the hymn of Ellen Douglas to the Virgin Mary.

reminded by his page that time is passing, he turns reluctantly away, sadly uttering these words, which are destined to be only too true—

> "'It is the last time—'tis the last,'—
> He muttered thrice,—'the last time e'er
> That angel voice shall Roderick hear!'"

He hurries away, and proceeds to the muster place of his clan at Lanrick, where they are all by this time assembled. The shout of welcome with which they receive the arrival of their chieftain closes the canto.

The fourth canto opens with the final arrangements of Roderick Dhu for the defence of his mountain stronghold; thence the narrative turns to our hero of the first canto, Fitz-James, who has for some time disappeared from the scene of action. We open with a meeting between two of our former acquaintances, the henchman, Malise, and young Norman of Armandave, two of the emissaries of the Fiery Cross; Angus, the third messenger, is not again mentioned, but we hear of his family and belongings Malise is returning from his scouting expedition, and encounters Norman, who is on sentry duty. Malise desires to see the chief at once; Norman conducts him thither, and on the way the henchman reports the presence of the Saxon troops at Doune, of which we have already spoken; while Norman, on his side, mentions the forethought of the chief in providing for the safety of the women and children of the clan, who have been removed to the island on Loch Katrine. Also, on Malise inquiring why the chief slept apart from his followers (for they are proceeding some distance up the glen), Norman reports that he (Roderick) is awaiting the result of an augury, termed the "Taghairm," which Brian, the weird priest before mentioned, has been engaged in invoking.

This rite is conducted as follows : the priest passes the night in the vicinity of a neighbouring waterfall in Glen Finlas, wrapped in the hide of a newly slain bull, which, in this instance, is a well-known, formidable beast, "Duncraggan's milk-white bull"—

> "His hide was snow, his horns were dark,
> His red eye glowed with fiery spark."

This animal, which evidently has the blood of the wild breed in his veins, is well known to Malise, who remembers the trouble they had with him when bringing him back from a raid. He had evidently been awarded as a portion of the spoil to the chief of Duncraggan, to whom Malise appears to have been related.[17] The hermit, therefore, wrapped in this animal's hide, has lain by the above-named cataract all night, and, all of a sudden, the two companions catch sight of him returning from his mission. Norman at once remarks—

> "Seems he not, Malise, like a ghost,
> That hovers o'er a slaughtered host?
> Or raven, on the blasted oak,
> That, watching while the deer is broke,
> His morsel claims with sullen croak?"

The priest has reached the chief before the two clansmen arrive, and reports the result of his nightly quest. Even to his hardened, fanatical spirit the ordeal has been terrible—

> "The shapes that sought my fearful couch,
> A human tongue may ne'er avouch;
> No mortal man,—save he, who, bred
> Between the living and the dead,
> Is gifted beyond nature's law,
> Had e'er survived to say he saw."

At length the priest receives his answer—

> "Not spoke in word, nor blazed in scroll,
> But borne and branded on my soul";

and this is the reported augury—

> "Which spills the foremost foeman's life,
> That party conquers in the strife."

Roderick, relying on his own prowess and that of his clansmen, looks upon this reply as favourable; he also mentions the fact of a supposed spy who has ventured into the stronghold of the clan, whom he decides to capture and slay, thus making

(17) The Lady of Duncraggan addresses Malise as "kinsman." See Canto III.

him the victim of the augury. He little guesses the identity of this spy and his real intentions; what was the result of this determination of the chief, we shall shortly learn; it is the prominent feature of the next phase of the poem, into which we shall shortly enter.

Malise and his companion now approach, and from the former Roderick at once demands the news. These are, the presence of the troops at Doune, under the Earls of Mar and Moray, of which we have heard, and that an attack might be expected from them the following day. There is no word, on the other hand, of any assistance from the neighbouring clans from Loch Earn, in which case Roderick would have stood battle on the side of Ben Ledi; as it is, he decides to make a stand in the Trossachs glen. Here, therefore, his troops are directed to move, a strong detachment, however, being still left on the side of Ben Ledi, as we shall hereafter see. A presentiment of evil comes over the mind of the chief, but he shakes it off—

> "But why?
> Is it the breeze affects mine eye?
> Or dost thou come, ill-omened tear!
> A messenger of doubt or fear?
> No! sooner may the Saxon lance
> Unfix Benledi from his stance,
> Than doubt or terror can pierce through
> The unyielding heart of Roderick Dhu."

The chief, having thus issued his orders, returns again to his private bivouac, in which, for the present, we leave him.

We now return to the Goblin Cave, and find Ellen, on the following morning, in a state of great distress concerning her father, who is now absent; on his parting, he had not mentioned the object of his departure, but she instinctively knows it, and the old minstrel vainly strives to quell her uneasiness. Deeming, as we have before shown, that he is the cause of this impending war, and also on account of a dream which old Allan-bane has underwent, revealing Malcolm Græme a prisoner in fetters, doubtless, on his account, Douglas has proceeded to Stirling to place himself in the hands of the king, and thus put an end to the conflict and save his friend. As Ellen says—

> "He goes to do what I had done,
> Had Douglas' daughter been his son !' "

He has left instructions to his daughter that, should he not return that evening, she should proceed to Cambuskenneth, near Stirling, and "make herself known"; though what this means, what he wishes her to do, is somewhat vague. What she actually did do, we shall see.

In the meantime, the old minstrel endeavours to console her, and offers to make her forget her grief in listening to his minstrelsy. She consents, but with little hope—

> "Well, be it as thou wilt; I hear,
> But cannot stop the bursting tear."

The lay which Allan-bane recites is one of the loveliest of Scott's productions. I have already drawn attention to the numerous small poems, inserted, as it were, so beautifully in the main poem of "The Lady of the Lake"; this one, "Alice Brand," as I think, exceeds them all in beauty; it is one of those, out of many portions of the poem, which I can repeat by heart from end to end.

It is a fairy tale; the subject is the adventure of two lovers, both, it would seem, of noble birth. For some reason or other, their union is disapproved of by the lady's family, and they proceed to elope. On the way, they are overtaken by the lady's brother; a combat at once takes place between him and her lover, in which the former is, as is supposed, slain. The lovers, "Lord Richard" and "Alice Brand," find themselves, at night, in a gloomy forest, haunted by fairies; and it is here that we are first introduced to them (the lovers), at the opening of the poem. Their sentiments towards each other are such as those of true lovers should be. Richard at first expresses his regret that he has brought her into this condition—

> "O Alice Brand, my native land
>   Is lost for love of you;
> And we must hold by wood and wold,
>   As outlaws wont to do.

> "And for vest of pall, thy fingers small,
>   That wont on harp to stray,
> A cloak must shear from the slaughtered deer,
>   To keep the cold away."

The lady replies nobly and loyally—

> "If pall and vair no more I wear,
>   Nor thou the crimson sheen;
> As warm, we'll say, is the russet grey,
>   As gay the forest green.

> "And, Richard, if our lot be hard,
>   And lost thy native land,
> Still Alice has her own Richard,
>   And he his Alice Brand." (18)

The lovers prepare to bivouac for the night, but they are exposed to a danger on which they have not reckoned. The wood, as I said, is haunted by fairies; and the "moody Elfin King" is highly incensed at these presumptuous mortals intruding on his territory, cutting down his trees, destroying the deer, "beloved by our Elfin Queen," and wearing "the fairies' fatal green." (19) He therefore despatches a hideous dwarf, who, having been "christened man"—*i.e.*, originally mortal, and stolen away by the fairies—will not heed the sign of the Cross, which no ordinary fairy could endure (20)—

> "For Cross or sign thou wilt not fly,
>   For muttered word or ban."

He enjoins his envoy to launch a terrible curse against the adventurous mortal—

(18) Some readers of the poem may consider that, with all her loyalty to her lover, Alice is somewhat indifferent to the fate of her brother; but it seems to have been a mischance. The combat was evidently fought in the dark, and Richard was unaware of the identity of his opponent until too late.

(19) As the note to the poem says, depriving the fairies of their rights of "vert" and "venison," like mortal proprietors of forests.

(20) Here, it is seen, the fairies are introduced as entirely evil beings; this, as we know, is not always the case. In the old fairy tales, we have good and evil introduced among fairies, as among men

> "Lay on him the curse of the withered heart,
>   The curse of the sleepless eye;
> Till he wish and pray that his life would part,
>   Nor yet find leave to die."

We shall see here, however, that the Elfin King has under-rated the power of the holy sign over his envoy; had Richard's hands been free from blood, the sign of the Cross would have overpowered the dwarf, as we shall see it did when made by Alice Brand.

The hideous dwarf, Urgan, appears, therefore, suddenly at the camp fire of the lovers, and, on Lord Richard crossing himself—

> "'I fear not sign,' quoth the grisly elf,
>   'That is made with bloody hands.'"

Alice, a thoroughly courageous woman, now intervenes, declaring that the blood on Richard's hands was but the blood of deer; this is indignantly denied by the dwarf, who asserts that it is the blood of her brother. Nothing daunted, however, she herself makes the holy sign—

> "And if there's blood on Richard's hand,
>   A spotless hand is mine;
> And I conjure thee, Demon elf,
>   By Him whom Demons fear,
> To show us whence thou art thyself,
>   And what thine errand here?"

The dwarf yields at once; he confesses his humanity, his detestation of fairyland, and his longing for deliverance, for which latter he reveals the means—

> "But wist I of a woman bold,
>   Who thrice my brow durst sign,
> I might regain my mortal mold,
>   As fair a form as thine."

The courageous Alice hesitates not a moment to undergo the ordeal, and the climax arrives—

> "She crossed him once—she crossed him twice—
>   That lady was so brave;
> The fouler grew his goblin hue,
>   And darker grew the cave."

Enough to check her, but she is not daunted—

> "She crossed him thrice, that lady bold:
> He rose beneath her hand
> The fairest knight on Scottish mold,
> Her brother, Ethert Brand!"

Ethert, after the combat, lying "'twixt life and death," is carried away by the fairies. As he owns it to be a "sinful fray," it is evident that he believes himself to have been in the wrong, and that he has undergone this ordeal on that account; all his objections, therefore, to the marriage of his sister to Lord Richard are at an end, and all ends happily, in the well-chosen words of the poet—

> "Merry it is in the good green wood,
> Where the mavis and merle are singing;
> But merrier were they in Dunfermline grey,
> When all the bells were ringing."

And now, in returning to our tale, we are again confronted with the hero of the first canto of the poem, of whom we have for some time lost sight, Fitz-James, as we shall still call him. Ellen suddenly sees her former guest in the island approaching; at this unexpected sight, she springs up in terror and amazement, and thus addresses him—

> "O stranger! in such hour of fear,
> What evil hap has brought thee here?"

Fitz-James at once avows his feelings towards her, and declares that his presence here is for the purpose of proposing an elopement—

> "I come to bear thee from a wild,
> Where ne'er before such blossom smiled,
> By this soft hand to lead thee far
> From frantic scenes of feud and war;
> Near Bochastle my horses wait;
> They bear us soon to Stirling gate.
> I'll place thee in a lovely bower,
> I'll guard thee like a tender flower."

We cannot help feeling some doubt here as to the king's

honourable intentions towards the maiden, for monarchs cannot
wed with their subjects. Ellen, however, unaware of the identity
of the stranger, receives the proposal as an honourable one, but
at once stifles all hopes. His return, she thinks, must be partly
through her own fault; she says—

> "Too much, before, my selfish ear
> Was idly soothed my praise to hear."

She says that her father, being an exiled, outlawed man, it
would be infamy for her to wed; but this confession not appearing sufficient, she avows the whole truth, viz., that she loves
another, saying—

> "Thou hast the secret of my heart,
> Forgive, be generous, and depart."

Fitz-James feels that there is no hope for him here; he
yields, but still offers her his protection. Ellen is now in a state
of great anxiety as to his safety; the same guide who had two
days before directed his way homewards, had now reconducted
him hither, and she entertains great doubts, not without reason,
as to the intentions of this man; she therefore dispatches Allan
to him with this message—

> "O haste thee, Allan, to the kerne;
> Yonder his tartans I discern;
> Learn thou his purpose, and conjure
> That he will guide the stranger sure!—
> What prompted thee, unhappy man?
> The meanest serf in Roderick's clan
> Had not been bribed by love or fear,
> Unknown to him, to guide thee here."

Her apprehensions are fully justified, for Fitz-James is the
supposed spy, of whom we have already heard, who is to be delivered into the hands of the clan and slain, to fulfil the augury
lately mentioned. Why Fitz-James has been suffered to proceed
thus far, through the midst of the enemy's stronghold, is somewhat inexplicable, and on this I will comment later.

Fitz-James, in the tumult of his feelings, little heeds Ellen's
warning, but, before parting, he presents her with the royal

signet ring, which he alleges to have received from King James, having on one occasion had the good fortune to preserve that monarch's life. This ring, he says, will ensure her admittance to the presence of the king—

> "Seek thou the King without delay;
> This signet shall secure thy way;
> And claim thy suit, whate'er it be,
> As ransom of his pledge to me."

On this, he hastily departs and rejoins his treacherous guide, Murdoch, who conducts him through the gorge of the Trossachs. No sign of anyone has as yet been seen, but we shall soon see how well the Highland clansmen could conceal themselves. Suddenly, in the midst of the glen, the guide utters a loud whoop; this at once arouses the suspicions of Fitz-James, who demands, "Murdoch! was that a signal cry?" The treacherous guide makes a stammering reply—

> "I shout to scare
> Yon raven from his dainty fare."

This "dainty fare" was none other than the knight's "gallant grey," on seeing which, he utters a word of regret. They proceed on their way, but Fitz-James's suspicions are now thoroughly roused—

> "Jealous and sullen on they fared,
> Each silent, each upon his guard."

We now enter upon a touching little episode of the poem. As the pair proceed, they encounter a strange maiden, evidently out of her mind—

> "When lo! a wasted female form,
> Blighted by wrath of sun and storm,
> In tattered weeds and wild array,
> Stood on a cliff beside the way."

She expresses great terror at the sight of the clansman's Highland plaid, but corresponding pleasure on seeing the stranger's Lowland garb; she breaks into a touching little song, one of the numerous beautiful little poems to which I have before drawn attention. The subject is her own unhappy fate, which Murdoch relates, on inquiry by Fitz-James. It was doubtless a too frequent story. Blanche of Devan had been—

> "Ta'en on the morn she was a bride,
> When Roderick forayed Devan-side.
> The gay bridgeroom resistance made,
> But felt our chief's unconquered blade."

This terrible incident has distorted her brain, but she still possesses some gleams of reason, more, indeed, than probably the clansmen believe. She instantly comprehends the relation between the stranger and his companion, and at once proceeds to warn the former, with another lovely little ballad, preceded by a low warning, which shows that she has evidently some of her wits about her—

> "Thou art wise, and guessest well."

She likens Fitz-James to a "stag of ten," advancing into an ambush laid by the hunters, and herself "a wounded doe, bleeding deathfully," who warns the stag of his danger, adding a final warning—

> "He had an eye, and he could heed,
> Ever sing warily, warily;
> He had a foot, and he could speed—
> Hunters watch so narrowly."

This song confirms the suspicions of Fitz-James, who turns fiercely on Murdoch—

> "Not like stag who spies the snare,
> But lion of the hunt aware."

The clansman, discovered, springs back, draws his bow, and sends an arrow at the knight; it misses its mark, however, and enters the breast of Blanche. Murdoch now flies, hotly pursued by his furious opponent. He vainly attempts to reach the ambush of his fellow-clansmen in front; before doing so, he is overtaken and slain.

Fitz-James now returns to the unfortunate maiden, who is mortally wounded; with her ebbing life, her reason brightens—

> "For, as these ebbing veins decay,
> My frenzied visions fade away."

She now, with her latest breath, urges the knight to inflict vengeance on the author of her wrongs, Roderick Dhu—

> "When thou shalt see a darksome man,
> Who boasts him Chief of Alpine's clan,
> With tartans broad and shadowy plume,
> And hand of blood, and brow of gloom,
> Be thy heart bold, thy weapon strong,
> And wreak poor Blanche of Devan's wrong."

These are her last words; sad, indeed, that her last words, her last thoughts, should have been of vengeance and not of better things; this I remember to have been remarked by one whose memory I revere. Such feelings, however, were probably entirely in accordance with those wild times.

They are indeed eagerly responded to by Fitz-James, who exclaims—

> "God, in my need, be my relief,
> As I wreak this on yonder Chief!"

The words, "Vengeance is mine; I will repay," were little heeded in those days.

He then takes a lock of Blanche's hair, to which he attaches one of her late unfortunate bridegroom, which she had possessed; he dips both in her blood, and takes a solemn oath—

> "By Him, whose word is truth! I swear
> No other favour will I wear,
> Till this sad token I embrue
> In the best blood of Roderick Dhu!"

Fitz-James is now in a dire strait; this adventure, fond as he is of them, is likely to prove his last, as he himself perceives. He wanders about during the whole day, being forced to avoid the beaten tracks, which, he feels sure, are guarded; he is compelled constantly to retrace his steps, on account of different obstacles; his foes are swarming round him, and at length, starving and weary, he hides himself in a thicket, resolving to wait there till nightfall—

> "I'll couch me here till evening grey,
> Then darkling try my dangerous way."

At dusk, he proceeds on his weary way again, but this time not for long; all at once he comes upon a lonely watch-fire, no less than that of Roderick himself, who, as we remember, was bivouacking alone in Glen Finlas. On the approach of the intruder, the chief springs to his feet, and the following dialogue takes place—

> "And up he sprung, with sword in hand—
> 'Thy name and purpose! Saxon, stand!'
> 'A stranger.'—'What dost thou require?'
> 'Rest and a guide, and food, and fire.
> My life's beset, my path is lost,
> The gale has chilled my limbs with frost.'
> 'Art thou a friend to Roderick?'—'No.'—
> 'Thou darest not call thyself a foe?'
> 'I dare! to him and all the band
> He brings to aid his murderous hand.'
> 'Bold words!—but, though the beast of game
> The privilege of chase may claim,
> Though space and law the stag we lend,
> Ere hound we slip, or bow we bend,
> Who ever recked, where, how, or when,
> The prowling fox was trapped or slain?
> Thus treacherous scouts—yet sure they lie,
> Who say thou camest a secret spy!'
> 'They do, by Heaven!—Come, Roderick Dhu,
> And of his clan the boldest two,
> And let me but till morning rest,
> I write the falsehood on their crest.'
> 'If by the blaze I mark aright,
> Thou bear'st the belt and spur of Knight?'—
> 'Then, by these tokens, mayst thou know
> Each proud oppressor's mortal foe.'
> 'Enough, enough; sit down and share
> A soldier's couch, a soldier's fare.'"

Roderick has evidently discovered that the stranger is no ordinary spy; he possesses the honour of knighthood, and is evidently "a foeman worthy of his steel," and therefore worthy to be dealt with by the chief himself and not by his clansmen. Here, therefore, the issue of the augury may well be decided.

But not at this moment; the stranger is hungry and weary—in fact, utterly worn out; he has thrown himself on the chief's hospitality, and this, from the sense of honour of those days, cannot be refused—

> "To assail a weary man were shame,
> A stranger is a holy name;
> Guidance, and rest, and food and fire,
> In vain he never must require."

Roderick, therefore, invites the stranger to share his "cheer," which is gladly accepted; but this is not all. It would be equally dishonourable to fight him here, even when rested, for, should the chief fall, the life of the stranger would not be worth an hour's purchase; he must convey him to a place of safety before he can engage with him in personal conflict. He, therefore, makes a proposition to his guest, but not until the latter has received food and has rested awhile. The stranger has declared himself to be a mortal foe to Roderick and his clan; he has spoken words against the honour of the chief, and these must be avenged; and also the fulfilment of the augury will be decided between honourable foes. This, then, the chief proposes. On the following morning, he will himself guide his guest through the dangerous country occupied by the Highlanders, until he has conducted him in safety past the utmost outposts of Clan Alpine—

> "As far as Coilantogle ford;
> From thence thy warrant is thy sword."

On reaching that spot, the issue must be decided by mortal combat.

This is an honourable proposition, showing us the better side of Roderick's character, and it is accepted as such without hesitation by Fitz-James. These two honourable foemen, therefore, now lie down to rest beside each other for the night.

Having thus conducted our hero to temporary safety, we would draw the attention of our readers to several facts which appear to be somewhat inexplicable. Roderick believes Fitz-James to have been a secret spy until he actually meets him, as we have seen, and, indeed, tells him that he has incurred his late peril in coming in this secret fashion—

> "Hadst thou sent warning fair and true,—
> I seek my hound, or falcon strayed,
> I seek, good faith, a Highland maid,—
> Free hadst thou been to come and go;
> But secret path marks secret foe."

Now, Fitz-James did not come secretly. He had engaged one of the chief's own clansmen to guide him, on a purpose which the latter well knew; the stranger did indeed "seek a Highland maid." Now, we ask, why did not the guide, Murdoch, report this fact to Roderick, instead of letting the chief remain in ignorance of the real object of the stranger? This, indeed, may be explained by the suggestion that Murdoch might have thought that he would be accused of an act of treachery towards his chief in thus assisting a stranger to abduct the woman whom he (the chief) loved. The feelings of Roderick towards Ellen were well known in the clan. We call to mind their song—

> "O! that the rosebud that graces yon islands,
> Were wreathed in a garland around him to twine."

Again, why was the capture of Fitz-James delayed? Why was he not seized when making his way through the Trossachs glen, where, as we know, the main body of the clan was assembled,[21] before his interview with Ellen? This proceeding would have obviated all suspicion of treachery on the part of Murdoch. And, lastly, why was the capture delayed for so long afterwards? This delay gave opportunity for Fitz-James to receive warning three times over—

> "Fitz-James's heart was passion-tossed,
> When Ellen's doubts and fears were lost;
> But Murdoch's shout suspicion wrought,
> And Blanche's song conviction brought."

These points are to me, as I have said, somewhat inexplicable, and this portion of the poem (*i.e.*, the narrative, not the verse) seems to have been somewhat carelessly written by the author.

At the first dawn of morning, the two warriors awake, and

shortly proceed on their way, the chieftain leading, in accordance with his promise. After some time, they arrive at a deep glen on the slope of the mountain Ben Ledi, down which they have to pursue their way to reach their destination. It is a wild, dreary spot—

> "Ever the hollow path twined on,
> Beneath steep bank and threatening stone;
> A hundred men might hold the post
> With hardihood against a host.
> The rugged mountain's scanty cloak
> Was dwarfish shrubs of birch and oak,
> With shingles bare, and cliffs between,
> And patches bright of bracken green,
> And heather black, that waved so high
> It held the copse in rivalry."

Through this weird glen the path is so rough that the chief slackens his pace, and, evidently somewhat chafed at his guest's bold defiance last night of himself and his clan, and his careless independence in thus boldly penetrating into their stronghold, suddenly asks the knight how it was that he had entered into these wilds without a pass from Roderick Dhu. The answer of the Saxon is as independent as ever—

> "Brave Gael, my pass, in danger tried,
> Hangs in my belt, and by my side."

He, however, somewhat turns off the chief's question, not divulging the real object of his adventure; the latter does not press him, but turns the subject, in his turn, asking him if he (Fitz-James) knew ought of the force at Doune arrayed against Clan Alpine. The knight replies that this force, as far as he knows, has been posted at Doune simply to guard King James's sports at Stirling, but that this sudden assembly of the clansmen might lead them to aggressive measures, of which previously they had had no intention. The chief, again not pressing his guest on this point, and being evidently in a somewhat aggressive mood, asks him how it is that he declares himself to be a mortal enemy to Roderick and his clan.

Fitz-James replies that, until the day before, he had known nothing of the chieftain—

> "Save as an outlawed desperate man,
> The chief of a rebellious clan,
> Who, in the Regent's Court and sight,
> With ruffian dagger stabbed a knight;
> Yet this alone might from his part
> Sever each true and loyal heart."

This arraignment naturally arouses the anger of Roderick, who sternly replies—

> "And heard'st thou why he drew his blade?
> Heard'st thou that shameful word and blow
> Brought Roderick's vengeance on his foe?
> What recked the Chieftain, if he stood
> On Highland heath or Holy-Rood?
> He rights such wrong where it is given,
> If it were in the court of Heaven."

Fitz-James, on his part, turns this off, and speaks of the "robber life" of the chieftain—

> "Winning mean prey by causeless strife,
> Wrenching from ruined Lowland swain
> His herds and harvest reared in vain."

The answer of the chief to this accusation shows the entirely different point of view taken on this subject by the Highlander and Lowlander. The former looks on every raid as a mere retribution; the land, formerly his, had been rent from him by the latter, and it was but his right—

> "To spoil the spoiler as we may,
> And from the robber rend the prey."

Into this matter I have fully entered at the commencement of this treatise, so I will not dwell on it further. The chief, having used the words which open the treatise,[22] concludes thus—

> "Seek other cause 'gainst Roderick Dhu."

Fitz-James, on this, speaks of his being treacherously waylaid, and his life attempted: the chief retorts that this was

[22] See page 147.

simply due to the stranger's rashness in entering the Highland country without giving due notice of his purpose, adding, however, that, but for the augury we know of, Fitz-James's life would not have been taken without inquiry.

Fitz-James, closing the argument, simply states that he has pledged himself to encounter this robber chieftain, and longs for the hour when he can do so—

> "Twice have I sought Clan-Alpine's glen
> In peace; but, when I come agen,
> I come with banner, brand, and bow,
> As leader seeks his mortal foe.
> For love-lorn swain, in lady's bower,
> Ne'er panted for the appointed hour
> As I, until before me stand
> This rebel Chieftain and his band."

To this boast Fitz-James receives a most startling reply. The chief exclaims, "Have then thy wish!" and utters a shrill whistle, on which a band of Highland clansmen, the detachment of which we made mention before,[23] suddenly springs up on all sides—

> "On right, on left, above, below,
> Sprung up at once the lurking foe;
> From shingles grey their lances start,
> The bracken-bush sends forth the dart,
> The rushes and the willow-wand
> Are bristling into axe and brand,
> And every tuft of broom gives life
> To plaided warrior armed for strife."

This formidable band, 500 strong, has thus sprung without warning into existence, and is now awaiting in silence the orders of its chieftain, who now turns to Fitz-James—

> "How say'st thou now?
> These are Clan-Alpine's warriors true;
> And, Saxon—I am Roderick Dhu!"

No wonder Fitz-James is terribly startled; he realises that he is in the deadliest peril; he has lately defied and insulted

(23) See page 183.

this formidable robber chieftain, who now has him at his mercy.
He is a thoroughly brave man, however, and is determined to
sell his life dearly—

> "His back against a rock he bore,
> And firmly placed his foot before:—
> 'Come one, come all! this rock shall fly
> From its firm base as soon as I.'"

He is in no danger, however; the sense of chivalry on the part
of the chieftain protects him, the latter expressing—

> "The stern joy which warriors feel
> In foemen worthy of their steel."

With a wave of the hand, the chief dismisses his clansmen,
who disappear as rapidly as they have come; and he assures the
stranger of the latter's safety until they have reached Coilantogle
ford, according to promise—

> "Nor would I call a clansman's brand
> For aid against one valiant hand,
> Though on our strife lay every vale
> Rent by the Saxon from the Gael.
> So move we on;—I only meant
> To show the reed on which you leant,
> Deeming this path you might pursue
> Without a pass from Roderick Dhu."

In spite of the chief's assurance, however, it is not to be
wondered at that Fitz-James feels some apprehension until they
are clear of this dangerous pass and have entered the open
country, where there is no possibility of ambush. They now
shortly reach their destination, Coilantogle ford, the spot where
the river Teith issues from Loch Vennachar—lovely in those
days doubtless, but now disfigured by a stone dam, built across
the outlet of the stream from the loch.

Here, at length, the chief halts, flings aside his shield and
plaid, and addresses his companion—

> "Bold Saxon! to his promise just,
> Vich-Alpine has discharged his trust.
> This murderous chief, this ruthless man,
> This head of a rebellious clan,

Hath led thee safe, through watch and ward,
Far past Clan-Alpine's outmost guard.
Now, man to man, and steel to steel,
A chieftain's vengeance thou shalt feel.
See, here, all vantageless I stand,
Armed, like thyself, with single brand:
For this is Coilantogle ford,
And thou must keep thee with thy sword."

The anger of Fitz-James against Roderick for the wrongs of Blanche has been considerably allayed by that chief's good faith and courtesy, and he is now quite willing to enter into terms, but Roderick is obdurate; he again mentions the augury, declaring that—

"The Saxon cause rests on thy steel."

On hearing the result of the augury, Fitz-James declares that it has been fulfilled by the death of Red Murdoch, and offers to conduct Roderick to the presence of the king at Stirling, promising that, if they could not come to terms, the chief should be restored to his fastness, with every advantage which he now held. This, however, only increases the anger of Roderick—

"Soars thy presumption, then, so high,
Because a wretched kerne ye slew,
Homage to name to Roderick Dhu?"

On his opponent still hesitating, he proceeds to taunt him with cowardice, saying—

"By Heaven, I change
My thought, and hold thy valour light,
As that of some vain carpet-knight,
Who ill deserved my courteous care,
And whose best boast is but to wear
A braid of his fair lady's hair."

This taunt recalls to Fitz-James his pledge to Blanche, and again arouses his anger against the chief—

"I thank thee, Roderick, for the word!
It nerves my heart, it steels my sword;
For I have sworn this braid to stain
In the best blood that warms thy vein."

Before commencing the fight, however, Fitz-James hastens to show Roderick that he is not the only one who can show courtesy—

> "Yet think not that by thee alone,
> Proud Chief! can courtesy be shown;
> Though not from copse, or heath, or cairn,
> Start at my whistle clansmen stern,
> Of this small horn one feeble blast
> Would fearful odds against thee cast."

All hope of truce, therefore, being at an end, the two warriors, thoroughly roused, proceed to enter into deadly conflict. Roderick Dhu, in throwing aside his shield, had declared himself to be "all vantageless," but he had done more than this, he had placed himself at an actual disadvantage, thereby, indeed, depriving himself of all means of defence, and placing himself almost at the mercy of his foe. The defensive weapon of the Highlander was the shield, or target, with which he warded off the blows of his assailant; the sword was entirely an offensive weapon, used only to strike, not to defend; he had no knowledge of what is now termed "fence." So, with Roderick, when he threw away his shield he was practically defenceless. Fitz-James, on the other hand, was a practised fencer—

> "He practised every pass and ward,
> To thrust, to strike, to feint, to guard."

The issue, therefore, of the combat is soon decided; the Highland chieftain attacks his foe with a shower of blows, "like wintry rain"; these are easily warded off by his skilled antagonist, who, on his side, brings in his blade with effect. The chieftain's blood is now flowing fast, and his strength is failing him. At length, by a skilful turn of his blade, Fitz-James wrenches the sword from his enemy's hand—

> "And backwards borne upon the lea,
> Brought the proud Chieftain to his knee."

The combat, however, is not yet ended, and Fitz-James has to find that he has a most desperate foe to deal with. The wounded chieftain, on being summoned to yield, savagely refuses, and, like a wounded wild cat, springs furiously at the throat of his antagonist.

A desperate struggle ensues; the chief bears his enemy to the ground; and well was it for Fitz-James that his assailant was desperately wounded, for—

> "The Chieftain's gripe his throat compressed,
> His knee was planted on his breast."

Roderick's dagger is now drawn, but, at the very moment of striking, his strength fails him—

> "Down came the blow! but in the heath
> The erring blade found bloodless sheath."

The chief faints, and Fitz-James manages to extricate himself from his now weakening grasp; then (as well he might)—

> "He faltered thanks to Heaven for life,
> Redeemed, unhoped, from desperate strife."

He had, indeed, had a narrow escape; and he must have felt that, among his numerous adventures, of which he was so fond, this was the most desperate. He proceeds to fulfil his vow, by dipping the braid of Blanche's hair in the blood of her antagonist, at the same time acknowledging the good faith and valour of the latter, an example at once of both the ruthlessness and cruelty and of the good faith, chivalry, and courage of this extraordinary man—

> "In Roderick's gore he dipped the braid,—
> 'Poor Blanche! thy wrongs are dearly paid;
> Yet with thy foe must die, or live,
> The praise that Faith and Valour give.'"

He now winds his horn, and the call is speedily responded to. Four mounted squires appear, two of them leading horses, one of which had been intended for the use of Ellen, the other being the knight's own charger. Fitz-James speedily gives orders to two of them to place the wounded chief on the steed intended for Ellen, and bring him to Stirling Castle, while he himself, directing the two other squires to follow him, mounts his own steed and gallops off towards Stirling.

Having now arrived at an important point in our narrative, we do not propose to continue it in the exact order of the poem, but to proceed with the fortunes of Clan-Alpine and their chieftain, and, when this part is completed, to conclude with those of our heroine, the "Lady of the Lake," and her father, Douglas, together with their relations with the king.

We proceed, then, first, to the conflict between the Clan Alpine and the royal troops, which latter, as we have seen, were stationed at Doune to guard the royal sports at Stirling. On hearing of the muster of the clan, and believing that they were assembled in the cause of the outlawed Douglas, the two earls, Mar and Moray, determine to attack them. Later, on the same morning on which the combat just described took place, this force is set in motion, and proceeds towards the Highland stronghold.

The battle which we are about to describe is told by the old minstrel, Allan-bane, to Roderick Dhu, on the latter's death-bed. This interview we will enter into later.

The Earls of Mar and Moray are evidently well skilled in mountain warfare; their force, preceded by a cloud of light-armed skirmishers, advances in perfect array, along the banks of Loch Achray, towards the Trossachs glen, which, as we have seen, Roderick has commanded his clansmen to defend in force. They are all assembled there, according to his order; but where was the chief ? His absence must have caused great astonishment, perhaps uneasiness, among his clansmen : they were never to see him more.

The approaching conflict is heralded by the signs of a gathering storm; the deep silence preceding it corresponds well with that observed by the Saxon troops on their march—

> "There is no breeze upon the fern,
>   No ripple on the lake,
> Upon her eyrie nods the erne,
>   The deer has sought the brake;
> The small birds will not sing aloud,
>   The springing trout lies still,
> So darkly glooms yon thunder-cloud,
> That swathes, as with a purple shroud,
>   Benledi's distant hill."

Equally impressive is the silent advance of the Saxon host—

> "No cymbal clashed, no clarion rang,
>   Still were the pipe and drum;
> Save heavy tread, and armour's clang,
>   The sullen march was dumb.
>
>   .   .   .   .
>
> The host moves like a deep sea wave,
> Where rise no rocks its pride to brave,
>   High swelling, dark, and slow."

No opposition has as yet been offered to their advance; not a sound breaks the stillness; no sign as yet of the enemy; and the army, unmolested, has passed the lake and formed upon the level ground in front of the Trossachs glen.

The light-armed skirmishers dive into the glen to explore it, and on that, all of a sudden, there is "hell broke loose." A wild yell arises from the depths of the glen; the skirmishers reappear, flying in disorder, driven back by the mad rush of the Highlanders, who now appear in hot pursuit. The poet well describes the scene—

> "Forth from the pass in tumult driven,
> Like chaff before the wind of heaven,
>   The archery appear;
> For life! for life! their flight they ply—
> And shriek, and shout, and battle-cry,
> And plaids and bonnets waving high,
> And broadswords flashing to the sky,
>   Are maddening in their rear."

The rush of the clan appears irresistible, but they have to encounter leaders who well know how to deal with their mode of warfare, formidable as it appears—

> "'Down, down,' cried Mar, 'your lances down!
>   Bear back both friend and foe!'
> Like reeds before the tempest's frown,
> That serried grove of lances brown
>   At once lay levelled low;
> And closely shouldering side to side,
> The bristling ranks the onset bide."

The Highlanders come on with their seemingly irresistible

rush, and dash themselves against the line of levelled lances, which successfully oppose them. While their rush is thus checked, and they are consequently thrown into disorder, the Earl of Moray suddenly wheels his rearward troop of horsemen round and attacks them on their flank. Then appears the inevitable result between regular troops and a wild, undisciplined force, when the first mad rush of the latter is successfully opposed.[24] The clansmen, deprived also of their chief, are driven back—

> "Where, where, was Roderick then!
> One blast upon his bugle horn
> Were worth a thousand men." [25]

The Highlanders are driven back through the pass, pursued by the Saxon troops, and the scene of the combat changes to the shore of Loch Katrine. The storm is now on the point of breaking forth—

> "The sun is set—the clouds are met,
> The lowering scowl of heaven
> An inky hue of livid blue
> To the deep lake has given;
> Strange gusts of wind from mountain glen
> Swept o'er the lake, then sunk agen."

A sort of truce seems now to have taken place between the opposing forces, after their desperate encounter in the Trossachs glen; the Saxons are posted on the shore of the lake, while the Highlanders man the sides of the mountains above.

It will be remembered that Roderick had removed all the women and children of the clan to the isle now termed "Ellen's Isle" (of which we have already made acquaintance in this treatise), for safety; and a thought now occurs to the Earl of Moray that, could the island be captured, it would be a strong advantage to the Saxon side—

---

(24) The battle of Culloden is a strong example of this; also the conflict between Sir Edward Stanley's troops and the Western Highlanders at the battle of Flodden, already related in my treatise, "Marmion."

(25) These lines remind one of the remark made by an Irish soldier in the Peninsular War. A detachment was stationed at a very perilous outpost, when suddenly the Duke of Wellington rode up. On this, the soldier exclaimed, "Bless his crooked nose! I'd rather see that than twenty thousand men!"

"Lightly we'll tame the war-wolf then,
Lords of his mate, and brood, and den."

Moray offers a reward to any man who will swim across to the island and loosen a boat from thence to convey troops across. A soldier at once springs forward, plunges into the lake, and swims for the island. Great excitement breaks forth on both sides; just as the outcry arises, the threatening storm breaks forth, and well it is for the swimmer that the waves run high and divert the aim of the enemy, who shower their arrows down upon him. He reaches the island in safety, and lays his hand upon a boat, but it is his last action. Above him suddenly appears "Duncraggan's widowed dame," the same who, as we have seen, sent her son on to carry out his duty in spite of the general grief at the funeral of his father. This grim woman awaits the approach of the Saxon, a dagger in her hand, and no sooner has the unfortunate man laid his hand on the boat, when down comes the blow, and his corpse is floating on the lake.

On this, wild cries arise on both sides, and the two forces are again rushing forward to the conflict when an envoy from the king appears, "bloody with spurring"; he stops the battle by declaring that Douglas, on whose account the war was supposed to be taking place, and Roderick himself, were both taken prisoner. Here the narrative stops abruptly; we do not know what terms, if any, are proposed; but I think we may conclude that matters are left *in statu quo*. The clan have also received a severe handling; their loss is probably greater than that of the Saxons; they have lost the strong hand of their chieftain; and they are, therefore, not likely to give trouble for some time to come.

And what of the chief? We left him desperately wounded in the hands of his foes. He is conducted to Stirling Castle, and there imprisoned. He is indeed, by order of the king, treated with the greatest care, but he is none the less a captive; and this position to one accustomed, as he is, to absolute freedom and the pure air of the mountains must have preyed terribly on his mind, and, perhaps, hastened his end. On the day following his captivity, a visitor is admitted to his prison, and he recognises the old minstrel, Allan-bane. How the latter came to be there, we will explain later.

The chief immediately assails his visitor with a torrent of questions, and we note that it is of Ellen that he inquires first, then of his mother, Douglas, and his clan. The old minstrel assures him that both his mother and Ellen are safe and well, that there are hopes for the safety of Douglas, and, lastly, he tells him of the gallant stand made by the clan, of which we have just heard—

> "And for thy clan—on field or fell,
> Has never harp of minstrel told
> Of combat fought so true and bold.
> Thy stately pine is yet unbent,
> Though many a goodly bough is rent."

The chief then desires the minstrel to relate to him in song the fight between his clan and the Saxon force—

> " I'll listen, till my fancy hears
> The clang of swords, the crash of spears !
> These grates, these walls, shall vanish then,
> For the fair field of fighting men,
> And my free spirit burst away,
> As if it soared from battle fray."

Old Allan obeys, and recounts the tale of the fight, which we have already described, but when he has come to the arrival of the envoy he perceives that the end has come; the fierce soul of the Highland chieftain has passed away—

> "At length, no more his deafened ear
> The minstrel melody can hear:
> His face grows sharp—his hands are clenched
> As if some pang his heart-strings wrenched;
> Set are his teeth—his fading eye
> Is sternly fixed on vacancy.
> Thus, motionless, and moanless, drew
> His parting breath, stout Roderick Dhu ! "

The coronach, or wailing, which the minstrel now pours forth over the body of the dead chief is so beautiful that we must repeat it at length—

"And art thou cold, and lowly laid,
   Thy foeman's dread, they people's aid,
   Breadalbane's boast, Clan-Alpine's shade!
For thee shall none a requiem say?
For thee, who loved the minstrel's lay,
For thee, of Bothwell's house the stay,
   The shelter of her exiled line,
   E'en in this prison-house of thine,
I'll wail for Alpine's honoured pine!

"What groans shall yonder valleys fill!
What shrieks of grief shall rend yon hill!
What tears of burning rage shall thrill,
When mourns thy tribe thy battles done,
Thy fall before the race was won,
Thy sword ungirt e'er set of sun!
   There breathes not clansman of thy line,
   But would have given his life for thine.—
O woe for Alpine's honoured pine!

"Sad was thy lot on mortal stage!—
   The captive thrush may brook the cage,
   The prisoned eagle dies for rage.
Brave spirit, do not scorn my strain!
And, when its notes awake again,
Even she, so long beloved in vain,
   Shall with my harp her voice combine,
   And mix her woe and tears with mine,
To wail Clan-Alpine's honoured pine."

Allan-bane speaks well when he says that Ellen will share
in his sorrow for the death of the chieftain; she cannot give
him her love; in fact, she has feared and shrunk from him;
but yet she appreciates his honourable love for her, and is deeply
grateful to him for his kindness and hospitality towards her
father and herself. This is shown in her subsequent interview
with the king; through the royal signet ring which she possesses,
she nobly petitions him for the pardon of the captive chieftain.
The answer of the monarch to her prayer is equally noble—

"Forbear thy suit:—the King of Kings
   Alone can stay life's parting wings,
I know his heart, I know his hand,
Have shared his cheer, and proved his brand:
   My fairest earldom would I give
   To bid Clan-Alpine's Chieftain live!"

And with this we take leave of Roderick Dhu, his faults, and his good qualities; ruthless, unsparing in his terrible raids, yet possessing distinct chivalrous qualities; he will not attack a foeman stealthily, unless, indeed, superstition steps in, as in the case of the augury. He rather, indeed, makes too much parade of his chivalry, which, on two occasions, draws upon him a retort—first, from Græme—

> "Thy churlish courtesy for those
> Reserve, who fear to be thy foes";

and, again, from Fitz-James—

> "Think not that by thee alone,
> Proud Chief! can courtesy be shown."

I have entered fully into the character of the chief at the outset of this treatise, so I need not go further here; the comments of the king, which I have already quoted, speak for themselves; and so, therefore, we now take leave of him.

We have now reached the concluding portion of the poem, which relates to Douglas and his daughter, Ellen, and to their relations with the king, to whom we now return.

Fitz-James—or, to give him now his proper title, King James—after his combat with Roderick Dhu, gallops off, as we have seen, accompanied by two of his squires, towards Stirling. He desires to reach that town in time for the royal sports, which take place at noon; he has not much time to do so, but his horse, Bayard, "lightly clears the lea." In due time, therefore, they reach the foot of the hill on which Stirling Castle is situated, and more slowly make their way up the rocky path.

Stirling, where the rest of the action of the poem takes place, is, next to Edinburgh, the most picturesque town in Scotland. Its situation is very similar to that of the Old Town of Edinburgh, lying on and around the slope of a hill, which is terminated and crowned by the Castle, beyond which the ground falls precipitately to the plain beneath. The view from the Castle and the adjoining height, on which the cemetery is now situated, is unsurpassed; while the Castle and town stand out a conspicuous landmark for miles around. Before the Union of the

Crowns, the Castle was a royal residence, and history speaks of many dark crimes committed within its walls.

While toiling up the steep ascent, James suddenly becomes aware of a man in front, also wending his way towards the town; he is disguised as a peasant, but the king recognises him at once—

> "Afar, ere to the hill he drew,
> That stately form and step I knew;
> Like form in Scotland is not seen,
> Treads not such step on Scottish green.
> 'Tis James of Douglas, by Saint Serle!
> The uncle of the banished Earl."

Glad to be thus forewarned of the presence of his enemy, as he deems him, the king turns off to the right, avoiding the sight of Douglas, and enters the Castle.

It is indeed Douglas, who, as we have seen, has determined to proceed to Stirling and place himself in the hands of the king, so as to put an end to this warfare, which he believes to be taking place on his account. His thoughts are, as we may imagine, not pleasant ones; he is placing his life in peril; and the sight of Stirling Castle, where, among the many foul deeds before alluded to, the murder of one of his ancestors was included, does not tend to comfort him. The sound of the preparations for the sports arouses him, and he determines, before giving himself up, to try his hand at the various competitions—

> "King James shall mark
> If age has tamed these sinews stark,
> Whose force so oft, in happier days,
> His boyish wonder loved to praise."

King James loved all such sports, and presently he appears with his nobles, wending his way through the town to the park where the sports were to be held. He receives a great ovation as he proceeds; his constant presence at these amusements rendered him highly popular with the people, by whom he was termed the "King of the Commons." But if he was thus popular with the common people, it was by no means the same with his nobles—

"But in the train you might discern
Dark lowering brow and visage stern:
There nobles mourned their pride restrained,
And the mean burghers' joys disdained;
And chiefs who, hostage for their clan,
Were each from home a banished man,
These thought upon their own grey tower,
Their waving woods, their feudal power,
And deemed themselves a shameful part
Of pageant, which they cursed in heart."

It may well be understood that the term, "Commons'
King," bestowed on James, would not, in those days, render
him popular with his nobles.

The games commence, and in every competition—archery,
wrestling, and stone-throwing [26]—Douglas carries off the chief
prizes, each of which he receives from the hand of the king.
But there is no interest, no sympathy displayed on the part
of the monarch: forewarned of Douglas's presence, he has made
up his mind how to treat him, and the prizes are presented to
him with the utmost coldness and indifference—

"From the King's hand must Douglas take
A silver dart, the archers' stake;
Fondly he watched, with watery eye,
Some answering glance of sympathy,—
No kind emotion made reply!
Indifferent, as to archer wight,
The Monarch gave the arrow bright."

And, again, in the wrestling competition—

"Prize of the wrestling match, the King
To Douglas gave a golden ring,
While coldly glanced his eye of blue,
As frozen drop of wintry dew."

It is the same thing in the stone-throwing, when Douglas
receives a purse of gold from the king, the contents of which he
tosses contemptuously among the spectators. He is deeply hurt
by the utter want of sympathy on the part of the monarch.

(26) The modern "putting the weight."

This stalwart stranger, who thus carries off all the prizes, soon attracts general attention, and his identity begins to be suspected. The next competition is that of hunting the stag, and testing the capabilities of the deer-hounds. The deer being let loose, two of the king's favourite hounds are sent after him, but Lufra, the hound of Douglas, starts off, outstrips the royal hounds, and pulls down the quarry. The king's huntsman, enraged at the sport being thus interrupted, strikes Lufra with his leash. On this, Douglas, already irritated at his treatment by the king, and infuriated by this last insult, strikes the huntsman down—

> " Needs but a buffet and no more,
> The groom lies senseless in his gore.
> Such blow no other hand could deal,
> Though gauntleted in glove of steel."

This incident brings matters to a climax; and, indeed, Douglas is hardly justified in his act, for his hound does not seem to have been injured. The royal attendants now advance to seize him, but he orders them back, and boldly avows himself to the king, who breaks forth into a fury, and, without inquiry, orders Douglas into confinement—

> " But shall a Monarch's presence brook
> Injurious blow and haughty look ?—
> What ho ! the Captain of our Guard !
> Give the offender fitting ward."

The prowess of Douglas has now brought him into favour with the fickle crowd, who begin to clamour on his behalf, forgetting their late favourite, the "Commons' King," who, seeing this, angrily stops the sports and orders his horsemen to clear the ground. A loud tumult ensues upon this, and the mob press hard upon the escort which is conveying Douglas to the Castle. On this, Douglas asks the commander of the escort to allow him to address a few words to the crowd ; these few words are so well spoken that they allay the fury of the people, which dissolves into tears—

> " The crowd's wild fury sunk again
> In tears, as tempests melt in rain."

Intense sympathy is expressed for Douglas, who is now conveyed in safety to the Castle.

The king, as may be imagined, is bitterly chagrined at this sympathy expressed for his enemy, and vents his anger and disgust on his lately beloved "commons," not without reason—

> "'O Lennox, who would wish to rule
> This changeling crowd, this common fool?
> Hear'st thou,' he said, 'the loud acclaim
> With which they shout the Douglas name?
> With like acclaim, the vulgar throat
> Strained for King James their morning note;
> With like acclaim they hailed the day
> When first I broke the Douglas sway;
> And like acclaim would Douglas greet,
> If he could hurl me from my seat.
> Who o'er the herd would wish to reign,
> Fantastic, fickle, fierce, and vain?
> Vain as the leaf upon the stream,
> And fickle as a changeful dream;
> Fantastic as a woman's mood,
> And fierce as Frenzy's fevered blood.
> Thou many-headed monster thing,
> O who would wish to be thy King!'"

The king's anger, however, is soon abated; he is met by a messenger from the Earl of Mar, reporting that he (the earl) had marched against Roderick Dhu's assembled clansmen, and that news of battle would probably soon be heard. James, on this, sends the messenger at once back to Mar, with orders to cease hostilities, as Roderick had been taken prisoner and Douglas had surrendered himself. The envoy starts, expressing, however, great doubt as to his arrival in time to stop the conflict; and, as we know, it had been going on for some time before his arrival.

It speaks well for the king that he was thus desirous of preventing bloodshed, instead of pressing the rebellious clan to the uttermost; but, in truth, there is no wonder that he is inclined to the merciful side, for he has great cause to be gratified with the existing circumstances and with the part taken in them by himself. Douglas has given himself up and Roderick has been taken prisoner, in the latter case, by the hand of the king himself in fair fight, and with a narrow escape to James of his own life. Roderick is mortally wounded, and the king, by his own personal prowess, has delivered the country from a great scourge. There will not be much danger, he thinks, from the clan now, without the guidance of their redoubtable leader—

> "The tidings of the leaders lost
> Will soon dissolve the mountain host,
> Nor would we that the vulgar feel,
> For their Chief's crimes, avenging steel."

In this better mood, therefore, James determines to give Douglas a fair hearing; and, that same evening, he assembles his council, and listens calmly and impartially to his prisoner's statement, with the happy result that he is quite convinced of Douglas's innocence, and the monarch and his powerful subject are entirely reconciled. With regard to Malcolm Græme, the danger to the latter appears to have been mere rumour; anything suspicious against the young man, if there were anything, would doubtless be explained then, but we have no particulars.

Matters are, therefore, in this condition when the heroine of the poem again makes her appearance on the scene.

On the morning following the events just related, Ellen Douglas, accompanied by her faithful Allan-bane and an old soldier belonging to the Earl of Mar's force, presents herself at the gate of the "Court of Guard," Stirling Castle. Filled with anxiety for the safety of her father and her lover, and being armed with the royal signet ring given to her by Fitz-James, she has determined to proceed to Stirling Castle and seek the presence of the king, to plead with him for their pardon. After the combat already described, she seeks the Earl of Mar, doubtless showing him the signet ring, and the earl at once places her under the escort of an old soldier of his force for safe conveyance to the Castle.

The "Court of Guard" is certainly not a desirable place for a young maiden, escorted only by two old men, to enter. It is occupied by a band of mercenary troops, employed by the king himself, in contradistinction to the feudal troops who followed the great nobles—

> "These drew not for their fields the sword,
> Like tenants of a feudal lord,

> Nor owned the patriarchal claim
> Of Chieftain in their leader's name."

They are a body of adventurers and refugees, drawn from the "riff-raff" of all nations, splendid in the battle-field, but otherwise "licentious, wild, and bold." They remind us of our own troops in the Peninsular War, under Wellington. This being holiday time, and discipline relaxed, their conduct is worse than ever. They have spent the night in debauchery, and the effects of the drink they have consumed have not yet left them.

Into the presence of this ruffianly crew, Ellen, with her slender escort, is now introduced. The men know the old soldier, Bertram, who is acting as escort, and at once assail him with questions as to the issue of the fight, the severity of which is evident to them by the number of wounded men who have been brought in, whose presence has not the slightest effect in restraining their debauchery.

On their questions concerning the battle, of which old Bertram can tell them little, being answered, they turn their attention to the maiden and harper, and now assail Bertram with their coarse gibes—

> " But whence thy captives, friend ? Such spoil
> As theirs must needs reward thy toil.
> Old dost thou wax, and wars grow sharp :
> Thou now hast glee-maiden and harp !
> Get thee an ape, and trudge the land,
> The leader of a juggler band."

Bertram at once declares that they are sent under his care by the Earl of Mar, and that no one must molest them. This by no means pleases these licentious men, and a rough Englishman, a refugee, named John of Brent, one of the most redoubtable of the band, loudly declares—

> " Shall he strike doe before our lodge,
> And yet the jealous niggard grudge
> To pay the forester his fee ?
> I'll have my share, howe'er it be,
> In spite of Moray, Mar, and thee."

He is advancing on the little band, who are desperately

preparing to defend their charge, when Ellen herself, throwing back her hood and revealing her face, steps boldly forward—

> "Boldly she spoke:—'Soldiers, attend!
> My father was the soldier's friend;
> Cheered him in camps, in marches led,
> And with him in the battle bled.
> Not from the valiant, or the strong,
> Should exile's daughter suffer wrong.'"

The beauty and courage of the maiden are not without effect on the rude band, and John of Brent, who, rough as he is, has an English heart, comes on her side at once, and declares that no one shall molest her—

> "Hear ye, my mates;—I go to call
> The Captain of our watch to hall:
> There lies my halbert on the floor;
> And he that steps my halbert o'er,
> To do the maid injurious part,
> My shaft shall quiver in his heart!
> Beware loose speech, or jesting rough:
> You all know John de Brent. Enough."

Their captain arrives, one young Lewis of Tullibardine; he addresses Ellen at first in tones of gallantry, but, on the production of the royal signet ring, he speedily alters his manner and apologises, and offers to conduct her to a suitable apartment, where she may remain until the king is ready to receive her.

She now gives money to the troops, who receive it with thanks, but Brent, with rude courtesy, prefers to wear the purse upon his cap—

> "Perchance, in jeopardy of war,
> Where gayer crests may keep afar."

On Ellen's departure with the young captain, old Allan begs John of Brent to conduct him to his lord, who, as he believes, is a prisoner. Brent, who seems to be in a position of authority in the troop, and has charge of the keys of the prison cells, at once acquiesces, and conducts the old man through various passages to a prison chamber—not a dungeon, but a room to which light is admitted, and is furnished well, as for the reception of a captive nobleman—

> "Such as the rugged days of old
> Deemed fit for captive noble's hold."

Here Brent leaves the old minstrel, assuring him that strict orders had been given "to tend the noble prisoner well." The captive is lying on a couch; and when old Allan approaches it he finds that it is occupied, not by Douglas, as he expected, but by the Highland chieftain, Roderick Dhu. Of the interview which now takes place, we have before entered into the details.

Ellen, in the meantime, is ushered into a suitable apartment to await her reception by the king. During this period she hears a lay from a turret chamber above, purporting to proceed from a captive. Who sings it we are not told; it is probably sung by some one sent thither by the king, who, knowing Ellen's feelings with regard to her father and her lover, strives to render them more intense, in order that the subsequent relief may be the greater.

However, she is not kept in suspense long. Scarcely has the song been concluded, when she hears a footstep behind her, and, turning, finds herself confronted with Fitz-James himself. She hails his appearance with the greatest relief, while he offers to conduct her to the king at once, and he gives her reassuring words as to her reception—

> "No tyrant he, though ire and pride
> May lead his better mood aside."

Conducted, then, by her friendly guide, she at length reaches the reception room, where the whole brilliancy of the Court bursts upon her. Timidly she raises her eyes, to seek among the glittering throng him who holds her father's fate in his hands; and then an overwhelming surprise takes possession of her. All the courtiers, in their gorgeous array, have their heads bare, while Fitz-James, in his simple costume of Lincoln green, alone remains covered. The truth flashes upon her; her conductor is no other than the king himself—

> "To him each lady's look was lent,
> On him each courtier's eye was bent;
> 'Midst furs, and silks, and jewels' sheen,
> He stood in simple Lincoln green,
> The centre of the glittering ring,—
> And Snowdoun's Knight is Scotland's King!'"

Overwhelmed by this unexpected discovery, Ellen throws herself at the monarch's feet, and shows the ring; he raises her at once with the utmost kindness, and loses no time in reassuring her as to the safety of her father, and, not only that, but his (the king's) perfect reconciliation with Douglas—

> "Ask nought for Douglas;—yester even,
> His prince and he have much forgiven:
> Wrong hath he had from slanderous tongue,
> I, from his rebel kinsmen, wrong.
> We would not to the vulgar crowd
> Yield what they craved with clamour loud;
> Calmly we heard and judged his cause,
> Our council aided and our laws.
> I stanched thy father's death-feud stern,
> With stout De Vaux and grey Glencairn;
> And Bothwell's Lord henceforth we own
> The friend and bulwark of our Throne."

But, for all this, Douglas is not present, and some doubt still appears in Ellen's eyes, on which the king adds—

> "But, lovely infidel, how now?
> What clouds that misbelieving brow?
> Lord James of Douglas, lend thine aid;
> Thou must confirm this doubting maid."

Douglas at once springs forth, and father and daughter fondly embrace; this completes the gratification of the king, on which we have already touched—

> "The Monarch drank, that happy hour,
> The sweetest, holiest draught of power,—
> When it can say, with godlike voice,
> Arise, sad Virtue, and rejoice!"

We cannot help thinking, however, that the revealing of the king's identity, and the affectionate meeting of father and daughter, need not have taken place in the presence of the whole Court. Such action, however, was quite in accordance with the character of the prince with whom we are dealing; he greatly loved display. James, however, himself now begins to perceive that there is too much publicity in the matter, and he interposes—

> "Nay, Douglas, nay!
> Steal not my proselyte away!
> The riddle 'tis my right to read,
> That brought this happy chance to speed."

He then explains to Ellen his assumed name and place of abode: Snowdoun is the old name of Stirling Castle, and James Fitz- (or son of) James is the name bestowed on the king by the Normans. He now proceeds to allay the uneasiness of Ellen as to her lover—

> "Thou still dost hold
> That little talisman of gold,
> Pledge of my faith,—Fitz-James's ring—
> What seeks fair Ellen of the King?"

Ellen, by the king's tone, feels that there is little or no fear now for her lover, Malcolm Græme; and, kindly and generously, she thinks of one who had been a benefactor to herself and her father, and who, she is sure, must have incurred the anger of the monarch through the bold rebellion of himself and his clan, the captive chieftain, Roderick Dhu. For him, therefore, she presents her claim. The reply of the king is equally noble and generous; with this we have dealt before.

James, however, is perfectly certain that her feelings are not principally with the Highland chief, and he presses her again—

> "Hast thou no other boon to crave?
> No other captive friend to save?"

Bashful at being thus closely pressed, Ellen hands the ring to Douglas, that he may plead for her; but the king will not have this, and puts on an assumed air of sternness—

> "Nay, then, my pledge hath lost its force,
> And stubborn justice holds her course."

He then summons Malcolm Græme, who kneels at the feet of his sovereign. Still continuing his assumed air of sternness, James addresses him—

> "For thee, rash youth, no suppliant sues,
> From thee may Vengeance claim her dues,
> Who, nurtured underneath our smile,
> Has paid our care by treacherous wile,
> And sought, amid thy faithful clan,,
> A refuge for an outlawed man,
> Dishonouring thus thy loyal name.—
> Fetters and warder for the Græme!"

Whether the king, in this, actually intended a rebuke to Græme, on account of his (being a royal ward) lending shelter to Douglas when the latter was an outlawed man, we cannot tell. But if there were any apprehension on the part of the lovers, it is speedily dispelled by the king's subsequent action, which, in a few well-chosen words, concludes the poem—

> "His chain of gold the King unstrung,
> The links o'er Malcolm's neck he flung,
> Then gently drew the glittering band,
> And laid the clasp on Ellen's hand."

And so, with this graceful action of the monarch, the poem closes: all here ends well. Scott certainly places the character of James V. in the best light possible; more favourably indeed than, as I think, he actually, according to historical facts, deserves; which facts I commented on at the opening of this treatise. But we are dealing with romance, and of this romance James is undoubtedly the hero; and an author must not be blamed for placing his hero in the most favourable light he can.

And so we bid farewell to "The Lady of the Lake," the most beautiful, in my opinion, of all Scott's poems; there is to me a charm in this work which none other of his poetical works possesses. One feature is the lovely descriptions of scenery which pervade the poem, descriptions which have made the district of the Trossachs and Loch Katrine the best known, the best favoured, spot by visitors to Scotland. The characters of the

poem are also superior to those of the others; there are none
that jar on one; there is no Goblin Page, as in "The Lay of the
Last Minstrel"; there is no forger, such as Marmion, in the
poem of that name; there is no unmitigated villain, such as
Oswald Wycliffe, in "Rokeby"; and the work has escaped the
scathing pen of Lord Byron. And, lastly, I have commented
on the beautiful little minor poems which appear at intervals
throughout the main work. In the first canto, we have Ellen's
beautiful "lullaby" to her guest, "Soldier, rest, thy warfare
o'er"; in the second, we have Allan-bane's farewell to the
guest—

> "Then, stranger, go! good speed the while,
> Nor think again of the lonely isle."

In the same canto, is the slogan of Clan Alpine, "Roderigh Vich
Alpine dhu, ho! ieroe!" In the third, we have three, on which
I have already commented—the coronach to the dead chief of
Duncraggan, Norman of Armandave's ode to his love, and Ellen's
hymn to the Virgin Mary. In the fourth, we have the gem of
all, "Alice Brand," into which I have entered in detail, and the
songs of Blanche of Devan. And, lastly, in the sixth, we have
the coronach of Allan-bane over the body of Roderick Dhu, and
two, which I consider inferior to the others, viz., the drinking
song of John of Brent and the lay of the supposed captive
knight.

Thus I end my treatise on my favourite poem, and conclude
it with regret. I think Scott himself must have considered it
his best poetical work, if we may judge from the beautiful lines
which open and conclude the poem. I end by quoting one of the
verses, which I may quite apply to myself, who know and love
the poem so well—

> "Yet once again, farewell, thou Minstrel Harp!
> Yet once again, forgive my feeble sway,
> And little reck I of the censure sharp
> May idly cavil at an idle lay.[27]

(27) Sir Walter Scott is evidently thinking of Lord Byron's hostile criticism
of his former works.

Much have I owed thy strains on life's long way,
  Through secret woes the world has never known,
When on the weary night dawned wearier day,
  And bitterer was the grief devoured alone.
That I o'erlive such woes, Enchantress! is thine own."

THE LORD OF THE ISLES.

VI.—THE LORD OF THE ISLES.

"Well is our country's work begun,
But more, far more, must yet be done !—
Speed messengers the country through;
Arouse old friends, and gather new;
Warn Lanark's knights to gird their mail,
Rouse the brave sons of Teviotdale,
Let Ettricke's archers sharp their darts,
The fairest forms, the truest hearts !
Call all, call all, from Reedswair-path
To the wild confines of Cape Wrath;
Wide let the news through Scotland ring,
The Northern Eagle claps his wing !"

IN this poem we are transported into a new country; we are still in Scotland, but, with the exception of the last canto, we traverse new ground altogether. We have visited the Lowlands of Scotland and the Perthshire Highlands, we are now transported to the Western Highlands and those lovely groups of islands that skirt the western coast of Scotland. We start in the Sound of Mull, that lovely strait that separates the island of Mull from the mainland; thence we are conveyed to the wild island of Skye; thence to the Isle of Arran, by Mull, Ulva, Colonsay, the well-known Staffa and Iona, Islay, and Jura; over the narrow isthmus of Tarbert into Loch Fyne; and thence to the island of Arran. We visit the Ayrshire coast, and, lastly, after a gap of several years, we find ourselves in the old ground we have already visited in the poem of "The Lady of the Lake," viz., the neighbourhood of the castle of Stirling.

The period of the poem extends from the year 1307 to 1314, representing the wanderings of Robert Bruce, afterwards King of Scotland. The last canto describes his crowning victory at Bannockburn.

The nominal hero of the poem, *i.e.*, the man from whom the poem is named, is Ronald, the young "Lord of the Isles," whose high characteristics are thus described—

> " Ronald, from many a hero sprung,
> The fair, the valiant, and the young,
> Lord of the Isles, whose lofty name
> A thousand bards have given to fame,
> The mate of monarchs, and allied
> On equal terms with England's pride."

The original of this young hero, who, in the poem, joins
Bruce at the outset and follows his fortunes throughout, is,
doubtless, Angus Og, who sheltered Bruce at his (Angus's) castle
of Donaverty, in Cantyre, at the time of the lowest point of the
king's fortunes, when the latter was flying from the pursuit of
his bitter enemy, the Lord of Lorn, who was kinsman to the Red
Comyn, whom Bruce had slain. From this refuge the king
escaped to the Isle of Rachrin, off the coast of Ireland. At the
opening of the present poem, Ronald is betrothed to Edith, sister
to the aforesaid Lord of Lorn, but, although the maiden's
affections are deeply bestowed on him, his love, as we shall see,
is centred elsewhere. The detail of all this we shall enter into
as we proceed with the treatise.

The real hero of the poem is, however, the great Scottish
king, Robert Bruce. His presence pervades the whole of the
poem ; it is with his fortunes that the other principal persons
of the work are involved ; during his ill-fortune, they are in the
midst of their own dangers and difficulties ; and, with his final
success, all the darkness disappears and the bright day dawns
at last.

The poem opens just as the fortunes of the great king begin
to take a turn for the better, viz., on his return from the Isle of
Rachrin, in the spring of the year 1307. Scott, however, as is
very frequently the case, does not adhere strictly to historical
fact. He makes the death of Edward I. take place immediately
after the return of Bruce from Rachrin, this event (Edward's
death) constituting the turn of fortune to the fugitive king. In
reality, the events in Arran and the attack on the castle of
Turnberry, in Ayrshire [1] (related in the poem), took place
before the death of the English king, which occurred in June,

---

(1) Turnberry was not captured by Bruce, as is mentioned in the poem. It
was an unsuccessful raid ; Scott owns this, in a note to the poem. See details
later.

1307. The turn in the fortunes of Bruce had, therefore, already commenced before that event.

The poem opens at the castle of Artornish, one of the strongholds of Ronald, the hero of the poem. It is situated in the Sound of Mull, near the entrance to Loch Aline, on the northern side. It was a place of considerable importance in the Middle Ages, it being the principal stronghold of the Lords of the Isles, where they held their "parliaments," or assemblages of vassals. It is now a mere ruin, and Baddeley remarks—"It is difficult for the passer-by to see anything more than yet another of the thousand-and-one little square strongholds which testify to the turbulence of former times in this part of Scotland." To this stronghold the Lord of Lorn, Bruce's bitter enemy, has brought his sister Edith to celebrate her wedding with the lord of the castle, Ronald, Lord of the Isles.

It is the wedding morning, and a band of minstrels has assembled to hail the bride. Their song arises, "Wake, Maid of Lorn!" and the lovely words of the song are well worthy of Scott—

> " O wake, while Dawn, with dewy shine,
> Wakes Nature's charms to vie with thine !
> She bids the mottled thrush rejoice
> To mate thy melody of voice;
> The dew that on the violet lies
> Mocks the dark lustre of thine eyes;
> But, Edith, wake, and all we see
> Of sweet and fair shall yield to thee ! "

But there is no response from the lady, and although the chief minstrel changes the note from that of flattery to a "softer spell," that of love, although—

> " More soft, more low, more tender fell
> The lay of love he bade them tell,"

it is unanswered. Edith is, indeed, not in a mood to respond to either flattery or love—

> " For not upon her cheek awoke
> The glow of pride when Flattery spoke,
> Nor could their tenderest numbers bring
> One sigh responsive to the string."

As little does she take interest in the ministrations of her handmaidens, who are decking her for the bridal; she is quite cold and indifferent. This does not escape the notice of her eldest attendant, Morag, her foster-mother—

> "Morag, to whose fostering care
> Proud Lorn had given his daughter fair."

The two stand quite in the position of mother and daughter—

> "Strict was that bond—most kind of all—
> Inviolate in Highland hall."

In the dialogue which follows, the aged attendant expatiates on the high qualities of Lord Ronald, an extract from which speech we have already quoted.[2] But this has no effect upon Edith; she checks her attendant, and divulges the insuperable reason why she is so sad and indifferent on her wedding morning, when others are gay—

> "But thou, experienced as thou art,
> Think'st thou with these to cheat the heart
> That, bound in strong affection's chain,
> Looks for return and looks in vain?
> No! sum thine Edith's wretched lot
> In these brief words—He loves her not!"

She explains how this has gradually dawned upon her, and points out that, even now, on their very wedding morning, he has not arrived—

> "Hunts he Bentalla's nimble deer,
> Or loiters he in secret dell
> To bid some lighter love farewell,
> And swear that though he may not scorn
> A daughter of the House of Lorn,
> Yet, when these formal rites are o'er,
> Again they meet, to part no more?"

Morag, on this, proceeds to reassure her, pointing out that the fleet of Lord Ronald is already in sight—

(2) See page 225.

> " Look, where beneath the castle grey
> His fleet unmoor from Aros-bay ! ' '

Aros Castle, another stronghold of the Lords of the Isles, is situated near Salen, in the island of Mull, and, therefore, on the opposite side of the sound, to Artornish Castle. From this point the fleet of Lord Ronald proceeds to unmoor, and to steer its course towards Artornish Castle. It sails with a favourable wind, and makes a gallant show during its progress—

> " Streamered with silk, and tricked with gold,
> Manned with the noble and the bold
> Of Island chivalry.
> Around their prows the ocean roars,
> And chafes beneath their thousand oars,
> Yet bears them on their way:
> So fumes the war-horse in his might,
> That field-ward bears some valiant knight,
> Champs till both bit and boss are white,
> But, foaming, must obey.
> On each gay deck they might behold
> Lances of steel and crests of gold,
> And hauberks with their burnished fold,
> That shimmered fair and free;
> And each proud galley, as she passed,
> To the wild cadence of the blast
> Gave wilder minstrelsy."

In strong contrast to this gorgeous pageant, which "bears on with mirth and pride," a small vessel is perceived by the maiden and her attendant labouring against the wind, tacking from shore to shore, and making but slow progress—

> " Amid the tide,
> The skiff she marked lay tossing sore,
> And shifted oft her stooping side,
> In weary tack from shore to shore.
> Yet on her destined course no more
> She gained of forward way."

Yet, strange to say, although the "sheltering haven" of Artornish Castle lay on her lee, the crew seems strenuously to steer clear of this point, making a fresh tack as the boat approaches the neighbourhood of the castle. This avoidance is easily explained when we know who compose the crew of the boat. Scott says—

> "And thou, Lord Ronald, sweep thou on,
> With mirth and pride and minstrel tone!
> But hadst thou known who sailed so nigh,
> Far other glance were in thine eye!
> Far other flush were on thy brow,
> That, shaded by the bonnet, now
> Assumes but ill the blithesome cheer
> Of bridegroom, when the bride is near."

The bark indeed contains the true hero of the poem, Robert Bruce himself, his brother Edward, and his sister Isabel, the latter in a fainting condition, "half dead with want and fear." They are indeed in a most hazardous condition, buffeted by the gale, against which they have been striving the whole day, with their boat damaged and leaking; and now it seems that there is no alternative between perishing in the waves or taking refuge in a hostile castle, for at present they doubtless deem Ronald to be their enemy, he being now about to wed the sister of Lorn, Bruce's most bitter foe.

The state of affairs has become so perilous that Edward Bruce, who is steering, at length, for their sister's sake, suggests taking refuge in Artornish Castle. Bruce consents; it is the only course open to them, dangerous as it is—

> "For if a hope of safety rest,
> 'Tis on the sacred name of guest,
> Who seeks for shelter, storm-distressed,
> Within a chieftain's hall."

Bruce evidently feels that he can trust to Ronald's honour, though the latter be a probable enemy. As it turns out, the king need have no fear: the chieftain, as we know, does not love his affianced bride; he is actually in love with Isabel, Bruce's sister, though where he had met her, the poet does not here say.

They change their course, and arrive safely beneath the wall of the castle, where they hear the sounds of merriment; the bridal feast is now in full course. They wind their bugle, and a warder soon appears. He greets them with "Thrice welcome,

holy sire!" evidently deeming that the priest had arrived who
was to perform the marriage rites, but who had evidently been
delayed by the storm. On learning his mistake, the warder
somewhat demurs, and inquires from whence they come: the
adventurers are careful not to reveal their identity, but state
that "they are known to fame," saying—

> "And these brief words have import dear,
> When sounded in a noble ear,
> To harbour safe, and friendly cheer,
>   That gives us rightful claim."

The warder, on this, states that Artornish Hall is open to
all, even to enemies; even (significant words) had they aided the
outlawed Bruce himself, whom he terms "that fell homicide."

Thereupon he admits the strangers, and conducts them to the
guardroom, where he leaves them for the present while he reports
their arrival to his lord. During his absence, the inmates of the
room crowd round the new arrivals, and continue to stare upon
the lady until Edward, who is of a fiery, impatient temperament,
intervenes roughly, which action might have roused strife had
not Bruce himself intervened, and the dignity of his bearing and
demeanour quells at once the strife which was now impending—

> "Proud was his tone, but calm; his eye
> Had that compelling dignity,
> His mien that bearing haught and high,
>   Which common spirits fear;
> Needed nor word nor signal more,
> Nod, wink, and laughter, all were o'er;
> Upon each other back they bore,
>   And gazed like startled deer."

The seneschal soon appears, and conducts the strangers to the
banqueting hall, and at this point the first canto of the poem
closes.

The banquet is at its height, with outward appearance of the
greatest mirth and glee, on the (supposed) joyful occasion, but
there are far different feelings in the hearts of the two principally
concerned—the future bride and bridegroom. Ronald is troubled,
he falls into deep fits of abstraction for a while, then, rousing
himself, he indulges in spasmodic fits of mirth—

> "And, for brief space, of all the crowd,
>   As he was loudest of the loud,
>   Seem gayest of the gay."

This, however, is unheeded by the guests, who think that his abstraction is due to a lover's rapture in his approaching marriage with the maid he loves, his fits of mirth to bridegroom's ecstacy. Edith, alas! knows better; she well knows that he is indifferent to her, and she watches his varying moods "with agony and fear." Her eyes and those of Ronald meet once, and this has a terrible effect on both; to hide this, Ronald rises, calls for "the mighty cup, first owned by royal Somerled," and pledges to his future brother-in-law, Lorn, the union of their houses; the latter responds, at present wholly unconscious of the indifference of Ronald towards his sister. A bugle sounding now without, Lorn remarks that it must mean the arrival of the abbot, who was to perform the marriage ceremony. On this, Ronald actually drops the cup from his hand on hearing that the evil hour (to him) is so nigh at hand, but he is relieved when the warder enters and informs him of the arrival of the strangers. The chieftain at once gives orders for their admission.

The three strangers are therefore introduced, and the seneschal, perceiving that, although their clothes were soiled with travel, their appearance denoted that they were no common persons, but people of good estate, places them in a high position, near, doubtless, to the chief. A murmur of discontent arises among the guests at this, but the seneschal at once proceeds to justify his act—

> "For forty years a seneschal,
>   To marshal guests in bower and hall
>   Has been my honoured trade.
>   Worship and birth to me are known,
>   By look, by bearing, and by tone,
>   Not by furred robe or broidered zone;
>   And 'gainst an oaken bough
>   I'll gage my silver wand of state,
>   That these three strangers oft have sate
>   In higher place than now."

In this the seneschal is supported by the senior minstrel,

who corroborates all that the former has said concerning the mien of the strangers, especially that of Bruce himself.

The guests, therefore, are allowed to take their seats without further comment, but the haughty Lorn regards them with suspicion, and whispers those suspicions in the ear of Sir Giles de Argentine, an English knight dispatched by Edward I. to cement the western league on his (the king's) side. Lorn suspects the identity of the strangers, and asks them a searching question as to whether they know of the whereabouts of that "rebellious Scottish crew" who went to the isle of Rachrin with the outlawed Bruce. Edward Bruce, fiery as ever, gives a defiant answer—

> "Of rebels have we nought to show;
> But if of Royal Bruce thou'dst know,
>   I warn thee he has sworn,
> Ere thrice three days shall come and go,
> His banner Scottish winds shall blow,
> Despite each mean or mighty foe,
> From England's every bill and bow,
>   To Allaster of Lorn."

Lorn's ire is naturally awakened at this, but Ronald interposes, and suggests a minstrel lay, as more suitable to this festive occasion than useless strife. Lorn acquiesces, and suggests a lay to his minstrel, at the same time whispering to Argentine—

> "The lay I named will carry smart
> To these bold strangers' haughty heart,
>   If right this guess of mine."

The subject of the lay is this incident. Bruce, in 1306, had sustained a severe defeat at Methven, which completely dispersed his followers, he himself having to flee for his life. He had got to the south-west of Scotland, to a place called Dalry, in Galloway, where he and his party were attacked by a superior force under Lorn. After a desperate conflict, Bruce managed to escape, but was forced to abandon his mantle and the brooch attached to it, which was torn from him. The lay glorifies this act of Lorn in exaggerated terms, but in very beautiful language—

> "Whence the brooch of burning gold,
> That clasps the Chieftain's mantle fold?"

And so on, with regard to the high value of the brooch, and then it proceeds—

> "While the gem was won and lost
> Widely was the war-cry tossed!
> Rung aloud Bendourish Fell,
> Answered Douchart's sounding dell,
> Fled the deer from wild Tyndrum,
> When the homicide, o'ercome,
> Hardly 'scaped with scath and scorn,
> Left the pledge with conquering Lorn!" (3)

The lay goes on in the same vainglorious style, ending, with regard to the outlawed Bruce—

> "Let him fly from coast to coast,
> Dogged by Comyn's vengeful ghost,
> While his spoils, in triumph worn,
> Long shall grace victorious Lorn!"

If this lay were sung for the purpose of discovering the identity of the three strangers, nothing could have been more successful. The fiery Edward, terribly enraged, is about to draw his sword, but Bruce checks him, at the same time mentioning some facts which had been carefully omitted from the song. He says to the minstrel—

> "Yet something might thy song have told
> Of Lorn's three vassals true and bold,
> Who rent their lord from Bruce's hold,
> As underneath his knee he lay,
> And died to save him in the fray.
> I've heard the Bruce's cloak and clasp
> Was clenched within their dying grasp,
> What time a hundred foemen more
> Rushed in and back the victor bore,
> Long after Lorn had left the strife,
> Full glad to 'scape with limb and life."

Bruce then hands the minstrel a chain of gold, with these words—

(3) It will be noted that Scott makes this incident take place near Tyndrum, in Argyleshire, but the attack by Lorn certainly occurred at Dalry, in Galloway, though Sir H. Maxwell, in his book, "Robert the Bruce," does not mention the capture of the brooch.

> "For future lays a fair excuse,
> To speak more nobly of the Bruce."

Bruce has clearly now revealed his identity, and his enemy, Lorn, springs to his feet and fiercely demands the instant death of the murderer of his kinsman, Comyn. Ronald, on the other hand, declares this shall not be: the laws of hospitality forbid it—while the three Bruces are under his roof their persons are sacred, he will never allow their blood to stain his hall. Lorn is not to be stayed by such arguments; he fiercely breaks out—

> "Talk not to me of sheltering hall,
> The Church of God saw Comyn fall!"

Comyn was slain at God's altar; no laws of hospitality should protect a murderer such as this. Lorn calls loudly on all present—

> "Up, all who love me! blow on blow!
> And lay the outlawed felons low!"

There were many chiefs present from the mainland who owned Lorn for their chieftain; these spring up and, with cries of vengeance, prepare to attack Bruce's party; but, on the other hand, there were many Island chiefs of importance present—these come to the side of Ronald for the protection of the threatened party. There were old feuds between the chiefs of the mainland and those of the islands, and these are remembered now.

The different parties stand opposed to each other, prepared for combat, but the laws of hospitality still restrain them, and neither party cares to strike the first blow. A dead, ominous silence ensues—

> "Such silence, as the deadly still,
> Ere bursts the thunder on the hill."

During this interval, the Lady Isabel (sister of Bruce) and Edith also strive "to pray for aid." They both cling to De Argentine, the English knight, instinctively aware of his nobility of character. Indeed, Isabel appears to have known the knight previously, having presented the prize to him in a tournament. She prays him to intervene, but at the same time turns her eye to Ronald, and on that a painful incident occurs. I have already mentioned the feelings of the chief towards this lady, and now, she having removed her veil, he sees the face of his love. He bursts out with, "Fear not, my Isabel!" then, recovering himself, he says, "What said I ?—Edith!—all is well." He then blunders on—

> "Nay, fear not—I will well provide
> The safety of my lovely bride—
> My bride ?"—

and then he preceptibly shudders. A terribly awkward, terribly painful incident.

We now turn to the English knight, De Argentine, who is a noble, pleasing character in the poem. We have seen how the two ladies have instinctively turned to him for aid; and he now rises to claim Bruce's party as prisoners, in the name of his sovereign, Edward I.; they, as—

> "Vassals sworn,
> 'Gainst their liege lord had weapon borne."

This was perfectly true; Bruce had, before this, sworn fealty to Edward, but Argentine looked on Bruce as a noble foe, as we shall constantly see; and Sir Walter Scott says—

> "Such speech, I ween, was but to hide
> His care their safety to provide;
> For knight more true in word and deed
> Than Argentine ne'er spurred a steed."

Ronald, guessing this intention, is inclined to support Argentine, but a certain Island chieftain, Torquil, "from Dunvegan, Lord of the misty Isles of Skye," one of those who have taken the side of Ronald, strongly opposes the claim. He contends that the claim of Bruce to the Scottish throne may be lawful, but, at any rate, in this place where Scottish chieftains are assembled "to bridal mirth and bridal cheer," an English representative, or Lorn himself, have no right to intervene, and he says—

> "Be sure, with no consent of mine,
> Shall either Lorn or Argentine
> With chains or violence, in our sight,
> Oppress a brave and banished knight."

The old chieftain here shows plainly on which side his sympathies lie.

This bold statement seems likely to waken the strife again, when a bugle call is again heard without. This evidently denotes the arrival of the abbot (doubtless from Iona), who is to perform the marriage ceremony. There is a great relief; to the Church shall the decision of the strife be entrusted—

> "He comes our feuds to reconcile,
> A sainted man from sainted isle;
> We will his holy doom abide,
> The abbot shall our strife decide."

The abbot shortly after enters, accompanied by an attendant train of monks. On his appearance, drawn swords and daggers disappear as if by magic, not soon enough, however, to escape the quick eye of the priest, who, after the usual blessing, sternly demands the reason of these unseemly tokens of warfare on a festal occasion such as this. Lorn, in reply, points out the presence of the outlawed Bruce—

> "A wretch, beneath the ban
> Of Pope and Church, for murder done
> Even on the sacred altar-stone!"

He places the fate of the offender in the hands of the abbot. Ronald, on the other hand, pleads the "stranger's cause"; Isabel supports this with tears, and prayers for mercy; Edith proffers the same prayer to her brother, only to receive a fierce reply from that furious chieftain, who is now evidently aware of the real state of Ronald's feelings towards Edith, having, doubtless, noticed the painful incident already recorded, also perceiving the evident leaning of Ronald to the cause of the Bruce. He declares that the contract with Ronald shall be broken off, and that Edith shall be wedded to an English baron, Clifford, Lord of Cumberland.

Argentine then speaks, again demanding Bruce and his party as prisoners in the name of his sovereign. This draws forth a fiery reply from Ronald, who now plainly shows to which party he is inclined. He mentions many eminent Scottish chieftains who had been put to death for defending their country, by order of Edward I.[4]   He positively refuses to give Bruce up—

> "What! can the English Leopard's mood
> Never be gorged with northern blood?"

He is supported by Torquil of Dunvegan, already mentioned, who speaks as boldly as before.   He declares that he will support Bruce, "with twice a thousand at his back," in spite of Rome or England, and he actually dares the abbot to do his worst.[5]

The abbot looks with severity on the bold speaker, but makes no remark; he then turns to the principal offender, and now ensues one of the most beautiful incidents of the poem—the most beautiful poetic language.

The abbot, although, like every Churchman, he strongly condemns the sacrilegious nature of the crime, evidently cannot help feeling that if he condemns Bruce he destroys the last hope of the liberty of Scotland.   The patriot within him struggles with the priest; he is greatly agitated when he turns to meet the gaze of the king, who encounters his glance steadily and bravely.   At length the abbot recovers himself for the time; his duties as a Churchman forbid him to overlook a crime of this nature, and he sternly demands of Bruce whether he has anything to plead why the terrible sentence of the Church (excommunication) should not be pronounced upon him; he enters into all the horrible consequences of such sentence—

> "And thou,
> Unhappy! what hast thou to plead,
> Why I denounce not on thy deed
> That awful doom which canons tell
> Shuts paradise and opens hell;
> Anathema of power so dread,
> It blends the living with the dead,
> Bids each good angel soar away,
> And every ill one claim his prey;

(4) It must be remembered, however, that all, or nearly all, of the Scottish chiefs mentioned in the poem had sworn allegiance to Edward.

(5) The note in the poem says that many of these Island chieftains were but imperfect converts to Christianity; they had Norwegian blood in their veins, and their old faith still clung about them.   Torquil here swears by Woden.   (Anyone who has read the fairy tales, "Tales of the Norse," will have noticed the extraordinary mixture of Christianity and heathenism which pervades the tales.)

Expels thee from the Church's care,
And deafens Heaven against thy prayer;
Arms every hand against thy life,
Bans all who aid thee in the strife,
Nay, each whose succour, cold and scant,
With meanest alms relieves thy want;
Haunts thee while living,—and, when dead,
Dwells on thy yet devoted head,
Rends Honour's scutcheon from thy hearse,
Stills o'er thy bier the holy verse,
And spurns thy corpse from hallowed ground,
Flung like vile carrion to the hound !
Such is the dire and desperate doom,
For sacrilege, decreed by Rome;
And such the well-deservèd meed
Of thine unhallowed, ruthless deed."

All the dire, fearful consequences of this most terrible ban are, indeed, here placed without disguise before the culprit. The answer of Bruce is noble, respectful, indeed, to the abbot, but firm. He does not deny the deed, but declares that it was not "selfish vengeance" that prompted it, but that Comyn had died an enemy to his country.[6] He does not deny the justice of the sentence against him—

"Nor censure those from whose stern tongue
The dire anathema has rung."

He also declares his intention of atoning for the deed as fully as he can—

"Heaven knows my purpose to atone,
Far as I may, the evil done,
And hears a penitent's appeal
From papal curse and prelate's zeal."

As soon as he has freed Scotland, he will see that requiem masses be said for the soul of Comyn, and that he himself, to expiate the crime, will proceed on a crusade to Palestine. He concludes by bidding defiance to both Argentine and Lorn, and, flinging the name of "traitor" back in their teeth, he concludes with dignity—

(6) I am now only following the poem; the details of the affair between Bruce and Comyn can be read in Sir H. Maxwell's "Robert the Bruce," "Heroes of the Nations" Series, Chapter VI. Bruce does not come out favourably in the matter; the author, indeed, is very impartial in dealing with his hero.

"These brief words spoke, I speak no more.
Do what thou wilt; my shrift is o'er." (7)

This noble, straightforward defence has a great effect upon the abbot. We have seen that he was evidently undecided in his mind, but by a strong effort had determined to fulfil his duty to the Church; but the words of Bruce destroy this decision altogether: he feels that the condemnation of Bruce means the ruin of his country, and patriotism now has the entire mastery of him—

"His breathing came more thick and fast,
And from his pale blue eyes were cast
Strange rays of wild and wandering light;
Uprise his locks of silver white,
Flushed is his brow, through every vein
In azure tide the currents strain,
And undistinguished accents broke
The awful silence ere he spoke:—
'De Bruce! I rose with purpose dread
To speak my curse upon thy head,
And give thee as an outcast o'er
To him who burns to shed thy gore;
But, like the Midianite of old,
Who stood on Zophim, heaven-controlled,(8)
I feel within mine agèd breast
A power that will not be repressed.
It prompts my voice, it swells my veins,
It burns, it maddens, it constrains!
De Bruce, thy sacrilegious blow
Hath at God's altar slain thy foe:
O'er-mastered yet by high behest,
I bless thee, and thou shalt be blessed!'"

At this unexpected outburst, intense astonishment prevails, "silence, awful, deep, and long"; exultation, doubtless, on the part of the adherents of Bruce; intense wrath on the part of Lorn and his followers, though at present suppressed. All the previous indecision on the part of the abbot has now disappeared; he continues in "vigorous manhood's lofty tone"; he becomes prophetic—

(7) The crime seems to have lain heavily on Bruce's mind during his lifetime, hence the sending of his heart to Palestine after his death.

(8) Balaam; Numbers xxiii., xxiv.

"Thrice vanquished on the battle-plain,
Thy followers slaughtered, fled, or ta'en,
A hunted wanderer on the wild,[9]
On foreign shores a man exiled,
Disowned, deserted, and distressed,
I bless thee, and thou shalt be blessed;
Blessed in the hall and in the field,
Under the mantle as the shield.
Avenger of thy country's shame,
Restorer of her injured fame,
Blessed in thy sceptre and thy sword,
De Bruce, fair Scotland's rightful Lord;
Blessed in thy deeds and in thy fame,
What lengthened honours wait thy name!
In distant ages, sire to son
Shall tell thy tale of freedom won,
And teach his infants, in the use
Of earliest speech, to falter Bruce.
Go, then, triumphant! sweep along
Thy course, the theme of many a song!
The Power, whose dictates swell my breast,
Hath' blessed thee, and thou shalt be blessed!" [10]

The abbot sinks back into the arms of his attendant monks; he sees at once that the proposed marriage cannot possibly be consummated now; he announces this, and gives orders to his train to embark immediately and sail away. The whole monastic train therefore retire, leaving the assembly in deep, spellbound silence and astonishment.

While this lasts, Ronald draws Lorn apart and endeavours to bring about an accommodation; but, as may be imagined, the latter vindictive chieftain is by no means inclined to give up his vengeance on account of the abbot's blessing upon his ememy. He, however, gives it up for the present, but declares all contract with Ronald at an end—

(9) See most interesting details of Bruce's wanderings in the work I have last quoted, Chap. VII.

(10) This interview between Bruce and the abbot is, of course, fictitious; he was excommunicated during the previous year, 1306, the ban of Rome not being removed until 1328. Bruce was, however, absolved by the Bishop of Glasgow, but this, of course, could not affect the Pope's edict. The curse of Rome, however, appeared to have little or no effect in Scotland: Bruce's greatest successes were gained while he was under that curse.

> " We nor ally nor brother know,
> In Bruce's friend, or England's foe."

Lorn determines to leave the castle at once with his followers, and sends for his sister to accompany him, but what is his rage on finding that Edith has disappeared and cannot be found. She, with her attendant, Morag, has fled, evidently in the abbot's ship. Lorn, foaming with rage, orders immediate pursuit, with threats to the abbot himself—

> " Man every galley !—fly—pursue !
> The priest his treachery shall rue !
> Ay, and the time shall quickly come
> When we shall hear the thanks that Rome
> Will pay his feignèd prophecy ! " (11)

He is at once obeyed by one of his retainers named Cormac Doil, a pirate, who is only too glad to be employed in such business—

> " For, glad of each pretext for spoil,
> A pirate sworn was Cormac Doil."

Lorn now calls his retainers together, and they leave the castle in a body; but De Argentine, before accompanying him, approaches Bruce. It will be remembered that the latter had lately flung back the term "traitor" to the former, and given him the lie. The English knight now requires satisfaction for this. He addresses Bruce sternly, but in courteous terms, acknowledging his worth, then tenders him his gauntlet, to be placed on his (Bruce's) brow when they shall meet in the field—

> " We need not to each other tell,
> That both can wield their weapons well;
> Then do me but the soldier grace,
> This glove upon thy helm to place
> Where we may meet in fight;
> And I will say, as still I've said,
> Though by ambition far misled,
> Thou art a noble knight."

(11) It must be remembered that Bruce was already excommunicated, and this blessing and prophecy of the abbot could not invalidate the edict of Rome. All that the abbot had to do was to pronounce the sentence on the culprit personally.

Bruce answers his honourable foe in the same spirit—

> "For your brave request,
> Be sure the honoured pledge you gave
> In every battle-field shall wave.
>   Upon my helmet-crest;
> Believe, that if my hasty tongue
> Hath done thine honour causeless wrong,
>   It shall be well redressed.
> Not dearer to my soul was glove,
> Bestowed in youth by lady's love,
>   Than this which thou hast given!
> Thus, then, my noble foe I greet;
> Health and high fortune till we meet,
>   And then—what pleases Heaven."

So part these gallant foes, with mutual respect; to meet again, in Argentine's last hour, on the field of Bannockburn.

Lorn being now Ronald's declared enemy, the latter sees to the defence of the castle, doubling the guards, and trebly barring the different doors, &c. The guests who remain retire to their chambers. Bruce and his brother, in theirs, have fallen asleep, when the king is aroused by the jarring of a secret door. He springs up and arouses Edward, but the next moment exclaims—

> "Nay, strike not! 'tis our noble host."

Ronald enters, accompanied by old Torquil of Dunvegan; both these chieftains go down on bended knee and tender allegiance to Bruce as king. Ronald has long been inclined to this, and he now gives himself entirely to the service of the monarch—

> "'And O,' said Ronald, 'Owned of Heaven!
> Say, is my erring youth forgiven,
> By falsehood's arts from duty driven,
>   Who rebel falchion drew,
> Yet ever to thy deeds of fame,
> Even while I strove against thy claim,
>   Paid homage just and true?'"

It need hardly be said that Bruce receives the homage of his new vassals most heartily. They enter then into consultation. Bruce intimates that he had wished to visit Carrick, his native shore, where his own ancestral mansion, Turnberry, was occupied by an English garrison. He was on his way to the Isle of Arran for this purpose, when a storm scattered his ships, and he, separated from the rest, had, with his brother and sister, eventually reached Artornish Castle, as we have seen.

Torquil advises Bruce to leave Artornish at once, as it is sure to be beseiged by Lorn, who had many adherents in this neighbourhood, to say nothing of the English ships, which were continually cruising about. He offers the king refuge in the Isle of Skye, which the latter accepts, Ronald volunteering to accompany him. Bruce, however, suggests that his sister Isabel, under charge of their brother Edward, should again withdraw to the Isle of Rachrin, off the coast of Ireland, in their boat. This is agreed to, and the two boats leave the castle and proceed to their different destinations. Here we take leave of Artornish Castle, and seek new ground.

We enter now, so to speak, into the second stage of the poem, which may be divided, roughly, into three divisions. The events of the first take place, as we have seen, within the castle of Artornish; the second, upon which we are now entering, comprises the wanderings of Bruce—first, to the Isle of Skye, thence to that of Arran, from which latter place he makes an attack upon the Carrick coast and captures (according to the poem) his ancestral seat, the castle of Turnberry.[12]

After this, there is a gap of seven years, and the third division of the poem enters into the details of the Battle of Bannockburn.

The two barks (the one belonging to Bruce, the other to Ronald) part for their different destinations, the first for Ireland, the second for the Isle of Skye; it is the latter, containing Bruce and Ronald, with the latter's page, Allan, that we accompany. Old Torquil remains behind to attend the councils of the Island chiefs, the old chieftain declaring—

> "And if my words in weight shall fail,
> This ponderous sword shall turn the scale."

Our adventurers sail with a favouring wind through the Sound of Mull, and clear the point of Ardnamurchan; after this, however, the circumstances are not so favourable—

(12) See page 226; also Note 1 of the treatise.

> " But then the squalls blew close and hard,
>   And, fain to strike the galley's yard,
>   And take them to the oar,
>   With these rude seas, in weary plight,
>   They strove the livelong day and night,
>   Nor till the dawning had a sight
>   Of Skye's romantic shore."

Though they sight the Isle of Skye at break of day, such is the delay caused by contrary · winds and waves that they are unable to effect a landing until the evening, when, in the words of the poem, they "moor in Scarigh bay," *i.e.*, Loch Scavaig.

The island of Skye possesses the wildest scenery in Scotland, and nowhere more so than at the spot where we have landed our travellers. They, doubtless, have landed at the extreme end of the loch, where a stream, called "The Mad Stream," empties itself into it; the only sheltered spot, indeed, as elsewhere Loch Scavaig is a wide arm of the sea. Baddeley says that this loch, "as seen by those who enter it from the open sea, approximates as nearly to the sublime as anything in Britain." About a quarter of a mile inland from the upper end of Loch Scavaig lies Loch Coruisk (called Coriskin in the poem), in the very heart of the Cuchullin (Coolin) mountains. These mountains are the wildest, roughest, and most difficult to climb in this country. I have been told that Alpine climbers have visited these mountains for the purpose of practising their climbing powers before proceeding to the more formidable heights of Switzerland. I myself was also told by a gentleman who knew the Cuchullins well, that, should anyone be caught in a mist in this wild district, it would be useless to attempt the usual method of following a stream downwards: it would be most dangerous, and would probably end in a fall over a precipice.

Our travellers, then, having landed at the spot above mentioned, proceed to cross the strip of land between the above two lochs, and come upon the shore of Loch Coruisk, where Bruce, who appears, according to the poem, never to have been in Skye before, expresses his wonder at the wildness and grandeur of the scene. Still more wild does it become as they proceed on their way and approach the base of the Cuchullin mountains—

"And wilder, forward as they wound,
Were the proud cliffs and lake profound.
Huge terraces of granite black
Afforded rude and cumbered track;
  For from the mountain hoar,
Hurled headlong in some night of fear,
When yelled the wolf and fled the deer,
  Loose crags had toppled o'er;
And some, chance-poised and balanced, lay,
So that a stripling arm might sway
  A mass no host could raise,
In Nature's rage at random thrown,
Yet trembling like the Druid's stone
  On its precarious base."

Bruce inquires of Ronald the name of the wild lake and wilder mountains; the chief replies—

"Coriskin call the dark lake's name,
Coolin the ridge, as bards proclaim,
From old Cuchullin, chief of fame."

Our travellers have not proceeded far when they meet with an adventure which costs one of them his life, while the others narrowly escape. This adventure also has a great effect upon the future events of the poem. They see five men advancing towards them; enemies evidently, for they wear the badge of Lorn; besides which, their ruffianly aspect proclaims them to be men of utterly unscrupulous character, whose trade is robbery and rapine. Two of them appear to be of higher rank than the rest, being better clad and better armed, the other three seem to be serfs, ill clad, and armed only with "a club, an axe, a rusty brand." The odds are considerably on the side of these ruffians—five to two, for Ronald's page can little count. The latter, however, can use bow and arrows, and Ronald wishes him to send two shots at the advancing party, thus, if successful, diminishing the odds, but this Bruce will not permit—he will have no blood shed if it can possibly be avoided.

This party of five, however, display no open hostility towards our travellers, although their looks belie them. On Bruce questioning them, they declare that they have been shipwrecked on the island, and they offer him and his party hospitality.

Bruce, mistrusting them, is not inclined to accept this offer; he says that his ship awaits him and his party in the bay, on which the chief of the party informs him that his (Bruce's) ship, on the appearance of an English vessel, had hoisted sail and borne away. This is a falsehood, as we shall see hereafter.

On hearing this bad news, Bruce and Ronald confer together and decide that there is no other way but to accept the hospitality of these strangers, but they determine to watch very carefully for any signs of treachery and to neglect no precautions. They refuse, therefore, to mix company with them, but insist upon their going in front and leading the way to their lodging. This they reach in due course. It consists of a—

> "Dreary cabin, made
> Of sails against a rock displayed."

Here they find, to their astonishment, a young boy (to all appearance)—

> "A slender boy, whose form and mien
> Ill suited with such savage scene,
>   In cap and cloak of velvet green,
>   Low seated on the ground.
> His garb was such as minstrels wear,
> Dark was his hue, and dark his hair,
> His youthful cheek was marred by care,
>   His eyes in sorrow drowned."

This apparent boy is, as all readers of the poem know, none other than Edith of Lorn, who, as we have seen, had fled with her attendant, Morag, in the abbot's ship from the castle of Artornish. I will comment later on the actions of this eccentric young adventuress; not only does she assume this disguise, but she also feigns dumbness. The chief of the party, on being questioned by Ronald as to who the boy may be, states that he was taken captive with his mother the day before, and that the latter was lost in their late shipwreck, hence the grief of the boy. This so-called "mother" is evidently Morag, the attendant, for we hear no more of her in the poem. The facts regarding Edith's disguise and capture by these brigands are very meagre; I will enter into them later; at present, I must proceed with my narrative.

The leader of the party, who is no other than the pirate Cormac Doil, whom we have seen Lorn dispatch in pursuit of the abbot's ship, now tries to induce Bruce and his party to take off their swords and sit down with them at their meal. To this Bruce will not consent for a moment; he insists that his party shall sit down separately, pleading that they are compelled to do this on account of a vow. Cormac ill brooks this, but, cowed by the looks of Bruce and Ronald, he at length gives a surly consent.

The two parties, therefore, sit down separately, Bruce and Ronald never relaxing their vigilance for a moment, as the looks of the party opposite appear more and more sinister as they contemplate them.

When the time for rest arrives, Bruce is careful to arrange that one of his party should keep watch during the night while the others sleep. The first watch is taken by Ronald, the second by Bruce himself, and the third by the page, Allan. Nothing occurs during the watch of the first two; they are both old campaigners, especially Bruce, and well used to keeping their eyes open at night. It is otherwise with the page; he is a boy, accustomed to his full night's rest, and therefore finds great difficulty in keeping awake. He does his best, however, loyally, but, as the dawn is beginning to break, he drops off into a doze, and, while in this condition, a murderous blow is delivered from the dagger of one of the ruffians, who has crept up treacherously behind the boy.

If the scoundrels, however, had hoped thus to surprise the whole party, they find themselves greatly mistaken. Bruce and Ronald are on their feet in an instant; the king snatches a brand from the fire, and with it deals the murderer a fatal blow, while two other of the ruffians are accounted for by the sword of Ronald. But, while the latter is thus engaged, the villainous leader of the band sneaks up behind him with his murderous weapon. Bruce is at this moment engaged with the last of the robber band: who is there to save Ronald ? There is one—the woman whom he has slighted. Edith, seeing the man she loves in such imminent danger, springs forward and seizes Cormac's arm; ere he can disengage himself, the precious moment is gained. Bruce has despatched his opponent, and now deals a crushing blow on the master miscreant, which stretches him on the ground mortally wounded.

Bruce now sternly demands the reason of this murderous attack upon unoffending strangers; Cormac confesses that he was aware of the identity of the king, and that he was acting on behalf of his chief, Lorn. Bruce then inquires, as Ronald had done, concerning the dumb boy, but the pirate knows (or says he knows) no more than he has already told—

> "We found him in a bark we sought
> With different purpose . . . and I thought"—

These are his last words—

> "Fate cut him short; in blood and broil,
> As he had lived, died Cormac Doil."

All of this pirate band have now been killed, and Bruce and Ronald, as we may imagine, have no desire to remain in this charnel house. They start, taking the mute boy with them, to whom Bruce speaks in these kindly words—

> "Yet scant of friends the Bruce shall be,
> But he'll find resting-place for thee."

Before they leave for their ship, Ronald delivers a beautiful word of farewell to his murdered page, Allan—

> "'Who shall tell this tale,'
> He said, 'in halls of Donagaile!
> Oh, who his widowed mother tell,
> That, ere his bloom, her fairest fell!—
> Rest thee, poor youth, and trust my care,
> For mass and knell and funeral prayer;
> While o'er these caitiffs, where they lie,
> The wolf shall snarl, the raven cry!'"

Before proceeding with my narrative, I must say a few words on this astounding escapade of Edith of Lorn, which pervades the whole poem. She has fled from Artornish, as we have seen, on account of her brother's threat to marry her to the English baron, Clifford. She takes refuge in the abbot's ship, assuming the disguise of a boy, though why she should have done so, and not come in her proper person, is incomprehensible. The abbot, it appears, is aware of her identity, and admits her to his ship in this disguise.[13] However, her borrowed garb proves of great service to her. Cormac Doil, as we know, was dispatched by Lorn in pursuit of the abbot's ship to recover the lady; he effects this, overtaking that ship the next morning; these pirates seize Edith, not, however, seemingly aware of her identity, *i.e.*, according to the word of Cormac Doil, which is not to be depended on. It certainly seems extraordinary that the pirates should have captured this apparent boy in minstrel garb, and held him to ransom, letting the abbot and the monks go free. Nevertheless, the abbot states that they captured the supposed boy, that he offered ransom for him, which was agreed to, but, ere the negotiations were concluded, a storm arose, which separated the abbot's ship from that of the pirates; these latter had the boy, together with his so-called "mother," Morag, on board their vessel. The abbot, who gives this account to Lorn, believes that the pirates' vessel was lost, and all drowned; this was indeed the case with Morag, and the fate of the others we know. Edith has now, by a happy chance, again met the man she loves; and how she obtains that love from him in return, we shall hear as the narrative proceeds.

We now reach the turning-point (in the poem) in the fortunes of the great Scottish king; though, as I have already shown, that point had already been passed before the event took place upon which I am now about to enter; but, at anyrate, after that event the fortunes of the Bruce improved by leaps and bounds. We no more see him a fugitive, hunted by, and h'ding from, his enemies; he now assumes the offensive, and his successes increase until they culminate in the crowning victory of Bannockburn.

To return to Bruce's party : they proceed towards the spot where they had left their boat, the king expressing a hope that the statement of the pirates regarding the departure of their ship was false.

Suddenly a bugle call rings out, followed by a loud shout,

(13) See Canto V., ver. 24.

which Bruce, to his astonishment, recognises as the voice of his brother Edward, whom he had believed to be well on his way to Ireland. Edward comes forward in a state of the greatest excitement. He exclaims—

> " What make ye here,
> Warring upon the mountain deer,
> When Scotland wants her King ? "

He relates that, on his way to Ireland, he has received news which bring him back to Scotland at full speed. Bruce's fleet has made its way safely to Brodick Bay, in the Isle of Arran, where—

> " Lennox, with a gallant band,
> Waits but thy coming and command
> To waft them o'er to Carrick strand." (14)

Other Scottish chiefs also are rising, Edward reports, in the cause of Bruce ; but the most important news of all is that of the death of their most formidable adversary, Edward I. of England—

> " There are blithe news !—but mark the close !
> Edward, the deadliest of our foes,
> As with his host he northward passed,
> Hath on the Borders breathed his last."

Bruce cannot avoid a feeling of great exultation at these news ; the liberation of Scotland now appears in view, but, at the same time, he feels regret at the death of one with whom he had been intimate in former days, and he does justice to the memory of the great monarch who has departed—

> " Now, Scotland ! shortly shalt thou see,
> With God's high will, thy children free,
>   And vengeance on thy foes !
> Yet to no sense of selfish wrongs,
> Bear witness with me, Heaven, belongs
>   My joy o'er Edward's bier ;
> I took my knighthood at his hand,
> And lordship held of him, and land,
>   And well may vouch it here,
> That, blot the story from his page
> Of Scotland ruined in his rage,
> You read a monarch brave and sage,
>   And to his people dear."

(14) See Canto III., ver. 9 ; also page 243 of treatise.

Edward Bruce is not so generous; in his usual fiery way, he declares that his hatred towards King Edward is as deep and enduring as that monarch's enmity towards Scotland. Bruce, however, rebukes him—

> " Let women, Edward, war with words,
> With curses monks, but men with swords :
> Nor doubt of living foes, to sate
> Deepest revenge and deadliest hate."

Bruce, in doing justice to the memory of King Edward, must have felt a twinge of conscience. It will be remembered that Bruce was only Scotch through the female line; he was a Norman baron, his ancestor having come over with the Conqueror; his claim to the Scottish throne came from his great-grandmother, daughter of David, Earl of Huntingdon, who was brother to William the Lion, King of Scotland.[15]   A descendant of the first baron, also through friendship with David I., King of Scotland, received the grant from that monarch of the lands of Annandale; Bruce's father also acquired the title of Earl of Carrick through marriage with the heiress of that fief.   The Bruces, therefore, held lands in Scotland, though also holding lands in England.

Bruce himself had been in the service of King Edward from his youth, and his record during this period is not good, as his biographer admits.   Twice did he swear fealty to that monarch, twice did he rebel, twice did he receive pardon.   He received many appointments from the king, and appears to have been treated by him with great consideration.[16]   His third revolt, accompanied by the murder of Comyn and his assumption of the Crown of Scotland, now renders his offence, in the eyes of Edward, unpardonable.   His biographer, Sir Herbert Maxwell, candidly says—"It is, in truth, a humiliating record, and it requires all the lustre of De Brus's subsequent achievements to efface the ugly details of it."   In fact, Bruce, like many other great men,

(15) The claims of John Balliol and of the Red Comyn (slain by Bruce) were superior to those of Bruce, the former being grandson of Isabella's elder sister, and the latter grandson of a sister of John Balliol.

(16) See Record on page 121, " Robert the Bruce," by Sir Herbert Maxwell.

greatly improves in character during the latter years of his life; the record of his later years far outshines those of his earlier ones. I hope to enter into the details of this before the conclusion of the treatise.

I think that the character of no monarch, until of late years, has been so underrated as that of Edward I., the great sovereign whose death I have just mentioned. In my childhood I was always led to regard him simply as a selfish, cruel tyrant; his subjugation of Wales, his attempt (partially successful) to subdue Scotland, were strongly condemned; [17] the supposed massacre of the Bards in Wales (since totally disproved) [18] was placed before me as a fact; Wallace and Bruce were perfect heroes, their faults being entirely suppressed; while the virtues of Edward, his statesmanship, his great qualities as a legislator (which latter obtained for him the name of the English Justinian), his other high attributes, which stamp him without doubt as the greatest of the Plantagenet kings, were placed in the background.

Among the people of Scotland, doubtless, the name of Edward was, and still is, the object of aversion, and we cannot blame them: he attempted to subdue their country; and although his motive was not that of selfish ambition, the mere acquiring of territory, but was owing to his far-sightedness in realising the great importance of the whole island being under the same ruler, nevertheless, it is not wonderful that the people he attempted to subdue should look with prejudice upon him, whatever his motive and whatever his good qualities may have been in other respects. Hume, however (a Scottish historian), admits him to be "the very model of a politic and warlike king," [19] and I think that the Scottish people, in general, are now beginning to re-

(17) It never occurred to these good people to condemn Henry V. for his attempt to obtain the Crown of France, to which he had no earthly right; nor was his motive as good as that of Edward's with respect to Scotland and Wales. The reason is not difficult to seek: Shakespeare's halo of romance surrounds Henry, while Edward is never mentioned.

(18) Here again comes in romance, and against Edward. See Gray's poem, " Ruin seize thee, ruthless king!"

(19) This comment, however, is, I think, given somewhat grudgingly; Edward was much more than that.

cognise the high qualities of their former enemy, while condemning his Scottish policy. Sir Herbert Maxwell, in the textbook which I have so often quoted, says—"From an English point of view, Edward was an ideal ruler for those times—a puissant knight, an experienced general, a kingly lawgiver." The same author also gives Edward credit for the motive by which he was actuated in his attempt to subdue Scotland; and altogether this Scottish writer gives a very fair estimate of the character of the great English king, concluding thus—"At this distance of time, Scotsmen may well afford to acknowledge that, if they had a splendid champion in Robert de Brus, they had a noble enemy in the first Edward." [20]

But it is the English people, my own countrymen, whom I condemn for their warped estimate (until of late years) of the character of one of our greatest sovereigns. I have shown how I was led to regard him in my childhood, and even, when studying with a tutor, I was led to believe that Edward's decision, when acting as arbiter for the disputed succession to the Crown of Scotland, was given in favour of Balliol, in place of Bruce (grandfather to King Robert), because he (Edward) thought the former would be easier to deal with than the latter. There seems to be no ground whatever for this suggestion; Edward appears to have entered very carefully into the matter,[21] and eventually decided in favour of Balliol, who was undoubtedly the rightful heir.[22] It was not until I was at Oxford, and had read a book, entitled, "The Greatest of the Plantagenets," and had also the privilege of attending lectures by the late Professor Goldwin Smith, that I began to appreciate the qualities of the great English king. Writers of late years, however, give a very fair estimate of Edward's character—both of his virtues and of his faults.

(20) "Robert the Bruce," by Sir H. Maxwell, Chap. VIII., pages 167 to 171.

(21) See "Edward Plantagenet," by Edward Jenks, M.A., Chap. X., "Scotland."

(22) See Note 15 to treatise. Also note that when Edward intimated the terms on which he was willing to act as arbiter, viz., that the Scottish barons should acknowledge him as their over-lord, Bruce, with the others, agreed at once; Balliol was the only one who hesitated. See above work.

Edward appears to have been possessed of a fiery, violent temper, and, when under its influence, to have been capable of harsh, even cruel, deeds. Submission and appeal for mercy, however, seem always to have entirely disarmed him; he is reported to have said, "No man ever kneeled to me in vain." The harsh side of his character appears more prominently in the last sixteen years of his life, which were years of great trial to him. The loss of his queen, Eleanor of Castile (his "Chère Reine"), in 1290, was a terrible blow to him. Then came the Scottish troubles, also troubles abroad, with the Church, and with his barons—"weary years of threefold strife," as one of his biographers terms this period.[23] The character and pursuits of his son (afterwards Edward II.) also troubled him greatly.

But the greatest trouble of all to Edward was that of Scotland; this it was that chiefly embittered the last days of his life. Over and over again had he imagined that country subdued; over and over again had they revolted as soon as his back was turned. The words on his tomb, "Scotorum Malleus; Pactum Serva," evidently refer to this; they intimate that, had the Scots kept faith with him, he would not have come down upon them with the heavy hand that he did, especially in the last year of his reign.

Indeed, the high qualities of this great monarch, as statesman and legislator, do not appear to have been properly appreciated by those over whom he ruled any more than the people of fifty years ago, as I have mentioned; and I recall the concluding words of that charming story by Miss Charlotte Yonge, "The Prince and the Page," in which the character of the great king is shown in a very high light. His relative, old Henry de Montfort (son of the great Simon), with his daughter and her husband, are depicted as standing before the tomb of the great Edward in Westminster Abbey. Henry comments on the high qualities of his royal relative, concluding with these words—"Alas, my cousin Edward! art thou indeed gone to Jerusalem,[24] and shall

(23) See "Edward I.," by Professor Tout, "Twelve English Statesmen" Series, Chap. XII.

(24) Edward is mentioned in the story as constantly expressing his intention to proceed on a crusade to Palestine as soon as all troubles were settled at home.

I follow thee there? Alack, that the Scottish temptation came between thee and the brightness of thy glory! Let us pray for the peace of his soul, my children, for a greater and better man lies there than England knows or heeds."

To return to our heroes. The good news which they have received at once determines Bruce as to his future course of action. He will at once sail for the Isle of Arran—

> "Hold we our way for Arran first,
> Where meet in arms our friends dispersed;
> Lennox the loyal, De la Haye,
> And Boyd the bold in battle fray."

Bruce then inquires of Ronald whether the latter will accompany him, or stay behind to raise his Islesmen; the chief replies that he himself will not leave the king's side, but, as they have two ships, he proposes to send his own to arouse the Islesmen and gather them to Arran. This is agreed to, and the adventurers embark, having first removed the body of the murdered boy, Allan.

The voyage of the ship bound for Arran is described in the usual glowing language of Scott; there is a joyous tone in the description, agreeing, doubtless, with the feelings of the voyagers, whose hearts are lightened by the good news which they have just received. The account of this voyage is, I think, one of the most beautiful parts of the poem—

> "Merrily, merrily, bounds the bark,
>   She bounds before the gale,
> The mountain breeze from Ben-na-darch
>   Is joyous in her sail!
> With fluttering sound like laughter hoarse,
>   The cords and canvas strain,
> The waves, divided by her force,
> In rippling eddies chased her course,
>   As if they laughed again.
> Not down the breeze more blithely flew,
> Skimming the wave, the light sea-mew,
>   Than that gay galley bore
> Her course upon that favouring wind,
> And Coolin's crest has sunk behind,
>   And Slapin's caverned shore."

They leave the Isle of Skye behind, but not without their rousing, by signal, the clansmen of "Sleat and Skaith," who are under Ronald's chieftainship, with instructions to join the main force in Brodick Bay, Arran.

The ship proceeds on its course, giving similar signals to the different islands as it passes—

> "Merrily, merrily, goes the bark
> On a breeze from the northward free,
> So shoots through the morning sky the lark,
> Or the swan through the summer sea.
> The shores of Mull on the eastward lay,
> And Ulva dark and Colonsay,[25]
> And all the group of islets gay
> That guard famed Staffa [26] round.
> Then all unknown its columns rose,
> Where dark and undisturbed repose
> The cormorant had found,
> And the shy seal had quiet home,
> And weltered in that wondrous dome,
> Where, as to shame the temples decked
> By skill of earthly architect,
> Nature herself, it seemed, would raise
> A Minster to her Maker's praise!"

Our heroes proceed on, signalling to their confederates in the different islands, and rousing them to assist in the general cause—[27]

> "Merrily, merrily, goes the bark,
> Before the gale she bounds;
> So darts the dolphin from the shark,
> Or the deer before the hounds.
> They left Loch-Tua on their lee,
> And they wakened the men of the wild Tiree,
> And the Chief of the sandy Coll;

(25) The "Colonsay" here mentioned must be "Little Colonsay," which lies about two miles south of the island of Ulva.

(26) I have so often taken the steamer round from Oban *via* Staffa and Iona (a round of the island of Mull) that this portion of the poem appeals to me more than any other. Often have I landed in Staffa, and the account in the poem describes the place in a truly graphic manner.

(27) This reminds us of the course of the "Fiery Cross" in "The Lady of the Lake."

> They paused not at Columba's isle,[28]
> Though pealed the bells from the holy pile,
>   With long and measured toll;
> No time for matin or for mass,
> And the sounds of the holy summons pass
>   Away in the billows' roll."

Our travellers now skirt the southern shore of the island of Mull, rousing "Loch Buie's fierce and warlike lord," and then strike due south for the islands of Islay and Jura, which are also within the call of Lord Ronald; also Scarba, to the north of Jura—

> "And Scarba's isle, whose tortured shore
> Still rings to Corrievreken's roar,[29]
> And lonely Colonsay."

They now proceed, doubtless, through the Strait of Islay, which runs between that island and that of Jura, and thence across to West Loch Tarbert, which pierces the peninsula of Cantyre. They avoid rounding that peninsula, for fear of meeting a hostile fleet; and they therefore proceed to the head of West Loch Tarbert, and from thence drag their vessel (by portage, as would be said in Canada) across the peninsula to Tarbert, on Loch Fyne, the distance being barely a mile.[30] Here they launch their vessel again, and steer towards the island of Arran, which now boldly rises from the sea in front of them.

The island of Arran presents a grand appearance on approaching it from the sea. It appears to be a mass of mountains, over which towers Goat Fell, the highest point in the island. Scott terms this mountain "Ben Ghoil, the Mountain of the Wind"—

> "The sun ere yet he sunk behind
> Ben-Ghoil, 'The Mountain of the Wind,'
> Gave his grim peaks a greeting kind,
>   And bade Loch Ranza smile."

Towards this beautiful arm of the sea (Loch Ranza) the travellers are now steering their course.

(28) Iona.

(29) The Strait of Corrievreken lies between the north part of the island of Jura and that of Scarba.

(30) I have myself walked across it.

Before they land, a conversation takes place between Bruce and Ronald. The latter makes a formal demand to the king for the hand of his sister, Isabel. He pleads that the flight of Edith from Artornish Castle, and the declaration of Lorn before the assembled chiefs that the marriage contract was at an end,[31] has freed him from any obligation towards the family of Lorn.[32] Bruce replies ambiguously, as might be expected, saying that he could not vouch for his sister's feelings in this matter, and as to the dissolution of Ronald's former marriage contract, this was a matter for the Church to decide. The king adds, however, that Isabel is now residing at the little convent of St. Bride, near Loch Ranza, where she will remain while the war lasts; to her there, therefore, will he submit Ronald's suit—

> " There, sent by Edward, she must stay,
> Till fate shall give more prosperous day;
> And thither will I bear thy suit,
> Nor will thine advocate be mute." [33]

They little deem who was overhearing this conversation; the supposed boy is standing beside them in speechless grief—

> " He stooped his head against the mast,
> And bitter sobs came thick and fast,
> A grief that would not be repressed,
> But seemed to burst his youthful breast."

This is no wonder! Terrible must it have been to Edith thus to hear the man whom she loves pleading for the hand of another. It is wonderful that this outburst did not suggest to Bruce and the others the true sex of this supposed boy.

They have no suspicion, however, and Edward Bruce,

(31) Canto III., ver. 3.

(32) Scott does not mention the circumstances under which this marriage was arranged. I have given my own conjecture on the subject on page 298 of the treatise. Also see Edith's words in Canto I., ver. 10.

(33) Scott in this poem often does not enter into details clearly. We left the Lady Isabel proceeding to Ireland under escort of her brother Edward. She is evidently not with the party now. How, then, did she reach Arran before them? The only solution is, that Edward sent her there in that boat from Lennox which " crossed their track," on their way to Ireland, bearing the welcome news before mentioned. See Canto IV., ver. 3.

roughly, though with kindly intent, rallies the boy on his weakness, and offers to take him with him as his page. Bruce, however, intervenes; he sees well that the boy is not fitted for that rough kind of life; [34] it would be better for him to tend their sister Isabel in her cell at St. Bride's. To this Edward at once acquiesces.

They now reach the shore, and proceed to land; and here occurs a well-known historical incident. [35] The king winds his horn thrice; his adherents, Douglas, De la Haye, and Lennox are in the neighbourhood, hunting a stag. Boyd joins them in haste, declaring that the enemy are upon them. Douglas, however, knows the call well, and soon reassures him—

> " ' Not so,' replied the good Lord James,
> ' That blast no English bugle claims.
> Oft have I heard it fire the fight,
> Cheer the pursuit, or stop the flight.
> Dead were my heart, and deaf mine ear,
> If Bruce should call, nor Douglas hear!
> Each to Loch Ranza's margin spring,
> That blast was winded by the King!' ''

The tidings spread fast, and the warriors and others assembled in the island hurry to the shore and give the king an enthusiastic greeting—

> "Around their King regained they pressed,
> Wept, shouted, clasped him to their breast,
> And young and old, and serf and lord,
> And he who ne'er unsheathed a sword,
> And he in many a peril tried,
> Alike resolved the brunt to bide,
> And live or die by Bruce's side!"

Bruce and his brother are deeply moved by this enthusiastic reception, each in his own way—

> "And blame ye then the Bruce, if trace
> Of tear is on his manly face,

(34) Edith, however, is quite capable of undergoing such hardship, as we shall shortly see.

(35) This incident seems, however, to have taken place at Brodick, not at Loch Ranza. See Sir H. Maxwell's " Robert the Bruce," Chap. VII., page 146.

> When, scanty relics of the train
> That hailed at Scone his early reign,
> This patriot band around him hung,
> And to his knees and bosom clung ?—
> Blame ye the Bruce ?—his brother blamed,
> But shared the weakness, while ashamed,
> With haughty laugh his head he turned,
> And dashed away the tear he scorned."

The following morning, Bruce, attended by the mute page, proceeds to St. Bride's convent, to interview his sister, Isabel, who had evidently arrived here in the "bark from Lennox," which had "crossed the track" of Edward Bruce on his way to Ireland, bearing the welcome news already mentioned.[36]

An aged sister reports to Lady Isabel that a princely knight, attended only by a single page, desires to see her. The lady is at first inclined to refuse, being unwilling to give audience to a stranger, but, on the sister's describing the princely mien of the visitor—

> "The form, the eye, the word,
> The bearing of that stranger Lord,"

Isabel is convinced that it is no other than her brother, the Bruce, who stands before the door—

> "'Enough, enough,' the Princess cried,
> '' 'Tis Scotland's hope, her joy, her pride.'"

Bruce is, therefore, instantly admitted; after the first affectionate greetings, the king expresses his regret that his misfortunes have brought his sister to the poor abode of a convent cell, but Isabel reassures him at once; she has gloried in sharing his dangers, and thoroughly approves his great attempt to liberate his country, but she adds that she has now entirely made up her mind to retire to the seclusion of a convent. Bruce, in reply, submits Ronald's suit—

> "Nay, Isabel, for such stern choice,
> First wilt thou wait thy brother's voice;
> Then ponder if in convent scene
> No softer thoughts might intervene—

(36) See Canto IV., ver. 3.

> Say they were of that unknown Knight,
> Victor in Woodstock's tourney-fight—
> Nay, if his name such blush you owe,
> Victorious o'er a fairer foe!" (37)

The princess, indeed, shows some signs of conscious feeling, but speedily recovers herself, and answers steadily—

> "I guess my brother's meaning well;
> For not so silent is the cell,
> But we have heard the Islesmen all
> Arm in thy cause at Ronald's call,
> And my eye proves that Knight Unknown
> And the brave Island Lord are one.—
> Had then his suit been earlier made,
> In his own name, with thee to aid,
> (But that his plighted faith forbade,)
> I know not—But thy Page so near ?—
> This is no tale for menial's ear."

Bruce reassures her, saying that the boy had saved his life, was perfectly trustworthy, and was also dumb, and that he proposed to place him in the convent to attend upon Isabel. He then again urges her to give an answer to Ronald's suit. She answers very firmly, with a refusal. Though, as has been seen, she has some tender feelings for Ronald, she also has sympathy towards Edith, whom she considers as still plighted to the Island chief, who, she also thinks, has not treated her (Edith) well—

> "If further press his suit—then say,
> He should his plighted troth obey,
> Troth plighted both with ring and word,
> And sworn on crucifix and sword."

She even reproaches her brother with his support of Ronald—

> "And wilt thou now deny thine aid
> To an oppressed and injured maid,
> E'en plead for Ronald's perfidy,
> And press his fickle faith on me ?"

(37) This is, I think, the first time in the poem where it is mentioned under what circumstances Ronald met Isabel. This is another instance of Scott's lack of detail in this poem.

She concludes that she will spurn any proffer that Ronald might make until he brought the ring and spousal contract from Edith, thus releasing him from his former troth—

> " I'd spurn each proffer he could bring,
> Till at my feet he laid the ring,
> The ring and spousal contract both,
> And fair acquittal of his oath,
> By her who brooks his perjured scorn,
> The ill-requited Maid of Lorn ! "

This noble and generous avowal has a thrilling effect upon Edith. Forgetting her disguise, she springs forward and flings herself upon Isabel's neck, then, recollecting herself, she kneels down, kisses Isabel's hand, and quits the cell.

Here, again, it is strange that this burst of feeling does not reveal the truth to either Bruce or Isabel, but neither suspect, and the latter is naturally indignant at the freedom of the supposed page.

Bruce now again urges his sister to consider well before committing herself to a monastic life; Isabel, however, repeats her decision, related above, adding that, even if Ronald should become free of his troth, she by no means commits herself as to changing her decision to enter the convent cell.

King Robert, therefore, takes his leave, acquainting his sister with his intention of recovering, if possible, their ancestral home of Turnberry, on the Carrick coast. He then leaves the convent, and returns to his camp.

We have now reached the fifth canto of the poem, in which is described the expedition of Bruce to recover Turnberry Castle, on the coast of Ayrshire, the seat of the Earls of Carrick, Bruce's ancestral home, and said to be his birthplace.[38] According to the poem, this expedition is successful, but, according to actual fact, all that Bruce accomplished was to attack and drive in the English outposts, stationed outside the castle. In fact, he had but 300 men,[39] and, with this small force,

---

(38) Bruce's father married the Countess of Carrick, thence receiving the title of Earl of Carrick.

(39) According to the poem, 5,400 men. See Canto V., ver. 11.

he could not accomplish the reduction of the fortress; but, having collected what spoil and arms he could, retreated into the hill country of Carrick.[40] Also, in the poem, Clifford (to whom, as will be remembered, Lorn intended to bestow the hand of his sister Edith) is represented as being the governor of the castle and being slain there, which was not the case, as Clifford was actually slain at Bannockburn. Percy was, in reality, the governor; and Lorn, also, is described as having been present, which was not the case. Scott acknowledges these misstatements, saying that he was following "a flattering and pleasing tradition." [41]

Bruce, therefore, having made up his mind to make the attempt, determines to move his force from Loch Ranza to Brodick Bay, where his fleet lies, it being the most convenient spot in the island, both for the harbourage of the ships and for its position, being on the eastward coast of Arran, facing the Ayrshire coast. At early dawn, then, Bruce's bugle rouses his men, and they start immediately for Brodick Bay—

> "At dawn a bugle signal, made
> By their bold Lord, their ranks arrayed;
> Up sprung the spears through bush and tree,
> No time for benedicite!"

We cannot take leave of Loch Ranza without quoting the beautiful opening lines of the fifth canto of our poem, which, as Baddeley says, are "too faithful a piece of word-painting for us to attempt an original one"—

> "On fair Loch Ranza streamed the early day,
>   Thin wreaths of cottage-smoke are upward curled
> From the lone hamlet, which her inland bay
>   And circling mountains sever from the world.
> And there the fisherman his sail unfurled,
>   The goat-herd drove his kids to steep Ben-Ghoil,
> Before the hut the dame her spindle twirled,
>   Courting the sunbeam as she plied her toil,—
> For, wake where'er he may, Man wakes to care and coil."

(40) Sir H. Maxwell's "Robert the Bruce," Chap. VII., page 148.

(41) See Canto V., note to ver. 33.

Before, however, following in the steps of Bruce and his party, we must return for a short space to the convent, where Bruce had that morning dispatched the young page, Amadine, *i.e.*, the changeling, as the pirates had termed their captive.

The Lady Isabel, on conclusion of her early devotions, sees a ring of gold, with a scroll attached, addressed to her, on the floor of her cell. She opens it and, with astonishment, reads the following words—

> " 'Twas with this ring his plight he swore,
> With this his promise I restore;
> To her who can the heart command,
> Well may I yield the plighted hand.
> And O ! for better fortune born,
> Grudge not a passing sigh to mourn
> Her who was Edith once of Lorn ! "

For a moment, Isabel cannot suppress a natural feeling of joy, but the next moment she reproaches herself for it. She then wonders how the missive had been placed in her cell; looking from the window, she perceives marks as if some one had climbed up the ivied buttress outside. She calls the old sister, Mona, and asks her if any stranger had entered the convent that morning. Mona replies that she had only seen the dumb page, whom Bruce had brought to the convent the day before, and that he seemed to be hurrying away—

> "I prayed him pass
> To chapel, where they said the mass;
> But like an arrow he shot by,
> And tears seemed bursting from his eye."

The truth flashes upon Isabel at once; the dumb page is no other than Edith herself. She begs Mona at once to go to Bruce and ask him to come to her, bringing the mute page with him. Mona replies that Bruce's party had left early that morning, she believes, for Brodick Bay—

> "Across the isle—of barks a score
> Lie there, 'tis said, to waft them o'er,
> On sudden news, to Carrick shore."

Isabel, on this, at once summons a devoted friend of hers in the convent, one Father Augustin, and dispatches him with a message to Bruce, begging the latter to give the page, Amadine, into the latter's charge, to be brought back to her. She fears that Bruce and his party may be on the point of sailing, so urges the priest to hasty dispatch—

> "Away, good father!—take good heed
> That life and death are on thy speed."

The good priest loses no time, but proceeds on his journey, following in the tracks of the force that had left that morning. He doubtless follows the course where the coach road now runs, from Loch Ranza to Corrie, on the east coast of the island—a lovely drive, which I well remember taking myself, from Corrie to Loch Ranza. The distance between these two places is nine miles, Brodick being about five miles to the south of Corrie. A terrible tramp for an old man, especially as the travelling must have been very different from what it is now—

> "Heavy and dull the foot of age,
> And rugged was the pilgrimage;
> But none was there beside, whose care
> Might such important message bear.
> Through birchen copse he wandered slow
> Stunted and sapless, thin and low;
> By many a mountain stream he passed,
> From the tall cliffs in tumult cast,
> Dashing to foam their waters dun,
> And sparkling in the summer sun."

Towards evening he reaches his destination, and finds Brodick Bay in a state of great animation; Bruce and his troops are preparing to start on their expedition to Carrick.

The good father seeks out Bruce, and delivers his message; the king replies that he had already sent the boy to the convent that morning, with orders to remain there. The priest answers that the boy had indeed been there, but had only stayed a short time. Edward Bruce now interposes, and says that he had seen the youth, at early dawn, at the convent, and that he (Edward), wishing, in accordance with Bruce's orders, to send a messenger over to Carrick to the Bruce's old retainer, Cuthbert, to find out whether the English garrison was unprepared for the contemplated attack, and, if so, to light a fire on the Carrick coast, offered the enterprise to the boy, who had accepted eagerly, and at once embarked, leaving with a favourable wind; and Edwards now remarks that the youth had well fulfilled his mission, for a beacon is already kindled on the Carrick coast.[42] Bruce rebukes his brother for thus dispatching this weak boy on such a dangerous errand—

> "On a part
> Of such deep danger to employ
> A mute, an orphan, and a boy!
> Unfit for flight, unfit for strife,
> Without a tongue to plead for life!"

Bruce, however, does not give Edith (as the supposed boy) credit for the courage and endurance which she really, as we shall see, possessed.[43]

Bruce then asks Father Augustin to bear these tidings to Isabel, assuring her that the page shall be restored as soon as possible, Ronald also adding that he will take the page under his especial charge—a strange upshot of events. Then, with the final blessing from the priest, Bruce gives the order to embark.

The force which Bruce is here described as having under his command is made out by Scott to be far stronger than it really was; there are thirty barks, each containing 180 men—the total would thus be about 5,400 men; and Scott adds—

> "With such small force did Bruce at last
> The die for death or empire cast!"

(42) Scott rather leads us to imagine that Turnberry is opposite to Brodick; in reality it lies about twenty-five miles to the south-east of the Isle of Arran, and is a little to the north of Ailsa Craig. As a matter of fact, they could not possibly have seen a light at Turnberry from Brodick Bay, for the land lies between; it could only have been seen from higher ground.

(43) It is, however, extremely improbable that Edward would have chosen such a messenger on such a dangerous errand. The boy had shown no fitness for it; in fact, there was every token about him of not only physical but mental weakness. In short, he showed no signs of manliness whatever. The voyage alone would be danger enough for a weak boy in an open boat. Turnberry, as I said, is twenty-five miles from Brodick Bay, and would be much farther from Loch Ranza. This is one of the several weak points in the poem, to which I so often draw notice.

As a matter of historical fact, Bruce had only 300 men; the attempt was unsuccessful; and he had many hardships yet to undergo before fortune smiled upon him.

They are quickly embarked, and, as they glide away—

> "Mingled with the dashing tide,
> Their murmuring voices distant died."

Father Augustin extends his hands, and delivers to them his final blessing—

> "'God speed them!' said the priest, as dark
> On distant billows glides each bark;
> 'O Heaven! when swords for freedom shine,
> And monarch's right, the cause is thine!
> Edge doubly every patriot blow!
> Beat down the banners of the foe!
> And be it to the nations known,.
> That Victory is from God alone!'"

The expedition proceeds on its way, gradually approaching the Carrick coast, with that wonderful beacon light to guide them. They imagine that it has been kindled by the page, Amadine, but they find later that in this they are mistaken—

> "As less and less the distance grows,
> High and more high the beacon rose;
> The light, that seemed a twinkling star,
> Now blazed portentous, fierce, and far."

There is a great mystery about this beacon light. Cuthbert, Bruce's retainer, had not kindled it, and he feared that it might be a trick to lead the king to his destruction; he, therefore (according to history), met the latter on his landing to warn him, or (according to the poem) sent the dumb page to do so. Sir H. Maxwell [44] considers it to be a "chance blaze," caused by the burning of the heather, this being the period of the "muirburn." This is probably the correct solution, but there seems to have been a tradition that the fire was lighted by supernatural power, and that the flame rose yearly, on the same night and at the same hour. [45] Howbeit, as Sir Walter Scott says—

(44) "Robert the Bruce," page 148.

(45) Canto V., note to ver. 17.

> " But whether beam celestial, lent
> By Heaven to aid the King's descent,
> Or fire hell-kindled from beneath,
> To lure him to defeat and death,
> Or were it but some meteor strange,
> Of such as oft through midnight range,
> Startling the traveller late and lone,
> I know not—and it ne'er was known."

Be it as it may, this wonderful light brightens the course of our adventurers as they approach the strand and disembark; then, just as they effect a landing, it suddenly dies away, probably on account of fresh gorse being thrown on the pile. But the invaders, however, look upon this sudden darkness in a supernatural light, and comments pass between them; Bruce, however, checks their talk and forms his force upon the beach, now, though that strange light had vanished, brightened by the rising of the moon.

And now the dumb page, who has arrived in safety, appears and hands the king a scroll from Cuthbert, who knows as little of the fire as the invaders do, and sends the boy to warn them of possible danger. Bruce reads the scroll, and finds in it bad news. Clifford's force is strong and quite prepared, and has lately been joined by a reinforcement, headed by Lorn himself; the country is in a state of deep depression, under the hand of the invader. On hearing this news, Bruce consults his leaders as to what course they should adopt. Should they hide in the woods for a time, or should they re-embark ? The answer from all is unanimous : there must be no retreat, the attempt must be made. Bruce, evidently relieved by their decision, at once acquiesces; they must take shelter in the meantime, and watch for a favourable opportunity.

They advance, therefore, further towards the castle, keeping under cover of the forest, and Ronald, according to his former promise, takes charge of the dumb page, and assists him up the rocky path—

> " Now cheer thee, simple Amadine !
> Why throbs that silly heart of thine ?
> . . . .

> Dost thou not rest thee on my arm ?
> Do not my plaid-folds hold thee warm ?
> Hath not the wild bull's treble hide
> This targe for thee and me supplied ?
> Is not Clan-Colla's sword of steel ?
> And, trembler, canst thou terror feel ?
> Cheer thee, and still that throbbing heart;
> From Ronald's guard thou shalt not part."

The chief little guesses whom he is thus supporting, and the feelings of the supposed page are past describing. They are not those of fear, for Edith has already shown her great courage in thus undertaking a lonely voyage of some forty miles in the cause of the man she loves; and her equally strong, but passive, courage under other circumstances she is yet, and soon, to show. They are very mingled feelings, but love predominates all; and I cannot explain them better than in the words of the poet, described in the following lines, which speak for themselves—

> "O ! many a shaft, at random sent,
> Finds mark the archer little meant !
> And many a word, at random spoken,
> May soothe or wound a heart that's broken !
> Half soothed, half grieved, half terrified,
> Close drew the page to Ronald's side;
> A wild, delirious thrill of joy
> Was in that hour of agony,
> As up the steepy pass he strove,
> Fear, toil, and sorrow, lost in love !"

The invaders have climbed the rocks above the coast, and enter the chase, a large park, interspersed with woods, which lay all around the castle, but which has now entirely disappeared, its place being occupied by the modern golf course. The castle itself, like that of Artornish, is now a mere ruin.

By the time the party has reached this spot, the powers of the mute page begin to fail. It is no wonder; he has endured a voyage of some forty miles, besides the exertions after landing; Ronald attempts to cheer him on, inflicting, unknowingly, a terrible mental wound as he does so—

> "Pass but this night, and pass thy care,
> I'll place thee with a lady fair,
> Where thou shalt tune thy lute to tell
> How Ronald loves fair Isabel !"

At this cruel thrust, added on to his weakness, the powers of Amadine's endurance entirely fail him; he quits his hold of Ronald, and falls to the ground, utterly worn out. Ronald is in a dilemma; he does not like to leave the boy, but he cannot desert his post; fortunately, he sees a hollow tree, where he places the weary page, leaving his plaid to wrap him round—

> "I will not be, believe me, far;
> But must not quit the ranks of war.
> Well will I mark the bosky bourne,
> And soon, to guard thee hence, return."

He, therefore, pursues his way with the troops, leaving the supposed boy behind, who now meets with an adventure which nearly costs him his life.

He has sobbed himself to sleep, when he is suddenly discovered by a party of the garrison, who are in chase of a deer. They recognise the boy, having seen him visit Cuthbert that day, but appear not to have molested him then. Obtaining no reply from him as to what brought him there, they imagine he is feigning dumbness, which was indeed the case, and declare their intention of taking him before their lord, who may soon remedy that—

> "Our Lord may choose the rack should teach
> To this young lurcher use of speech."

They convey, therefore, the supposed boy to the castle, but, on account of his weakness, do not bind him.

Lorn, Edith's brother, is, as we have heard, now staying with Clifford, the governor of the castle, to whom he has brought a reinforcement, which shows that they are evidently prepared for a possible attack from Bruce. It will be remembered that Lorn, after breaking off the contract with Ronald, had declared his intention of bestowing the hand of his sister upon Clifford.

These two nobles are now conversing in the courtyard of the castle, and the subject of their conversation is Edith herself, who now overhears it. Lorn is relating to his companion the account of Edith's escape with the abbot, and her subsequent death by drowning, as is supposed.[46] Her heartless brother concludes—

(46) See page 250 of this treatise.

"So let it be, with the disgrace
And scandal of her lofty race!
Thrice better she had ne'er been born,
Than brought her infamy on Lorn!"

Lord Clifford [47] now perceives the captive, and inquires who he is; the men reply that he is a spy, whom they had found lurking in a hollow oak. Clifford, without further question, orders them to hang the boy at once, but, noticing the plaid the prisoner wears, which Ronald had left with him, he asks Lorn if that plaid had any connection with him, and if the boy should be spared on that account. Lorn, glancing indifferently at the prisoner (at his dress, fortunately, not at his face), recognises the Clan Colla tartan, and disclaims all connection with it. [48] He supports Clifford in his intention of hanging the boy at once, unless the latter had any important information, which he might be tempted to divulge to avoid death. Poor Edith, thus condemned to death by her own brother, cannot help murmuring, "O brother! cruel to the last!"

So they lead her forth to her death, playing the "dirge of Clan Colla," and here the most noble traits of the girl's character manifest themselves. All her weakness is now gone; rather than betray the man she loves, she will gladly lay down her life. Her courage, her devotion, now stand forth gloriously—

"Love, strong as death, his heart hath steeled,
His nerves hath strung—he will not yield!
Since that poor breath, that little word,
May yield Lord Ronald to the sword."

They have reached the destined spot, beneath the bough of an oak; the executioner is by the captive's side, the rope is around her neck, the death agony is upon her, but, in that last moment rescue is at hand.

Bruce's party have now reached this point, and are lying under cover. They hear the death dirge, and Ronald, looking

(47) Such is the title Scott gives him in the poem; he was really Sir Robert de Clifford.

(48) In fact, it is evidently Ronald's clan, and with him Lorn was now at enmity.

forth from the bushes, sees the page being led to death. He is about to rush forth to the rescue, when Bruce checks him. Not a hair of the boy's head shall fall, the king assures him; only let him wait a few minutes, until a party be sent out to cut off that of the garrison from retreat to the castle. Bruce then orders Douglas, with 50 men, to make circuit, placing themselves between the garrison party and the castle, and to hold up a spear over the bushes as soon as they are posted. He also orders his brother Edward, with 40 men, to approach the castle gates under cover, and, when he hears the sound of battle, to rush forward, secure the drawbridge, force the gate, and hold the courtyard.[49]   Bruce himself, with the remainder of his force, will advance slowly, until he sees the signal from Douglas.

Ronald's feelings are terrible during this delay; he can scarcely contain himself as the death party approaches the fatal tree. They have assembled beneath it, the last moment of the captive is at hand, when the expected signal is seen above the bushes—

> "'Now, noble Chief! I leave thee loose;
> Upon them, Ronald!' said the Bruce."

The attack now commences in all quarters with the greatest fury; the party of the garrison now outside the castle is evidently a large one, and they are here attacked on both sides—

> "'The Bruce, the Bruce!' to well-known cry
> His native rocks and woods reply.
> 'The Bruce, the Bruce!' in that dread word
> The knell of hundred deaths was heard.
> The astonished Southern [50] gazed at first,
> Where the wild tempest was to burst,
> That waked in that presaging name.
> Before, behind, around it came!
> Half-armed, surprised, on every side
> Hemmed in, hewed down, they bled and died.

(49) Scott now writes as if Bruce had only the 300 men he actually had; he might have spared a considerably greater number of men for these two detached parties, his force being, according to the poem, above 5,000 men. See page 263 of the treatise.

(50) These, however, are more likely to be Lorn's men than English; the fresh reinforcement would probably be quartered outside the castle, and, in this case, all the more deadly would be the conflict.

> Deep in the ring the Bruce engaged,
> And fierce Clan-Colla's broadsword raged!
> Full soon the few who fought were sped,
> Nor better was their lot who fled,
> And met, 'mid terror's wild career,
> The Douglas's redoubted spear!
> Two hundred yeomen on that morn
> The castle left, and none return."

During the conflict, Ronald has rescued the captive, who, while he tends her, nearly reveals herself.

While Bruce is thus obtaining unqualified success, a harder task awaits Edward. Impatient as ever, he has attacked the castle gates before the signal is given—

> "Upon the bridge his strength he threw,
> And struck the iron chain in two
>   By which its planks arose;
> The warder next his axe's edge
> Struck down upon the threshold ledge,
> 'Twixt door and post a ghastly wedge!
>   The gate they may not close."

A desperate fight ensues; a desperate resistance is offered, but Edward, now reinforced by Bruce's victorious party, forces his way in. Fearful is the slaughter—

> "Mad with success, and drunk with gore,
> They drive the struggling foe before,
>   And ward on ward they win.
> Unsparing was the vengeful sword,
> And limbs were lopped and life-blood poured,
> The cry of death and conflict roared,
>   And fearful was the din!'"

The garrison is utterly routed; Clifford is slain by Ronald, while Lorn manages, with a few men, to escape to his ship, which is moored below the castle, and clears off.

Great rejoicings now take place on the occasion of Bruce's recovering his ancestral hall; a hearty welcome is given by the king to all his followers, and his joy is manifest at being once more within the home of his childhood. He forgets not, however, to render due thanks to Heaven for his victory. He orders the "mazers four," or drinking cups, to be brought—

> " Thrice let them circle round the board,
> The pledge, fair Scotland's rights restored ! "

He then gives orders to send messengers throughout the country, to " arouse old friends, and gather new "—

> " Call all, call all ! from Reedswair-path
> To the wild confines of Cape Wrath ;
> Wide let the news through Scotland ring,
> The Northern Eagle claps his wing ! "

I have already mentioned the actual facts of Bruce's Carrick expedition ; [51] in the poem, it is looked upon as the turning-point in the monarch's career ; it was not so in reality. After his failure here, Bruce retired to the hill country of Carrick, and was a hunted fugitive for some time afterwards. The actual turning-point in his career was the battle of Loudon Hill, where he defeated the Earl of Pembroke. This battle took place shortly before the death of Edward I., which latter event, therefore, occurred after—not before—the Carrick expedition, as stated in the poem. Scott honestly owns that his account is not strictly historical, and he relates the attack in the poem in his most beautiful style, but I confess I greatly dislike seeing historical facts warped, whether in novel, drama, or poem. [52]

Nevertheless, wherever the turning-point in the career of the great monarch took place, the end was the same ; and into this we are now about to enter.

The events of the first five cantos of the poem take place in the year 1307, and embrace the period from Bruce's return from Ireland up to the death of Edward I., though, as I have shown, the different events are not mentioned in their strictly historical order. There is a lapse of seven years from the end of the fifth canto to the beginning of the sixth, which latter canto commences in 1314, the year of Bannockburn, the description of which great battle is the principal subject of the canto.

(51) See page 263 of the treatise.

(52) Many writers are not so honest as Scott. Shakespeare is a most flagrant example of scamping history ; what he writes regarding historical facts is utterly unreliable. But the most flagrant example of all is that of Miss Porter, in the " Scottish Chiefs," where the authoress makes Edward I. defeated at Bannockburn, and dying of chagrin at Carlisle afterwards. Lord Lytton, on the other hand, is very careful ; see his preface to " The Last of the Barons."

The events of these seven years may be related in a few words. After the death of Edward I., the English grip on Scotland gradually slackened. Edward II. was a very different man to his great father. Although possessed, personally, of many amiable qualities, he was of a weak, irresolute nature, and totally unfitted for a throne, at anyrate in such a period as that with which we are now dealing. He cared little about retaining his hold on Scotland, or even for the welfare of his own country; all he cared for was the society of his unworthy favourites. He disregarded his father's injunctions to carry on the Scottish war to the utmost.[53] He advanced as far as Cumnock, in Ayrshire, then withdrew his army from Scotland, and he himself returned to London. The first years of his reign were occupied with quarrels between, on the one side, himself and his unworthy favourite, Piers Gaveston, and, on the other, the English barons. This ended in the triumph of the latter, and the execution of the favourite. During this period, Edward had indeed made one or two desultory invasions of Scotland, but they came to nothing, Bruce adopting the usual Scottish policy of refusing battle and wasting the country before the invader, thus starving him out and forcing him to retire.

On the other hand, the fortunes of Bruce had increased year by year in his favour. The battle of Loudon Hill and the death of Edward I. were the "turn of the tide" for him. Year after year he made progress; town after town in Scotland fell before him. At length, in the memorable year 1314, Stirling was the only fortress still in English hands—

"Such news o'er Scotland's hills triumphant rode,
    When 'gainst the invaders turned the battle's scale,
When Bruce's banner had victorious flowed
    O'er Loudon's mountain and in Ury's vale;
When English blood oft deluged Douglas-dale,
    And fiery Edward routed stout St. John,
When Randloph's war-cry swelled the southern gale,
    And many a fortress, town, and tower was won,
And Fame still sounded forth fresh deeds of glory done."

(53) Edward I. is said to have given orders that after his death his flesh should be boiled, and his bones carried into Scotland before the army. This mandate was disregarded by his son; and Bruce is reported to have said that he feared the bones of Edward I. more than the living body of Edward II.

The castle of Stirling was now being closely invested by a Scottish force, under Edward Bruce, and the garrison were becoming in danger of starvation; and Sir Philip de Mowbray, the governor, made an arrangement with Edward Bruce that he would deliver up the castle if he were not relieved before Midsummer Day—

> "Of all the Scottish conquests made
> By the first Edward's ruthless blade,
> His son retained no more,
> Northward of Tweed, but Stirling's towers,
> Beleaguered by King Robert's powers;
> And they took terms of truce,
> If England's King should not relieve
> The siege ere John the Baptist's eve,
> To yield them to the Bruce."

King Robert was greatly displeased with his brother for making this agreement; he believed that it would bring on a formidable invasion from England, which he was anxious to avoid at present, if possible; events turned out as he expected. Edward Bruce is reported to have replied, "Let the King of England bring all the men he has; we will fight them and more." "Be it so," answered the king; "we will abide the battle like men." [54]

But before proceeding with the events of the ensuing campaign, we must turn to those of the poem, and inquire into the doings of the different characters of that work.

After the capture of Turnberry Castle, Bruce returns the dumb page to the care of his sister Isabel at the convent of St. Bride; and there Edith remains, having resumed the dress of her sex, up to the period at which we have now arrived. Isabel, princess no longer, has, with Bruce's consent, assumed the veil and convent vows. Lorn has fled to England, and died there; Edith, therefore, succeeds to his lands by right, that right being guarded by Ronald, who is now fighting by the side of Bruce. The king had been made acquainted with the identity of the supposed page, but the poem does not state clearly whether Ronald had or not; he seems, however, to have been aware that Edith was still living. This I gather from the ensuing con-

(54) "A Short History of Scotland," by P. Hume Brown, page 23.

versation between Isabel and Edith, which takes place in the convent.

It is just at the time when news reaches the convent of the agreement made at Stirling and the impending invasion from England, and when Bruce had gathered all the available troops he could muster in the neighbourhood of Stirling, that this conversation takes place.

Lady (or, as we should now call her, Sister) Isabel commences it by expressing the pleasure she has derived from her intercourse with Edith, and her regret that now they must part; the convent cell was not for her (Edith). Isabel then pleads for Ronald; the heart of the latter, she declares, is returning to the one to whom he has been betrothed from childhood—[55]

> "Nor, Edith, judge thyself betrayed,
> Though Robert knows that Lorn's high Maid
> And his poor silent page were one.
> Versed in the fickle heart of man,
> Earnest and anxious hath he looked
> How Ronald's heart the message brooked,
> That gave him, with her last farewell,
> The charge of Sister Isabel,
> To think upon thy better right,
> And keep the faith his promise plight.
> Forgive him, for thy sister's sake,
> At first if vain repinings wake—
>   Long since that mood is gone:
> Now dwells he on thy juster claims,
> And oft his breach of faith he blames—
>   Forgive him for thine own!"

It appears to me that the above appeal would hardly, indeed, make a favourable impression on Edith; it implies that Ronald is only returning to his troth with Edith when all chance of obtaining Isabel is gone. Edith, accordingly, answers hotly and proudly—

> "No! never to Lord Ronald's bower
> Will I again as paramour."

Isabel, on this, checks her at once—

> "Nay, hush thee, too impatient maid,
> Until my final tale be said!"

(55) Canto I., ver. 10.

Isabel was indeed right to check her, for Edith had no right to use the term "paramour" to herself in connection with Lord Ronald, who, whatever his feelings towards her might have been, had no intention of dealing dishonourably with her; he had full intention of marrying her; and it was not until Lorn had himself broken off the marriage contract that he (Ronald) had sought the hand of Isabel. It must be said of him, however, that he seems to have had little care for the pain which he was inflicting on his betrothed; Edith, therefore, had good cause for her anger with him.

Isabel then brings forward to Edith an extraordinary suggestion, for which I myself can see little reason; no less than that the maiden should again disguise herself, and, in the character of the page, Amadine, seek the camp of Bruce, and there make trial of Lord Ronald's penitence—

> "The good King Robert would engage
> Edith once more his elfin page,
> By her own heart, and her own eye,
> Her lover's penitence to try—
> Safe in his royal charge, and free,
> Should such thy final purpose be,
> Again unknown to seek the cell,
> And live and die with Isabel."

Edith, as might be supposed, is somewhat taken aback by this proposal; she hesitates, and proffers many reasons against it which, indeed, were indisputable, but she is accustomed to escapades. Love eventually prevails; she will dare anything for the sake of seeing Ronald again, if only for the last time; if her journey is fruitless, she will return to solitude again. Isabel, noble, as ever, reads her thoughts—

> "But Isabel, who long had seen
> Her pallid cheek and pensive mien,
> And well herself the cause might know,
> Though innocent, of Edith's woe,
> Joyed, generous, that revolving time
> Gave means to expiate the crime.
> High glowed her bosom, as she said,
> 'Well shall her sufferings be repaid!'"

Edith, therefore, sets out again, disguised as the page Amadine, under escort, ostensibly to be employed as page to King Robert. They arrive eventually at the field of Bannockburn, on the very eve of the battle, and find the forces of the Scottish king drawn up in presence of the enemy. Here we leave our heroine for the present, and return for a while to history.

The Battle of Bannockburn is one of the most famous battles in mediæval history, and it is remarkable for the fact that it was one of the few occasions on which the Scots defeated the English in a regular pitched battle; and in this case, as at Stirling Bridge, the victory was won more through the blunders of the English commander than by the good generalship of the Scottish leader, though in this case (Bannockburn) I am not attempting to deny that Bruce was a great general, which Edward II. certainly was not, and the former showed great ability in the disposition of his troops before, and in the handling of them during the battle, while the latter, as we shall see, actually courted defeat, which he suffered accordingly.

The number, on both sides, of the men engaged in the battle is still uncertain. Barbour states that the English army numbered 100,000 men, of which 40,000 were cavalry, while the Scottish force was about half that number. Hume Brown [56] supports this, but most writers agree that this is an exaggeration. Sir H. Maxwell estimates the numbers as 50,000 English and 20,000 Scots; while Mr. W. M. Mackenzie, in his book, "The Battle of Bannockburn," recently published, after a long calculation, goes as low as 20,000 English and 7,000 Scots. I myself am inclined to accept Sir H. Maxwell's estimate as nearest the truth; but, in any case, it is evident that the English numbered at least two to one against their foes, especially in the matter of cavalry, of which Bruce had but 500.

An advantage, however, lay on the side of the Scots to compensate them for their want of numbers. Their "morale" was certainly superior to that of their opponents. They were composed of native Scots, fighting in a good cause, the defence of their country; they were well organised, each division (or "battle") being under a competent leader, and the whole being

(56) "A Short History of Scotland," page 23, "Bannockburn."

under the command of one of the greatest generals of that age, in whom they had every confidence. The English, on the other hand, were a very heterogeneous body; besides native English, there were Welsh and Irish, and also foreigners, such as Gascons, Poitevins, &c. Also, they had no great general on their side; from Edward downwards the leaders, though brave enough, had little or no military skill.

In describing this battle, which I am now about to attempt, I shall for the present confine myself to hard, historical facts; I shall pass by all the romantic incidents until I deal with the events of the battle as related in the poem.

Bruce had chosen his position well. His front was covered by the famous Bannock Burn, which gives its name to the battle, which stream was a more formidable obstacle to the English than has generally been supposed. His right rested on what was afterwards termed the "Gillies' Hill," and his left on St. Ninian's Kirk. He divided his force into four divisions, or "battles." These lay in a sort of echelon formation from the front: the first, under the king himself, in front; the second, under his brother Edward, a short distance in rear; then, a greater distance behind, the third, under Douglas; while, on the latter's left and slightly in rear, lay the fourth, under Randolph, Earl of Moray. These were all infantry, with the exception of a small force of cavalry, 500 strong, under Sir Robert Keith.[57]

The English army, composed of ten divisions, had arrived at Falkirk (about 9 miles from Stirling) on the evening of Saturday, June 22nd, and their vanguard appears to have reached the Bannock on the morning of Sunday, the 23rd. The two armies now confronted each other, facing respectively north and south, with the Bannock flowing between them. It is on this ground that, until recently, the main battle was supposed to have taken place, but my above-mentioned text-book, which I am now principally following, shows that it was fought on quite

(57) I am taking the dispositions from the first map in my present text-book ("The Battle of Bannockburn," by W. M. Mackenzie, M.A.), which would seem to be the correct one. In Sir H. Maxwell's map, Douglas is placed on the left, in which case *he* would be the one to engage Clifford in the contest which I am about to relate, not Randolph. The position of the small body of cavalry is not entered in the map.

different ground, and under circumstances which entirely explain the defeat of the English, which previously I had not considered satisfactorily explained.

Now, the great object of King Edward was to relieve Stirling Castle, and there were two routes which were available to him for that purpose. The first was by a Roman road, which crosses the Bannock at a place where that stream makes a double bend outwardly from the Scottish position, thence through that position and a portion of ground called the New Park, and on direct to Stirling. The other road was more circuitous; it crossed the Bannock more than a mile below the first crossing, thence traversing a piece of ground called the "Carse," before reaching Stirling. Boggy ground rendered the stream inaccessible at any other point. Edward attempted to force his way through by both these routes, and in both attempts he failed.

Sir Robert Clifford, with 300 men (according to Barbour, 800), was dispatched by the "Carse" route to communicate with the garrison of Stirling. They approached close to Randolph's position, who attacked them with 500 infantry.[58] Here is an example of infantry beating off cavalry; and, indeed, this is the great feature of the battle. The Scottish infantry was formed in a "schiltrom" (corresponding to the modern square). The English cavalry attacked them furiously on all sides, but in vain. At length Randolph assumed the offensive, advanced, and cut the English in two, which separate parts, on this, retired in disorder, the one to Stirling Castle and the other back to the main body.

In the meantime, another attempt had been made to break through to Stirling by the Roman road, and with a like result. In the gap between the bends of the Bannock before mentioned, about 500 yards wide, called the "entry," Bruce had laid down several rows of shallow pits, or "pots," as they are called, to hinder the manœuvring of the enemy's cavalry. These "pots" have been considered, until the recent publication of the book I before mentioned, to have been a great factor in the defeat of the

---

(58) I quote from Mackenzie for the Scottish numbers; the number of the English is corroborated; therefore Scott's statement in the poem (Canto VI., ver. 18) as to Randolph's being outnumbered by ten to one is glaringly incorrect.

English. It will, therefore, be a surprise to my readers, as it was to myself, to know that the English cavalry never penetrated the "pots" at all, or, if any of them did, it must have been on this occasion (the 23rd), not on the day of the main battle.

The English vanguard, under Sir Henry de Bohun, nephew of the Earl of Hereford, approached the "entry," and prepared to advance, under the impression that the Scots were retreating; but finding, on the contrary, that they were standing firm, and that their force outnumbered his, he gave orders for a retreat. At that moment King Robert himself rode out in front of his troops: a distinct challenge, which De Bohun could not refuse to accept; he therefore spurred his horse against the king, and met his death, as we shall see when we come to the narrative of the poem.

It will be here seen that the circumstances were somewhat different from what has before been believed; De Bohun was not merely an independent knight on the staff of King Edward, but held a separate command in the English army.

The fall of the English leader disheartened his force, already preparing to retreat, and the Scottish force advancing drove them back in disorder.

These two repulses considerably dispirited the English troops, and Edward, still bent upon reaching Stirling, took a step that evening which proved fatal to his army. He brought them across the Bannock, lower down, towards the Forth; not without considerable difficulty, for bridges had to be improvised, and there was not a great amount of the proper materials for that purpose. However, they were got over that evening, and stationed in the "Carse," a piece of ground about a mile in width, with the river Forth on the right and in rear, and the Bannock burn on the left; in the immediate rear, a piece of marshy ground, interspersed with pools of water, called the "Pools." Here, then, was this vast army, cooped up on three sides, and so cramped for room that they were unable to manœuvre; their very numbers were a hindrance to them. Edward was indeed courting defeat, and Bruce must have exulted when he saw the English king lead his army into such a position.[59] But why did not "well-skilled

---

[59] Mackenzie's "Battle of Bannockburn," Chap. IV., page 1.

Bruce" attack Edward during this hazardous move ? He seems to have missed an opportunity, like James IV. at Flodden.

The battle of the following day, the memorable 24th June, 1314, may be described in a few words. On seeing the enemy in the position above described, Bruce determined to attack.[60] He had, in accordance with the movement of the enemy, changed front to the left, so that the hostile armies were now facing respectively east and west. He had also changed the position of some of his divisions : Edward Bruce was still on the right, then came Randolph, then Douglas, while the king himself had shifted his division to the left of this line, which now advanced in echelon from the right—*i.e.*, each division slightly in advance of the one on its left. Each division then, falling upon the enemy, came on in succession until the whole were engaged. Edward Bruce, on the right, was the first to encounter the English vanguard, under the Earl of Gloucester, which seems to have been slightly in advance of the main body. In the conflict which ensued, Gloucester was slain.

Another fatal blunder was here made by Edward II. He posted his archers at the right-hand corner of the front of his huge column. Now, the English archers were a very formidable body for offensive purposes, but in defensive warfare they were almost helpless, especially against cavalry. They had no defensive armour, and seem only to have been armed with short swords. Posted, however, as they now were, they could enfilade the Scottish invading columns, and no doubt in this way they harassed them considerably, but they were quite exposed to any attack from the enemy. Edward might easily have placed them within the main body, under cover of his men-at-arms. Bruce now utilised his small force of cavalry, 500 strong, under Sir Robert Keith; he sent them to attack the archers, whom they speedily dispersed. The most important arm on the English side was, therefore, now put out of action.[61]

---

(60) In former accounts it was the English who struck first.

(61) Bannockburn was a lesson to the English archery. In after battles, each archer carried a stake, which he planted in the ground in front of him as a defence against cavalry attack.

The remainder of the fight may be described in a few words. The English force, cooped up in this corner, were practically helpless; their very strength in numbers made it all the worse; they could neither clear their front nor could they retire. While in this disheartened condition, there came the well-known rush of the Scottish camp followers from the Gillies' Hill. This clinched matters. The confused mass of the English force, believing this new body to be a Scottish reinforcement, began to break up, and, on the retreat of King Edward from the conflict, fell into confusion. Some fled across the Bannock, some took refuge in the crags of Stirling rock. The slaughter at the Bannock was frightful. King Edward made for the castle of Stirling, but De Mowbray, the governor, very rightly refused to admit him; that would mean that the King of England would have to surrender himself a prisoner, as the castle would now, according to agreement, have to be given up.

Such seems to be the true version of the battle, and the author of the book I quote (Mackenzie) puts this very pertinently before us in several ways. The chief point that impressed me in reading the book was this—King Edward proceeded to Stirling after the battle, also, some of the fugitives fled there. If the battle was fought on the ground south of the Bannock, as has hitherto been supposed, how did Edward and those fugitives get to Stirling? Their line of retreat would naturally be towards Falkirk; to go to Stirling, would mean advancing in the teeth of a victorious army. I think this cannot be disputed. King Edward, after his visit to Stirling, doubtless slipped off by the New Park and the other side of the Gillies' Hill.

I now return to the events of the poem, and I am about to run through the different features of this battle as related there. These are, generally, fairly correct, though, of course, the battle is placed on different ground; and there are several inaccuracies, which I shall point out as I proceed. Be it noted that, up till now, I have kept strictly to historical facts, in my own opinion accurate; now I follow the poem and the romantic details (mostly accurate) which it exhibits.

Scott describes the gathering of the English for the invasion, and of the Scots for the defence, of Scotland very finely—

> " Right to devoted Caledon
> The storm of war rolls slowly on,
>   With menace deep and dread;
> So the dark clouds, with gathering power,
> Suspend a while the threatened shower,
> Till every peak and summit lower
>   Round the pale pilgrim's head."

On the other hand—

> " O who may tell the sons of fame
> That at King Robert's bidding came
>   To battle for the right!
> From Cheviot to the shores of Ross,
> From Solway-Sands to Marshal's-Moss,
>   All bouned them for the fight."

The disposition of Bruce's forces for the battle are very fairly rendered—

> " In battles four beneath their eye,
> The forces of King Robert lie.
> And one below the hill was laid,
> Reserved for rescue and for aid;
> And three, advanced, formed vaward-line,
> 'Twixt Bannock's brook and Ninian's shrine.
> Detached was each, yet each so nigh
> As well might mutual aid supply."

Scott somewhat exaggerates the numbers of the English army, which has often been done—

> " Beyond, the Southern host appears,
> A boundless wilderness of spears,
> Whose verge or rear the anxious eye
> Strove far, but strove in vain, to spy.
> Thick flashing in the evening beam,
> Glaives, lances, bills, and banners gleam;
> And where the heaven joined with the hill,
> Was distant armour flashing still,
> So wide, so far, the boundless host
> Seemed in the blue horizon lost."

Such is the scene which presents itself to the eyes of Edith on her arrival, with her escort, at the field of Bannockburn.

It is the 23rd June, the evening before the battle. She notes the reserve "battle," composed of the Islesmen and men of the western coast. Bruce's banner floats here, and she specially notes that of Lord Ronald, "a galley driven by sail and oar." She looks anxiously for the chief himself—

> "But he was far
> Busied amid the ranks of war."

Her escort, Fitz-Louis, guides her past the remaining "battles" to the king, who is now at the front. But, before she reaches him, that well-known incident, the attack of De Bohun on Bruce, occurs. I have already written the true account of the affair.[62] I now proceed with the incident as rendered in the poem.

Bruce, mounted on "a palfrey, low and light," is riding in front of the line, inspecting his troops and noting the position of the enemy. He is conspicuous by wearing a gold diadem on his helmet, and he carries a battle-axe. King Edward is also riding in front of his troops, accompanied by De Argentine and other knights, and Scott says—

> "And who, that saw that monarch ride,
> His kingdom battled by his side,
> Could then his direful doom foretell !—
> Fair was his seat in knightly selle,
> And in his sprightly eye was set
> Some spark of the Plantagenet."

The king notices Bruce, and asks De Argentine who he is. The knight, seeing the gold crown, and also his glove, which Bruce is wearing on his helmet, according to their compact,[63] at once replies that it is the Bruce. The king then says—

> "And shall the audacious traitor brave
> The presence where our banners wave ? "

Argentine replies that, were Bruce as well horsed as he himself was, he would certainly try issue of battle with him.

(62) See page 283 in treatise.

(63) See Canto II., vers. 5 and 6 of the poem, and page 242 of the treatise.

The king replies that, in battle, "nice tourney rules" may be set aside, and calls on some one to sweep the "rebel," as he terms Bruce, from his path. On this, Sir Henry de Bohun, who is here described as being with the king—"on his staff," as we should now say—dashes forth, and, with lance in rest, spurs his war steed in full career against the Scottish king. The latter is, however, prepared for him. He wheels his light palfrey to one side, thus avoiding the headlong rush, and, as the English knight passes, raises his battle-axe and deals him a fatal blow. The assailant falls from his horse, dead—

> "Such strength upon the blow was put,
> The helmet crashed like hazel-nut;
> The axe-shaft, with its brazen clasp,
> Was shivered to the gauntlet grasp.
> Springs from the blow the startled horse,
> Drops to the plain the lifeless corse;—
> First of the fatal field, how soon,
> How sudden, fell the fierce De Boune!"

On Bruce's return within his lines, his leaders crowd round him and expostulate with him for thus placing his life in danger, but he replies carelessly—

> "My loss may pay my folly's tax;
> I've broke my trusty battle-axe."

It is at this moment that Fitz-Louis approaches and informs the king of the arrival of the page Amadine. Bruce addresses the maiden by her assumed name, and directs her to proceed to the Gillies' Hill, where the camp followers are. She plays a very prominent part there later on, as we shall see. The king does not omit to speak of Ronald favourably—

> "For brave Lord Ronald, too, hath sworn
> Not to regain the Maid of Lorn,
> (The bliss on earth he covets most,)
> Would he forsake his battle post,
> Or shun the fortune that may fall
> To Bruce, to Scotland, and to all."

As the maiden leaves, the king says to her, in a low voice—

> "Be of good cheer—farewell, sweet maid!"

We now come to the second incident which occurs on the evening before the battle, viz., the conflict between Sir Robert de Clifford and Randolph, Earl of Moray, which I before described.[64] Clifford, be it remembered, was trying to push through to Stirling, to obtain communication with the garrison there, and he appears to have passed Randolph's position without the latter observing it. Bruce perceives this, and says to Randolph—

> "Lo! round thy station pass the foes!
> Randolph, thy wreath has lost a rose."

Moray, on this, marches off his division and charges down upon the enemy. Douglas then begs the king to allow him to go to Randolph's assistance, as the latter was outnumbered by ten to one.[65] Bruce refuses at first, but afterwards gives permission, but as Douglas is proceeding on his way he perceives that Randolph is getting the best of it, so he says to his men—

> "Rein up; our presence would impair
> The fame we came too late to share." [66]

This shows the good accord existing among the Scottish leaders, in contrast with the English chiefs, between whom, in this very conflict, there was bickering.[67]

This closes the events of this day, and we now proceed to the account of the main battle on the following day.

The first event mentioned is the well-known incident which took place before the battle began. The English army advances,

(64) See page 282 of the treatise. In the poem, Scott, as we have seen, makes out Clifford to have been slain at Turnberry, and he therefore makes Sir William Deyncourt command the English force on this occasion. Deyncourt was, indeed, present, and was slain there, but he was not in command.

(65) This is glaringly incorrect. Randolph had 500 men, Clifford but 300. This latter number is corroborated by Sir Thomas Gray, who was actually in the conflict on Clifford's side, and was taken prisoner. The only advantage Clifford had was that he commanded cavalry against Randolph's infantry.

(66) Scott more than once speaks of the Scottish leaders as if they were commanding cavalry, when we know that Bruce had none with the exception of the 500 men under Sir Robert Keith.

(67) See Mackenzie, page 56: Randolph's stand.

King Edward being in the centre, accompanied by De Argentine and by De Valence, Earl of Pembroke. All at once, the whole Scottish host appears to sink down before him—

> " Upon the Scottish foe he gazed—
> At once, before his sight amazed,
> Sunk banner, spear, and shield;
> Each weapon-point is downward sent,
> Each warrior to the ground is bent."

On this, the king exclaims—

> " ' The rebels, Argentine, repent !
> For pardon they have kneeled.'—
> ' Aye !—but they bend to other powers,
> And other pardon sue than ours !
> See where yon barefoot Abbot stands,
> And blesses them with lifted hands !
> Upon the spot where they have kneeled,
> These men will die, or win the field.' " (68)

The king answers—

> " Then prove we if they die or win !
> Bid Gloster's Earl the fight begin."

The Earl of Gloucester, who is here represented as being in command of the English archers, now gives the signal for that force to commence action. They halt, and commence a heavy discharge of arrows upon the Scottish line—

> " To the right ear the cords they bring—
> At once ten thousand bowstrings ring,
> Ten thousand arrows fly !
> Nor paused on the devoted Scot
> The ceaseless fury of their shot;
> As fiercely and as fast,
> Forth whistling came the grey-goose wing,
> As the wild hailstones pelt and ring
> Adown December's blast.

---

(68) It was not De Argentine who said this, it was Sir Ingelram de Umfraville, a Scottish knight fighting on the English side. This knight advised Edward to feign retreat, so as to draw the Scots out of their position, and thus encounter them on the open plain south of the Bannock, but the king refused. If Mr. Mackenzie's account of the battle be the correct one (and I accept it as such), this counsel must have been given on the evening before the battle, before Edward made his fatal move to the "Carse"; after that, on the actual day of the battle, we have seen that it would have been impossible for him to have retired in good order

> Nor mountain targe of tough bull-hide,
> Nor Lowland mail, that storm may bide;
> Woe, woe to Scotland's bannered pride,
>   If the fell shower may last!"

Formidable indeed was this force, as I said before, when acting on the offensive, but almost helpless when attacked by cavalry, which arm is now about to be brought against them. Edward Bruce, with his division, is waiting until the archers gain an exposed position; then he lets loose his force upon them. He exclaims, "Mount, ye gallants free!" and as they vault into the saddle, he again urges them on to the attack—

> "Forth, Marshal, on the peasant foe!
> We'll tame the terrors of their bow,
> And cut the bowstring loose!" [69]

This cavalry attack on the archers is well described. The latter had little or no defensive armour, and they had not yet adopted the method of planting stakes in front of them, as they did on future occasions—

> "Then spurs were dashed in chargers' flanks,
> They rushed among the archer ranks.
> No spears were there the shock to let,
> No stakes to turn the charge were set,
> And how shall yeoman's armour slight
> Stand the long lance and mace of might?
> Or what may their short swords avail
> 'Gainst barbèd horse and shirt of mail?
> Amid their ranks the chargers sprung,
> High o'er their heads the weapons swung,
> And shriek and groan and vengeful shout
> Give note of triumph and of rout!"

(69) Here again is gross inaccuracy; Scott writes for effect, as he often does. It was not Edward Bruce who dispersed the English archers: it was Keith, with his 500 horse. Again, as in the case of Douglas before mentioned, Scott represents Edward Bruce as commanding cavalry: his division was, like those of the other leaders, infantry; Keith's small force was, as we know, the only cavalry which Bruce possessed. However, the lines are very fine. The term "peasant," also, is not applicable to the class from whence the English archers sprang; it represented the middle class of England, a class which neither France nor Scotland possessed, and therefore, although both these countries tried it, they never could raise this formidable arm, at least to any extent. (See Alison's "History of Europe," Chap. I.)

The archers are utterly cut down and dispersed. King Edward now, indignant at the dispersal of the archery, orders up his cavalry—

> "Forward, each gentleman and knight!
> Let gentle blood show generous might,
> And chivalry redeem the fight!"

Ten thousand horsemen, on this, come charging down on the Scottish cavalry, but they become entangled in Bruce's military pits, or "pots," which, in reality, appear to be mythical, at least in the case of the English cavalry being entangled in them—[70]

> "Down! down! in headlong overthrow,
> Horseman and horse, the foremost go,
> Wild floundering on the field!
> The first are in destruction's gorge,
> Their followers wildly o'er them urge;—
> The knightly helm and shield,
> The mail, the acton, and the spear,
> Strong hand, high heart, are useless here!"

Edward, then, has failed as yet, both with his archers and his men-at-arms. But it is only the vanguard of these latter who have been discomfited in the "pots"; there is yet a strong body of mounted men behind, under command of the noblest of the English peers—

> "Names known too well in Scotland's war,
> At Falkirk, Methven, and Dunbar,
> Blazed broader yet in after years,
> At Cressy red and fell Poitiers."

These advance with more caution, and a desperate conflict ensues, which lasts for some time. The English cavalry, however, is hampered for want of room in the narrow "entry," being unable to deploy. This is certain, whether we accept the last account of Mr. Mackenzie or that of Sir Herbert Maxwell. This desperate fight goes on, according to the poem, till midday,

---

(70) See page 282 of treatise. I also see by Scott's note to the verse we are now dealing with (Canto VI., ver. 24) that Barbour does not mention any entanglement of the English horse in the " pots."

when both sides begin to tire, especially on the side of the English, hampered as the latter were by their greater numbers, crowded into this small space. Bruce sees this, and calls up his reserve, consisting of his own Carrick men and Lord Ronald's Islemen. He now calls upon the Island chief—

> "One effort more, and Scotland's free!
> Lord of the Isles, my trust in thee
> Is firm as Ailsa-rock;
> Rush on with Highland sword and targe,
> I, with my Carrick spearmen, charge;
> Now, forward to the shock!" [71]

This new force presses forward desperately, and drives the foe back a considerable distance, but here the latter are rallied by De Argentine, and make a temporary stand. It is at this critical moment that the well-known incident of the charge of the camp followers takes place and decides the day, and here we return to our heroine.

Edith has all this time been with the camp followers on the Gillies' Hill, watching eagerly the events of the battle. She has just seen Ronald's force brought into action, and has exulted at its success; but now it seems to be checked, the English have recovered themselves, and seem, as she thinks, to be hemming the Islesmen round. On this, forgetting her assumed dumbness, she calls out distractedly to those around her—

> "O God! the combat they renew,
> And is no rescue found!
> And ye that look thus tamely on
> And see your native land o'erthrown,
> O! are your hearts of flesh or stone?"

This apparent miracle of the mute page suddenly recovering his speech has an immediate effect on the multitude. It is a superstitious age, and the real truth never occurs to them, and this miracle, as they deem it, stirs them up to immediate action. They fly to arms—any arms that they had—

(71) Scott in his note (Canto VI., ver. 28) states that these words were actually addressed by Bruce to the Lord of the Isles—Angus of the Isles, I presume, the original of Ronald.

> "And, like a bannered host afar,
> Bear down on England's wearied war."

We know the result. Already shaken considerably, the English force, seeing this new reinforcement, as they conceive it to be, advancing upon them, become entirely disheartened, and break up on all sides. King Edward in person endeavours desperately to rally them, but all his efforts are in vain; at length, the Earl of Pembroke takes his bridle and leads him away from the lost battle-field.

De Argentine remains; he is determined not to survive defeat—

> "'Now then,' he said, and couched his spear,
> 'My course is run, the goal is near;
> One effort more, one brave career,
> Must close this race of mine.'"

Then, shouting loud his battle-cry, he charges into the midst of the pursuing foes; he slays five of them, not, however, without being desperately wounded himself.

Bruce, in the meanwhile, is following up his victory, giving orders to press the flying foe to the uttermost, when he hears the war-cry of De Argentine. Instinctively he knows what it means—

> "'Save, save his life,' he cried, 'O save
> The kind, the noble, and the brave!'"

He penetrates the throng, but finds that he is too late. De Argentine is desperately wounded; he strives to charge against Bruce, but his strength fails him, and he falls to the ground. The king is down by his side in a moment, and loosens his vizor, and the dying knight says—

> "Lord Earl, the day is thine!
> My sovereign's charge, and adverse fate,
> Have made our meeting all too late;
> Yet this may Argentine,
> As boon from ancient comrade, crave—
> A Christian's mass, a soldier's grave."

It is a touching scene, this last meeting between these two gallant foes, who press each other's hands for the last time. As De Argentine dies, Bruce thus pronounces his requiem—

"And ' O farewell !' the victor cried,
' Of chivalry the flower and pride,
  The arm in battle bold,
The courteous mien, the noble race,
The stainless faith, the manly face !—
Bid Ninian's convent light their shrine
For late-wake of De Argentine.
O'er better knight on death-bier laid,
Torch never gleamed, nor mass was said !' "

The number of the slaughtered on the English side, both in
the battle and in the flight which followed, is not known, but
it must have been something frightful. The loss fell the heaviest
on the knights and men-at-arms; the infantry, with the exception
of the archers, seem not to have been engaged at all—this is,
of course, accepting Mackenzie's account as the correct one.
An immense booty was taken from the English camp. Bruce
appears to have behaved with great humanity; he gave the dead
honourable burial and treated the prisoners with kindness.
Scott remarks, with regard to the slain—

"Not for De Argentine alone
Through Ninian's church these torches shone,
And rose the death-prayer's awful tone.
That yellow lustre glimmered pale
On broken plate and bloodied mail,
Rent crest and shattered coronet
Of Baron, Earl, and Banneret,
And the best names that England knew
Claimed in the death-prayer dismal due."

One of the greatest charms to me in the writings of Sir
Walter Scott is his marked impartiality when he deals with the
contentions between England and Scotland. Dearly as he loves
his own nation, Scotsman as he is to the very core, he has a warm
corner in his heart for England; he evidently has a respect and
affection for that nation; and he must win the heart of every
English reader by his appeal to their good feeling and sense of
right, after relating the defeat at Bannockburn, in the following
words—

"Yet mourn not, Land of Fame !
Though ne'er the leopards on thy shield
Retreated from so sad a field
Since Norman William came.

> Oft may thine annals justly boast
> Of battles stern by Scotland lost;
>   Grudge not her victory,
> When for her free-born rights she strove;
> Rights dear to all who freedom love,
>   To none so dear as thee!"

But, however we may now look upon it in the above light, it cannot be denied that the defeat, at the time, was a terrible blow to England. So greatly was the disgrace felt that, as one author says, the English said it was a punishment for their sins.[72] The effects of the defeat were felt in England for a long period. During the reign of Edward II., and the early years of Edward III., the Scots were the aggressive power. Many times did they invade England, wasting, plundering, burning, and carrying off booty; and it was not until after the death of Bruce that the glory of England revived, and the dark clouds of Bannockburn were dispersed by the glorious sunlight of victory on the fields of Halidon Hill and Neville's Cross.

We have but a few more words to say in the narrative of the poem. Edith, as we have seen, has concluded her various escapades by forgetting her assumed dumbness and inciting the camp followers to their famous charge, on account of the apparent miracle. Now that the battle is over, Fitz-Louis (Edith's escort) and others crowd round Bruce and tell him of this marvellous event—

> "With him, a hundred voices tell
> Of prodigy and miracle,
>   'For the mute Page had spoke.'—
> 'Page!' said Fitz-Louis, 'rather say,
> An angel sent from realms of day
>   To burst the English yoke.
> I saw his plume and bonnet drop,
> When hurrying from the mountain top;
> A lovely brow, dark locks that wave,
> To his bright eyes new lustre gave,
> A step as light upon the green,
> As if his pinions waved unseen!'"

Bruce inquires if the page spoke with anyone. Only, Fitz-Louis says, one word (what, is not mentioned) with Lord Ronald,

(72) "A Short History of Scotland," by Hume Brown: "Bannockburn," page 23.

returning from the battle-field. The king eagerly inquires what answer the chief made. This was the reply—

> " He kneeled,
> Durst not look up, but muttered low
> Some mingled sounds that none might know,
> And greeted him, 'twixt joy and fear,
> As being of superior sphere."

At this satisfactory news, the king, in spite of the melancholy surroundings—relics of the late battle, dead, dying, and wounded—cannot help laughing for joy—

> " ' And bore he such angelic air,
> Such noble front, such waving hair ?
> Hath Ronald kneeled to him ? ' he said,
> ' Then must we call the Church to aid—
> Our will be to the Abbot known,
> Ere these strange news are wider blown,
> To Cambuskenneth straight he pass,
> And deck the church for solemn mass,
> To pay, for high deliverance given,
> A nation's thanks to gracious Heaven.
> Let him array, besides, such state
> As should on princes' nuptials wait.
> Ourself the cause, through fortune's spite,
> That once broke short that spousal rite,
> Ourself will grace, with early morn,
> The bridal of the Maid of Lorn.' "

Here the poem ends satisfactorily, though somewhat abruptly, as does also the poem of "Rokeby," as we shall see later. Publicly, Scotland is delivered; privately, the lovers are united.

With the exception of the great Scottish king, there are, as I think, no characters in this poem of any especial consequence. Ronald, the nominal hero of the poem, is brave and chivalrous, and thoroughly loyal to the cause to which he has attached himself; but, apart from this, his conduct towards his fiancée appears rather heartless. He is certainly ready to fulfil his contract with Edith, but he shows that he has no love for her— nay, more, that he loves another, and, as we have seen, lets out that fact in her very presence. The fact appears to be that formerly there was alliance between the houses of Lorn and the

Lord of the Isles, and, to cement that alliance, a marriage was arranged by the parents between Ronald and Edith, the representatives of the two houses, their children. The children grow up, looking on their future marriage as a matter of course, until Ronald meets with Isabel Bruce in England, and his affections are at once transferred to her. How far she reciprocated these feelings, and how far the two became acquainted, we know not; this is one of the instances of the vagueness in details which often occurs in this poem, to which I have several times alluded.[73]

The escapades of Edith do not appeal to me, especially the latter one, when she appears in disguise on the battle-field. This adventure appears to me entirely unnecessary: Bruce, I should think, might easily have reconciled the two fiancés without requiring Edith to enter upon this escapade. Edith is an extraordinary character. She exhibits a weakness in her disguise as a boy such as, we should think, must have exposed her true sex; on the other hand, when dispatched on her mission to Carrick, she displays the utmost courage and promptitude, and she faces death bravely, rather than betray the man she loves. Nothing is said of the course of life of Ronald and Edith after the poem ends, so we may only hope that their union was a happy one, though we cannot help feeling some doubt when we remember the previous circumstances.

Isabel presents a most noble and unselfish character, perhaps too much so for ordinary human nature. Her feelings of affection towards Ronald cannot, however, have been very strong. The fiery and impetuous Edward Bruce, in contrast with the more steady, calculating character of his elder brother is, I think, well represented in accordance with historical facts. De Argentine is a fine example of a brave, noble, and chivalrous English knight. Torquil, the rough old chief of Skye, is a pleasing character, but we see no more of him after his parting with Bruce and Ronald at Artornish Castle, in Canto III. The impetuous, overbearing character of Lorn, and his bitter hostility to Bruce, are depicted well.

---

(73) Instances which I have already quoted, such as Isabel's arrival in Arran, the circumstances of Edith's presence in the robber's cave, &c.

But the character which dominates the whole poem, round which the other characters revolve as planets round the sun, is that of the great Scottish king, Robert the Bruce, and we cannot close our treatise without a few words regarding him.

Robert Bruce was undoubtedly the greatest monarch who ever ruled Scotland—eminent as a great sovereign, soldier, and statesman. The record of his earlier years, however, is not good; he there appears in the character of a time-server. He had been in the service of Edward I. from his youth; and, as I pointed out in a former page, twice did he swear fealty to that monarch, twice did he rebel, twice did he receive pardon [74]—"a most humiliating record," says his biographer, Sir H. Maxwell. The culminating point of this disgraceful career was the murder of Comyn, which the same biographer describes as "a brutal, bloody murder, aggravated, as there is too much reason to suspect, by its being committed under trust." [75] There is no doubt that Bruce committed a treacherous murder, but in those days this would not have been thought of much consequence, had the crime not been committed in a sacred place. This latter fact it was that brought the curse of Rome on his head, which clung to him for nearly the whole of his life.

After this act, a brighter light shines upon his record. He had now "burned his boats," as the saying is, and before him lay two extremes, "the throne or the scaffold." He hesitated not a moment; he threw himself into the cause of his country (on his mother's side), and from that cause he never again swerved. Defeated at first, "a hunted wanderer on the wild," in daily risk of his life, his courage never forsook him. The tide of fortune was already turning in his favour at the time of the death of his great opponent, Edward I.; from that period it steadily progressed. His progress, unlike the spasmodic effort of Wallace in 1298, which ended in defeat, was steady and methodical. Taking advantage of the dissensions between the weak King of England and his barons, which turned away their attention from Scotland, he proceeded on his way, taking fortress

(74) See page 252 of treatise.

(75) Sir H. Maxwell's " Robert the Bruce," page 129.

after fortress from the invaders, until their retention of Stirling alone brought on the crowning victory of Bannockburn. This practicallly delivered Scotland from her invaders, and that country may thank Bruce for it. The king, however, was too great a man to be unduly elated over his victory. He had a marvellous opportunity there, and, like a great general, he at once availed himself of it. But he knew well that such an opportunity was not likely to occur again, and for the remainder of his reign he preserved the old strategy against the English, on any invasion of theirs, by retiring, wasting the country, and starving them out. He harassed England throughout his reign by frequent incursions, but, through it all, he was ever ready to enter into terms of peace with that country, but always on the terms that he was to be acknowledged rightful King of Scotland. Both the Pope and the King of England, however, would never consent to this; the former, probably, on account of the murder of Comyn, which still hung over the life of Bruce, and, it appears, preyed on his mind—hence the sending of his heart to Palestine after his death. At length, however, in 1328, Edward III. renounced all claim to the Lord Paramountcy of Scotland hitherto claimed by the English king, at the same time acknowledging Robert Bruce to be rightful King of Scotland. In the same year, the ban of excommunication was removed by the Pope from the Scottish king. The great monarch had, therefore, completed his work, and in the following year ended his earthly career. Under his reign, Scotland had a prosperous time, and it was the only period in which she appeared to dominate over her southern neighbour.

It is an interesting thing to note, in studying the relations between England and Scotland in the thirteenth and fourteenth centuries, to see that there are three periods affecting the two countries, each commencing with the death of a great king, which death has a great influence on the welfare of the country over which he ruled. We commence with the death of Alexander III. of Scotland, in 1286, the greatest ruler, next to Bruce, of that country. During this first period, which lasts till 1307, there was a disastrous time for Scotland. It comprised the attempt of Edward I. to subjugate that country, which attempt nearly succeeded. With the death of that great monarch (1307), affairs changed. In this second period, Scotland recovered her liberty, and not only that, but retained a certain superiority over her former invader, until the death of her own great king, Robert Bruce. After that event (1329), in the third period, England recovers her former prestige; she wins the battle of Halidon Hill, and, finally, proves her superiority over her northern foe in her victory at Neville's Cross, won at a time when she was also engaged in a war with France.

I have now concluded, and have but a word to say of the poem itself. I have already commented on the characters represented in it. It does not appeal to me as do those poems which I have already commented upon, possibly because I have not studied it as I have the others. But there are beautiful pieces in it; Scott is unequalled in his description of scenery—those of the isles of Skye and Arran, and, more than all, the voyage of Bruce and his companions between the above-named islands are hard to beat. The account of the Battle of Bannockburn is also very beautiful, but not, as I think, equal to that of Flodden in "Marmion."

We are sorry here to part with Scotland; the scenes of the former poems, with the exception of that of "The Bridal of Triermain," all lie in that country. We have visited the Border country, the Central Highlands, and the Western Isles: all are laid before us in glowing colours. In the last poem on which I am attempting to comment, we change our ground, and proceed to English soil.[76] In concluding the poem, we add the following lines of Scott in comment of it—[77]

> " So shalt thou list, and haply not unmoved,
>   To a wild tale of Albyn's warrior day;
>   In distant lands, by the rough West reproved,
>   Still live some reliques of the ancient lay.
>   For, when on Coolin's hills the lights decay,
>   With such the Seer of Skye the eve beguiles,
>   'Tis known amid the pathless wastes of Reay,
>   In Harries known, and in Iona's piles,
> Where rest from mortal coil the Mighty of the Isles."

(76) " The Vision of Don Roderick " stands apart; it is a short epitome of the history of Spain.

(77) " Lord of the Isles," opening verses.

THE VISION OF DON RODERICK.

VII.—THE VISION OF DON RODERICK.

> " Lives there a strain, whose sounds of mounting fire
>   May rise distinguished o'er the din of war,
> Or died it with yon Master of the Lyre
>   Who sung beleaguered Ilion's evil star ?
> Such, Wellington, might reach thee from afar,
>   Wafting its descant wide o'er ocean's range;
> Nor shouts, nor clashing arms, its mood could mar
>   As it swelled 'twixt each loud trumpet change,
> That clangs to Britain, victory, to Portugal, revenge ! "

THESE lines, which form the opening verse of the "Introduction" to the above poem, show undoubtedly the main principle which pervades it. Though the events of the poem are laid down as taking place centuries ago, they are in reality subordinate to those of the early years of the nineteenth century. The Peninsular War, the heroes of that war, and especially Wellington himself, are at the front throughout; and, at the end of the poem, they swamp all the other events which precede the period in which they live. Sir Walter Scott has evidently a great admiration for Wellington, also for that general's subordinates, especially (as might be expected) for those who belong to Scotland, the poet's own country.

However, we must now turn to the period in which the events of the poem take place. This is at the beginning of the eighth century, about the years 710-11, the final years of the reign of Roderick, the last representative of the Gothic kingdom of Spain, which was to be followed by many centuries of Moorish domination, the latter to fall, in its turn, finally, at the capture of Granada, in the fifteenth century; this city being the last stronghold of any consequence held by the Moors in Spain.

Roderick, the last of the Gothic kings, was himself an usurper. He had overthrown the reigning family of Witiza— by intrigue, certainly, or, as the poem hints, by murder.[1] He

---

(1) Gibbon's " Decline and Fall of the Roman Empire," Chap. LI.

seems to have been a weak, profligate, and licentious prince, and his violation of the daughter of one of his chief generals, Julian, brought the enmity of that chief upon him. The name of the daughter is given as Florinda in the poem—in Moorish writings, as Cava. Julian, in revenge, turned to the Saracens, and offered to aid them in an invasion of Spain, thus betraying his country and his religion. This is the tradition, but Gibbon says—"This well-known tale, romantic in itself, is indifferently supported by external evidence; and the history of Spain will suggest some motives of interest and policy more congenial to the breast of a veteran statesman." Whatever may have been the cause, he invited the Moors to invade Spain, and the result was the entire subjugation of the peninsula. The Goths were no longer what they had been, the victorious invaders of the Roman Empire; they had degenerated, as the Romans before them; and though, according to Gibbon, they had an overwhelming force to oppose the invader, they were yet entirely defeated at Xeres. Roderick, fleeing from the fight, was drowned in the Guadalquiver. This is, doubtless, what actually occurred, but readers of "Lockhart's Spanish Ballads" will remember the tradition which tells that the fugitive king was imprisoned in a cellar swarming with serpents, and that it was not until he had been fatally bitten by these that he could receive pardon for his sins.

The subject of the poem is founded on a tradition which says that there was, within the cathedral of Toledo, a "fated room," where the King of Spain might behold his future destiny. The "spell-bound portal" of this room, however, would not open to any king—

> "Save to a King, the last of all his line,
> What time his empire totters to decay,
> And treason digs, beneath, her fatal mine,
> And, high above, impends avenging wrath divine."

The poem opens, then, in the cathedral of Toledo, where King Roderick is making his confession to the Archbishop of Toledo, which prelate, according to Gibbon, afterwards proved a traitor to his king, going over to the enemy at the battle of Xeres. The king's troops are without, and Scott corroborates the words of Gibbon as to their deterioration—

> "The chosen soldiers of the Royal Guard
>   Their post beneath the proud Cathedral hold:
> A band unlike their Gothic sires of old,
>   Who, for the cap of steel and iron mace,
> Bear slender darts, and casques bedecked with gold,
>   While silver-studded belts their shoulders grace,
> Where ivory quivers ring in the broad falchion's place."

The king confesses to many a hidden crime, and makes matters worse by weakly attempting to excuse himself, first, as to the murder of Witiza, his predecessor—

> "'Thus royal Witiza was slain,' he said;
>   'Yet, holy father, deem not it was I.'—
> Thus still Ambition strives her crimes to shade—
>   'O rather deem 'twas stern necessity!
> Self-preservation bade me, and I must kill or die.'"

Still worse than this is his excusing his vile conduct in the violation of the Lady Cava, or Florinda—

> "And, if Florinda's shrieks alarmed the air,
>   If she invoked her absent sire in vain,
> And on her knees implored that I would spare,
>   Yet, reverend priest, thy sentence rash refrain!—
> All is not as it seems—the female train
> Know by their bearing to disguise their mood."

A more lame excuse for a foul crime could not have been conceived, and even the hardened king himself is ashamed of it.

The prelate has listened to these confessions in horror, and no wonder, especially as these excuses show that there is little penitence in the culprit. At the close, he speaks very sternly—

> "O hardened offspring of an iron race!
>   What of thy crimes, Don Roderick, shall I say?
> What alms, or prayers, or penance can efface
>   Murder's dark spot, wash treason's stain away!
> For the foul ravisher how shall I pray,
>   Who, scarce repentant, makes his crime his boast?
> How hope Almighty vengeance shall delay,
>   Unless, in mercy to yon Christian host,
> He spare the shepherd, lest the guiltless sheep be lost."

Roderick is utterly hardened; he cares little for this

denunciation, and is ready to face the consequences of his crimes; but, in reply, he desires the prelate to lead him to that hidden chamber above mentioned, where he may learn the secrets of the future. The priest warns him that this hidden room will only disclose its secrets to a monarch who is the last of his line and is on the brink of his overthrow. The king, however, persists in his determination, and the prelate leads the way.

They reach an "ancient gateway," which the king unlocks, and opens with some difficulty. They find themselves in a large, vaulted hall, the walls of which are all of black marble, covered with "signs and characters unknown." Two bronze figures face them, standing against the opposite wall—one holds an hourglass, the other a mace: they represent Destiny and Time. The eyes of that representing Destiny are fixed upon the hour-glass of the other, in which the sand is fast falling. When the whole of the sand has fallen into the lower portion of the glass, the figure representing Destiny raises its mace and strikes the wall a heavy blow, on which the wall opens, and to Roderick are now exposed the visions of the future. Into these, which comprise the history of Spain from the eighth to the nineteenth century, we will now enter.

These visions are divided into three portions. The first opens with the Moorish invasion of Spain in A.D. 711, the defeat and death of Roderick, and the conquest of the country by the invaders. The second portion represents the period of the sixteenth century when Spain was at her highest pitch of power; she had expelled the Moslem, and extended her conquests over a great part of the world, the glory of this period, however, being dimmed with bigotry and the cruelties of the Inquisition. The third portion represents the earlier years of the nineteenth century, when Napoleon, in his attempt to subjugate Spain and Portugal, brought on the Peninsular War.

First, then, appears to Roderick the country of Spain laid out before him like a map; the inhabitants also move before him, "in various forms and various equipage," with various intermittent sounds—one of which, suggestive indeed to the king, is a female shriek, followed by the crash of eastern musical instruments and Moorish war-cries, significant of the violation of Cava and the Moorish invasion which followed, brought about by her enraged father. Roderick knows well what these sounds mean; he looks on with great excitement, and, carried away by his feelings, urges on his troops to resist the invader—

> "They come! they come! I see the groaning lands
> White with the turbans of each Arab horde,
> Swart Zaarah joins her misbelieving bands,
> Allah and Mahomet their battle-word,
> The choice they yield, the Koran or the sword.—
> See how the Christians rush to arms amain!—
> In yonder shout the voice of conflict roared;
> The shadowy hosts are closing on the plain—
> Now, God and St. Iago strike, for the good cause of Spain!"

But, alas! the scene which opens before him contains nothing but disaster and defeat to the Christian troops, their leader himself setting the example of flight. The king exclaims—

> "'By Heaven, the Moors prevail! the Christians yield!—
> Their coward leader gives for flight the sign!
> The sceptred craven mounts to quit the field—
> Is not yon steed Orelia?—Yes, 'tis mine!
> But never was she turned from battle line;
> Lo! where the recreant spurs o'er stock and stone!— '
> Curses pursue the slave, and wrath divine!
> Rivers ingulf him!'—'Hush,' in shuddering tone,
> The Prelate said, 'rash Prince, yon visioned form's thine own.'"

Yes, it is himself the king sees flying before the enemy, and in attempting to cross the flooded stream of the Guadalquiver, both steed and rider perish.

The invaders spread over the land, and for centuries Moslem rule is dominant in Spain—

> "Berber and Ismael's sons the spoils divide,
> With naked scimitars mete out the land,
> And for their bondsmen base the freeborn natives brand."

With this the scene closes. There is a momentary darkness, the prospect being blotted out by flames and smoke, accompanied by sounds like thunder, this representing a period of war; then gradually the smoke clears away, and the scene again opens to the view. This is the commencement of the second period of the vision.

Scott places before us in glowing colours the cruelties and barbarities of the Moorish occupation of Spain—the imprisonment of Christian women in the harem, the Cross hurled down from the altar, and the Mohammedan worship introduced into Christian churches; but, if we turn to history, we find that this is somewhat exaggerated: although, at first, in the first fervour of conquest, there may have been some outrages by the invaders, the Moslem rule in Spain appears to have been generally tolerant, and, indeed, it appears that in all the countries conquered by the Mohammedans, the vanquished, on payment of a moderate tribute, were permitted the free exercise of their own religion without molestation.[2] In fact, the rule of Moslem in Spain, in this case, contrasts favourably with that of the Christian sovereigns, Ferdinand and Isabella, under whose reign the horrors of the Inquisition were introduced; which latter period is shown in the second portion of the vision, into which we are about to enter.

The Moors were not permitted long to remain in undisputed possession of Spain; in fact, the tide of their conquests was now approaching its flood. They had swarmed over India, Africa, and Spain, and they now attempted to carry their conquests further into Europe. In A.D. 732, an Arab force crossed the Pyrenees and invaded France, but here they were met at Tours by a Christian force under Charles Martel, totally defeated, and driven back into Spain. This was the first check to their victorious career; here the Divine fiat went forth to their devouring tide of conquest—"Thus far shalt thou come, and no farther, and here shall thy proud waves be stayed." Sir Edward Creasy rightly includes the Battle of Tours in his book on the "Decisive Battles of the World."

From this date, the Mohammedan tide of conquest in Spain gradually receded, while the Christian power by slow degrees obtained the superiority. A small body of Christian refugees had fled to the mountains of Asturias; these gradually formed themselves into a small kingdom, which was strengthened and

(2) Gibbon's "Decline and Fall of the Roman Empire," Chap. LI., page 590.

enlarged as time grew on. For several centuries a state of war continued between Christians and Moslems, in which, although there were varying successes, the former by degrees drove the latter back towards the south. In the eleventh century, which marks the centre period of these wars, appeared the famous warrior, the Cid Rodrigo Diaz, whose prowess contributed greatly to the Christian cause.[3] In the fifteenth century, the possessions of the Moors in Spain were confined to the kingdom of Granada, and when the capital town of that kingdom, Granada, was captured by the Christian host of Castilians and Arragonese, under Ferdinand and Isabella, in 1492, the Moorish power in Spain was finally destroyed—

"There was crying in Granada, when the sun was going down,
Some calling on the Trinity, some calling on Mahoun:
Here passed away the Koran, in here the Cross was borne,
And here was heard the Christian bell and there the Moorish horn." [4]

The period which now ensues, shown in the second portion of the vision, represents the kingdom of Spain in its highest glory. It was then that she, like the Moorish kingdom before her, stretched the arms of conquest over a great portion of the world. It was then that new countries, never before dreamed of, were discovered by Columbus and other daring explorers, to be followed by the conquest of these countries under such men as Cortes and Pizarro—

"Oft his proud galleys sought some new-found world,
That latest sees the sun, or first the morn."

In the sixteenth century, in the reign of Philip II., Spain was the most powerful kingdom in the world. In Europe, she possessed Spain and Portugal, the Netherlands, part of the present France ("Franche Comté"), a large portion of Italy, and Sicily; in Asia, the Philippine Islands, a portion of the south-west of India, and other islands; while, in America, she possessed Mexico and Peru and a part of the present southern United

(3) It is strange that Scott makes no mention of this hero in his " Vision."

(4) Lockhart's " Spanish Ballads."

States.[5] Lord Macaulay, in the essay quoted in the above note, does not omit to say that the empire of Philip II. was more powerful than that of Napoleon, for the latter, while dominant over the greater portion of Europe, was entirely confined to land; for the British fleet rode the sea unopposed, and no French ship dare show itself out of harbour; while Philip was practically unopposed by sea or land until his invasion of Britain in 1588, when his Armada received that crushing defeat which proved the turning-point in the career of Spanish conquest, as the battle of Tours proved to be that of the Moors.

But before this external blow took place, a certain fatal element was slowly and secretly sapping the power of the Spanish kingdom. This was Bigotry, as represented by that terrible institution, the Spanish Inquisition; this gradually obtained entire influence over the Spanish nation, and, through its deadly work internally, the external power of the nation declined, until, a century later, the greater portion of her conquests had been lost, and Spain had fallen low in the list of nations.

Scott well explains this by representing Spain, during the period of her greatness, as being under the influence of two genii, Valour and Bigotry; and well does he show how these two influences worked in the country in the hour of her glory, while the predominating influence of the latter caused her fall—

> "Before the Cross has waned the Crescent's ray,
> And many a monastery decks the stage,
> And lofty church, and low-browed hermitage.
> The land obeys a Hermit and a Knight—
> The genii these of Spain for many an age;
> This clad in sackcloth, that in armour bright,
> And that was Valour named, this Bigotry was hight."

The poet well shows how the sackcloth-clad genie was more powerful than the one in armour—

> "Haughty of heart and brow the Warrior came,
> In look and language proud as proud might be,
> Vaunting his lordship, lineage, fights, and fame,
> Yet was that bare-foot Monk more proud than he;

(5) Lord Macaulay's Essay on the "War of Succession in Spain."

> And, as the ivy climbs the tallest tree,
>   So round the loftiest sóul his toils he wound,
> And with his spells subdued the fierce and free,
>   Till ermined Age, and Youth in arms renowned,
> Honouring his scourge and hair-cloth, meekly kissed the ground."

Well, indeed, here does the poet describe how Valour "veiled his crest to Bigotry," how he—

> "Stooped ever to that Anchoret's behest,
>   Nor reasoned of the right nor of the wrong,
> But at his bidding laid the lance in rest,
>   And wrought fell deeds the troubled ꞏꞏ .d along,
> For he was fierce as brave, and pitiless as strong"

—a true estimate of the Spanish character at that period. Scott concludes this portion of the vision with a comment on the cruelties of the Inquisition, and their terrible *autos-da-fé*—

> "And at his [Bigotry's] word the choral hymns awake,
>   And many a hand the silver censer sways.
> But, with the incense-breath these censers raise,
>   Mix steams from corpses smouldering in the fire;
> The groans of prisoned victims mar the lays,
>   And shrieks of agony confound the quire,
> While, 'mid the mingled sounds, the darkened scenes expire."

Here closes the second portion of the vision, and I cannot help thinking that Scott somewhat slurs over it in his desire to get on to the third period, that of Napoleon and Wellington. I think it a pity that he did not go more into detail in describing one of the most interesting periods in Spanish history.

A lapse of two hundred years takes place before we enter into the third portion of the vision. This brings us to the early years of the nineteenth century, just before the opening of the Peninsular War. It is now a very different Spain to that of the sixteenth century. King Roderick hears strains of secular music in place of the former religious chants, dances are taking place, gaiety reigns supreme instead of the grim *autos-da-fé* before described. The poet says—

> "And well such strains the opening scene became;
>   For Valour had relaxed his ardent look,
> And at a lady's feet, like lion tame,
>   Lay stretched, full loth the weight of arms to brook;

And softened Bigotry, upon his book,
  Pattered a task of little good or ill:
  But the blythe peasant plied his pruning-hook,
  Whistled the muleteer o'er vale and hill,
  And rung from village green the merry seguidille."

The above lines clearly show the degeneracy existing at this period among the nobility and clergy of Spain, but the national spirit still existed among the peasantry, as future events were soon clearly to prove.

It was at this period (A.D. 1808) that Napoleon entered into that disastrous attempt to subjugate Spain and Portugal which was the principal cause of his fall. He owned this himself—"It was the Spanish ulcer," he said, "which destroyed me." He determined to oust the royal family of Spain, and to place his brother Joseph on the throne of that country.[6]

Spain, indeed, lay open at this time to Napoleon's iniquitous designs. The Court was divided against itself. On the one hand were the weak old king, Charles IV., his queen, and her infamous favourite, Godoy; on the other, Ferdinand, Prince of Asturias, the heir-apparent to the throne—

"Grey Royalty, grown impotent of toil,
  Let the grave sceptre slip his lazy hold,
  And careless saw his rule become the spoil
  Of a loose female and her minion bold."

I need not enter into the details of these plots and quarrels, and the infamous means by which Napoleon accomplished his purpose; suffice it to say that, by July, 1808, the Royal Family had been removed to France, and Joseph Bonaparte was established on the throne at Madrid, that city being occupied by French troops under Murat—[7]

"Even so upon that peaceful scene was poured,
  Like gathering clouds, full many a foreign band,
  And he, their leader, wore in sheath his sword,
  And offered peaceful front and open hand,

(6) See my treatise, "The Decisive Campaign of Torres Vedras," Chap. II., "Napoleon and Spain."

(7) I entered into the details of these occurrences, in my treatise, mentioned in the last note.

Veiling the perjured treachery he planned,
    By friendship's zeal and honour's specious guise,
Until he won the passes of the land;
    Then, burst were honour's oath and friendship's ties!
He clutched his vulture-grasp and called fair Spain his prize."

Scott describes Napoleon as being accompanied by a "shadowy form," bearing a torch, which she waves abroad : this figure represents Ambition. He then describes the installation of Joseph to the Spanish throne, the mere puppet of Napoleon—

"The ruthless leader beckoned from his train
    A wan, fraternal shade, and bade him kneel,
And paled his temples with the crown of Spain,
    While trumpets rang, and heralds cried, 'Castile!'
Not that he loved him—No!—in no man's weal,
    Scarce in his own, e'er joyed that sullen heart;[8]
Yet round that throne he bade his warriors wheel,
    That the poor puppet might perform his part,
And be a sceptred slave, at his stern beck to start."

But if Napoleon thought that his object was now accomplished, he found himself greatly mistaken. He did not know the Spanish people. They are the most extraordinary people in the world : before an invader they have more than once appeared utterly to collapse, but, when that invader considers himself to be settled victoriously in a conquered country, he finds that his work is only just beginning. The country rises from end to end, and the invader finds himself master only of the ground on which his troops stand. So it was now—

"But on the natives of that land misused,
    Not long the silence of amazement hung,
Nor brooked they long their friendly faith abused,
    For, with a common shriek, the general tongue
Exclaimed, 'To arms!' and fast to arms they sprung;
    And Valour woke, the genius of the land!
Pleasure, and ease, and sloth aside he flung,
    As burst the awakening Nazarite his band,
When 'gainst his treacherous foes he clenched his dreadful hand."

(8) Scott, I think, lets his hatred of Napoleon here go too far. The latter was not wholly devoid of personal affection.

Had the Spanish people been united, they might have driven the invaders from the land, but each province acted independently, each forming its own Junta (Assembly) and following its own course; this was the Spanish weakness throughout. Even as it was, however, they did well: a terrible disaster befel the French at Baylen, in Andalusia, where a whole army laid down their arms, on which Joseph fled from Madrid and retired with his whole force behind the Ebro.

Scott here gives a very good account of the nature of this war; the ruthless march of the invaders, victorious, indeed, in general, over the inferior Spanish troops, but harassed at all times by the guerilla bands, which—

> "Came like night's tempest, and avenged the land,
> And claimed for blood the retribution due."

Scott also touches upon the glorious defence of the cities of Zaragoza and Gerona—

> "Then Zaragoza—blighted be the tongue
> That names thy name without the honours due!
> For never hath the harp of minstrel rung
> Of faith so felly proved, so firmly true!
> Mine, sap, and bomb thy shattered ruins knew,
> Each art of war's extremity had room,
> Twice from thy half-sacked streets the foe withdrew,
> And when at length stern Fate decreed thy doom,
> They won not Zaragoza, but her children's bloody tomb."

Also, regarding the city of Gerona—

> "Nor thine alone such wreck. Gerona fair!
> Faithful to death thy heroes should be sung,
> Manning the towers while o'er their heads the air
> Swart as the smoke from raging furnace hung;
> Now thicker darkening where the mine was sprung,
> Now briefly lightened by the cannon's flare,
> Now arched with fire-sparks as the bomb was flung,
> And reddening now with conflagration's glare,
> While by the fatal light the foes for storm prepare."

We now enter into another stage of the conflict, when a British force enters the scene of action, to help the Spanish

people in their hour of need. As from Asturias came the first
light that brightened the darkness of the Moorish invasion of
Spain, so from the same province came the appeal to Great
Britain for help, which appeal indicated the first step towards
the deliverance of Spain from the French invader—

> "While all around was danger, strife, and fear,
>   While the earth shook, and darkened was the sky,
> And wide Destruction stunned the listening ear,
>   Appalled the heart, and stupified the eye,—
> Afar was heard that thrice-repeated cry,
>   In which old Albion's heart and tongue unite
> Whene'er her soul is up and pulse beats high,
>   Whether it hail the wine-cup or the fight,
> And bid each arm be strong, or bid each heart be light."

The approach of the British force is now exposed to Don
Roderick's view. He sees "a gallant navy stemming the billows
broad," displaying our national flag, the Union Jack—

> "From mast and stern St. George's symbol flowed,
>   Blent with the silver cross to Scotland dear."

The landing of the host is grandly described—

> "It was a dread, yet spirit-stirring sight!
>   The billows foamed beneath a thousand oars,
> Fast as they land the red-cross ranks unite,
>   Legions on legions brightening all the shores.
> Then banners rise, and cannon-signal roars,
>   Then peals the warlike thunder of the drum,
> Thrills the loud fife, the trumpet-flourish pours,
>   And patriot hopes awake, and doubts are dumb,
> For, bold in Freedom's cause, the bands of Ocean come!"

Scott then comments on the different nationalities comprising
this auxiliary force, and their several characteristics; first,
England—

> "A various host—from kindred realms they came,
>   Brethren in arms, but rivals in renown—
> For yon fair bands shall merry England claim,
>   And with their deeds of valour deck her crown.

Hers their bold port, and hers their martial frown,
  And hers their scorn of death in Freedom's cause,
Their eyes of azure, and their locks of brown,
  And the blunt speech that bursts without a pause,
And freeborn thoughts, which league the soldier with the
  laws." (9)

The poet naturally becomes more enthusiastic when he goes on to speak of his own countrymen; it is a fine description of the Highlanders—

"And O! loved warriors of the Minstrel's land!
  Yonder your bonnets nod, your tartans wave;
The rugged form may mark the mountain band,
  And harsher features, and a mien more grave;
But ne'er in battlefield throbbed heart so brave
  As that which beats beneath the Scottish plaid,
And when the pibroch bids the battle rave,
  And level for the charge your arms are laid,
Where lives the desperate foe that for such onset stayed!"

These are grand lines, and quite true; but Scott writes as if the Scottish contingent was entirely composed of Highlanders; there were surely as many Lowland Scotsmen in the ranks, as good soldiers, in their way, as their Highland brethren. The Welsh contingent is not mentioned at all.

In proceeding to his comment on the Irish contingent, Scott does not omit to mention that Wellington was, on the mother's side, of that nationality, he also having been born in that country—

"Hark! from yon stately ranks what laughter rings,
  Mingling wild mirth with war's stern minstrelsy,
His jest while each blithe comrade round him flings,
  And moves to death with military glee:
Boast, Erin, boast them! tameless, frank, and free,
  In kindness warm, and fierce in danger known,
Rough Nature's children, humorous as she:
  And he, yon chieftain—strike the proudest tone
Of thy bold harp, Green Isle!—the hero is thine own."

(9) Scott gives here the best side of the British soldier, and in his general comment he is right; but it cannot be denied that Wellington's men, although excellent fighting machines, were not in other respects always "leagued with the laws."

And here the poem ends abruptly—too abruptly, as I think, for Scott closes his work just as the rescuing force appears on the scene. Surely he should have made King Roderick see the deliverance of his country from this final invader. Scott himself says—

> "Now on the scene Vimeira should be shown,
> On Talavera's fight should Roderick gaze,
> And hear Corunna wail her battle won,
> And see Busaco's crest with lightning blaze."

It will be noticed that Scott here only makes mention of the earlier battles, which took place before the enemy were checked at the lines of Torres Vedras, which check proved to be the turning-point in the war; the above battles were looked upon as barren victories, no favourable result occurring from them. He does, indeed, in his "Conclusion," mention Fuentes d'Honoro—

> "Behold, where, named by some prophetic seer,
> Flows Honour's Fountain, as foredoomed the stain
> From thy dishonoured name and arms to clear—
> Fallen Child of Fortune,[10] turn, redeem her favour here!"

Scott's lines on Busaco are good; he refers to the boast of Masséna that he would never rest until he had planted the French standard on the towers of Lisbon, and driven the British into the sea—in his own words, "drowned the leopard"—

> "And shall the boastful Chief maintain his word,
> Though Heaven hath heard the wailings of the land,
> Though Lusitania whet her vengeful sword,
> Though Britons arm, and Wellington command!
> No! grim Busaco's iron ridge shall stand
> An adamantine barrier to his force!
> And from its base shall wheel his shattered band,
> As from the unshaken rock the torrent hoarse
> Bears off its broken waves, and seeks a devious course."

It will be noted, however, that the above verses would more fitly apply to the lines of Torres Vedras than to Busaco. After his defeat at the latter place, Masséna managed to turn Wellington's flank; the latter had, therefore, to retreat on Torres Vedras,

(10) Masséna, termed by Napoleon "The Spoilt Child of Fortune."

and it was not until Masséna had reached the lines there that the French received their first permanent check. Scott, however, afterwards well describes that check—

> "Four moons have heard these thunders idly rolled,
>   Have seen these wistful myriads eye their prey,
> As famished wolves survey a guarded fold—
>   But in the middle path a lion lay!
> At length they move—but not to battle-fray,
>   Nor blaze yon fires where meets the manly fight;
> Beacons of infamy, they light the way
>   Where cowardice and cruelty unite
> To damn with double shame their ignominious flight." (11)

Scott mentions Albuera and Barossa shortly—

> "Hark! Albuera thunders Beresford,
>   And red Barossa shouts for dauntless Græme!"

He gives Beresford too much credit for the former victory; in fact, he expends several divisions of verses in this general's praise. I will not say that they are undeserved, but, certainly, Beresford, great organiser as he was, was not equal to Wellington as a general, or, indeed, to Soult, his opponent at Albuera; and had it not been for the dauntless valour of the British soldiers, that victory would have been a defeat.(12)

Scott never mentions Wellington's greatest victories, such as Salamanca, Vittoria, and the Pyrenees.(13)

Taking the poem as a whole, it is a good conception, and the lines are very beautiful and inspiring, but the fault is, as I think,

(11) Masséna, after his check at Torres Vedras, being forced to retreat, vented his rage on the unhappy inhabitants of the districts through which he passed—country utterly laid waste, towns burnt, and people murdered.

(12) It was after this battle that Soult made the well-known remark, which has generally been ascribed to Napoleon, that the British soldier never knew when he was beaten.

(13) Scott, however, mentions the battle of Vittoria in one of his lesser poems: mark his comment on the different British nationalities—

> "The English Rose was ne'er sae red,
>   The Shamrock waved where glory led,
> And the Scottish Thistle raised its head,
>   And smiled upon Vittoria."

that it does not go far enough. I have drawn attention to this more than once; the events of the second portion of the vision were, as I said, somewhat slurred over and many events of that period omitted; and I have just pointed out how, in the third period, the poem ends abruptly, just as the interesting portion was commencing. I think it is a pity that Scott did not go further into the details of the history of Spain, which history is one of the most interesting of all among the European nations. However, as I said, the lines are beautiful, and the poet concludes in his usually lovely style—

> "But all too long, through seas unknown and dark,
>   (With Spenser's parable I close my tale,)
> By shoal and rock hath steered my venturous bark
>   And landward now I drive before the gale:
> And now the blue and distant shore I hail,
>   And nearer now I see the port expand,
> And now I gladly furl my weary sail,
>   And, as the prow light touches on the strand,
> I strike my red-cross flag, and bind my skiff to land."

ROKEBY.

VIII.—ROKEBY.

In entering into a comment on the above poem, and the characters introduced into it, I find myself confronted with a more difficult task than I have hitherto experienced, and for these reasons—first, that I know less of this poem than I do of any other of Scott's poetical works, some of which I could comment upon with the greatest ease and with but little reference to the text-book; but, in the case of "Rokeby," I find that I have to study the poem carefully before attempting to enter into any of the details. Again, the scene is laid in an entirely new country, and one which is strange to me; it is the portion of country surrounding the rivers Tees and Greta, in the county of York. This district, with the exception of a visit of an hour or two to Barnard Castle, I have never traversed. Scott, however, had visited it more than once, and was evidently greatly impressed by its beauties, as we shall see as we proceed with our comment; but Baddeley, in his guide book, does not seem to have been impressed so greatly, for he says—"Exquisitely pretty as the scenery so attractively described undoubtedly is, it will probably strike every visitor that the popular poet (Scott) has somewhat erred in the direction usually taken by irresponsible writers—exaggeration." [1] How this may be, I cannot say, not knowing the country, but I remember greatly admiring the view of the valley of the Tees from the top of the keep at Barnard Castle. Here again, however, Baddeley criticises Scott; he says—"We forbear quoting Scott's fanciful description of the view from the castle ('Rokeby,' Canto II.), because not more than a quarter of the objects therein mentioned are to be seen." [2]

The scene, therefore, is laid entirely in England, in contradistinction to those of Scott's other poems, which, with the

(1) Baddeley's "Yorkshire," Part II., page 138.

(2) Baddeley's "Yorkshire," Part II., page 134.

exception of "The Bridal of Triermain" (the scene of which, indeed, lies not far from the Scottish Border), and, of course, of "The Vision of Don Roderick," which stands quite apart from the other poems, are laid altogether in Scotland. Another peculiarity of the poem is that the characters introduced are, with the exception of the young Irish chief, Redmond O'Neale, entirely English; and, indeed, Redmond is only Irish on the mother's side. A great feature of the poem, like that of "The Lady of the Lake," to which I have already drawn attention, lies in the beautiful short pieces of poetry which occur at intervals throughout it.

The period in which the events of the poem take place is the seventeenth century, at the time of the great Civil War; and it opens just at the time of the great battle of Marston Moor, in July, 1644, which battle-field lies, as we know, in Yorkshire, about six miles west of York. This battle is the only historical fact mentioned in the poem; the general events are quite fictitious, as Scott himself owns.

The scene of the poem opens, then, at Barnard Castle, in the castle from which the town takes its name—a ruin now, but, doubtless, garrisoned and in full preservation in those days. The governor is one Oswald Wycliffe, who holds the castle for the Parliament, but he is not the kind of man, as we shall see, to be swayed either by feelings of loyalty towards his king or by patriotic feelings regarding the freedom of his country. He takes the side which he thinks likely to be the most profitable to himself, nor does he care much about exposing himself in the battlefield, but rather prefers remaining safe within the ramparts of his castle—

> "While Wycliffe, bound by many a train
> Of kindred art with wily Vane,
> Less prompt to brave the bloody field,
> Made Barnard's battlements his shield,
> Secured them with his Lunedale powers,
> And for the Commons held the towers."

In commencing our treatise, then, we come into the presence of this worthy, who is evidently in a very disturbed state of mind. He lies on his couch in a restless state, tossing from side to side, with intervals of perturbed snatches of sleep. The poet describes the condition of this Oswald Wycliffe in his usual glowing language, far more descriptive than any words of mine can portray—

> "Ere sleep stern Oswald's senses tied,
> Oft had he changed his weary side,
> Composed his limbs, and vainly sought
> By effort strong to banish thought.
> Sleep came at length, but with a train
> Of feelings true and fancies vain,
> Mingling, in wild disorder cast,
> The expected future with the past.
> Conscience, anticipating time,
> Already rues the enacted crime,
> And calls her furies forth to shake
> The sounding scourge and hissing snake;
> While her poor victim's outward throes
> Bear witness to his mental woes,
> And show what lesson he may read
> Beside a sinner's restless bed."

As the above lines imply, Oswald's sleep may well be disturbed, for he is expecting the news of a great crime—no less than murder, devised by himself, the execution of which he has transferred to another, being too cowardly to undertake it himself. Such is the character of this man—utterly unscrupulous, shrinking from no crime, but shrinking from the consequences to himself; but also, not being entirely hardened, subjected to the tortures of remorse. He is undoubtedly the villain of the poem, rather than the man by whom the crime above alluded to is committed, and to whom we shall shortly be introduced.

Oswald is startled from his uneasy slumbers by the tramp of a horse, which approaches the castle gate. He hears the warder's challenge, the fall of the drawbridge, and soon the voices of men below ushering the newcomer to Oswald's chamber—

> "The cry was—'Tidings from the host,
> Of weight—a messenger comes post.'"

This is the messenger whom Oswald expects, ostensibly with news from the battle-field of Marston Moor, where the hostile armies are now facing each other; but of the result of the battle the governor cares little, his anxiety being to know whether the foul deed which he had commissioned the stranger to accomplish had been committed. He gives orders to admit the stranger, and to bring food, &c., for him.

The stranger, one Bertram Risingham, strides into the room with little ceremony, and in him we are confronted with one of the principal characters of the poem—one who would generally be considered the "villain" of the piece, until the last canto, when he suddenly changes and shows that he has some good in him.[3] Scott hints at this even now, when he first introduces Bertram; he says—

> "Even now, by conscience unrestrained,
> Clogged by gross vice, by slaughter stained,
> Still knew his daring soul to soar,
> And mastery o'er the mind he bore;
> For meaner guilt, or heart less hard,
> Quailed beneath Bertram's bold regard."

Such is the case, now, with the two men with whom we are dealing. We see the great distinction between Bertram and Oswald, between the bold and the cowardly villain, which will be fully depicted in the conversation which follows and in the future events of the poem. The appearance of Bertram is not one to inspire confidence, but rather suspicion and fear. He has the undoubted mien of a soldier, brave indeed, but truculent—

> "But yet, though Bertram's hardened look
> Unmoved could blood and danger brook,
> Still worse than apathy had place
> On his swart brow and callous face;
> For evil passions, cherished long,
> Had ploughed them with impressions strong.
> All that gives gloss to sin, all gay,
> Light folly, passed with youth away,
> But rooted stood, in manhood's hour,
> The weeds of vice without their flower."

(3) I well remember reading "Rokeby" for the first time as a boy. Through the first five cantos I detested Bertram, looking upon him as an unscrupulous, hardened villain, with no redeeming point about him except his courage. In the sixth canto my opinion of him changed (to my great surprise at the time), and my sympathy was with him when he fell, fighting bravely against overwhelming odds.

His had been a life of crime; he had been a buccaneer in the Spanish Main, utterly unscrupulous, shrinking from no crime, but withal brave as a lion. In this latter characteristic he is superior to Oswald, the weak, cowardly villain, who—superior to this adventurer in birth and station, should on that account be above such conduct—is equally callous to crime, but without the courage to undertake it himself. Bertram, as we shall see, thoroughly despises Oswald, and makes no attempt to conceal his contempt; he treats him without the slightest ceremony, which is most galling to Oswald, the buccaneer's superior in birth and station.

Bertram, as I have said, clanks into the room without ceremony, and falls to the food and drink like a ravenous wolf, without a "by your leave." He takes his time over the repast, disregarding Oswald, who paces the room impatiently—

> "In feverish agony to learn
> Tidings of deep and dread concern,"

but he fears his guest, and dares not interrupt him—

> "Then did his silence long proclaim
> A struggle between fear and shame."

At length Oswald attempts to lure from his guest the news which he is so anxiously expecting—*i.e.*, of the deed which he had incited Bertram to commit—trusting that the latter might make the statement without a direct question from the former. This is thoroughly characteristic of Oswald; Bertram quite understands this, and baffles him—he "returns him answer dark and short"—

> "Or started from the theme, to range
> In loose digression wild and strange."

Oswald, thus driven to speak more plainly, now ventures to ask if a battle has been fought, hoping that this would lead to an admission of the deed on the part of Bertram, but the latter still baffles him, and enters into a detail of the battle of Marston Moor, from which battle-field he has just returned, having fought on the side of the Parliament. The description is fine—

"Wouldst hear the tale ?—On Marston heath
Met, front to front, the ranks of death;
Flourished the trumpets fierce, and now
Fired was each eye and flushed each brow;
On either side loud clamours ring—
' God and the Cause!'—' God and the King!'
Right English all, they rushed to blows,
With nought to win, and all to lose."

Bertram is evidently opposed to the Royalist wing which defeated the opposing Parliamentary wing; and the victorious Royalist charge (led, however, in fact, by Lord Goring, not by Prince Rupert, as the poem intimates) is described finely—

"The battle's rage
Was like the strife which currents wage,
Where Orinoco, in his pride,
Rolls to the main no tribute tide,
But 'gainst deep ocean urges far
A rival sea of roaring war;
While, in ten thousand eddies driven,
The billows fling their foam to heaven,
And the pale pilot seeks in vain,
Where rolls the river, where the main.(4)
Even thus, upon the bloody field,
The eddying tides of conflict wheeled
Ambiguous, till that heart of flame,
Hot Rupert, on our squadrons came,
Hurling against our spears a line
Of gallants, fiery as their wine;
Then ours, though stubborn in their zeal,
In zeal's despite began to reel.
What would'st thou more ?—in tumult tossed,
Our leaders fell, our ranks were lost.
A thousand men, who drew the sword
For both the Houses and the Word,
Preached forth from hamlet, grange, and down,
To curb the crosier and the crown,
Now, stark and stiff, lie stretched in gore,
And ne'er shall rail at mitre more."

It was at this period of the fight that Bertram left the

(4) I have read, however, that while the Orinoco sends its waves far into the ocean, its tide is quite distinguishable from the ocean wave, and that it was this fact that brought Columbus the discovery of South America.

battle-field, having accomplished the deed to which he had been commissioned, the details of which we will now enter into.

Bertram also relates the news he heard at first of the rout of the Parliamentary forces and their Scottish auxiliaries (which rout is, as I shall show, at least exaggerated), and, later, of the turning of the fate of the day by Cromwell's "barbed horse"—

> " But ere I cleared that bloody press,
> Our northern horse ran masterless;
> Monckton and Mitton told the news,
> How troops of Roundheads choked the Ouse,
> And many a bonny Scot, aghast,
> Spurring his palfrey northward, passed,
> Cursing the day when zeal or meed
> First lured their Lesley o'er the Tweed."

This was the state of things when Bertram left the battle-field; he had accomplished his purpose, and he cares no more for the result of the battle than does Oswald, to whom he does not hesitate to tell that fact—

> " Yet when I reached the banks of Swale,
> Had rumour learned another tale;
> With his barbed horse, fresh tidings say,
> Stout Cromwell has redeemed the day;
> But whether false the news or true,
> Oswald, I reck as light as you." (5)

(5) I have often remarked on Scott's writing " for effect," setting aside historical facts. He appears to have done so here, confusing in some particulars the battles of Marston Moor and Naseby. In the former battle, the victorious Royalist left wing, which defeated the opposing Parliamentary right wing, was led by Lord Goring, not Prince Rupert, the latter wing being under Fairfax. Cromwell commanded the left Parliamentary wing, consisting of his own troopers (48 troops) and the Scottish contingent (22 troops) under David Lesley. These were opposed to the Royalist right wing, under Prince Rupert. A desperate strife ensued. " They stood at the sword's point," says an eye-witness, " a pretty while, hacking one another, but at last he (Cromwell) brake through them, scattering them like a little dust." Far from being routed, as the poem describes (see page 331 of treatise), Lesley and his Scots supported Cromwell loyally throughout. Cromwell, having thus defeated Rupert, leaves the Scots to engage the Royalist centre, while he proceeds to the other flank, occupying the ground originally held by Goring, which chief, returning from the pursuit of Fairfax's wing, is charged and defeated by Cromwell, the victory being completed by the destruction of the Royalist

These last words were spoken by Bertram later. I go back to the time when he left the fight. Oswald again attempts to insinuate hints, so as to extract a direct answer, affecting to look upon the report as "disastrous news," and asks concerning any chief who may have fallen, in these words, which show the utter hypocrisy and falseness of the man, in contradistinction to the plain-spokenness, utter recklessness of the ruffian before him—

> "What leaders of repute and name
> Bought by their death a deathless fame!
> If such my direst foeman's doom,
> My tears shall dew his honoured tomb."

No answer from Bertram, who thoroughly understands this hypocrisy. Oswald insinuates again, getting nearer to the final question—

> "No answer?—Friend, of all our host,
> Thou know'st whom I should hate the most,
> Whom thou, too, once wert wont to hate,
> Yet leavest me doubtful of his fate."

Bertram now bluntly desires a plain question; it must come from Oswald himself, and in plain words he demands this. On this reply, Oswald can contain himself no longer, but in anger bursts forth with the direct question—

---

infantry. With regard to the Scots, Goring in his charge had attacked a Scottish contingent under Lord Leven; that nobleman, indeed, thinking the battle lost, left the field, but his men held firm. Thus the rout of the Scots, mentioned in the poem, appears to be entirely incorrect, and it is a marvel to see Sir Walter Scott thus deteriorating his own countrymen; this is not like him.

With regard to Naseby, the Royalist right wing under Prince Rupert defeated the opposing wing under Ireton, but then fell into disorder, plundering, &c. Before Rupert could gather together again what men he could, and return, Cromwell, on the right, had defeated the Royalist left wing; he then turns on the flank of the Royalist centre, at that time assailed in front by Fairfax. The Royalists are then utterly defeated.

It will be seen, therefore, that the victorious charge under Prince Rupert took place at Naseby, not at Marston Moor, and that the Scottish contingent in the latter battle were not routed, but behaved well throughout. In both battles, Cromwell's "barbed horse" had the principal share in deciding the result.

(See account of battles in the "Encyclopædia Britannica," also "Biography of Cromwell," in the "Dictionary of National Biography.")

> " Wretch ! hast thou paid thy bloody debt ?
> Philip of Mortham, lives he yet ?
> False to thy patron or thine oath,
> Trait'rous or perjured, one or both.
> Slave ! hast thou kept thy promise plight,
> To slay thy leader in the fight ?"

On this, Bertram springs up with a harsh laugh, wrings Oswald's hand till the grasp "forces the red blood-drop from the nail," and exclaims (showing his disregard and contempt of Oswald in every word; he recks nothing of the higher caste and position of the latter)—

> " Now, Oswald Wycliffe, speaks thy heart !
> Now play'st thou well thy genuine part !
> Worthy, but for thy craven fear,
> Like me to roam a buccaneer.
> What reck'st thou of the Cause divine,
> If Mortham's wealth and lands be thine ?
> What carest thou for beleaguered York,
> If this good hand have done its work ?
> Or what, though Fairfax and his best
> Are reddening Marston's swarthy breast,
> If Philip Mortham with them lie,
> Lending his life-blood to the dye ?"

Straightforward words these, and eminently applicable to the character of the man to whom they are addressed.

Bertram then describes, in his usual straightforward manner (entirely opposite to that of Oswald), how, during the confusion caused by the thundering charge of Prince Rupert, he treacherously shoots his leader, Mortham (formerly his patron and friend), sees him fall, and, as he thinks, dead. He then clears out of the battle, as we have before seen.

The motives of the two villains, in causing the death of this man, are different. Oswald desires the lands and heritage of Mortham, of which he seems to be heir-presumptive. Bertram is actuated by a feeling of revenge for an imagined injury from his former patron and friend; he is indeed doubtful at first, but in a man like him revenge for an injury comes before gratitude and former friendship; the evil predominates over the good in him, and his resolve is soon decided—

> "When purposed vengeance I forego,
> Term me a wretch, nor deem me foe;
> And when an insult I forgive,
> Then brand me as a slave, and live!"

These words are strongly characteristic of the speaker, as those quoted above are of Oswald.[6]

And now, before continuing my narrative, I must make some explanation as to the events, the characters connected with them, and their relation to each other, which as yet have been only casually brought before my readers.

The families of Rokeby and Mortham occupy a prominent position in the poem. A glance at the map[7] will show that Rokeby Park and Mortham Tower[8] are in the immediate neighbourhood of each other, separated by the river Greta, a short distance above the junction of that river with the Tees. The representatives of these two families, at the period of the poem, are the Knight of Rokeby, Sir Richard, and Philip Mortham, already mentioned. These two are related to each other, Mortham having married Rokeby's sister. There exists also a close friendship between them, until the outbreak of the Civil War, when that friendship is broken by the two taking opposite sides—Rokeby that of the King, Mortham that of the Parliament—and these two old friends and relatives find themselves opposed to each other at Marston Moor. Oswald Wycliffe also, being, it appears, a relative of Mortham, seems to have been on terms of friendship with his two neighbours; his son Wilfrid, whom we shall shortly meet, is in love with Matilda, Rokeby's daughter and heiress, the heroine of the poem, whom we shall also meet soon; his love, however, is not returned, as we shall see. Such a match would, of course, be greatly advantageous to Oswald, and Rokeby himself is in favour of it, when the Civil War breaks out, and Oswald joins the side of the Parliament, for his own advantage, not actuated by any feeling either of loyalty or patriotism. Hereupon Rokeby, a staunch Royalist, like most of his class and position, declares that his daughter shall never

(6) See page 333 of treatise.

(7) Baddeley's "Yorkshire," Part II., Section Map No. 8.

(8) A peel tower restored, according to Baddeley.

wed the son of a rebel. Such cases of severed friendships must
have occurred only too frequently at the disturbed period with
which we are dealing.

And now to show how Bertram Risingham comes into the
story, and what reasons induced him to attempt the murder of
Mortham, his old friend and associate, and latterly his patron
and benefactor.

In the war with Ireland, towards the end of the reign of
Queen Elizabeth, Rokeby and Mortham took part. The Irish,
under O'Neale, Earl of Tyrone, defeated an English force under
the Earl of Essex at Avon Duff. Our two chiefs, being taken
prisoner in this engagement, received quarter at the hands of
the Tanist (heir-apparent) of O'Neale, were treated well, and
finally sent home unransomed. "Hereby hangs a tale," which
is an important feature of the poem, and into which we shall
enter later in the treatise.

On their return, the two friends spend their lives very
differently. Rokeby lives quietly on his estate—

> " Calm he enjoyed, by Greta's wave,
> The peace which James the Peaceful gave,
> While Mortham, far beyond the main,
> Waged his fierce wars on Indian Spain."

Mortham remains for years abroad, leading a wild kind of
life, that of an adventurer—a buccaneer, indeed. He falls in
with this Bertram Risingham, when or where, we are not told,
but it is certain that they were bosom friends and allies. Strange
it is that a man of Mortham's rank and position should thus link
himself with one like Bertram, but so it was. Bertram stuck
faithfully to his ally; he saved his life more than once, and,
remembering this, he says—

> " These thoughts like torrents rushed along,
> To sweep away my purpose strong."

And now for the reason why this faithful comrade of
Mortham, who for years had stuck to him "through thick and
thin," should have so changed in feeling towards his former
associate as to attempt to murder him. Strange, but quite
characteristic of the man we are dealing with.

Mortham returns home from his "years of piratical wandering," and Bertram with him. Mortham invites his old comrade to his house, as "partner of his wealth and home." But this condition of things does not last long. Mortham's character changes, through circumstances into which we will enter later, and also remorse appears to have seized him for his former piratical doings—

> "Doubts, horrors, superstitious fears,
> Saddened and dimmed descending years;
> The wily priests their victim sought,
> And damned each free-born deed and thought."

In fact, the piratical adventurer, which has not been unfrequently the case, becomes a religious fanatic.

It soon becomes very evident that such a household as this is no place for Bertram. There is no remorse in him for what he has done; he is still the same reckless, unscrupulous ruffian as ever; in fact, to the last he glories in what he has done. His conduct disgusts his former friend; he has to leave the house, doubtless at the command of Mortham himself—

> "Then must I seek another home,
> My licence shook his sober dome;
> If gold he gave, in one wild day
> I revelled thrice the sum away.
> An idle outcast then I strayed,
> Unfit for tillage or for trade,
> Deemed, like the steel of rusted lance,
> Useless and dangerous at once.
> The women feared my hardy look,
> At my approach the peaceful shook:
> The merchant saw my glance of flame,
> And locked his hoards when Bertram came;
> Each child of coward peace kept far
> From the neglected son of war."

These lines show clearly, far better than any words of mine could do, the position of Bertram; apart from his scandalising this Puritanical household, he is, in any circumstances, out of place in time of peace. His dismissal from the house, however, rankles deeply in his soul; he nourishes a bitter grudge against Mortham, his old associate in former days.

More congenial times arrive for Bertram when the Civil War breaks out. Mortham takes the side of the Parliament, and this is not to be wondered at, considering his present Puritanical temperament. He calls upon Bertram (who still appears to be a kind of retainer of his, though dismissed the house) to join him and his vassals, and the latter obeys, though here the grudge is increased. Bertram considers that he is placed in an entirely subordinate position; all places of trust are given to canting fanatics; he is left simply to run the risk of battle—

> " What guerdon waited on my care ?
> I could not cant of creed or prayer;
> Sour fanatics each trust obtained,
> And I, dishonoured and disdained,
> Gained but the high and happy lot,
> In these poor arms to front the shot!"

This latter grudge decides him. Scott, in his usual beautiful style, depicts the feelings of this man's mind, wavering between old reminiscences and recent grudges—

> " Philip of Mortham is with those
> Whom Bertram Risingham calls foes,
> Or whom more sure revenge attends,
> If numbered with ungrateful friends."

His mind is made up; evil has the mastery, and the fatal deed is done.

We return to the two villains. It would be well expected that Bertram would make his terms as to the division of Mortham's property, and this he at once proceeds to do. We must notice that he is in a very dangerous position, in the power of a man as unscrupulous as himself. Oswald might call his guards and arrest Bertram on the confession which the latter had just made; Oswald's word would assuredly be taken before that of this ruffian of truculent appearance; the latter could be speedily put out of the way. But Bertram has no fear whatever of this; his own courage is indisputable, and Oswald is a coward. The buccaneer proclaims his terms—he will not interfere with Oswald's inheritance of the lands and heritage of Mortham, but in the caverns which lie under Mortham's castle are stored hoards of plunder from South America—gold, jewels, plate, &c.; these Bertram claims for himself, according to what he terms "buccaneers' law."

It is not an unreasonable request, and Oswald, though chafing at the ruffian's haughty "laying down of the law," and anxious to acquire this "loot" himself, dares not refuse. Bertram declares his intention of proceeding to Mortham's castle at once, and insists on Oswald's accompanying him, as, without the presence of the heir-presumptive, he would not be admitted. Oswald, in his usually cowardly fashion, fearing to trust himself alone with Bertram, excuses himself, saying that his duties will not permit him to leave the castle, but suggests that his son Wilfrid should accompany "his friend," as he sneakingly terms Bertram. The latter quite comprehends Oswald's craven fear, and says that he cares not whether it be Wilfrid or his father, at the same time contemptuously remarking that he could easily have slain Oswald now, without danger to himself, had he been so minded. Wilfrid, therefore, is summoned, and the ill-assorted pair start on their mission. With this, the first canto of the poem ends.

Wilfrid, Oswald's son, is an entire contrast to his father. He is no warrior, neither is his nature sullied by crime. Physically weak and sickly, he has no wish, had he the power, to take part in any manly exercises; but he is devoted to study, especially poetry, and loves to wander about in solitude and dreamy meditation—

> "In youth he sought not pleasures found
> By youth, in horse, and hawk, and hound,
> But loved the quiet joys that wake
> By lonely stream and silent lake;
>
> .   .   .   .
>
> Such was his wont; and there his dream
> Soared on some wild, fantastic theme
> Of faithful love, or ceaseless spring,
> Till Contemplation's wearied wing
> The enthusiast could no more sustain,
> And sad he sank to earth again."

Wilfrid is the only survivor of a numerous progeny of sons of hardier type than he, and it is not wonderful that Oswald did not favour this sickly, dreamy boy. This boy, however, as is so often the case, was the darling of his mother. At the period, however, with which we are dealing, mother and sons, save Wilfrid, are all dead; therefore, Oswald now takes more notice of the youth, the latter being the only instrument to forward his ambitious schemes.

We have seen that Oswald was anxious to unite his son in marriage with Matilda, the heiress of Rokeby. Wilfrid is deeply in love with this maiden, but his love is not returned; she loves another, whom we shall shortly meet. But, if she cannot give the youth the love he longs for, she gives him everything else that she can—

> " Yet all Matilda could, she gave
> In pity to her gentle slave—
> Friendship, esteem, and fair regard,
> And praise, the poet's best reward!
> She read the tales his taste approved,
> And sang the lays he framed or loved;
> Yet, loth to nurse the fatal flame
> Of hopeless love in friendship's name,
> In kind caprice she oft withdrew
> The favouring glance to friendship due,
> Then grieved to see her victim's pain,
> And gave the dangerous smiles again."

This conduct on her part, however, must have caused terrible pain to Wilfrid, who was bound heart and soul in chains of love for her. It might have been done, as the poet suggests, with good intentions on her part, but, on the other hand, it might be called by a more unfavourable name. It does not also appear whether Matilda, at the time, disclosed to Wilfrid the fact that she loved another, probably she did not.

We have seen that both parents were favourable to the proposed match between the pair, until it was broken off by Rokeby on the outbreak of the Civil War, when Oswald joined the side of the Parliament. This seems to have preyed deeply upon Wilfrid's mind, for the last verses of the first canto of the poem describe his moody, dreamy state of mind. He is in this condition when his father rouses him to dispatch him on the mission to Mortham Castle—not without a warning—

> "Take thy sword!
> Bertram is—what I must not tell.
> I hear his hasty step—farewell!'"

The second canto opens with the poet's glowing description of the view from the summit of Barnard Castle, the principal feature being the course of the river Tees. This I myself have seen, and that, unfortunately, is all I know of the country in which the scene of the poem is laid. I have already commented upon this at the commencement of this treatise,[9] so I will only repeat that the route taken by the two wayfarers we are dealing with is unknown to me, and the description is taken entirely from the poem, not from my own personal observation, as it has been in many of my former treatises.

Bertram leaves the castle before dawn, and, accompanied by Wilfrid, crosses the bridge to the south bank of the Tees; thence, turning eastward, passes the ruins of Eglistone Abbey, towards Rokeby Park, which, however, he shuns; and, leaving the park on the left, crosses Greta Bridge; thence, descending into the valley beneath, follows the right bank of the river Greta towards its junction with the Tees.

Scott well describes the different feelings which occupy the thoughts of these two ill-assorted companions towards each other; the bold, truculent, and unscrupulous adventurer, and the mild, visionary recluse—

> "Each on his own deep visions bent,
> Silent and sad they onward went.
> Well may you think that Bertram's mood
> To Wilfrid savage seemed and rude;
> Well may you think bold Risingham
> Held Wilfrid trivial, poor, and tame;
> And small the intercourse, I ween,
> Such uncongenial souls between."

They descend the valley of the Greta, the scenery of which is beautifully described by Scott, which description is, in the opinion of Baddeley, exaggerated; as to this, never having been there, or, as far as I know, seen any photograph of the place, I cannot give any opinion.

(9) See page 325 of treatise.

The glen seems to be deep, and darkly wooded; in a part which they are now approaching it is so dark and gloomy that the sun, even at noonday, can barely penetrate through the overhanging boughs. The dell is believed to be haunted. Many grisly tales are told of it in the winter nights round the Christmas fires, and no peasant ventures to enter it after nightfall. Bertram, as we know, is bold and reckless, knowing no fear in any encounter with mortal man, but his otherwise bold spirit quails when superstition exerts its influence over it. There is no wonder in this; he is a native of the place, he is brought up from a child in the knowledge of these tales; and, besides this, there comes upon him the recollection of the many crimes he has committed, and especially, doubtless, that of the last and worst recently committed. Thus, on entering the so-called haunted glen, his otherwise bold soul is attacked by a pang of fear—

> "Thus, as a man, a youth, a child,
> Trained in the mystic and the wild,
> With this on Bertram's soul at times
> Rushed a dark feeling of his crimes;
> Such to his troubled soul their form,
> As the pale death-ship to the storm,
> And such their omen dim and dread,
> As shrieks and voices of the dead.
> That pang, whose transitory force
> Hovered 'twixt horror and remorse;
> That pang, perchance, his bosom pressed
> As Wilfrid sudden he addressed."

He informs the youth that he has seen twice, in this glen, a form lurking in the bushes by the path, and seemingly dogging their steps; e'er Wilfrid can reply, Bertram sees this form again, and, conquering his superstitious fear, with a threatening shout, draws his sword and dashes off in pursuit. The object of his pursuit appears to have climbed the cliffs bordering the glen; here Bertram follows, scaling the height with marvellous activity, up a very dangerous ascent, with constant risk of his neck; indeed, at one point, he loses his footing, and only saves himself by the hold of his hands. Eventually, he gains the summit in safety.

Wilfrid follows by a safer route, and the two now find themselves in front of the gateway of Mortham Castle, the situation of which, as the note to the poem says, "is eminently beautiful, occupying a high bank, at the bottom of which the Greta winds out of a dark, narrow, and romantic dell, of which a description has been attempted in the text, and flows onward through a more open valley to meet the Tees, about a quarter of a mile from the castle."

The castle, as the pair approach it, seems utterly deserted; not a sound rises from within, no neighing of horses or baying of hounds is heard, there is no porter at the gate, no attendants at their wonted offices, walks and orchard utterly neglected—

> "All spoke the master's absent care,
> All spoke neglect and disrepair."

Bertram pauses in front of an ancient tomb, a bowshot from the gate, shadowed by two huge elm trees. He says that the form which he has been following had vanished behind this tomb, where he had often thought that Mortham's treasure from the Indies was stored, which, from what he had heard from an old fellow-buccaneer, was often used as a hiding-place for their ill-gotten treasures—

> "Trust not, would his experience say,
> Captain or comrade with your prey;
> But seek some charnel, when, at full,
> The moon gilds skeleton and skull:
> There dig, and tomb your precious heap,
> And bid the dead your treasure keep;
> Sure stewards they, if fitting spell
> Their service to the task compel."

Bertram then states his belief that the apparition he had just seen was that of one who had been sacrificed at the hiding-place of this treasure, according to the horrible custom of the buccaneers, in order that his spirit might keep guard over the hidden treasure. Wilfrid, while disbelieving this superstitious fancy, and—

> "Much marvelling that a breast so bold
> In such fond tale belief should hold,"

makes inquiry of Bertram as to the appearance of this apparition which he had seen. That villain answers incautiously, with that infatuation which often compels a murderer to reveal his crime; he, indeed, half speaks to himself, forgetting that he is overheard—

> " 'Twas Mortham's form, from foot to head!
> His morion, with the plume of red,
> His shape, his mien—'twas Mortham, right
> As when I slew him in the fight."

Fatal admission! He had forgotten Wilfrid, who exclaims with horror, "Thou slew him? Thou?" The ruffian, though startled, recovers his hardihood, and, thoroughly despising Wilfrid, replies brutally—

> " I slew him?—I!—I had forgot
> Thou, stripling, knew'st not of the plot.
> But it is spoken—nor will I
> Deed done, or spoken word, deny.
> I slew him; I! for thankless pride;—
> 'Twas by this hand that Mortham died."

Wilfrid, meek, gentle, peace-loving as he is, is by no means without courage, and being, unlike his father, of blameless character and embued with hatred of crime, is horrified at this bold, shameless avowal. That latent spark of courage which animated him flames forth, and he dauntlessly flings himself upon the formidable ruffian with sword drawn, exclaiming—

> " Should every fiend, to whom thou'rt sold,
> Rise in thine aid, I keep my hold.—
> Arouse there, ho! take spear and sword!
> Attack the murderer of your lord!"

There were none, as we know, in the castle to aid, and the result to Wilfrid would soon have been fatal, for Bertram, roused to fury at the slight touch of the youth's weapon, turns upon him; in a moment he has struck the sword from Wilfrid's hand, and stretched him on the ground; in another moment his sword would have been in the youth's heart, when an unexpected intervention takes place.

The apparition of the morning steps between the antagonists, and with drawn sword parries Bertram's descending blow; he has, as the latter had said, the exact appearance of the (supposed) murdered Mortham—

> " 'Twas Mortham's bearing, bold and high,
>   His sinewy frame, his falcon eye,
>   His look and accent of command,
>   The martial gesture of his hand,
>   His stately form, spare-built and tall,
>   His war-bleached locks—'twas Mortham all."

The apparition looks steadily upon Bertram, and, with lifted hand, motions him away, saying sternly—

> " ' Go and repent,' he said, ' while time
>   Is given thee; add not crime to crime.' "

The cowed ruffian, not yet entirely certain whether he beholds the ghost of his murdered lord or that lord himself in "living flesh and blood," either of which is equally terrible to him, and also influenced by that habit of obedience which he had rendered for years to his lord, makes no attempt at resistance; he retreats step by step—

> "Oft stopped, and oft on Mortham stared,
>   And dark as rated mastiff glared."

Of a sudden, however, the trampling of horse is heard; Bertram turns, and plunges again into the glen; Mortham also retires from the spot, first, however, warning Wilfrid with the words, "Tell thou to none that Mortham lives."

The trampling of horse is caused by a party of horsemen, who, with Oswald Wycliffe himself at their head, draw up before the castle gate. Oswald eagerly inquires of his son why the latter has his sword drawn, and where Bertram is. Wilfrid replies, little dreaming of his father's share in the crime—

> "Bertram is gone—the villain's word
>   Avouched him murderer of his lord !
>   Even now we fought—but, when your tread
>   Announced you nigh, the felon fled."

Oswald attempts to set this aside, saying that Mortham

died in battle, and that Bertram, or Wilfrid himself, was raving, and tries to end the matter, saying that pursuit is vain; thankful, for his own sake, if Bertram gets clear off.

Unfortunately for Oswald, however, there is one riding beside him who has actually seen the crime committed. This is Redmond O'Neale, a young Irish chieftain, the page (or squire) of the Lord of Rokeby, who will in future take a prominent place in the events of the poem. He has come on an embassy to Barnard Castle, the purport being no less than to report that the Lord of Rokeby had been taken prisoner at Marston Moor, and was on his way to Barnard Castle, to be placed under Oswald's charge as a prisoner at large, until he could procure a ransom. This arrangement suits Oswald's plans exactly. He, as we know, desires an union in marriage between Wilfrid and Matilda, heiress of Rokeby, which union would, later on, bring the Rokeby estates into the Wycliffe family. He will now have the Lord of Rokeby in his power, and he says, later on, to Wilfrid—

> "Right heavy shall his ransom be,
> Unless that maid compound with thee!"

His train is, doubtless, now on its way to meet the illustrious prisoner, and to take him over from the escort now conducting him.

We must return, however, to the young Redmond, whose personality and history we will enter into later; at present, I will not interrupt the course of events. This fiery, warm-hearted young Irishman is indignant at the cold reply and indifference of Oswald too (as he thinks) to the murder of his (Oswald's) kinsman. He bursts forth impetuously—

> "Yes! I beheld his bloody fall,
> By that base traitor's dastard ball,
> Just when I thought to measure sword,
> Presumptuous hope! with Mortham's lord.
> And shall the murderer 'scape, who slew
> His leader generous, brave, and true?
> Escape! while on the dew you trace
> The marks of his gigantic pace?
> No! ere the sun that dew shall dry,
> False Risingham shall yield or die."

Without waiting for any authority from Oswald, he calls on the troopers to disperse and surround the wood, adding—

> "But if among you one there be
> That honours Mortham's memory,
> Let him dismount, and follow me!
> Else on your crests sit fear and shame,
> And foul suspicion dog your name!"

Like Wilfrid, little did the troopers of Wycliffe know of the foul share which their lord had in this deed; so, when Redmond springs from his horse, twenty men of Wycliffe's band spring to the ground with him. He and these twenty men bound into the wood, while the remainder, mounted, disperse in all directions to watch every outlet of escape. This is done, as we have seen, without any authority from Oswald, who, however, acquiesces, seeing now, doubtless, the advantage and safety to himself should Bertram be slain, not taken prisoner. He shouts out, therefore, to the men—

> "Suspicion!—yes—pursue him—fly!—
> But venture not, in useless strife,
> . On ruffian desperate of his life.
> Whoever finds him, shoot him dead!
> Five hundred nobles for his head!"

While Redmond and his party are scouring the wood and the remainder are watching the outlets, Oswald remains behind, in a terrible state of mind, as we may well understand. He is as guilty of his kinsman's blood as much as if he had murdered him with his own hands. On Bertram's life or death hangs the discovery of the crime. Should that ruffian be captured, Oswald knows well that he would betray him, even if that would not save his (Bertram's) own life—

> "Leaning against the elmin tree,
> With drooping head and slackened knee,
> And clenchèd teeth, and close-clasped hands,
> In agony of soul he stands!
> His downcast eye on earth is bent,
> His soul to every sound is lent;
> For in each shout that cleaves the air
> May ring discovery and despair."

At length the troopers return, one by one, reporting that all traces of the fugitive were lost, though Redmond and his party were still continuing the search farther up the Greta glen, towards Brignal. Wilfrid, who has been with Redmond, arrives last, and reports this news to his father; and now a different mood comes over Oswald—

> "O, fatal doom of human race !
> What tyrant passions passions chase !
> Remorse from Oswald's brow is gone,
> Avarice and pride resume their throne."

He now enjoins his son to renew his addresses to Matilda. She is in love with young Redmond, but Oswald tries to persuade Wilfrid that she shows more signs of affection for him than for the young Irishman; what these signs in reality meant, I have already explained.[10] He also points out that her father will now be in his power, using the words above stated.[11] With this, he leads his troops onward on their mission.

In the meantime, the pursuers of Bertram have failed in their object. They have to deal with a man whose knowledge of woodcraft is as keen as that of a Red Indian. In far away South America Bertram had learnt such woodcraft in confronting many a peril more deadly than this. The poet well describes the different artifices of the fugitive, according to varying circumstances. At times he is inclined to rush out and sell his life dearly, but caution prevails, and he withdraws again into his concealment.

Redmond is all this time leading the chase with all the fire and impetuosity of his Irish blood. Bertram, who, of course, knew Redmond well—the one having been in the service of Rokeby, the other in that of Mortham—appears to have a deadly grudge against the youth, for what reason is not here specified— probably the hatred and jealousy towards one whose character is far superior to his own. Twice, when Redmond approaches him, he is prepared to plunge his dagger into his heart, but each time caution prevails. At last, Bertram manages to elude his pursuers, their cries die away in the distance, and at length the fugitive

(10) See page 339 of the treatise.
(11) See page 345 of the treatise.

finds his way into Scargill wood, near Brignal Banks, higher up the Greta valley. Here, wearied out, he lies down to rest.

It is at this point, I think, that a fitting opportunity occurs of entering into the history and personality of the young Irish chieftain, Redmond O'Neale; and as his history is, as we shall see, bound up with that of Philip of Mortham, we shall also enter into the events of the latter's life. We have seen that he has escaped the assassin's hand, the treacherous shot having slain his horse, missing him, so that he has escaped scot free, barring, perhaps, bruises from the fall. The assassin did not wait to ascertain the result of his shot, but, taking it for granted that Mortham was slain, cleared out of the battle-field at once.

We have already [12] alluded to the expedition to Ireland of Rokeby and Mortham, and the kindness they received from the Tanist O'Neale, who sends them home unransomed. I said that "hereby hangs a tale," and into the details of this "tale" we are now about to enter. Turlough O'Neale, the Tanist, who had treated the two English chiefs so well, had a daughter Edith. Mortham falls in love with this daughter; she, returning his love, flies from her country, whether with Mortham or independently is not said; but, at anyrate, she marries him. O'Neale is highly enraged at first at her marrying a heretic, but, later, his resentment cooling, he sends his son across to Yorkshire to inquire about his daughter and to try to bring about a reconciliation, enjoining him, however, in the meantime, not to make himself known to any but his sister until he receives further instructions. This dispatch, though well intended, gives rise to a dreadful tragedy.

Mortham weds his wife in secret—

> "We wedded secret—there was need—
> Differing in country and in creed;
> And when to Mortham's tower she came,
> We mentioned not her race and name,
> Until thy sire,[13] who fought afar,
> Should turn him home from foreign war,
> On whose kind influence we relied
> To soothe her father's ire and pride."

[12] See page 335 of treatise.

[13] Rokeby; Mortham is relating this to his niece, Matilda, as we shall mention later.

There is one exception; to one man alone does Mortham confide his secret; to a dear friend, as he believes—a "darling" friend, indeed, he terms him; and this trusted friend is none other than that arch-scoundrel, Oswald Wycliffe, the true "villain" of the poem, as I have before mentioned—

> "Few months we lived retired, unknown
> To all but one dear friend alone,
> One darling friend—I spare his shame,
> I will not write the villain's name!"

Edith is kindly to all, especially to this supposed friend, because, doubtless, he *was* the "darling" friend of her husband. The villain misconstrues this, and makes foul advances towards her, which are indignantly repulsed; on this, the scoundrel vows revenge. It is at this period that her brother appears on the scene, and he, being forbidden, as we have seen, by his father to make himself known to any but his sister, naturally meets her clandestinely. Mortham, one evening, is sitting at table with Oswald over their wine, of which they have partaken freely, when they perceive Edith going stealthily along the alleyed walk outside, as if unwilling to be seen. The villain Oswald takes the opportunity of hinting to Mortham that she is going to meet a lover. Mortham, heated with wine, and utterly thoughtless, seizes a cross-bow and rushes out into the alley, where he finds his wife in the arms of a stranger. In his mad rage, without attempting to ascertain the identity of the stranger, he lets loose his bow and slays both. He then finds out that the man whom he has slain is her brother—

> "He came in secret to enquire
> Her state, and reconcile her sire."

Mortham, by this fearful deed, becomes simply maddened. Oswald, with his usual cowardice, flies from his former friend's rage, and escapes into a foreign country. This act of Mortham's is hushed up, it being ascribed to accident, but he himself is seized for a time with madness, and, on recovering, finds further sorrow awaiting him; his and Edith's infant son—

> "Have I not written, that she bare
> A boy, like summer morning fair ?"—

has been abducted by a party of armed men, who carry him and
his nurse away. This has been done by old O'Neale, in his rage
at the murder of his son and daughter. He conveys the boy to
Ireland, and brings him up as an O'Neale, "murdered Connal's
child," this Connal being probably the son who had been killed
by Mortham.

It is no wonder that gloom and despair settle down upon
the unhappy Mortham, and draw him away from his country to
distant South America, where—

> "Over distant land and sea
> I bore my load of misery."

He embarks in desperate adventures, with a "daring crew
and dread"—

> "With whom full oft my hated life
> I ventured in such desperate strife,
> That even my fierce associates saw
> My frantic deeds with doubt and awe."

At length, one night, after a desperate battle, when he and
his ruffians are sleeping on the field, a voice sounds in his ear—

> "'Ah, wretch!' it said, 'what makest thou here,
> While unavenged my bloody bier,
> While unprotected lives mine heir,
> Without a father's name and care ?'"

On this, Mortham returns home, bringing with him some of
the most desperate of his crew (Bertram among them) for the
purpose of revenge, but better thoughts prevail—

> "But, humble be my thanks to Heaven,
> That better hopes and thoughts has given,
> And by our Lord's dear prayer has taught,
> Mercy by mercy must be bought!"

He confronts Oswald, who, during Mortham's absence has
returned, and charges him with the abduction. The villain
denies it, but in such a manner that Mortham does not believe
him; however, actuated by his better frame of mind, he spares
him, and says—

"All praise be to my Maker given!
Long-sufferance is one path to heaven."

Mortham, now returned, becomes "a man of sadness and woe." He separates himself from his former friend, Rokeby. Indeed, he at times suffers from a mental malady, which affects his brain for a time. Through it all, he bestows all the affection he retains on his niece Matilda,[14] whose very presence seems to exercise on him a similar influence to that which the harp of David exercised upon King Saul. Such was the state of things which existed for some years, until the outbreak of the Civil War, and here, for a while, we take leave of Philip of Mortham.

We have already mentioned that, while Mortham was absent, pursuing his wild adventures in South America, Rokeby remained at home, residing quietly on his estate. Some years pass, when, one winter's night, the knight is startled by a thundering knocking at the castle gate, while a voice in foreign accents plaintively craves for admission and succour. On the gate being opened, a man rushes in, whose appearance startles the knight and his guests—

"His plaited hair in elf-locks spread
Around his bare and matted head;
On leg and thigh, close stretched and trim,
His vesture showed the sinewy limb;
In saffron dyed, a linen vest
Was frequent folded round his breast;
A mantle long and loose he wore,
Shaggy with ice, and stained with gore."

This, as the note to the poem says, is an attempt to describe the ancient Irish dress.

This Irish "kerne" staggers up the hall, carrying a burden, which turns out to be a boy of rare beauty. He introduces the child as Redmond O'Neale, grandson of Turlough O'Neale, Rokeby's former benefactor. He bears a message from that chieftain to the effect that he hands over the boy to Rokeby's charge—

(14) It will be remembered that Mortham married Rokeby's sister; she would probably be his second wife, but it is not recorded when he married her; it is only stated that she died before the opening of the poem.

"He bids thee breed him as thy son,
  For Turlough's days of joy are done.;
And other lords have seized his land,
  And faint and feeble is his hand;
And all the glory of Tyrone
  Is like a morning vapour flown."

Turlough declares that this charge was first due to Mortham, but, in the latter's absence, it is handed to Rokeby. The reader can have no difficulty in surmising who this boy is, though, in the poem, the fact is not known till near the end. Turlough, as we have seen, has brought up Mortham's son as his grandson (which, indeed, he was, but through his daughter, not through his son, Connal); he seems to have had no intention of restoring the boy to his native country until the troubles above mentioned came upon him, and rendered him unable any more to protect the child. He, therefore, reluctantly sends the boy across the water, under charge of this wild attendant, to be placed in Mortham's (his father's) hands, but, the latter being absent, he is delivered over to Rokeby. O'Neale does not reveal the identity of the boy, and probably never intends to; neither Mortham nor Rokeby suspect the truth, for, probably, neither knew of the hand which the old Irish chieftain had in the abduction of the child; indeed, Mortham, as we know, suspected Oswald.

The messenger (the child's foster-father) has been attacked by robbers on the way, plundered, and mortally wounded, as now appears.[15] He has only time to deliver his message when he falls dead, amid the bitter grief and tears of the boy. His last words are, "Bless thee, O'Neale!"

The Lord of Rokeby is true to his trust; he brings up the boy as his own son. The child is at first, of course, sad and homesick, but this feeling in course of time dies away. He is so kindly treated by his new protector that he soon entertains a sincere regard for him, but especially is this feeling evinced towards Rokeby's little daughter, Matilda. The children grow up together with the sincerest affection towards each other; what this feeling grows into may be easily anticipated. As the years pass by, the lad grows up into a fine, lusty youth, brave,

[15] Of this attack we shall hear more in the last Canto of the poem.

gallant, and excelling in all the sports of the time; while still, predominant in all this, is his affection for Matilda, which is fast developing into a warmer feeling—

> " Thus from their childhood blending still
> Their sport, their study, and their skill,
> An union of the soul they prove,
> But must not think that it was love."

Another turn of affairs, however, opens the eyes of the lovers. Wilfrid, Oswald Wycliffe's son, is also in love with Matilda. Oswald is, of course, greatly in favour of this match, which would eventually bring the Rokeby estate into the Wycliffe family; and Rokeby himself is favourable to it, for, naturally, the son of Oswald Wycliffe is a better match than Redmond, grandson of a disinherited Irish chieftain. But the Civil War breaks out; Rokeby, on Oswald's taking the side of the Parliament, breaks off the proposed match, declaring that no rebel's son should wed his daughter.

Redmond, on the other hand, is highly in favour with the Knight of Rokeby, and the latter has appointed him to be his page, the first order of chivalry. The youth has by this time made his name—

> " Seek the North Riding broad and wide,
> Like Redmond none could steed bestride;
> From Tynemouth search to Cumberland,
> Like Redmond none could wield a brand;
> And then, of humour kind and free,
> And bearing him to each degree
> With frank and fearless courtesy,
> There never youth was formed to steal
> Upon the heart like brave O'Neale."

Redmond O'Neale is indeed the " paragon " of the poem, as Oswald Wycliffe is the " villain."

Redmond accompanies his lord in the Civil War, fighting on the Royalist side. He saves Rokeby's life twice in the battle of Marston Moor, and when his lord is taken prisoner, he yields himself up with him; and we have last seen him riding with Oswald from Barnard Castle, where he had been sent to arrange for the reception of the Knight of Rokeby, who had been assigned, as before mentioned, to Oswald's charge. They are now riding to meet the noble prisoner. At Mortham Castle, then, we see him starting off in pursuit of Bertram, which pursuit, as we have seen, proves fruitless.

Here, then, we resume the narrative of the poem, and, to myself, with relief. I have lately attempted to place before my readers the argument of the poem. It has been a somewhat difficult task, for the different details in the life of Mortham and other characters of the poem are so scattered over the whole work that it has been a matter of some difficulty to bring the detached pieces together, and I think I cannot describe it better than to compare it with an attempt to elicit the solution of a dissected puzzle. I only trust that I have made the whole argument clear to my readers. This is one of the peculiarities of this poem; there are others, which I shall hope to point out at the end of the treatise.

We left Bertram in Scargill wood, resting after the wearying pursuit had ceased. He little heeds the beauty of the flowing river and surrounding woods, so ably, as always, described by the poet; his thoughts are gloomy and sullen—his late crime, the unexpected apparition of his victim, Oswald's seeming treachery in setting Redmond upon him (Bertram), so as to secure Mortham's treasure for himself (Oswald) [16]—these thoughts pass through his mind—

> "In sullen mood he lay reclined,
> Revolving, in his stormy mind,
> The felon deed, the fruitless guilt,
> His patron's blood by treason spilt;
> A crime it seemed, so dire and dread,
> That it had power to wake the dead. [17]
> Then, pondering on his life betrayed
> By Oswald's art to Redmond's blade,
> In treacherous purpose to withhold,
> So seemed it, Mortham's promised gold, [18]

[16] Bertram, however, does not appear to have overheard Oswald's offer of 500 nobles reward for the fugitive's head. See page 346 of treatise.

[17] Bertram appears to be still in doubt whether the apparition of Mortham is his ghost or himself in the flesh.

[18] Here Bertram is wrong. We know the reason of Oswald's presence with his troop at Mortham. See page 345 of treatise.

> A deep and full revenge he vowed
> On Redmond, forward, fierce, and proud;
> Revenge on Wilfrid—on his sire
> Redoubled vengeance, swift and dire!''

Scott well describes the dire state of mind of this wretch—

> "If, in such mood, (as legends say,
> And well believed that simple day,)
> The Enemy of Man has power
> To profit by the evil hour,
> Here stood a wretch, prepared to change
> His soul's redemption for revenge!''

But there is no response to the wretch's vows; there is no response needed—

> "The Demon knew his vassal's heart,
> And spared temptation's needless art."

The Fiend, however, does respond to his "vassal's" vow, by furnishing the latter with the means to commit more crime, as we shall shortly see.

Bertram for some time continues in this gloomy vein of thought, when he is roused by a voice from behind, saying, "Bertram! well met on Greta side." Bertram springs to his feet, sword in hand, but then he lowers it. He recognises the speaker, whom he addresses as "Guy Denzil," but evidently does not trust him, as he orders him to "stand back a pace."

This Denzil has been an old comrade of Bertram's in many an unlawful act; of late, he has been a soldier in Rokeby's band, but has been dismissed with disgrace for marauding; this through the intervention of Redmond, against whom, therefore, he has a bitter grudge. He informs Bertram that he has a project in hand, more profitable than soldiering, and quite of the kind to suit Bertram's liking, if the latter will join in it. Bertram at once acquiesces, and demands what the project is.

Guy then informs Bertram that, nigh at hand, he has a band of comrades utterly lawless and unscrupulous, drawn from the worst elements of the soldiers fighting on both sides—

"Gleaned from both factions—Roundheads, freed
From cant of sermon and of creed;
And Cavaliers, whose souls, like mine,
Spurn at the bonds of discipline.
Wiser, we judge, by dale and wold,
A warfare of our own to hold
Than breathe our last on battle-down,
For cloak or surplice, mace or crown.
Our schemes are laid, our purpose set,
A chief and leader lack we yet."

Guy then informs Bertram that he himself is the very man they need, and he is, without doubt, right. Bertram is now a proscribed man; he is also bold as a lion, utterly unscrupulous, and will hesitate at no crime, risk or no risk. Denzil says—

"Join, then, with us; though wild debate
And wrangling rend our infant state,
Each, to an equal loath to bow,
Will yield to chief renowned as thou."

Bertram agrees, and desires Denzil to lead him to where his comrades lie, ordering him, however, to lead the way: Bertram knows the man well, and does not trust him. While the two proceed on their way, Bertram remembers his late vow to the Fiend, and, characteristic of himself, sees that he has received a response—

"'Even now,' thought Bertram, 'passion-stirred,
I called on Hell, and Hell has heard!
What lack I, vengeance to command,
But of stanch comrades such a band?
This Denzil, vowed to every evil,
Might read a lesson to the devil.
Well, be it so! each knave and fool
Shall serve as my revenge's tool.'"

The pair proceed down a steep descent to the level of the Greta, and cross the river. At the base of the cliff fronting them, Guy draws aside some brambles, and discloses a small entrance leading to a winding passage, into which they enter. Sounds are now heard, which become louder as they advance; at length they emerge into a cavern, which had formerly been a slate mine, now deserted, and become—

> " The banquet-hall and fortress too
> Of Denzil and his desperate crew."

These outlaws, who boisterously salute the entrance of their leader, are thus terribly described by the poet—

> " There Guilt his anxious revel kept;
> There, on his sordid pallet, slept
> Guilt-born Excess, the goblet drained
> Still in his slumbering grasp retained;
> Regret was there, his eye still cast
> With vain repining on the past;
> Among the feasters waited near
> Sorrow, and unrepentant Fear,
> And Blasphemy, to frenzy driven,
> With his own crimes reproaching Heaven,
> While Bertram showed, amid the crew,
> The Master-Fiend that Milton drew."

Amid this wild and lawless crew, however, there appears one who seems to be singularly out of place among them. He is but a stripling; he has not been brought up among such men; his youth has been innocent; but in some manner or another he has been led away by Denzil, and has now become a member of this robber band. He is not entirely hardened, however; the remembrance of his boyish days sometimes brings tears to his eyes; but this passes, and he joins in the revelry of the lawless crew, "drowning sorrow in the bowl." In real truth, he is as weak as water; he detests this life of crime, yet he joins in it; he aids the band in their treacherous schemes, as we shall soon see. He is the minstrel of the band, described as the "life of all their revelry"—

> " Peals his loud song! The muse has found
> Her blossoms on the wildest ground,
> 'Mid noxious weeds at random strewed,
> Themselves all profitless and rude."

His name is Edmund of Winston; he is not an important character in the narrative of the poem; of little importance, indeed, beyond his minstrelsy, which is brought forward from time to time while the poem proceeds.

Here I will remark on the fact that Scott in this poem, as

in "The Lady of the Lake," brings in lesser poems at intervals, but not, to my mind, equal to those in the last-named poem. There are some, however, in "Rokeby" which appeal to us, such as those which I am now about to mention, and that stirring Royalist song, which has been set to music, "When the dawn on the mountains rose misty and grey." All these songs, with the exception of one sung by Matilda and one by Wilfrid, are sung by this youth, this extraordinary mixture of good and evil, who enters into the schemes of this robber band without any hesitation, yet hating them all the while. He is wayward, and, as is to be seen throughout, weak as water. Denzil, on Bertram's inquiry concerning this youth, thus describes him—

> "I watch him well—his wayward course
> Shows oft a tincture of remorse.
> Some early love-shaft grazed his heart,
> And oft the scar will ache and smart.
> Yet he is useful;—of the rest,
> By fits, the darling and the jest,
> His harp, his story, and his lay
> Oft aid the idle hours away."

Of this harper's songs, sung during the scene in this cave, two evidently refer to an outlaw's life—the first, perhaps, referring to Edmund himself. It represents a maiden singing, thus—

> "O Brignal banks are fresh and fair,
>   And Greta woods are green;
> I'd rather rove with Edmund there,
>   Than reign our English queen."

She evidently does not know the character of her lover, who is an outlaw; she thinks he is either a ranger or a soldier. He is neither, and, honestly, he warns her off—

> "And O! though Brignal banks be fair,
>   And Greta woods be gay,
> Yet mickle must the maiden dare
>   Would reign my Queen of May!"

Plainly, honestly, he speaks out—

"Maiden! a nameless life I lead,
    A nameless death I'll die;
The fiend, whose lantern lights the mead,
    Were better mate than I!
And when I'm with my comrades met
    Beneath the greenwood bough,
What once we were we all forget,
    Nor think what we are now."

This very adequately describes the position of Edmund himself, who has thrown in his lot with this robber band.

The second song mentioned in this canto describes the departure of a young soldier, taking farewell of his lady-love and expressing the thought that he will return no more. There seems to have been but a casual acquaintance between these two lovers, but in the short time in which they have been acquainted they have lost their hearts to each other, only to part for ever—

"'A weary lot is thine, fair maid,
    A weary lot is thine!
To pull the thorn thy brow to braid
    And press the rue for wine!
A lightsome eye, a soldier's mien,
    A feather of the blue,
A doublet of the Lincoln green,—
    No more of me you knew,
                My love!.
    No more of me you knew.

"'This morn is merry June, I trow,
    The rose is budding fain;
But she shall bloom in winter snow
    Ere we two meet again.'
He turned his charger as he spake
    Upon the river shore,
He gave his bridle-reins a shake,
    Said, 'Adieu for evermore,
                My love!
    And adieu for evermore.'"

The third song again relates to the life of an outlaw, but is of a more lively character. One, Allen-a-dale, like the lover in "Brignal Banks," is in love with a maiden, but, far from warning her off, as the other does, he is determined, like "young Lochin-

var," to take her off with him. He is a thorough outlaw of the
"Robin Hood" type [19]—

> "Come, read me my riddle, come hearken my tale!
> And tell me the craft of bold Allen-a-Dale."

His "craft" comes out gradually—first, among his other
delectable occupations, that of poacher—

> "The fish of the lake, and the deer of the vale,
> Are less free to Lord Dacre than Allen-a-Dale!"

He was "ne'er belted a knight," "no baron or lord," but—

> "Twenty tall yoemen will draw at his word;
> And the best of our nobles his bonnet will vail,
> Who at Rere-cross on Stanmore meets Allen-a-Dale."

A clear example of "Stand and deliver!"

This bold outlaw demands his bride: the parents ask of his
resources, naturally; he, in modern slang, makes "no bones
of it"—

> "'Though the castle of Richmond stand fair on the hill,
> My hall,' quoth bold Allen, 'shows gallanter still;
> 'Tis the blue vault of heaven, with its crescent so pale,
> And with all its bright spangles!' said Allen-a-Dale."

This is plain speaking; the parents of his lady-love turn
him from their doors, but what is the use of that? Their
daughter's heart is set on the handsome, bold-speaking outlaw—

> "But loud, on the morrow, their wail and their cry:
> He had laughed on the lass with his bonny black eye,
> And she fled to the forest to hear a love-tale,
> And the youth it was told by was Allen-a-Dale!"

We return now to the course of the narrative, entering into
the conversation between Bertram and Denzil as to the proposed
project.

While all this revelry has been proceeding, the two leaders,
Bertram and Denzil, have been earnestly conferring together.

[19] This Allen-a-Dale appears in Scott's novel of "Ivanhoe" as one of the
band of Robin Hood.

Bertram, still bent on gaining Mortham's treasure, relates to his comrade the tale of his expedition to Mortham Tower, and the apparition of Mortham, as to which he is still in doubt, having his old superstition in his mind as to the spectre of the owner of the treasure acting as sentry over the buried gold. Denzil, who has no belief in apparitions, somewhat sneeringly remarks that the spectre has "chosen ill his ghostly haunt," for the treasure in question had been removed to Rokeby Castle—

> "For why his guard on Mortham hold,
> When Rokeby Castle hath the gold
> Thy patron won on Indian soil,
> By stealth, by piracy, and spoil ?"

This would seem to quite dispose of the question of a ghastly apparition, and Bertram is ashamed to have displayed his superstitious fears to his seeming associate; this also rouses his wrath, which he turns to another account, viz., that of Denzil wronging the memory of Mortham, whose old influence still clings to him (Bertram). As for fear, he reminds Denzil, who has not the courage of Bertram, that he (Denzil) had feared Mortham in the latter's lifetime—[20]

> "For, while he lived, at Mortham's look
> Thy very soul, Guy Denzil, shook!
> And when he taxed thy breach of word
> To yon fair Rose of Allenford,
> I saw thee crouch like chastened hound,
> Whose back the huntsman's lash hath found.
> Nor dare to call his foreign wealth
> The spoil of piracy or stealth:
> He won it bravely with his brand
> When Spain waged warfare with our land."

He also resents the suggestion of want of courage—a hint of which, as we see throughout the poem, he always resents, and no wonder, as courage (up, at least, to the last canto) is the only good quality which he appears to possess—

> "Mark, too,—I brook no idle jeer,
> Nor couple Bertram's name with fear;
> Mine is but half the demon's lot,
> For I believe, but tremble not—
> Enough of this."

(20) Bertram still appears to keep up the idea of Mortham having been slain.

These words speedily silence Denzil, who dreads nothing so much as the wrath of Bertram. The latter then inquires as to Denzil's knowledge of the removal of the treasure. Denzil relates what we already know: Mortham's moodiness, his estrangement from his friend Rokeby, and his affection towards his niece, Matilda, to whose charge the treasure was consigned. On the outbreak of the Civil War, it was conveyed to Matilda's bower in Rokeby keep, with certain instructions (into which we will enter later) should he be slain in the war.

This naturally arouses Bertram's indignation—

> "Destined to her! to yon slight maid!
> The prize my life had well nigh paid,
> When 'gainst Laroche, by Cayo's wave,
> I fought, my patron's wealth to save!"

Bertram remarks that Denzil was doubtless after this treasure; the latter acknowledges this, but adds that he has still another object in view—no less than the abduction of Rokeby's daughter and the holding of her for ransom, that ransom being the treasure itself. He has already sent out spies to ascertain her whereabouts—

> "My rangers go
> E'en now to track a milk-white doe
> By Rokeby Hall she takes her lair,
> In Greta wood she harbours fair,
> And when my huntsman marks her way,
> What think'st thou, Bertram, of the prey?
> Were Rokeby's daughter in our power,
> We rate her ransom at her dower."

Bertram eagerly agrees to this villainous project, for he has a grudge against Matilda, who has always regarded him with dislike and dread, and no wonder—

> "She told to Mortham she could ne'er
> Behold me without secret fear,
> Foreboding evil; she may rue
> To find her prophecy fall true!"

Bertram then points out that, should the above scheme fail, they have enough men to storm Rokeby Castle (now left only to the care of a few old retainers), secure the treasure and the lady, and set fire to the castle. Denzil, a more cautious and less courageous villain, points out to his companion the difficulties to be overcome—

> "The menials of the castle, true,
> And stubborn to their charge, though few;
> The wall to scale—the moat to cross—
> The wicket-grate—the inner fosse."

Bertram, the bolder ruffian, dismisses this cautious advice with contempt, but Guy now points out an easier method than that of open attack—treachery. If one of their number could be admitted to the castle on some pretext or other, there is a certain postern which Guy knows of which the spy could open, and admit the robbers to the interior.[21] Bertram at once consents; be it by force or guile, he cares little. Denzil is now about to propose the minstrel, Edmund, as a suitable person to do the spy's work, when one of Denzil's scouts comes in from the wood. Denzil at once addresses him—"Speak, Hamlin, hast thou lodged our deer?" He answers—"I have, but two fat stags are near." He explains that he has dogged Matilda to Thorsgill glade,[22] but that she was there joined by Wilfrid and Redmond, adding—

> "Much, as it seemed, was theirs to say:
> There's time to pitch both toil and net,
> Before their path be homeward set."

Bertram and Denzil, on this, start on their villainous errand of abduction—and, if necessary, of murder—taking four of the boldest of the band with them.

We turn now to the little party which these ruffians are now waylaying. Here we are for the first time introduced to the heroine of the poem, Matilda, heiress of Rokeby, and the only female character depicted in the poem, for Edith, Mortham's wife, belongs to a period prior to the date on which the first canto opens. She is joined in Thorsgill glade by her two constant

---

(21) It will be remembered that Denzil had been one of Rokeby's followers, and would know the castle well.

(22) This glade is not marked in the map: it is probably a portion of Rokeby Park.

companions, Redmond and Wilfrid. We have already entered into the relations between the three; both young men are in love with Matilda, who returns Redmond's love, but has esteem and affection towards Wilfrid. These young men are her constant companions, and, as they possess a common feeling towards the maiden, there is, naturally, a certain amount of jealousy between them, but there is no actual enmity, for they are both generous and kind-hearted. Redmond appears not, as yet, to share his lord's captivity; indeed, he has not yet been to Barnard Castle since he left it with Oswald that morning.

Matilda is glad to meet these two, as she requires their advice, and on a subject no less than that of the treasure which Mortham has committed to her charge—

> "Chance-met, we well may steal an hour
> To friendship due from fortune's power.
> Thou, Wilfrid, ever kind, must lend
> Thy counsel to thy sister-friend;
> And, Redmond, thou, at my behest,
> No farther urge thy desperate quest.
> For to my care a charge is left,
> Dangerous to one of aid bereft,
> Well nigh an orphan, and alone,
> Captive her sire, her house o'erthrown."

She relates to her hearers the tale that we have heard more than once: that of the gloom, and even madness, of Mortham, tempered, however, with deep love towards herself. On his leaving for the war, he leaves, as we have seen, in her charge "a treasure huge of gems and gold," and, with that, a—

> "Disjointed, dismal scroll,
> That tells the secret of his soul,
> In such wild words as oft betray
> A mind by anguish forced astray."

This scroll contains Mortham's confession as to the murder of his wife and her brother, into which we have already entered. She reads this scroll to her two companions, and has reached the period of Mortham's return from South America when an interruption occurs.

A rustling is heard in an adjoining thicket; Redmond springs to his feet; Guy Denzil, who is lurking there, draws back; he dares not, coward as he is, face Redmond, who resumes his seat, with the remark that "some roe was rustling in the shade." Bertram, who is with Denzil, laughts to scorn the cowardice of his associate, having no fear himself—

> "Give me thy carabine—I'll show
> An art that thou wilt gladly know,
> How thou may'st safely quell a foe."

Bertram levels the piece direct upon Redmond, but he is suddenly stopped by Denzil, who warns him of an armed force coming down the dell. The two villains, therefore, sneak off, and regain the cave in safety.

In the meantime, Matilda continues the reading of the scroll, showing how Mortham steadfastly adheres to the belief that his son lives; and he prays Matilda to preserve the treasure which he is handing over to her for his heir, for whom, he says, when the war is over, he will search "through Europe wide." He leaves the following instructions—

> "My wealth, on which a kinsman nigh
> Already casts a grasping eye,
> With thee may unsuspected lie.
> When of my death Matilda hears,
> Let her retain her trust three years;
> If none, from me, the treasure claim,
> Perished is Mortham's race and name;
> Then let it leave her generous hand,
> And flow in bounty o'er the land;
> Soften the wounded prisoner's lot,
> Rebuild the peasant's ruined cot;
> So spoils, acquired by fight afar,
> Shall mitigate domestic war."

These revelations excite the sympathy of the two generous youths to whom they are told, each equally noble in his own way. Matilda now declares that she will share her father's captivity. Wilfrid then anxiously inquires if she is coming to Barnard Castle, where her father now is. Matilda replies that, wherever her father may be, there will she be also. Wilfrid feels that, in that case, Rokeby Hall, "dismantled and forsook by all," is not a safe place for the keeping of the treasure. He, therefore, suggests that as he has, by his father's authority, a band of troops under his own command, a portion of these might be sent at night to bear away the treasure to whatever place Matilda may wish to transport it. Matilda eagerly consents, saying that the treasure should be removed at once and placed in Wilfrid's own hands, than whom, as she says, none can be more trust-worthy—

> "O be it not one day delayed!
> And, more, thy sister-friend to aid,
> Be thou thyself content to hold,
> In thine own keeping, Mortham's gold—
> Safest with thee."

Safe indeed, as far as Wilfrid is concerned, but Matilda forgets that, in removing the treasure to Barnard Castle, she is practically placing it in the hands of Oswald.

At this juncture, the armed party whom we have before mentioned arrives on the scene. These are evidently part of Wilfrid's own band, and the latter asks, with surprise, why they are thus entering the glade in force? The captain of the band replies that, while they were exercising manœuvres on Barninghame Moor, a stranger appeared, telling them that their commander, Wilfrid, was, with others, in danger of his life. The captain reports of the stranger—

> "He had a leader's voice, I ween,
> A falcon glance, a warrior mien.
> He bade me bring you instant aid;
> I doubted not, and I obeyed."

This stranger is, without a doubt, Mortham himself.

The party are startled, and Redmond, searching around, discovers Denzil's musket, which the villains had left in their hurried flight. They therefore decide to quit the glade at once, Redmond and Matilda, with "fitting guard," repairing to Rokeby; Wilfrid, at nightfall, would attend with a body of troops at Rokeby, to conduct Matilda and the treasure to Barnard Castle. Though they know that there is danger about, they, unfortunately, do not know that Bertram and Denzil, with their ruffian band, are about to make a treacherous attack on Rokeby that night, otherwise they would, doubtless, either have retained some troops with them or have set out for Barnard Castle with the least possible delay.

We now enter into the fifth canto of the poem, which is filled with more exciting events than any other. They take place in the night following the day whose events we have been just describing.

Night has fallen, but the moon is shining brightly, when Wilfrid wends his way from Barnard Castle to Rokeby Hall. On arriving at his destination, he finds that, although the defences of the castle had for some time been neglected, of late some attempts to strengthen them had been made, the garrison evidently being aware that there was danger abroad, though they did not know that an attack was to be made that very night; and, had it not been for treachery, Bertram's attack would very probably have failed. Wilfrid also finds considerable difficulty in obtaining admission; he is questioned carefully before the gate is opened, although he must have been known—

> "And when he entered, bolt and bar
> Resumed their place with sullen jar." (23)

Also, the old porter scans him over carefully with the light of his torch before admitting him to the interior of the hall.

Here Matilda meets him, and greets him cordially, saying that they were only awaiting the arrival of the guard from Barnard Castle to set out for the latter place; and here Wilfrid delivers his mission, which was to say that, to hide the treasure more securely from any prying eye, it were better not to remove it until late in the night, and that, therefore, he had given orders to his troop to set out so as to arrive at Rokeby about midnight. The "prying eye" which Wilfrid fears is that of his father, of

---

(23) The reader will call to mind the similar lines in " The Bridal of Triermain," when Sir Roland de Vaux enters the Castle of St. John—

> " And bolt and bar
> Spontaneous took their place once more,
> And the deep arch, with sullen roar,
> Returned their surly jar."

whose avarice he is well aware, but he little deems how many
lives, including his own, would be sacrificed through that unfortunate order for delay.

Wilfrid now receives an equally cordial greeting from
Redmond, and it is very pleasing to see how these two noble-
hearted youths lay aside their rivalry in the common cause of
protecting the mutual object of their love. Their hands meet in
a cordial grasp of friendship and alliance—

> "Seemed as between them this was said,
> 'Awhile let jealousy be dead;
> And let our contest be, whose care
> Shall best assist this helpless fair.'—
> There was no speech the truce to bind,
> It was a compact of the mind;
> A generous thought, at once impressed
> On either rival's generous breast."

Matilda fully comprehends this generous state of feeling
between her two lovers, and with great relief, for she had been
somewhat apprehensive of jealousy and angry feeling between
the two rivals. In this happy state of affairs, the three sit in
pleasant conversation for a while—

> "Two lovers by the maiden sate,
> Without a glance of jealous hate;
> The maid her lovers sat between,
> With open brow, and equal mien:—
> It is a sight but rarely spied,
> Thanks to man's wrath and woman's pride."

Their conversation is interrupted by a knock at the outer
gate, followed by the tinkling of a harp, accompanied by a song
from one who evidently desires admission to the castle—

> "Summer eve is gone and passed,
> Summer dew is falling fast;
> I have wandered all the day,
> Do not bid me farther stray!
> Gentle hearts of gentle kin,
> Take the wandering Harper in!"

But old Harpool, the porter, has no ear for music; he is
also cautious, as we have seen, and if he made difficulty in

admitting Wilfrid, whom he must have known well,[24] still more would he do so in the case of a stranger, a vagrant minstrel. A conversation ensues, the Harper replying in verse, but old Harpool is obdurate.

Wilfrid being, as we know, of a minstrel turn himself, now intercedes on behalf of the Harper: another mistake which poor Wilfrid makes to-night, leading to fatal consequences. Matilda also is inclined to be hospitable, and the Harper clenches this feeling by another song in praise of the house of Rokeby, especially with regard to their hospitality, concluding thus—

> "Rokeby's lords had fair regard
> For the harp and for the bard;
> Baron's race throve never well,
> Where the curse of minstrel fell.
> If you love that noble kin,
> Take the weary Harper in!"

Harpool is still obdurate; he yields so far, however, as to say that lays of comic minstrelsy might induce him to open the door to this wandering singer. All this discourse is overheard by the three within, and Matilda now turns to Redmond for his advice, as to whether to admit this Harper or not. Redmond gives no direct answer, but he acknowledges his love for minstrelsy; oft has he heard it in Ireland, and the mention of it brings back reminiscences of his early childhood in that country; of the old bard, Owen Lysagh, the filea (bard) of O'Neale, who transported his audience with his melody—

> "I've seen a ring of rugged kerne,
> With aspects shaggy, wild, and stern,
> Enchanted by the master's lay,
> Linger around the livelong day,
> Shift from wild rage to wilder glee,
> To love, to grief, to ecstasy,
> And feel each varied change of soul,
> Obedient to the bard's control."

And then follows a burst of regret for the loss of the old home,

(24) It must be remembered, however, that the families of Rokeby and Wycliffe took opposite sides in the Civil War.

the old heritage of the O'Neales overrun by strangers, as we have heard before—

> "Ah, Clandeboy! thy friendly floor
> Slieve-Donard's oak shall light no more;
> Nor Owen's harp, beside the blaze,
> Tell maiden's love or hero's praise!
> The mantling brambles hide thy hearth,
> Centre of hospitable mirth;
> All undistinguished in the glade,
> My sires' glad home is prostrate laid,
> Their vassals wander wide and far,
> Serve foreign lords in distant war,
> And now the stranger's sons enjoy
> The lovely woods of Clandeboy!" [25]

Matilda sympathises with his grief, in accordance with her own regret at now having to leave the home of her fathers, but she impresses upon him, amidst his and her own sufferings, submission to the will of the Almighty—

> "And think'st thou, Redmond, I can part
> From this loved home with lightsome heart,
> Leaving to wild neglect whate'er
> E'en from my infancy was dear?
>
> .   .   .   .
>
> Yet is this consolation given,
> My Redmond;—'tis the will of Heaven."

It is Matilda's last night at her old home; indeed, that night she will see the last of the old building; but that last evening, she says, "the hospitable hearth shall flame" in Rokeby Castle. She sends orders to Harpool to admit the stranger Harper (fatal order), and "relieve each need."

She now asks Wilfrid, in the meantime, to entertain them with a song, kindly saying that, though she has to leave Rokeby and share her father's captivity, she knows that she will have no "rigid jailer" in Wilfrid. The reader will notice, in all these beautiful dialogues, the wonderful way in which the heroine

---

(25) It is not often the case that Scott enters into the beauties of the scenery of Ireland. I have gone somewhat out of my way to enter these lines, for, contrary to the locality of the main poem, I know this part of Ireland. I have been in the woods of Clandeboy, and have climbed to the summit of Slieve-Donard.

of the poem displays both her love to Redmond and her kind, pitiful, and sisterly feelings towards Wilfrid.

Wilfrid takes her lyre from her hands, and sings a very mournful lay, indicative of his feelings towards Matilda and his hopeless love, to which, as I pointed out at the commencement of the treatise, he was much addicted. The song opens thus—

> "O lady, twine no wreath for me,
> Or twine it of the cypress tree!"

And so the mournful strain runs on through the song; it even mentions Matilda's name, which, I think, should have been omitted—

> "Yes! twine for me the cypress bough,
> But, O Matilda, twine not now!
> Stay till a few brief months are passed,
> And I have looked and loved my last!
> When villagers my shroud bestrew
> With pansies, rosemary, and rue,—
> Then, lady, weave a wreath for me,
> And weave it of the cypress tree."

I myself think that this was the last subject that Wilfrid should have brought forward in his song, considering the relations of the three present, but Redmond, understanding the feelings of his rival, makes a cheery speech in reply, to win him from his melancholy; and Matilda, to change the subject, suggests the admission of the stranger minstrel, also the calling in of the household, at the same time, for the last evening in the old hall—

> "So let the horn and beaker flow
> To mitigate their parting woe."

The reader can have no doubt as to the personality of this so-called wandering minstrel. He is Edmund of Winston, member of the robber band, detailed by the leaders to act the spy, obtain entrance into the castle, and admit his confederates by the postern gate already mentioned. He has been admitted to the castle, as we have seen, by Matilda's order, has received hospitality, and, doubtless, has taken advantage of some opportunity to open the postern gate.[26] This young scoundrel is now ushered into Matilda's presence, and his mien and features are well and characteristically described by Scott—

> "He made obeisance with a free
> Yet studied air of courtesy.
> Each look and accent, framed to please,
> Seemed to affect a playful ease;
> His face was of that doubtful kind
> That wins the eye, but not the mind;
> Yet harsh it seemed to deem amiss
> Of brow so young and smooth as this.
> His was the subtle look and sly,
> That, spying all, seems nought to spy;
> Round all the group his glances stole,
> Unmarked themselves, to mark the whole;
> Yet sunk beneath Matilda's look,
> Nor could the eye of Redmond brook.
> To the suspicious or the old,
> Subtle and dangerous and bold
> Had seemed this self-invited guest;
> But young our lovers,—and the rest,
> Wrapt in their sorrow and their fear
> At parting of their mistress dear,
> Tear-blinded to the castle hall
> Came, as to bear her funeral pall."

This is an excellent description of this youth, a strange mixture of good and evil, engaging recklessly in an act of the most infamous treachery, and, at the same time, loathing it in his heart.

When called upon to exercise his minstrelsy, however, a different expression is displayed upon his features; his soul now is all in his work; but, when that influence is past, the worse expression again displays itself—

> "His soul resumed, with habit's chain,
> Its vices wild and follies vain,
> And gave the talent, with him born,
> To be a common curse and scorn."

(26) Scott is very vague about this. When did Edmund obtain the opportunity of opening the postern gate? Old Harpool, as we have seen, was very cautious: he would hardly have left this vagrant minstrel alone for long, and even if he had, would surely have seen that there was some supervision. We have seen his caution even with Wilfrid, whom he, doubtless, well knew.

His first song is characteristic of the remarks above; it is all about his harp; how that instrument has cheered him through all the troubles of his life; the principle is—

> " Yet rests one solace to my heart,—
> My harp alone."

Matilda approves, but old Harpool cares not for it, and is preparing to return to his guardroom, when Edmund strikes up a lay of a very different kind—a lay which constrains Harpool, a staunch Royalist like his master, to pause and listen. This song is the most stirring Royalist poem ever composed. It represents a young gallant setting forth, at the outset of the war, to fight for Church and King. It is purported to be sung by the young soldier's lady-love, and is set to music in an equally stirring melody, which calls forth to the utmost the enthusiasm of any upholder of the Royalist cause.[27] "God strike with the gallant that strikes for the Crown" is the theme which runs throughout the whole song—

> "For the rights of fair England that broadsword he draws,
> Her King is his leader, her Church is his cause;
> His watchword is honour, his pay is renown,—
> God strike with the gallant that strikes for the Crown."

This stirring air, however, only brings down silence upon Matilda; times are indeed changed since that song was first sung; the Royalists have suffered a heavy defeat, and worse, she feels, is to follow. Her father also is a prisoner in the hands of the enemy, and that enemy an unscrupulous one.

She, however, gives the Harper a bounty for his song, which he receives not without a twinge of conscience, but, "pride of art," the poet says, "had steeled him to his treacherous part," and Scott illustrates this by examples of the sportsman in feeling no pity for the creature which he has just shot—

> " Each feeling of his victim's ill
> Drowned in his own successful skill ";

(27) However, anyone who does not entirely support the cause cannot help admiring the song: such may notably be said also of the Jacobite songs relating to Prince Charles Edward.

and of the veteran soldier who takes delight in battles fought, towns captured, &c.; he feels no pity for the killed and wounded—

> "What against pity arms his heart?—
> It is the conscious pride of art."

But Scott places Edmund in a lower grade than these; he is weak, shifting, and unstable—

> "But principles in Edmund's mind
> Were baseless, vague, and undefined.
> His soul, like bark with rudder lost,
> On passion's changeful tide was tossed;
> Nor Vice nor Virtue had the power
> Beyond the impression of the hour;
> And, O! when passion rules, how rare
> The hours that fall to Virtue's share!"

But now Matilda, who had borrowed Edmund's harp, breaks forth into a plaintive lay, bemoaning her misfortune in having to leave the home of her fathers, but, at the same time, proudly declaring that no misfortune shall shake the constancy of her family to the cause which they have adopted.

This noble lay again awakens the conscience of the wretched Edmund, in which the noble, steadfast character of Matilda is brought before him, evidently so much superior to his own; her beauty also reminds him of one, superior to the village maidens whom he knew, one whom he had often pictured in his boyish fancy, and now it comes home to him that is about treacherously to betray such an one as this. He has unbarred the postern door to admit his murderous comrades, and the time is now come for their attack; they are in the castle, and only awaiting for a certain strain which he was to sing as a signal for their attack. He may, therefore, thus delay the attack for a short time until Wilfrid's troops arrive, who must now be well upon their way. But he cannot wait long; Bertram and his ruffians are expecting the sign, and for his own safety he dare not delay.

The signal song is weird, and suggestive of a crime which is not actually described; the hearers can only imagine what it may be. A "friar of orders grey" is ordered by two ruffians to attend the bedside of a dying woman, and is taken there blindfolded. On arrival, he finds the lady, with a child in her arms, to all appearance, well. He is ordered, however, with threats, to shrive her, and he dare not refuse. The lady dies during the night; how, is not said, nor is the child mentioned, but there has evidently been foul play, for the remorse of the lord of the castle, termed "Wild Darrell," is mentioned—

> "Wild Darrell is an altered man,
> The village crones can tell;
> He looks pale as clay, and strives to pray,
> If he hears the convent bell.

> "If prince or peer cross Darrell's way,
> He'll beard him in his pride—
> If he meet a friar of orders grey,
> He droops and turns aside." (28)

Matilda remarks that this weird lay seems to have called up phantoms; she believes that she sees a human form at the porch at the farther end of the room. It proves only too true, for Bertram rushes in, accompanied by his robber train, who commence forming a semi-circle to hem their victims in; they stand with their muskets levelled, ready to fire at Bertram's signal. On the other hand, the retainers of Rokeby, though greatly terrified, draw together, placing themselves in a close band between their mistress and the robbers. It was fortunate for Matilda that she had called these retainers into the hall for the last night, and also that these latter were armed, for the purpose of attending their mistress, with Wilfrid's escort, to Barnard Castle.

Redmond does not lose his presence of mind; he calls on Wilfrid eagerly to remove Matilda through a handy wicket gate to the outside of the castle, there to await the arrival of Wilfrid's troop, who cannot now be far off, while he himself, with the retainers, will strive to hold the robbers back in the meantime.

Wilfrid accomplishes his mission successfully, and the lady stands safe outside the castle. She misses Redmond, however,

(28) The particulars contained in this song seem to be facts, and the details of them are entered in a note in the larger edition of Scott's poems; but, as they had nothing to do with the poem, I did not think it necessary to enter into them.

and turns furiously on Wilfrid, charging him with having left the former to die—

> "I know it well!—he would not yield
> His sword to man—his doom is sealed!
> For my scorned life, which thou hast bought
> At price of his, I thank thee not."

Poor Wilfrid, thus unjustly reproached, turns away in shame and grief—

> "'Lady,' he said, 'my band so near,
> In safety thou may'st rest thee here.
> For Redmond's death thou shalt not mourn
> If mine can buy his safe return.'"

Matilda, at this, sees her error, and calls on him to return, but he heeds not, and re-enters the castle.

The maiden now is left alone, all being silent at present in the castle—but not for long. A shot is heard, succeeded by a volley; then the clashing of arms and other sounds denoting a fearful fight. At this moment, the trampling of horse is heard, and Wilfrid's troopers approach at a gallop, having doubtless seen and heard the commotion within the castle. Matilda flies to the leader, and urges him to hasten to the garrison's aid. The troopers spring from their horses, leaving them to run as they will, and rush on into the castle.

And none too soon, for, on marking Matilda's flight, Bertram gives the signal for attack, and Redmond and the little band of Rokeby's retainers are now sorely pressed. The latter, though brave and true, are old veterans, and no match for the robber band, who are all recently deserted soldiers and in the prime of their strength. Redmond urges his little force on; he charges more than once, but the bandits, though driven back, renew the attack, and their superior numbers begin to tell. Wilfrid has fallen wounded; Redmond stands over him, defending him, and urging Rokeby's men to make a last stand—

> "Stand to it yet! renew the fight
> For Rokeby's and Matilda's right!
> These slaves! they dare not, hand to hand,
> Bide buffet from a true man's brand."

He makes a last desperate attack upon the bandits, who give way before him; but now Bertram confronts him, and before that gigantic ruffian he might have fallen, but old Harpool, the porter, though lying mortally wounded on the floor, gives timely aid: he grasps Bertram's knees and checks him. That momentary delay saves Redmond, for assistance is nigh. At this moment, in rush the troopers. At their onslaught the villains give way in panic: these trained soldiers are a far more formidable foe than the old retainers of Rokeby, brave though the latter were; and doubtless, also, the robbers are taken by surprise: they had had no idea of the force coming to Rokeby that night, so—

"In panic dread,
They broke, they yielded, fell, or fled."

Bertram in vain attempts to rally them; his voice rings out above the roar of fight, but to no effect.

And now another enemy appears upon the scene: the castle is on fire, by what means no one knows, but there can be no wonder at it after all the firing which has gone on within. A general clearance now takes place, the female servants, first of all, rushing with shrieks outside, and the fear soon spreads to the combatants themselves. The flames have seized the very hall in which they are fighting; they have to clear out of it. But the fight still continues in front of the castle. The robbers are hewn down by the troopers; all are slain, with the exception of Guy Denzil, who is taken alive, for the purpose, probably, of bringing him before Oswald, on the chance of obtaining information from him. The wretched Edmund, deficient in physical as in moral courage, being now threatened by the troopers, clings abjectly to Matilda's dress; she, with pitiful heart, intercedes for the young scoundrel, and his life is saved.

All are now accounted for, save the arch-ruffian of all. Every one thinks that he has perished in the flames, but they have not done with him yet. All of a sudden, the gigantic ruffian bursts out of the midst of the flames, plunges into the thick of his foemen, and, after a desperate conflict, breaks through them and escapes to the forest. We cannot omit the lines, so splendidly descriptive—

"And where is Bertram ?—Soaring high,
The general flame ascends the sky;
In gathered group the soldiers gaze
Upon the broad and roaring blaze,
When, like infernal demon, sent
Red from his penal element,
To plague and to pollute the air,
His face all gore, on fire his hair,
Forth from the central mass of smoke
The giant form of Bertram broke!
His brandished sword on high he rears,
Then plunged among opposing spears;
Round his left arm his mantle trussed,
Received and foiled three lances' thrust;
Nor these his headlong course withstood,
Like reeds he snapped the tough ash-wood.
In vain his foes around him clung;
With matchless force aside he flung
Their boldest—as the bull, at bay,
Tosses the ban-dogs from his way.
Through forty foes his path he made,
And safely gained the forest glade."

A robber, an unscrupulous ruffian indeed, but a gallant and fearless one; he stands, I think, in a grade above Oswald, Denzil, or the wretched, pusillanimous Edmund.

Redmond now appears, bringing forth the wounded Wilfrid; as the latter is laid down, he meets Matilda's kind glance, filled with regret for her late unjust reproach of him; he says, "I could have wished e'en thus to die."

The troops now prepare to take their departure for Barnard Castle; there is no occasion to delay longer, for the castle is now given over to the flames, and there are no appliances in these days; the treasure, also, for which they have come, is evidently destroyed in the ruins of the castle. They have horses ready for the lady and Redmond; three troopers attend to Wilfrid, two supporting him on his horse, the other leading his bridle rein. They then proceed on their way to Barnard Castle, but Matilda often looks behind to take a last look at the mansion of her fathers, now brightening the night with its flames. It is perhaps as well, doubtless she thinks; better let it be destroyed than given into the hands of the enemies of Rokeby. Its destruction, indeed, represents that of the family's falling cause—

"But oft Matilda looked behind,
As up the vale of Tees they wind,
Where far the mansion of her sires
Beaconed the dale with midnight fires.
In gloomy arch above them spread,
The clouded heaven lowered bloody red;
Beneath, in sombre light, the flood
Appeared to roll in waves of blood.
Then, one by one, was heard to fall
The tower, the donjon-keep, the hall.
Each rushing down with thunder sound,
A space the conflagration drowned;
Till, gathering strength, again it rose,
Announced its triumph in its close,
Shook wide its light the landscape o'er,
Then sunk—and Rokeby was no more!"

We have arrived now at the opening of the sixth and last canto of the poem, and the principal subject of this canto is the nefarious doings and treachery of Oswald Wycliffe, of whom we have lost sight for some time. We left him at Mortham Tower, as the reader will remember, in terrible agony of mind during the pursuit of Bertram, fearing that that desperado, if captured, would betray him and disclose their mutual crime; and how, when that danger was past, he returns to his usual avaricious plans.[29]

We know that his great object was to unite his son Wilfrid in marriage with Matilda, thereby gaining eventually the Rokeby estates, and how this was frustrated by Rokeby refusing to give his daughter to the son of a rebel. As matters stand now, it appears that every chance lies in his favour as to his attaining his object, for Rokeby is a prisoner at large under his charge, and Matilda and young Redmond have also arrived, after the burning of Rokeby Castle. All these, therefore, are in Oswald's hands, and he feels that he can make his own terms; and, in accordance with his own infamous, treacherous character, he determines, by a false charge, to get Rokeby more completely in his power.

It will be remembered that the robber, Guy Denzil, and the young harper, Edmund, had been taken prisoners at the affray at Rokeby Castle; they are confined in a dungeon together at

(29) See pages 346 and 347 of treatise.

Barnard Castle, and here pass two days. On the third morning, Oswald enters the prison, and accosts Denzil, whom he knows, and Guy confesses as to his identity. Oswald then suggests that, if the robber would serve him faithfully in a certain matter, his (Guy's) life might be spared—

> "List to me, Guy. Thou know'st the great
> Have frequent need of what they hate;
> Hence, in their favour, oft we see
> Unscrupled, useful men like thee.
> Were I disposed to bid thee live,
> What pledge of faith hast thou to give?"

Denzil, as may be expected, eagerly accepts the offer, and says that his own son (as he falsely terms Edmund) should "rest his pledge." Oswald then tells Denzil of his desire to unite Wilfrid with Matilda in marriage, and of Rokeby's refusal; to gain the latter's consent, therefore, he (Rokeby) must be placed under more strict restraint—

> "Gentle restraint, he said, would lead
> Old Rokeby to enlarge his creed."

Oswald then instructs Denzil to make a report to the effect that Rokeby had broken his parole,[30] by leaguing with certain Royalists in the north in a plot to surprise Barnard Castle. Denzil makes no difficulty about this; Edmund, with his usual vacillation, shows scruples, until Oswald swears that his prisoners' lives (*i.e.*, Rokeby and his train) shall be safe, when he weakly yields—

> "I scrupled, until o'er and o'er
> His prisoners' safety Wycliffe swore,
> And then—alas! what needs there more?
> I knew I should not live to say
> The proffer I refused that day;
> Ashamed to live, yet loth to die,
> I soiled me with their infamy!"

(30) Scott does not explain clearly under what conditions Rokeby was a prisoner. He is described as a prisoner "at large," and "on parole"; also "ransom" is spoken of. It is not shown whether he was allowed to quit the precincts of the castle or not

In these words, Edmund confesses his weakness to Bertram later, and the latter's comment is a just one—

> "'Poor youth,' said Bertram, 'wavering still,
> Unfit alike for good or ill!'"

The above charge is signed by the two prisoners, and Oswald at once breaks forth into feigned rage; he summons the garrison to arms, throws Rokeby and all his train into prison, and warns each suspected Royalist to assemble at noon on the following day at the Abbey Church of Eglistone.

This was the confession made by Edmund to Bertram in the robbers' cave, where Denzil and his company had before lain. How the young minstrel came to be there will shortly be related. At present, it is sufficient to say that he has been digging for and has at last secured the object of his search, when a heavy hand is laid on his shoulder. He starts up and confronts Bertram, on which he gives a shriek of terror. Bertram says, "Fear not!" with some contempt—

> "Fear not! by Heaven, he shakes as much
> As partridge in the falcon's clutch!"

Bertram seizes the casket in Edmund's hand, and discovers a "chain and reliquaire of gold." He then inquires of the youth how he came to have escaped, as Bertram knew that he had been imprisoned with Denzil; he also inquires as to this "toy" that Edmund had found. Edmund relates to Bertram all that we have already heard. Bertram, on hearing of this intended meeting at Eglistone Church, remarks that he had passed that church and had heard and seen sinister preparations, leaving no doubt that some dire deed was to be performed—

> "Torches and cressets gleamed around,
> I heard the saw and hammer sound,
> And I could mark they toiled to raise
> A scaffold, hung with sable baize,
> Which the grim headsman's scene displayed—
> Block, axe, and sawdust ready laid."

Bertram quite comprehends Oswald's intentions in this—

> "Some evil deed will there be done,
> Unless Matilda wed his son.
> She loves him not—'tis shrewdly guessed
> That Redmond rules the damsel's breast.
> This is a turn of Oswald's skill;
> But I may meet and foil him still!"

Bertram then further questions Edmund as to the latter's escape, and the meaning of the article which he had discovered. The latter continues his tale as follows:—

Oswald, in the midst of his outburst of feigned rage, receives a scroll, delivered, as he is told, late the night before. On opening it, he appears overcome with violent emotion—

> "His hand like summer sapling shook,
> Terror and guilt were in his look."

He announces to Denzil, as "fit counsellor for evil deed," the contents of the scroll, which contains the fact that his intended victim, Mortham, is alive; he, however, carefully conceals his own share in the attempted murder—

> "Slain by a bravo, whom, o'er sea,
> He trained to aid in murdering me,
> Mortham has 'scaped; the coward shot
> The steed, but harmed the rider not."

Bertram, on hearing this falsehood and the libel on his own courage, which latter charge angers him more than all else, as we have once before seen,[31] springs up in a rage, and paces the cavern furiously—

> "'Thine own grey head, or bosom dark,'
> He muttered, 'may be surer mark!'"

He signs to the terrified Edmund to continue his tale.

Oswald reads the contents of the scroll, which is written by Mortham himself—

> "Ruler of Mortham's destiny!
> Though dead, thy victim [32] lives to thee.

(31) See page 361 of treatise.

(32) The word "victim" would, I think, apply to the suffering which Mortham had endured through Oswald's treachery in regard to his (Mortham's) wife. Mortham, it would seem, is not aware of Oswald's share in his attempted murder.

Once had he all that binds to life,
A lovely child, a lovelier wife;
Wealth, fame, and friendship were his own—
Thou gav'st the word, and they are flown.
Mark how he pays thee:—to thy hand
He yields his honours and his land,
One boon premised—Restore his child!
And, from his native land exiled,
Mortham no more returns to claim
His lands, his honours, or his name;
Refuse him this, and from the slain
Thou shalt see Mortham rise again."

Mortham evidently still thinks that Oswald had a hand in the abduction of the child, in which, as I before said, he does not appear to have been implicated. It was the work, I think, of old O'Neale alone. Oswald now disclaims all knowledge of the child, saying, with his usual hypocrisy—

"Heaven be my witness! wist I where
To find this youth, my kinsman's heir,—
Unguerdoned, I would give with joy
The father's arms to fold his boy,
And Mortham's lands and towers resign
To the just heirs of Mortham's line."

Denzil, who, like Bertram on a former occasion,[33] thoroughly appreciates the value of this cant, replies, with a "cynical sneer"—

"'Then happy is thy vassal's part,'
He said, 'to ease his patron's heart!
In thine own jailer's watchful care
Lies Mortham's just and rightful heir;
Thy generous wish is fully won—
Redmond O'Neale is Mortham's son.'"

At this unexpected, overwhelming intimation, Oswald starts up in a frenzy of rage, exclaiming—

"Is Hell at work? or dost thou rave?
Or darest thou palter with me, slave?
Perchance thou wotest not, Barnard's towers
Have racks, of strange and ghastly powers."

(33) See page 329 of treatise.

Denzil assures Oswald that his statement is true, and gives the following explanation. .

It will be remembered that, on the night on which Redmond was brought to Rokeby Castle, he and his escort, the Irish kerne, were attacked and plundered by robbers, the Irishman being mortally wounded.[34] Guy Denzil was one of this robber band, and, among the plunder they obtained, was the reliquary and chain which we have seen Edmund searching for and discovering in the robbers' cave. This portion of the plunder was evidently assigned to Denzil, who thus states—

> "That very night, when first of all
> Redmond O'Neale saw Rokeby Hall,
> It was my goodly lot to gain
> A reliquary and a chain,
> Twisted and chased of massive gold.—
> Demand not how the prize I hold!
> It was not given, nor lent, nor sold.—
> Gilt tablets to the chain were hung,
> With letters in the Irish tongue."

Denzil, having to flee the country, hides this booty without attempting to decipher the tablets, not knowing the language; but later, having sojourned in Ireland, he becomes sufficiently acquainted with the native tongue to be able to read, but not thoroughly to understand the words, for—

> "Darkling was the sense; the phrase
> And language those of other days,
> Involved of purpose, as to foil
> An interloper's prying toil.
> The words, but not the sense, I knew,
> Till fortune gave the guiding clue."

This clue is obtained by Denzil's overhearing the conversation of Matilda with Redmond and Wilfrid, as related in an earlier part of the treatise.[35] The tale thus told, Denzil here relates to Oswald. It is not likely, however, that the latter will easily relinquish his hold on the lands of Mortham. With his usual

(34) See pages 351 and 352 of treatise.

(35) See page 364 of treatise; also pages 348 to 354, relating the histories of Mortham and Redmond.

hypocrisy, he again declares that he will willingly restore the lands to his kinsman Mortham or his heir, but adds—

> "But Mortham is distraught. O'Neale
> Has drawn for tyranny his steel,
> Malignant to our rightful Cause,
> And trained in Rome's delusive laws."

Oswald now attempts to strike a bargain with Denzil, so as to get these proofs into his own hands. A conversation ensues between them in whispers, so that Edmund cannot hear what they say; at length, however, Denzil speaks aloud, declaring that nothing on earth shall induce him to discover the hiding-place of the reliquary, &c., unless he receives a free pardon—

> "Free me from peril and from band,
> These tablets are at thy command."

Oswald, however, will not release him until he has obtained the tablets in question, so he intimates to Denzil that he will retain him as a hostage while his son (*i.e.*, Edmund) should go and bring them, also bearing a scroll in reply to Mortham. We are not informed of the actual contents of the latter, but they were evidently intended to lure Mortham into some snare—

> "A scroll to Mortham shall he bear
> From me, and fetch these tokens rare.
> Gold shalt thou have, and that good store
> And freedom, his commission o'er;
> But if his faith should chance to fail,
> The gibbet frees thee from the jail."

Denzil, therefore, reluctantly dispatches Edmund to the robbers' cave, which he reaches, obtains the reliquary, &c., and there encounters Bertram, as we have before said.

Bertram now demands to see Oswald's letter to Mortham; on reading it, he tears it into scraps, and remarks—

> "All lies and villainy! to blind
> His noble kinsman's generous mind,
> And train him on from day to day,
> Till he can take his life away."

Bertram's mind is now reverting to its old allegiance to his former friend and patron, and it is also now possessed by a bitter hatred towards Oswald. He then sternly demands of Edmund his intentions in this matter—

> "And, now, declare thy purpose, youth,
> Nor dare to answer, save the truth;
> If aught I mark of Denzil's art,
> I'll tear the secret from thy heart!"

Edmund replies, unhesitatingly, that he is determined to renounce all connection with Denzil; he cares not what becomes of him, for he (Denzil) was the man who originally led him, when a thoughtless youth, away from the right path. He also declares that it was his intention to hand the tablets over to Mortham, acquainting him, at the same time, of the relation that Redmond bears to him. Bertram at once acquiesces, observing that this youth (Edmund) was quite out of place in a robbers' band.

It is at this point that we see the extraordinary change in Bertram, in this last canto of the poem. He softens wonderfully, and this is seen from the commencement of this interview between these two persons, so extremely opposite in all respects. Bertram shows no brutality towards this timorous youth, and, though he shows some contempt for the youth's terror at his appearance, his words are somewhat kind and pitiful.[36] His actions also now point to the change we have mentioned. It is an undoubted fact that he feels deep sorrow for his attempted murder of his former friend and patron; disgust with himself that he had so lowered himself as to be the accomplice of such a man as Oswald; and he has now determined that he will make what reparation he can. He also feels a presentiment of approaching death. Scott well describes the change which has taken place in him—

> "He paused, and, stretching him at length,
> Seemed to repose his bulky strength.
> Communing with his secret mind,
> As half he sat, and half reclined,
> One ample hand his forehead pressed,
> And one was dropped across his breast.
> The shaggy eyebrows deeper came
> Above his eyes of swarthy flame;

[36] See page 381 of treatise.

His lip of pride awhile forbore
The haughty curve till then it wore;
The unaltered fierceness of his look
A shade of darkened sadness took,—
For dark and sad a presage pressed
Resistlessly on Bertram's breast,—
And when he spoke, his wonted tone,
So fierce, abrupt, and brief, was gone,
His voice was steady, low, and deep,
Like distant waves when breezes sleep;
And sorrow mixed with Edmund's fear,
Its low, unbroken depth to hear."

At length, he speaks to Edmund, and his words are touching. He says that he will not himself see Mortham again, but he will send him a message through Edmund—

"Mortham must never see the fool
That sold himself base Wycliffe's tool!
Yet less from thirst of sordid gain,
Than to avenge supposed disdain.
Say, Bertram rues his fault—a word,
Till now, from Bertram never heard."

He also desires Edmund to remind Mortham of the former days, of their wanderings and adventures in the Spanish Main, adding—

"Perchance my patron yet may hear
More that may grace his comrade's bier."

He mentions also his presentiment of approaching death; as his life had been stormy, violent, and terrible, so will his end be sudden, equally violent, equally terrible—

"And now, my race of terror run,
Mine be the eve of tropic sun!
No pale gradations quench his ray,
No twilight dews his wrath allay;
With disk like battle-target red,
He rushes to his burning bed,
Dyes the wide wave with bloody light,
Then sinks at once—and all is night."

Bertram then enjoins Edmund to seek out Mortham, who is

either at Mortham Castle or in a forester's hut in Thorsgill glade, urge him to go to Richmond, where he has troops, and lead them to the aid of his son, Redmond, and his old friend, Rokeby, at Eglistone Church, adding this—

> "Say, till he reaches Eglistone,
> A friend will watch to guard his son."

Edmund, though still in fear, cannot forbear a touch of pity for the grim, gigantic ruffian, who now shows traces of a better nature, and attempts to repair, as far as he can, the wrong he has done. A tear shines in the boy's eye, and Bertram himself is touched by this exhibition of feeling—

> "'I did not think there lived,' he said,
> 'One who would tear for Bertram shed.'"

He loosens a golden buckle from his baldric, and presents it to Edmund, speaking to him even with affection—

> "And this, dear Edmund, thou shalt take,
> And wear it long for Bertram's sake."

Edmund departs, and this is the last we see or know of him in the poem, except that he fulfils his mission faithfully. He has expressed his intention of leading a new life, and we trust that he may adhere to this purpose; but we cannot help thinking that the same prophecy will apply to him as it did to the patriarch Reuben of old, "Unstable as water, thou shalt not excel."

On the following morning, Oswald, who is impatiently awaiting the return of his messenger, asks his retainers whether "Denzil's son" has returned. Unfortunately for Denzil, one of the train knows young Edmund, and informs Oswald who he is. Wycliffe, in a fury at Denzil's deception, at once concludes that either the robber's tale is a false one, or, worse still, that the lad has been despatched to Mortham to tell the truth. However that might be, the tale rests entirely on Denzil's evidence; the latter, therefore, must be silenced at once. He thereupon orders Denzil's immediate execution—

"Ho! Provost Marshal! instantly
Lead Denzil to the gallows-tree!
Allow him not a parting word;
Short be the shrift and sure the cord!"

And so the wretch is hurried off to instant death.

Oswald then dispatches one of the domestics to direct his son
Wilfrid to attend him at the castle gate, to ride to Eglistone
Church. This old domestic, Basil by name, replies that Wilfrid
is not fit for the saddle; he had been wounded, as we know, at
Rokeby Castle, and now, following on the wound, comes some
internal complication, affecting mind as well as body, which the
medical attendant is unable to cope with. Oswald, however,
disregards his son's state of health, and repeats his order to him
to attend him at Eglistone. He has fully determined now to
carry out the marriage of Wilfrid to Matilda, which he had so
long contemplated. We have here his nefarious plan, shown
clearly in his own thoughts—

"Now comes my fortune's crisis near!
Entreaty boots not—instant fear,
Nought else, can bend Matilda's pride,
Or win her to be Wilfrid's bride.
But when she sees the scaffold placed,
With axe and block and headsman graced,
And when she deems, that to deny
Dooms Redmond and her sire to die,
She must give way. Then, were the line
Of Rokeby once combined with mine,
I gain the weather-gage of fate!
If Mortham come, he comes too late,
While I, allied thus and prepared,
Bid him defiance to his beard."

All circumstances, therefore, seem favourable to Oswald's
plans, but he still has some hesitation as to proceeding to extremities should Matilda continue firm in her refusal. Mortham
has to be reckoned with; and it occurs to Oswald now that,
although he has silenced Denzil, the youth Edmund had been
present, and had overheard the robber's tale, and could, therefore, give evidence in that matter; indeed, he might have by
now placed the casket in Mortham's hands, which was indeed the

case. However, Oswald trusts that the maiden will yield when her father's life is threatened, and with that he and his train proceed to Eglistone Abbey Church to carry out his nefarious design.

And now we come to the final scene of the poem, which takes place in the above-named church; though to close in joy, it opens in gloom. The church is crowded with people who have come to view the tragic event, which is no less than the execution of the Lord of Rokeby and his associate, Redmond, on the trumped-up charge we have already mentioned.[37] The scaffold, with all its dread appurtenaces, is now prepared in the church, and, with trumpet-call, a herald announces the sentence of death on the two men above mentioned. This announcement, however, is by no means received with approbation by the crowd—

> "Till from the crowd begin to rise
> Murmurs of sorrow and surprise,
> And from the distant aisles there came
> Deep-muttered threats, with Wycliffe's name."

Oswald, however, is guarded by a powerful band of retainers, and he sternly bids silence, on pain of death. He then addresses himself to Rokeby, who bears himself calmly and manfully, in contrast to Oswald, who dares not meet his eye—

> "And said, with low and faltering breath,
> 'Thou know'st the terms of life and death.'"

These were, as we have heard, the sanction of the Lord of Rokeby to the marriage of his daughter to Oswald's son, and the consent of Matilda to that marriage. The knight, however, holds firmly to his former decision—

> "The maiden is mine only child,
> Yet shall my blessing leave her head,
> If with a traitor's son she wed."

Then Redmond speaks, gallantly, as is his wont—

> "The life of one
> Might thy malignity atone;
> On me be flung a double guilt!
> Spare Rokeby's blood, let mine be spilt!"

(37) See page 380 of treatise.

Oswald would willingly have assented to this proposition, but "dread prevailed," doubtless dread of the vengeance of Mortham. He now proceeds to urge Matilda to consent to the marriage, showing the advantages that would follow from such union—

> "An union formed with me and mine
> Ensures the faith of Rokeby's line.
> Consent, and all this dread array,
> Like morning dream, shall pass away;
> Refuse, and, by my duty pressed,
> I give the word—thou know'st the rest."

A terrible moment it is for Matilda—on the one hand, her father and her lover condemned to death; on the other, a marriage repugnant to her, and which would bring her father's curse upon her. But the sight of the scaffold and death appliances prevails; she cannot bring upon herself the death of her father and lover, and, although she has no love for Wilfrid, yet she has respect and sisterly affection for him. She says, therefore—

> "I make my choice!
> Spare but their lives!—for aught beside,
> Let Wilfrid's doom my fate decide.
> He once was generous!"

She could not indeed have made a better decison. Oswald, in triumph, calls forth his son to greet his betrothed, but he receives an unexpected reply from Wilfrid—

> "O hush, my sire! to prayer and tear
> Of mine thou hast refused thine ear;
> But now the awful hour draws on,
> When truth must speak in loftier tone."

And now follows a most touching scene. Poor Wilfrid, suffering from his wound, mortal as it proves, with other physical and mental injuries, now acts like the true gentleman that he is—

> "He took Matilda's hand. 'Dear maid,
> Could'st thou so injure me,' he said,
> 'Of thy poor friend so basely deem
> As blend him with this barbarous scheme?

> Alas! my efforts, made in vain,
> Might well have saved this added pain.
> But now, bear witness, Earth and Heaven,
> That ne'er was hope to mortal given
> So twisted with the strings of life
> As this—to call Matilda wife!
> I bid it now for ever part,
> And with the effort bursts my heart!'"

These noble words are his last; not only his wound, but the "agony of mental pain" proves too much for him. He kneels with difficulty and kisses Matilda's hands; then, with this final effort, the last moment comes—he sinks down and dies.

Terrible is the commotion: Matilda throws herself in an agony of tears on the body, while the wretched Oswald is almost driven to madness. All his schemes have been centred on Wilfrid alone, and the latter's death has utterly frustrated them. He becomes mad with fury; Mortham will doubtless be here shortly to claim his heir and his lands, and then assuredly marriage will take place between Matilda and the hated Redmond. He forgets all fear of consequences, and in his mad rage determines on the instant death of the prisoners—

> "And shall their triumph soar o'er all
> The schemes deep-laid to work their fall?
> No!—deeds, which prudence might not dare,
> Appal not vengeance and despair.
> The murderess weeps upon his bier—
> I'll change to real that feignèd tear!
> They all shall share destruction's shock;—
> Ho! lead the captives to the block!"

The provost marshal, however, seeing the utter madness of his lord, hesitates to deliver the signal, but Oswald exclaims furiously—

> "Slave, to the block!—or I, or they,
> Shall face the judgment seat this day!"

These are his last words, spoken in his last moments, and the words are now immediately to be fulfilled.

It is a critical moment for the prisoners; Mortham and his troops have not arrived in time, but unexpected succour is at hand. The galloping of a horse is heard, which quickly approaches the church and passes through the churchyard; then a horseman, clothed in black, dashes in; he charges up the nave, drawing a pistol as he rides, and scattering all before him—

> "All scattered backward as he came,
> For all knew Bertram Risingham!" (38)

He is grimly determined; straight at Oswald Wycliffe he rides, pistol in hand—

> "Full levelled at the Baron's head,
> Rung the report—the bullet sped—
> And to his long account, and last,
> Without a groan dark Oswald passed!"

Passed! in the midst of his sins, at the very moment of ordering the committal of a murder; all in an instant, with no time for repentance; his last words had come true.

His slayer speedily follows him. Bertram promptly wheels his horse round to escape while the onlookers have as yet not recovered from their amazement; but, unfortunately for him, the horse stumbles and falls, bursting the saddle girths; and while he strives to set himself free, and is just rising, Oswald's soldiers recover from their trance of amazement, and attack him on all sides. A desperate conflict ensues; Bertram defends himself like a lion, as he did at Rokeby a few days before, but here his assailants are too many for him—

> "Sword, halbert, musket-butt, their blows
> Hailed upon Bertram as he rose;
> A score of pikes, with each a wound,
> Bore down and pinned him to the ground;
> But still his struggling force he rears,
> 'Gainst hacking brands and stabbing spears;
> Thrice from assailants shook him free,
> Once gained his feet, and twice his knee.
> By tenfold odds oppressed at length,
> Despite his struggles and his strength,

(38) Bertram had probably been in the neighbourhood the whole time, knowing what was going on. Finding that Mortham's troops would not be in time to save the prisoners, he makes this desperate attempt, which otherwise he might not have made.

He took a hundred mortal wounds,
As mute as fox 'mongst wrangling hounds;
And, when he died, his parting groan
Had more of laughter than of moan!''

The retainers gaze with wonder on the body for a while, but are then proceeding to blows and insults, and even to cutting off the head from the body, but Basil, the old retainer, intervenes; he covers the body with a mantle, saying—

"Fell as he was in act and mind,
He left no bolder heart behind:
Then give him, for a soldier meet,
A soldier's cloak for winding-sheet.''

And thus we part with this extraordinary character, a bold, unscrupulous ruffian, but yet not without an element of good in him; and Scott himself lays down, early in the poem, the suggestion that, had Bertram been brought up under better influences, the good might have predominated. His courage is indisputable, and he resents any imputation upon that quality, as we have seen once or twice in the course of the poem. I have already commented upon the extraordinary change depicted in him in the last canto of the poem, so I will say little on that subject. Some of my readers may indeed consider that this change is somewhat overdrawn: I myself do not think that it is unnatural. The strong point of Bertram's change seems to me to be his returning loyalty to his old friend, also his bitter hatred against Oswald, who has seized the estates of that old friend, and is threatening the life of the son of the latter; and he indeed probably still thinks that Oswald had intended to steal the treasure from Mortham Tower when the latter had proceeded with a troop of soldiers to that place.[39] I think that all will agree that his character is superior to that of Oswald, who has all Bertram's unscrupulousness without the latter's courage, and also a strong element of disgusting hypocrisy, which Bertram never stoops to. Bertram is as he has been brought up; Oswald is in a superior position, and, as we now say, "ought to have known better." In the character of the latter, we fear that we can find no redeeming trace.

[39] See page 354 of treatise.

The poem now ends somewhat abruptly. Mortham soon arrives with a large body of troops, who might easily have overcome any opposition from Wycliffe's troops; they would not have been in time, however, to save the captives' lives but for the interposition of Bertram. Mortham meets his long-lost son, and greets him with the utmost affection; the dominant wish of his life has at last been fulfilled.[40]

All, then, ends happily, as may be expected. Redmond is wedded to Matilda, with, we presume, the Lord of Rokeby's consent, although Mortham, be it remembered, is on the side of the Parliament. Redmond, however, has fought on the side of the Royalists under Rokeby himself, having also been brought up as a son by the latter; this, therefore, would doubtless reconcile the old Cavalier to the marriage. The young pair are married, and, to all appearance, "live happily ever afterwards," for the poet says—

> "And Teesdale can remember yet
> How Fate to Virtue paid her debt,
> And, for their troubles, bade them prove
> A lengthened life of peace and love."

With regard to the poem, the treatise of which I have now completed, I would refer the reader to my comments on the first page of the treatise, which I need not repeat. I have only to add a few remarks in addition to those mentioned before. I have not the same feeling towards this poem as I have towards others, such as "The Lay of the Last Minstrel," "Marmion," "The Lady of the Lake," &c. It is recorded in an entirely different style; the "history" of it leads up to the facts, and this "history" is inserted into different parts of the poem and is difficult to unravel, so as to set the argument of the piece flowing in regular order. The history of Mortham, containing his connections with Rokeby, Oswald Wycliffe, Bertram, and Matilda, is an example of this; all these connections have had to be picked out and attached together: this has been a matter of some difficulty.

(40) A doubtful feeling occurs, however, as to how Redmond may have looked upon Mortham, who, although his father, is also the murderer of his mother.

I must point out one extraordinary feature of the poem, viz., that the principal characters very seldom appear on the actual stage. For instance, the Lord of Rokeby, who gives his name to the poem, and of whom we hear a great deal, never appears personally on the scene at all until the end of the last canto, when we have seen him awaiting his execution in Eglistone Church. The life of Philip of Mortham, in its details, springs up in batches throughout the whole poem, but we never see him in person except twice, and then only for a few minutes—once at Mortham Tower, when he confronts Bertram,[41] and, again, at the last scene of all, when he welcomes his son at Eglistone Church.[42] Matilda, the heroine of the poem, does not appear in person until the fourth canto.

As to the characters of the poem, I have already commented upon some of the principal ones, viz., Bertram, Oswald, and Edmund. Wilfrid, Redmond, and Matilda are all pleasing, each in their different way; Wilfrid is particularly so, for he stands in striking contrast to his father, and his sad end calls forth our sincere sympathy. It must be striking to the reader to note how his end and that of Bertram agree so plainly with the attributes of these diametrically opposite characters.

The songs of the poem, although inferior, in my opinion, to those of "The Lady of the Lake," are very pleasing and attractive to one's feelings, especially the old Royalist song, "When the dawn on the mountains," and "Allen-a-Dale."

Scott's opening lines to all the cantos are very beautiful; the description of the scenery, as in all his works, is unrivalled; and if it is declared to be exaggerated, and that certain features of the scenery described are not to be seen from certain points mentioned,[43] yet no one can question the beauty of the lines, which describe so glowingly the beauties of English scenery, so lovely in their own way. The description of the burning of Rokeby is very grand.

And thus we conclude our treatise. It ends indeed with considerable tragedy; several of our principal characters die in

(41) See page 344 of treatise.

(42) See page 395 of treatise.

(43) See Baddeley's notes, page 325 of treatise.

the last hour, chiefly by violent deaths, but for the others the poem ends happily. Our lovers are joined together in happy union, all the long years of trouble are over and brighter days dawn, to be made all the happier through the remembrances of past sorrows, which have now cleared away. And thus the poem concludes well—

> "Time and Tide had thus their sway,
> Yielding, like an April day,
> Smiling noon for sullen morrow,
> Years of joy for hours of sorrow!"

CONCLUSION.

IX.—CONCLUSION.

I HAVE at length reached the conclusion of my treatise, and look back with pleasure on my work—that of running through the beautiful works of one of my most favourite poets, Sir Walter Scott, and I also feel regret that my task is now concluded. I have termed the work, "The Poetical Heroes of Sir Walter Scott," and I have carefully commented on the characters of those heroes as I have proceeded in my narration, so that there is not much more to be said regarding them. I have also commented on the merits of the different poems in which they appear.

The poems all end well, which cannot always be said of Sir Walter's novels. There is invariably "a lover and his lass," who pass through various troubles in the course of the poem in which they appear, to be happily united at the end, and with every prospect of "living happily ever afterwards"; and very beautifully Scott presents this at the close of all his poems. At that of "The Lay of the Last Minstrel," he tells us how—

> "Brave sons and daughters fair
> Blessed Teviot's Flower and Cranstoun's heir."

In "Marmion," he shows us the wedding of Wilton and Clare graced by the presence of the King and Queen themselves; a wedding that proves a most happy one, as he says that—

> "And afterwards, for many a day,
> That it was held enough to say,
> In blessing to a wedded pair,
> ' Love they like Wilton and like Clare!'"

In "The Lord of the Isles," the course of our lovers runs by no means smooth; there is devoted love on the part of Edith of Lorn, indifference on that of Ronald, who loves another; but all comes right in the end. They plight their troth on the battle-field, and the King (Bruce) declares that he will grace the wedding with his presence—

> "Ourself the cause, through fortune's spite,
> That once broke short that spousal rite,(1)
> Ourself will grace, with early morn,
> The bridal of the Maid of Lorn."

In "The Bridal of Triermain," I need not repeat the romantic tale of how the hero won his bride; the result here also is reported to be happy—

> "Our lovers, briefly be it said,
> Wedded as lovers wont to wed,
>   When tale or play is o'er;
> Lived long and blessed, loved fond and true,
> And saw a numerous race renew
>   The honours that they bore."

In "Rokeby," also, the end is the same—

> "'Twas then the Maid of Rokeby gave
> Her plighed troth to Redmond brave;
> And Teesdale can remember yet
> How Fate to Virtue paid her debt,
> And, for their troubles, bade them prove
> A lengthened life of peace and love."

And last, and best of all, is the ending of "The Lady of the Lake," where the generous King, like the true gentleman that he is, conquers the love which he himself feels towards the maiden, and unites the two lovers—

> "His chain of gold the King unstrung,
> The links o'er Malcolm's neck he flung,
> Then gently drew the glittering band,
> And laid the clasp on Ellen's hand"—

thus feeling in—

> "That happy hour,
> The sweetest, holiest draught of Power."

The female characters of Sir Walter's poems are not numerous. In "Rokeby," there is but the one, Matilda, the

---

(1) See "Lord of the Isles," Canto III.

heroine; in the others, there are seldom more than two, consisting of the heroine herself, with the second, a stronger, sterner female character in the background—such as, in "The Lay of the Last Minstrel," Margaret of Branksome, pining for her lover, and her stern, haughty mother, her soul imbued with the family feud, and therefore stubbornly withstanding her daughter's wish. In "Marmion," there is the Lady Clare, and, in contrast with her, the unhappy Constance, discarded, and meeting with a tragic end. In "The Lord of the Isles," Edith of Lorn, with her romantic escapades, and Isabel, sister of Robert Bruce, the latter lady a stronger character. In "The Bridal of Triermain," Gyneth and her stern mother, Guendolen, whose art "warped" her daughter's "unsuspicious heart." Lastly, in "The Lady of the Lake," appears Ellen Douglas, the greatest, as I think, of Scott's heroines, and, in the background, though quite unconnected with the heroine of the poem in this case, stands out "Duncraggan's widowed dame."

All Scott's heroines are pleasing, with the exception, indeed, of Gyneth, in "The Bridal of Triermain"; but none, except, indeed, Ellen, the "Lady of the Lake," are, as I think, in any way remarkable. Ellen's courage on behalf of her father must attract readers of the poem in which she is depicted. The escapades of Edith of Lorn, on the other hand, are not attractive—at least, not to myself. The ladies Clare, Margaret of Branksome, and Matilda of Rokeby are examples of what I have just said—pleasing, endowed with good and amiable qualities, but in character not particularly remarkable.

The male characters of the poems are more numerous, and, generally speaking, more interesting. In every poem, as I have said, there is the usual lover; in "The Lady of the Lake," indeed, there are three: the successful one, Malcolm Græme, is the least important of the three, his rivals in the poem being the two principal characters, King James V. (Fitz-James) and the formidable Highland chieftain, Roderick Dhu. In "Marmion," there are two, the principal character here, Lord Marmion, being the unsuccessful suitor. In "Rokeby," also, there are two, Redmond and Wilfrid, the former being the favoured lover. In the other poems, there is but one lover—

Lord Cranstoun, Ronald, Lord of the Isles, and, greatest character of all, as I think, Sir Roland de Vaux of Triermain.[2]

It will be seen also, as appears from the above paragraph, that these lovers are not generally the principal characters of the poems in which they are depicted; it is so in the case of Marmion and De Wilton, though the latter, indeed, nearly equals the former in importance. In "The Lord of the Isles," the personality of the great king, Robert Bruce, dominates the poem, although the nominal hero, Ronald, gives his name to it. In "The Lay of the Last Minstrel," Lord Cranstoun is decidedly a prominent character, but I am doubtful whether to give the precedence to him or to William of Deloraine. I do not reckon the Elfin Page, whose presence in the poem appears to me to be a blemish on it. In "Rokeby," the prominent characters are very numerous, and it is hard to say to which one the precedence should be given; they are all prominent in the several parts of the poem in which they appear; such characters as Bertram, Oswald Wycliffe and his son, Wilfrid, and Redmond O'Neale. Rokeby and Mortham are important characters in the narrative of the poem, but they hardly ever appear on the actual scene. I should be inclined, on the whole, to give the precedence to Bertram. In "The Lady of the Lake," I have already shown that Malcolm Græme is without doubt an inferior character; the precedence is divided equally between King James V. (Fitz-James) and Roderick Dhu, Lord James of Douglas coming next to them. In "The Bridal of Triermain," Sir Roland de Vaux, of course, predominates, the only other male character of importance in the poem being King Arthur.

To turn now to the doubtful characters, or "villains," of the poems (although the latter term hardly applies to all of them), we often find a great similarity of character in such persons depicted in the different poems. If we take William of Deloraine, the hardy, rough, moss-trooping Borderer, and Roderick Dhu, the formidable, marauding Highland chieftain, we find each typical of the class to which he belongs; neither of them look upon their marauding, plundering life as wrong-

(2) I only mention the names of these heroes here; I have already commented upon their characters in my narration of the poems in which they severally appear.

doing; they consider that they are acting quite within their rights—Deloraine in plundering the English Borderers, who do the same on the Scottish side whenever they get the chance; and Roderick in pursuing the same course with the Lowland Saxons, who, as he asserts, originally robbed his ancestors of the lands which they once possessed. With all their robbing and marauding tendencies, it will be seen that each of these two has his good qualities. We see, as an example, in the case of William of Deloraine, his courtesy towards his feudal foe, Lord Cranstoun, and his honourable remarks over the body of his former "deadly enemy," Richard Musgrave; in the case of Roderick Dhu, the chivalrous conduct of that chief towards Fitz-James, a declared enemy, and now flying for his life from Roderick's clan. The chief shows the fugitive hospitality, and subsequently conducts him in safety beyond the Highland position; then, and not till then, does he try the issue with the enemy in single combat. In "Rokeby," also, Bertram, though showing himself an unmitigated ruffian in the first five cantos, softens considerably in the sixth, showing strong traits of a better nature. The courage, also, of all these three characters is indisputable.

We must now descend the ladder a little. Marmion is a worse character than the three above depicted, and deserves the hostile criticism of Lord Byron—

> "Now forging scrolls, now foremost in the fight,
> Not quite a felon, yet but half a knight."

He is of a higher position than the above-mentioned three,[3] and, as I before pointed out, it is not fair on William of Deloraine to compare him with Marmion. The latter is a villain; at the same time, he also has his good side; he is a valiant soldier, and thoroughly devoted to his country, as is seen in his last moments.

The only character of this kind who is depicted without any good qualities to modify his villainy is Oswald Wycliffe, in "Rokeby." He is an unmitigated scoundrel, capable of any

---

(3) Roderick Dhu is indeed a knight, but is not of the position, nor would he have the education, of Marmion.

villainy, and also devoid of courage, showing also, which makes it worse, a disgusting spirit of hypocrisy. Roderick, the Gothic king, in "The Vision of Don Roderick," is of a somewhat similar character. This latter poem, however, stands apart from these others; it is a short epitome of Spanish history.

Three Scottish sovereigns appear in the course of the poems—Robert Bruce, in "The Lord of the Isles," James IV., in "Marmion," and James V., in "The Lady of the Lake." All these are depicted favourably, the latter especially so.

So much for the "heroes" of the poems, who are the subjects of the treatise, but I cannot conclude without a few words on the poems themselves. Here and there, as my readers have seen, I, or others, have criticised some incorrect statements of the poet, either with regard to scenery or to history; under the former are such mistakes as the mention of the "huge, nameless rock" on the Red Tarn, near the summit of Helvellyn, and the "huge rampart barring the way" at the entrance of the Trossachs glen, neither of which exist; and his terming the mountain Saddleback (or, poetically, Blencathra), fronting St. John's Vale, "Glaramara," which latter mountain is in Borrowdale, and not near the Vale of St. John at all. Baddeley's remarks regarding the view from the top of Barnard Castle will be remembered, when he says that not half the objects mentioned by Scott can be seen from that point. With regard to his historical mistakes, I have, more than once in the treatise, remarked that he writes for effect; this, indeed, to do him justice, he often admits himself, as, for instance, in "The Lord of the Isles," the several incorrect statements regarding Bruce's landing at Turnberry. The narrative, too, in the same poem does not run generally in accordance with historical facts, at least in the order in which they occur.

But no unfavourable criticisms can dim the beauty of Scott's poetry, which has from childhood so deeply appealed to me. His description of scenery is unrivalled. Most of the cantos of his poems open with the description of some lovely spot: take, for instance, the description of Loch Katrine at the opening of the third canto of "The Lady of the Lake," and the opening of several cantos in "Rokeby." I have also before drawn notice to the beautiful description of the voyage of Bruce and Ronald in the Western Islands of Scotland, in the fourth canto of "The Lord of the Isles." His descriptions of the two great battles of Flodden and Bannockburn, also, are wonderfully drawn, especially that of the former.

In the "Introduction" to the treatise, I said that Scott was not the favourite poet with the Scottish people, as compared with Burns, at least with the lower classes, and the reason appears to me to be this—Burns's poems, written in the national dialect, and depicting the life and manners of the Scottish peasantry, appeal to the hearts of that class; while those of Scott depict the beauties of the scenery of Scotland, the love of which is undoubtedly his great characteristic; not that he is not thoroughly patriotic and does not dearly love his native country, witness those lovely lines which I quoted early in the treatise, "Breathes there a man with soul so dead." [4] I have also commented upon his impartiality towards the English people, which, naturally, greatly appeals to myself.

The writer of a memoir of Sir Walter Scott [5] says of the poet—"Sir Walter Scott is undoubtedly the most remarkable writer that figures in the literary annals of the nineteenth century. As a poet, historian, novelist, and critic, he achieved a lofty reputation; and if his productions in each department are not superior to those of all his contemporaries, they possess merits that entitle them to a high rank. In romantic fiction he is altogether without even a rival."

This is a very fair estimate of his abilities. As poet and novelist, he stands in the first rank; as a critic, I am not prepared to say; as an historian, he is inferior; at least, the only historical works of his I know are "The Tales of a Grandfather" and the "Life of Napoleon"—the first is a history of Scotland for children, addressed to his grandson, John Lockhart, good in its way, but not, as I think, in any way above the average; the second is certainly inferior to many biographies of the marvellous man whose career it portrays. There are many minor

---

(4) Scott, however, brilliantly depicts types of Scottish character in his novels. See his inimitable characters in "Guy Mannering," "The Antiquary," &c.

(5) G. H. T. He only gives his initials. ("Sir Walter Scott's poems," Excelsior Series.)

poems of Scott upon which I have not touched, as well as "Harold the Dauntless," the last of his greater poems, and, as all agree, inferior to the others.

We have noticed the criticisms of Lord Byron on Sir Walter Scott's earlier poems. These seem to have touched him rather quickly, although he dissembles the fact, but it is clear enough—

> "And little reck I of the censure sharp
> May idly cavil at an idle lay."

Scott is generally considered a greater novelist than poet, and this appears to have been understood by himself, at least, in his later years, for the biographer whom I have quoted above states that, after 1817 (in which year he published "Harold the Dauntless," inferior to his former works), he issued no poem of any length. The biographer says that "he had, in fact, opened a new and to him a richer vein"—doubtless, his novels; "and," says the same writer, "the wonderful popularity of Lord Byron's poems dismayed him. Sir Walter Scott himself, in the later years of his life, admitted that he had relinquished poetry because Byron beat him 'in the description of the strong passions, and in deep-seated knowledge of the human heart.'" This may be true, but Scott, I think, need not have disparaged himself with regard to Byron; the latter may have been superior in genius, but undoubtedly the poetry of Scott was of a higher and purer order.

And so we take leave of our poet, and with regretful leave indeed; but his works remain, and will continue unforgotten while the world lasts; they have rendered his name immortal, and that they do so cannot be better shown than by the rendering of his own beautiful lines—[6]

> "Call it not vain:—they do not err
> Who say that, when the Poet dies,
> Mute Nature mourns her worshipper,
> And celebrates his obsequies;
> Who say, tall cliff, and cavern lone,
> For the departed bard make moan:
> That mountains weep in crystal rill;
> That flowers in tears of balm distil;

(6) "Lay of the Last Minstrel," Canto V., vers. 1-2.

> Through his loved groves that breezes sigh,
> And oaks, in deeper groan, reply;
> And rivers teach their rushing wave
> To murmur dirges round his grave."

These lines indeed testify to the departed poet's deep love of the beauties of nature, and will occur to those who visit his grave in the ruins of Dryburgh Abbey.

And now I have finished my task, and lay down my pen with regret: it has been the greatest pleasure to me thus to dive into the glories of the poetical works of that eminent man, which bring back to me the reminiscences of the readings and recitings of my earlier childhood—readings and recitings which have now come back so vividly to me while engaged in the pursuit of my now concluded work. If it stirs the hearts of any of my readers, if it leads them to study the works of the great poet in the same spirit as myself, I may exclaim, with him—

> "If one heart throb higher at its sway,
> The wizard note has not been touched in vain."

I look back upon my task with the same pleasure and regret as did the poet himself at the end of the greatest of his poems, in the lines with which I now finally conclude—[7]

> "Hark! as my lingering footsteps slow retire,
>   Some Spirit of the air has waked thy string!
> 'Tis now a Seraph bold, with touch of fire,
>   'Tis now the brush of Fairy's frolic wing.
> Receding now, the dying numbers ring
>   Fainter and fainter down the rugged dell,
> And now the mountain breezes scarcely bring
>   A wandering witch-note of the distant spell—
> And now, 'tis silent all!—Enchantress, fare thee well!'"

ROBERT H. ANSTICE.

---

(7) Ending stanza of " The Lady of the Lake."